PEKINGESE

BEVERLY PISANO

Title page: *The unique personality of the Pekingese—confident and somewhat haughty—has remained a point of intrigue and delight for dog fanciers everywhere.*

Photography: *Paulette Braun, Isabelle Francais, Herlich Hamburg, Ron Moat, Robert Pearcy, Vince Serbin, Robert Smith, Sally Anne Thompson , Louise Van der Meid, and Ake Wintzell.*

Drawings: *Scott Boldt, Richard Davis, Annmarie Freda, Scott Holwick, E. Michael Horn, Andrew Prendimano, John Quinn, and Alexandra Suchenka.*

The text of this book is the result of the joint efforts of the author and the editorial staff of T.F.H. Publications, Inc., which is the originator of all sections of the book except the chapters dealing with the history and character of the Pekingese, the breed standard, and grooming. Additionally, the portrayal of canine pet products in this book is for general instructive value only; the appearance of such products does not necessarily constitute an endorsement by the author, the publisher, or the owners of the dogs portrayed in this book.

Distributed in the UNITED STATES to the Pet Trade by T.F.H. Publications, Inc., One T.F.H. Plaza, Neptune City, NJ 07753; distributed in the UNITED STATES to the Bookstore and Library Trade by National Book Network, Inc. 4720 Boston Way, Lanham MD 20706; in CANADA to the Pet Trade by H & L Pet Supplies Inc., 27 Kingston Crescent, Kitchener, Ontario N2B 2T6; Rolf C. Hagen Ltd., 3225 Sartelon Street, Montreal 382 Quebec; in CANADA to the Book Trade by Vanwell Publishing Ltd., 1 Northrup Crescent, St. Catharines, Ontario L2M 6P5 ; in ENGLAND by T.F.H. Publications, PO Box 15, Waterlooville PO7 6BQ; in AUSTRALIA AND THE SOUTH PACIFIC by T.F.H. (Australia), Pty. Ltd., Box 149, Brookvale 2100 N.S.W., Australia; in NEW ZEALAND by Brooklands Aquarium Ltd. 5 McGiven Drive, New Plymouth, RD1 New Zealand; in Japan by T.F.H. Publications, Japan—Jiro Tsuda, 10-12-3 Ohjidai, Sakura, Chiba 285, Japan; in SOUTH AFRICA by Lopis (Pty) Ltd., P.O. Box 39127, Booysens, 2016, Johannesburg, South Africa. Published by T.F.H. Publications, Inc.
MANUFACTURED IN THE UNITED STATES OF AMERICA
BY T.F.H. PUBLICATIONS, INC.

Contents

1995 EDITION

Introducing the Pekingese

HISTORY

This intriguing little breed from the Orient, long a favorite with royalty, has become just as popular in our society today as it was in the imperial courts of the ancients. It is a charming canine companion who offers its master an abundance of loving affection and amusing antics.

The Pekingese, truly an "imperial" dog, has a history that takes it back to ancient times, as far back, some say, as 2000 B.C. For centuries, the Pekingese, or "Peke," was worshipped in the temples of China, and it was a custom of the emperor to select four Pekes who were to become his "bodyguards." These four Pekes would precede the emperor to the Chamber of Ceremonials on occasions of state; two of them announcing his approach at correct intervals with sharp piercing barks, the other two daintily holding the hem of his royal robe in their mouths. Theft of or damage to one of the royal dogs was considered to be a crime punishable by death.

There are myriad legends concerning the origin of the Pekingese. Among the most colorful is that of the romance of "the Lion and the Marmoset."

One day while the mighty king of all beasts, the Lion, was walking through the Magic

The Pekingese makes a charming canine companion, offering an abundance of loving affection and amusing antics. Owner, Gloria Henes.

4

Legend and myth trace the Pekingese's origins back to a magical cross between the Lion and the Marmoset monkey. Whatever the origin, the Peke is a fascinating and wonderful creature.

Forest, he stopped by a pool to rest and have a cool drink from the pool. As he stepped to the edge of the pool, he saw the reflection of a beautiful little Marmoset monkey perched in the tree nearby. Immediately he found himself madly in love with the exquisite creature, but after some meditation, he became very sad. He realized how large and mighty he was and how tiny and delicate the little Marmoset looked. But as the days passed, he still could think only of his love for the Marmoset. The Fairy Godmother came upon the Lion, and seeing him so downcast, asked if she could help him. After listening to his story, the Fairy Godmother said, "Oh King of All Beasts, I will grant your wish." The Fairy Godmother waved her magic wand and the Lion was made as small as the little Marmoset. To this day, the little Monkey-faced Pekingese has some of the characteristics of the lion about him—the regal bearing and profuse mane.

As to the *true* origin of the Pekingese, we find that the

Introducing the Pekingese

Kenet's Black Magical Peke-a-Boo and Kenet's Ivy League owned by Gloria Henes.

name of "Pekingese" has been given to the rough-coated dog whose smooth-coated relative has been known as the Chinese Pug Dog. Opportunities for research in bygone Chinese lore have been very limited, but there is sufficient evidence to establish what we have stated as authentic.

In the Metropolitan Museum of Art in New York, there are many Chinese porcelains, the Bishop collections of jade, and the Pierpont Morgan collections, all of which contain data regarding these dogs. The oldest of these is the carved crystal in the Bishop collection entitled "Lions," a Pekingese bitch with two puppies. Each has a pendant or drop ear and a tail plumed over the back. The heads are massive and flat across the top of the skull; the muzzle is short but very full. The mane is indicated as profuse. The date on this piece is given as the Ming Dynasty, 1368-1644. In the same Bishop collection, there can be found a dog and puppy, also called "Lions"; the date for this is 1736-1795

The Morgan collection is all porcelain or earthenware. The

AmCan. Ch. St. Aubrey Pavarotti of Elsdon owned by Edith N. Jones.

Introducing the Pekingese

porcelain pieces show the best illustrations of Pekingese dogs to be found, with beautiful plates having a pattern of the Pekingese in "biscuit color." On other porcelain plates are two Pekingese dogs with black and white coloring; on another the coloring is principally white. These plates are also placed in the 1736-1795 collection.

Although the circle of information is very limited, the Pekingese, both rough and smooth, were known to England a century ago, specimens having been brought to that country as loot from the imperial palaces.

In October, 1860, four small Pekingese were presented to Queen Victoria by Lieutenant Dunne. However, three of these dogs found their way to the "Goodwood" Castle, property of the Duke of Gordon and Lord

Without a moment's doubt, the Peke is full of himself, possessed of self-esteem and boldness.

Pekingese develop quickly and smoothly. This Peke puppy can grow to weigh up to 14 pounds.

John Hay. It was from these dogs that the English get their "Goodwood" line of Pekingese.

THE PEKE COMES TO AMERICA

In 1898 the first Pekingese came to America. They were admitted to AKC registry in 1906, and to show classification in 1907. The Pekingese Club of America was formed in 1909 and gave its first Specialty Show in January, 1911.

Pekes have continued to capture the fancy of American dog lovers, and as testimony to their popularity, they now occupy a high ranking on the AKC's registrations listing—being in the top 25.

CHARACTER

Pekingese are the aristocrats of dogdom, with many different characteristics in one little parcel. A fascinating breed, they are lovable, haughty, and bold,

Introducing the Pekingese

The Pekingese, in any color, should possess a black mask and black spectacles.

with a quaintness that is irresistible. These small companions are suited to most environments, and are loyal to child and adult alike.

Having lovable dispositions, Pekes are not bad tempered, as some people have been led to believe. In fact, they are quite anxious to please. However, many are quite haughty with strangers, for they seem to know they are of royal ancestry and merit due respect from everyone! While they may be resentful if strangers make advances first, if you give them time they will make friends. They will come to you freely when they are convinced of your good intentions. Then, when you make a return visit, they will greet you as if they had always known you.

Pekingese are obedient little dogs, and are easy to train. Speak to them in a gentle but firm tone and they are willing to do anything for you. Kindness goes a long way with these royal little dogs.

The Pekingese is often called the Lion Dog, and with his flowing mane and pear-shaped body he does resemble the king of the forest. If he should come face to face with his namesake, he may well be undaunted, for he has no fear of animals many times his size. Pekingese make

Lionshadow's Queen Guinevere owned by Edith N. Jones.

wonderful watch-dogs who bark at any strange noises, but never bark just to be barking.

They love to romp and play; they can take long walks or sit quietly by your side for many hours, happy just to be near you. They love to go places and are a source of great fun. Alert, seeing everything that is going on around them, many delight in watching television!

Pekingese are rather jealous by nature and like all the attention they can have. Yet, they can easily be trained to share the affection with a cat or another dog. Once they become friends, they will sleep and eat together, sharing the affection of their master and mistress.

Pekes are hardy little dogs with a stamina much greater then their size. The Pekingese is anything but a silk pillow dog, as he is so often pictured. He can romp and play for a long while without tiring easily.

These tiny dogs have clean habits, which means that they are easily housebroken. Most Pekingese are very fastidious, unhappy if their lovely coats become soiled, delighted after they are washed or groomed. Some show their pleasure at

Given the opportunity to run about the back yard, your Pekingese will show you how much they enjoy exercise and play.

This pair of Pekingese from England is taking a much needed rest after a fun-filled afternoon.

being groomed by rolling over on their backs so their stomach coat can be gently brushed.

Quite the show-offs when they want to attract your attention, Pekes will sit up, wave their paws and "speak." They use their paws in play a great deal like a kitten; in fact, tricks seem to be second nature to them, and puppies barely past weaning age will sit up to attract attention.

Their characters are to a great extent formed by their owners, for they seem to sense your every mood. Many times a little Pekingese with his great devotion has eased the pain of illness or another's grief. And many Peke owners have said that their loyal companion carried them through an almost unbearable time.

Usually there is one member of the family that the pet is more fond of and will obey more readily. Occasionally you will

L & E's Damien's Leprechaun and L & E's Damien's Sparkle Plenty owned by Lorraine Moran.

find a Pekingese that gives all of his affection to one member of the family, simply ignoring everyone else when their person is present. But when this favorite is absent, he will be very friendly with the rest of the family. Then again there will be one who is very loving and friendly with all members of the household, but when company arrives, he will completely ignore the family and give all his attention to the guests. Maybe he is trying to be a good host. One fascination of the Pekingese character is that you never quite know exactly what they are thinking.

Pekingese come in many colors, ranging from whites, creams, many shades of fawn, reds, sables, and brindles to blacks and blacks with tan, gray, fawn or red markings.

The Breed Standard

If you plan to enter your Pekingese into show competition, you should become thoroughly familiar with the official standard of the national club under which your dog is registered, and also with those standards of other jurisdictions if you are considering international exposure for your Pekingese.

Even if you do not desire to show or breed your Pekingese (and instead want simply a beloved household pet), you may indeed be interested in knowing about those attributes that exemplify the perfect Pekingese.

AMERICAN AND BRITISH STANDARDS

The official standards as approved by the American Kennel Club and The Kennel Club (of Great Britain) have very much in common. Despite differences in wording, both call for essentially the same requirements. It must be noted, however, that the British standard calls for maximum weights to be only 11 pounds for dogs and 12 pounds for bitches.

For sake of brevity, we are including only the American Kennel Club standard in this book. If your Pekingese is

Pekingese come in many colors. Here is an example of a red and a sable owned by Linda Nolker.

registered with a different national club, write to that club and request a copy of the official standard. Considering that these standards have a tendency to change in the way they are worded from time to time, serious show persons are advised to contact their local club for the most up-to-date standard available.

THE PEKINGESE STANDARD (AKC)

Expression: Must suggest the Chinese origin of the Pekingese in its quaintness and individuality, resemblance to the lion in directions and independence and should imply courage, boldness, self-esteem and combativeness rather than prettiness, daintiness or delicacy.

Skull: Massive, broad, wide and flat between the ears (not dome-shaped), wide between the eyes. **Nose:** Black, broad, very short and flat. **Eyes:** Heart-shaped, not set too high, leather never long enough to come below the muzzle, nor carried erect, but rather drooping, long feather. **Muzzle:** Wrinkled, very short and broad, not overshot nor pointed. Strong, broad underjaw, teeth not to show.

Shape of Body: Heavy in front, well-sprung ribs, broad chest, falling away lighter behind, lion-like. Back, level. Not too long in body; allowance made for longer body in bitch. **Legs:** Short forelegs, bones of forearm, bowed, and well shaped. **Feet:** Flat, toes turned out, not round, should stand well up on feet, not on ankles.

Action: Fearless, free and strong, with slight roll.

Coat, Feather, and Condition: Long with thick undercoat, straight and flat, not curly nor wavy, rather coarse, but soft; feather on thighs, legs, tail and toes long and profuse. **Mane:** Profuse, extending beyond the shoulder blades, forming ruff or frill round the neck.

Color: All colors are allowable. Red, fawn, black, black and tan, sable, brindle,

A relative of the Chinese Pug Dog, the Pekingese possesses the same short, flat muzzle.

white and parti-color well defined: black masks and spectacles around the eyes, with lines to ears are desirable.

Definition of a Parti-Color Pekingese: The coloring of a parti-colored dog must be broken on the body. No large portion of any one color should exist. White should be shown on the saddle. A dog of any solid color with white feet and chest is not a parti-color.

Tail: Set high; lying well over back to either side; long, profuse straight feather.

Size: Being a toy dog, medium size preferred, providing type and points are not sacrificed; extreme limit, 14 pounds.

FAULTS: *Protruding tongue, badly blemished eye, overshot, wry mouth.*

DISQUALIFICATIONS: *Weight: over 14 pounds. Dudley nose.*

The imperial Pekingese is quaint and highly individualistic, undeniably Chinese with resemblance to the lion in boldness and impression.

Grooming the Peke

A well-groomed Pekingese is a beautiful sight to behold, with his glossy coat, long plume tail and fringes. Pekingese stay as nature intended them to, with no cropping of ears or docking of tails. The only trimming done is to whiskers on the muzzle, and then only if the dog is to be entered at a show. The whiskers are clipped close the day of the show, with blunt-end scissors, to protect the eyes from injury should the dog move suddenly or give a struggle. Clipping the whiskers gives a neater, smoother finish to the muzzle.

Grooming should start as soon as the new pet is settled in his home. The most important part of the grooming equipment is the brush, and it should be used every day if possible. Genuine bristle brushes are preferred, especially those that are not too stiff. A coarse-toothed steel comb should be used just to work any tangles

A well-groomed Pekingese is a sight to behold, with his glossy coat, long plume tail and fringes.

For a Pekingese, the most important grooming accessory is the brush. Genuine bristle brushes are preferred.

out, not for rough combing that might pull out the coat.

Place a blanket or rug on the table on which you'll groom your pet. Start with your pet on his back, so the "underneath" coat can be groomed first. If the coat is soiled, wring a cloth out in warm water and rub the soiled places, sprinkle with talcum powder and rub it well into the coat. Now rub dry with a towel and then brush briskly until each hair seems to stand alone. If the coat is not soiled, just brush well.

Turn your pet over and stand him firmly on his feet. This will accustom your dog to posing on a table as would be required at a dog show. If in the future you decide to show your Peke, this will be an important part of his training. Brush briskly, using light strokes against the lay of the coat. Start at the back of the neck and brush forward from the skin to the end of the hair and always toward the head. By the time you have covered the whole body, each hair will be glossy and clean.

Lift the ear and gently brush the hair underneath and in back of it. Now take your steel comb and gently work out any tangles. Don't ever cut out the tangles that form behind the ears or on any part of the coat, as this will leave an ugly, ragged place that is not at all becoming to a lovely little Pekingese.

Clean the ears gently inside (not probing too far into the ear) with a damp cloth and carefully remove any wax accumulation with a cotton swab, then dust a pinch of medicated powder into each ear. While you have the ear pulled up, place it flat against the head and brush the fringe on the edge of it, let the ear drop in place and brush the fringe down and a little forward to make a lovely frame for the face.

The fringes on the legs are to be brushed as well, and if necessary they can be combed. This can be done easily while the dog is lying on his back for grooming underneath.

Hold the tail out in back and comb any tangles; then place the plume over the back and brush gently toward the head until it resembles a silken fan. Brush the hair flat on the top of the skull to give the proper flatness between the ears. The

In order to groom your Pekingese, you will need various grooming instruments. Grooming kits provide you with all the essentials and are available at your local pet store. Photo courtesy of Hagen.

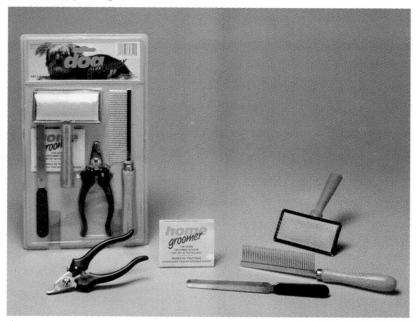

The Peke proves an easycare companion. His plush coat requires on average a couple hours of weekly care, but no special skills or clipping are required. Owner, Lorraine Moran.

skirts (bitches-females) or pants (dogs-males) can be lifted and held with one hand while a little at a time is brushed down from underneath until they are all brushed.

Dampen a cloth with warm water and wash the face, being careful to wash under the wrinkle and drying it well, as a damp wrinkle can become very sore. Dust a little medicated powder under the wrinkle to keep it dry.

Drop any good eye wash, preferably one that your veterinarian recommends, into each eye to wash away any dust or hair that may have accumulated during the grooming of your pet.

Keep the toenails trimmed or they will grow long, sometimes curving right back into the pad of the foot, causing extreme pain and great difficulty in walking. An eye can be badly damaged by an uncut toenail. For this purpose, a special clipper for dogs can be obtained from your retail pet supplier.

See to it that you don't cut too far down and injure the "quick," which will cause pain and bleeding. Have your vet show you the proper way to clip the nails. Trim the hair between the pads of the feet, for accumulated dirt there will often cause soreness. Dust a little powder between the pads after cleaning and drying them.

Examine your pet's mouth at least once a week, and clean out anything that might have lodged between the teeth. Take a soft damp cloth and wipe the teeth clean. Some Pekes do not object to a small toothbrush. If tartar forms, have it removed by your veterinarian.

To keep your pet free from fleas and other such parasites, a liquid solution rubbed into the coat is better than powder. Because of the Pekes' flat noses and large eyes, a powder can be harmful unless used very carefully. Flea powder also tends to dry the skin.

BATHING

Don't bathe your Pekingese unless absolutely necessary, as soap and water baths take the oil out of the coat and cause it to be flat and lifeless. It also can cause the skin to become dry and scaly. A towel dampened in lukewarm water and rubbed briskly all over your pet and right down to the skin will clean the coat and skin and keep it in much better condition. A brisk rub with a dry towel, a good brushing and your pet is as clean as he would have been with a soap and water bath and much more beautiful, with a sparkle and gloss to the coat.

The only time a good bath is recommended is before a show appearance, or after your pet has completed a shedding of his coat. As soon as you notice your Peke starting to shed, brush and comb the coat every day until all the loose coat is shed out. Now, a good bath will give the new coat clean start. Brushing briskly every day will bring the new coat in glossy and healthy and much faster.

If your pet has been ill or, if a bitch is in season, and you don't want to dampen the coat for fear of chilling, a dusting with talcum powder and a good brushing will clean your pet nicely.

Remember: if a Peke is not brushed every day, there will be tangles in the coat. A well-groomed pet is a happy pet!

Facing page: Remember: A well-groomed Peke is a happy Peke!

Tribute to Wonderful Pekes

Each Pekingese has a character and personality all his own. No two are alike.

When a family decides to buy a house pet and the mother and children decide they would like a little Pekingese, the man of the house goes along to help select it, but often under protest. The puppy is selected to the great joy of the mother and children, but father has an expression on his face that says, "If you must have one of those silly little things, I will pay for it but don't expect me to like it." If you could drop in on the family of a new pet a week or so later, you would find that the puppy has taken complete possession of father. He was the first to suggest to mother that the puppy would be happier if his little bed were moved to their bedroom at night. He is the one who sits in the easy chair with the puppy sleeping on his lap while he reads the evening paper or watches television. He is the one down on his hands and knees rolling a ball for the puppy. And who is the first one to spoil the pup at the dinner table by sneaking him tidbits when he sits up or speaks? And when the puppy is trained to a leash, guess who takes him for a walk? Father! When he is old enough, father is the first one to suggest that he should be entered at a dog show. Why? Because there is no other dog that can compare with him. The "silly thing" is now the smartest, most beautiful little dog in the world. At least the father thinks so!

As an example of the Pekes' wonderful devotion, a bedridden little girl was given a Pekingese puppy after her mother had tried everything to keep up her morale and make her happy. The little girl had previously been very active and soon tired of dolls, games and other toys. The doctor suggested a pet, and after a family conference, it was decided a Pekingese puppy would be best. A little bitch puppy was selected, one that was more reserved and quieter than the other puppies in the litter; she was brought home and given to the little girl. That day was the turning point in this little girl's life. She never tired of watching the cute antics of her friend, and when she became tired, the puppy was willing to be cuddled close to her mistress

Like the many other breeds from the Orient, the Pekingese is a patient and collected dog. Owner, Jeannine Joyal.

and nap when she did. The little girl ate her meals eagerly now, for the puppy was fed at the same times each day in a dish by the bed with milk between meals. No more coaxing or worry for the mother, a much happier little girl, and a very very happy puppy.

The little lion dogs are rather jealous by nature, or maybe possessive would be a better word. Once they take over a master and mistress, they are reluctant to share them unless they are taught to do so.

An English war bride came to America with her husband to live. In England she had lived with her mother, and they had raised Pekingese. She was unable to bring one of her pets with her, and after several months in this new, strange land she became very lonesome for her Pekingese. She decided, then, to buy one here. After visits to many kennels, she finally found a bitch that was very tiny and the type she liked. To the young bride, having this Pekingese was almost like having a baby in the home, and the young couple loved her very much. When she was almost four years old, a new baby—a "real" one—arrived in the family. Shortly after the mother came home from the hospital with the baby, she noticed her pet acting strangely: she didn't eat well and

hid away in dark corners. The mother, being very busy with the new baby, didn't pay too much attention to her Pekingese until she absolutely refused to say anything at all and wouldn't even come out of her bed to greet them in the mornings. They became alarmed and took her to their veterinarian; after an examination and many questions he told them their pet was starving from lack of enough food, but also from lack of love and attention. He told them to take her home and try to give her the same attention they had given her before the new baby arrived. The first thing in the morning, they would pick her up, pet her, and make quite a fuss over her. They would feed her by hand, and soon she was eating as usual. They were very careful not to let her see them make a fuss over the baby unless one of them made a fuss over her at the same time. After a short time she was gaining weight and getting back her usual pep and personality. In a very few weeks she had made up her mind that the baby was one of her possessions too. And she was no longer jealous. When the baby was old enough to be put in a play pen, the little Pekingese was her constant guard. They are the greatest of pals, and the baby and the little pet are very happy together.

Adorned with jewels and flowers, this Peke seems to be living life in the manner afforded him by his royal ancestry.

Ch. Jomar Teddy Bear, owned by Jomar Pekingese, Margaret Zuber.

A SPECIAL "OBEDIENCE" PEKE

The Pekingese are obedient dogs and do well in obedience trials. At an obedience trial where a Pekingese was trying to complete his Companion Dog Championship, there was a very interesting episode. The little toy dog had gone through the trial with a very good score, and the final test of the long "down" was ready to start. He followed his master and trainer up the ring and his master turned and stopped; the Peke crossed in back of him and sat down at his side, all in the proper procedure. Then the "down" signal was given and the "stay," and his master proceeded back to the other end of the ring and stood facing his little pal for the timing of the "down." There were a number of other dogs in this trial, and some were of the lager breeds; right next to the little Pekingese was a large German Shepherd Dog. Everything was very quiet and the dogs were going through their final test perfectly. The spectators were quiet, for everyone wanted to see them all finish with good scores. With less than a minute to go, the German Shepherd Dog started working his way forward on his stomach inch by inch. He would proceed a way, then he would stop, and then go forward again. The little Peke, never moving out of position, was intently watching this procedure. Glancing at his master, he wagged his tail as if he was trying to ask permission to do as the other dog. All of a sudden the German Shepherd Dog jumped to his feet and dashed toward his master. With pleading eyes and wagging tail, but still in the proper down position, the little guy watched his master. Everyone now was watching the little Peke, for no one wanted to see him make a move and spoil his chances. Still, with pleading eyes and

Although hailed by dogdom as an "imperial" dog, the Pekingese is hardly a lazy pillow-sitting dog. This Peke, however, does not seem too concerned with breaking the stereotype.

wagging tail and now a faint whine, he begged to come to his master, but there was no signal; he knew he must not move. Everyone there must have been saying a prayer for him; it was so quiet you could have heard a pin drop. The final time was up; the signal was given by the judge; the Peke had kept his position all the time and finished in the proper form with a very good score. The applause from the crowd was deafening, and the trainer could not have been any happier than the spectators at seeing this tiny toy stay, while a larger breed walked to his master. At six months of age this Peke was trained so well that his master could take him to town and tell him to "stay" by the entrance to a store. He could be gone a half hour or more, and when he returned the puppy would still be sitting in the same position.

OTHER MEMORABLE PEKES

A Pekingese bitch had a litter of puppies that she was very proud of. She would dash out of the bedroom where her little brood lived whenever she heard the doorbell, greeting the visitors as soon as the door was opened. Then she would run toward the bedroom, all the time wagging her tail and coaxing the folks to follow her. When the

A beautiful parti-colored Peke owned by Gloria Henes. The parti-color should have a broken color pattern on the body.

As a favored animal of the Buddhist, the Pekingese was regularly portrayed in their art: tapestries, paintings, silk, and sculptures.

visitors came into the bedroom and showed their pleasure at seeing her lovely family, she would stand by, actually beaming with pride.

The owner of a lovely show Pekingese was unable to take him to an out-of-town show, so she had a friend take him. While at the show, the friend wanted to take this little fellow outside to exercise. Instead of going to his grooming case and getting the leash he was used to, she had the one that belonged to her own Peke handy and decided to use it. Each time she tried to slip this leash over the head of this Peke, he would growl and snap at her; when she decided to get

his own leash, he barked, wagged his tail, and practically pushed his head into the loop.

In a home where the baby was just old enough to play in a play pen with his toys, another Peke was taught to play with certain toys and never to touch the ones that belonged to the baby. He would even carry his toys in to the play pen with the baby, but never carried or touched the ones that didn't belong to him.

It is easy to understand why this tiny oriental dog was the sacred dog of China, and why he is one of the most popular dogs in the world.

Pekingese make wonderful companions for children. Make sure to instruct your child on how to properly handle a young puppy.

Selecting Your Dog

Now that you have decided which dog breed suits your needs, your lifestyle, and your own temperament, there will be much to consider before you make your final purchase. Buying a puppy on impulse may only cause heartbreak later on; it makes better sense to put some real thought into your canine investment, especially since it is likely that he will share many happy years with you. Which individual will you choose as your adoring companion? Ask yourself some questions as you analyze your needs and preferences for a dog, read all that you can about your particular breed, and visit as many dog shows as possible. At the shows you will be surrounded by people who can give you all the details about the breed you are interested in buying. Decide if you want a household pet, a dog for breeding, or a show dog. Would you prefer a male or female? Puppy or adult?

If you buy from a breeder, ask him to help you with your decision. When you have settled on the dog you want, discuss with him the dog's temperament, the animal's positive and negative aspects, any health problems it might have, its feeding and grooming requirements, and whether the dog has been immunized. Reputable breeders will be willing to answer any questions you might have that pertain to the dog you have selected, and often they will make themselves available if you call for advice or if you encounter problems after you've made your purchase.

Energetic and friendly, the Pekingese will stand on his hind legs to please you! He is very happy to please his master.

33

A bit too big?
A little **too** small.
Too fuzzy for me!
Too fat to crawl.

Before you wrap it tight
And crate it home,
Behold its appetite
And room to roam.

A sloppy yap, a barking slur,
Puppy eyes to be let free,
A him? a her? an unmarked cur,
Let's pout to see its pedigree.

The perfect pet quest:
Which pup for me is best?

ANDREW DE PRISCO

Most breeders and sellers want to see their dogs placed in loving, responsible homes; they are careful about who buys their animals. So as the dog's new owner, prepare yourself for some interrogation from the breeder.

Buying a puppy should not be an impulsive endeavor; it is never wise to rush out and buy just any puppy that catches your shopping eye. The more time and thought you invest, the greater your satisfaction with your new companion. And if this

This English-bred Peke is High Foo March Morning. The candid and vulnerable expression of the breed makes it most irresistible.

new companion is to be purely a pet, its background and early care will affect its future health and good temperament. It is always essential that you choose a properly raised puppy from healthy, well-bred stock.

You must seek out an active, sturdy puppy with bright eyes and an intelligent expression. If the puppy is friendly, that's a major plus, but you don't want one that is hyperactive nor do you want one that is dull and listless. The coat should be clean and plush, with no signs of fleas or other parasites. The premises should be clean, by sight and smell, and the proprietors should be helpful and knowledgeable. A reputable seller wants his customers satisfied and will therefore represent the puppy fairly. Let good common sense guide your purchase, and choose a reliable, well-recommended source that you know has well-satisfied customers. Don't look for a bargain, since you may end up paying many times over in future veterinarian bills, not to mention disappointments and heartache if your pet turns out not to be well. If you feel that something is lacking in the care or condition of the dogs, it is better to look elsewhere than to buy hastily and regret it afterward. Buy a healthy dog with a good disposition, one that has been

Pekingese, when given the opportunity to be outdoors, will frolic and romp about on the lawn. Size does not necessarily dictate the amount of exercise a dog may need. An energetic Peke is a fair indicator of that.

properly socialized and likes being around people.

If you cannot find the dog you want locally, write to the secretary of the national breed club or kennel club and ask for names of breeders near you or to whom you can write for information. Puppies are often shipped, sight unseen, from reputable breeders. In these instances, pictures and pedigree information are usually sent beforehand to help you decide.

Breeders can supply you with further details and helpful guidance, if you require it. Many breed clubs provide a puppy referral service, so you may want to look into this before making your final decision.

PET OR SHOW DOG

Conscientious breeders strive to maintain those desirable qualities in their breed. At the same time, they are always working to improve on what they have already achieved, and they do this by referring to the breed standard of perfection. The standard describes the ideal dog, and those animals that come close to the ideal are generally selected as show

Owners of purebred dogs too often forget that all breeds of dog are interrelated. The ancient canine that is the believed ancestor of all dogs is known as Tomarctus. As packs traveled and inhabited various lands, types evolved through the process of adaptation. Later, as dogs and man joined forces, type became further diversified. This chart sketches one commonly accepted theory of the domesticated dog's development. Where does your dog fit in? With a few exceptions, dogs evolve or change as a result of a specific functional need.

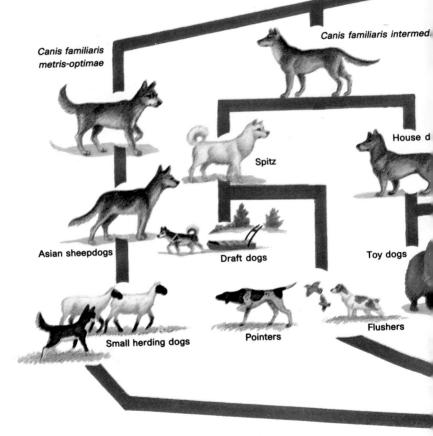

Canis familiaris intermed

Canis familiaris metris-optimae

House d

Spitz

Asian sheepdogs

Draft dogs

Toy dogs

Small herding dogs

Pointers

Flushers

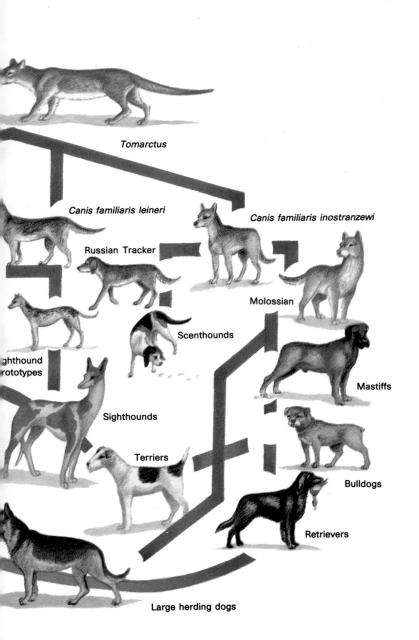

Tomarctus

Canis familiaris leineri

Canis familiaris inostranzewi

Russian Tracker

Molossian

Scenthounds

Sighthound prototypes

Mastiffs

Sighthounds

Terriers

Bulldogs

Retrievers

Large herding dogs

stock; those that do not are culled and sold as pets. Keep in mind that pet-quality purebred dogs are in no way less healthy or attractive than show-quality specimens. It's just that the pet may have undesirable features (such as ears that are too large

A proud Peke sits amid his laurels on his master's favorite chair. Dogs who have shined in the show ring make very loving and gracious home companions as well.

or eyes that are the wrong color for its breed) which would be faults in the show ring. Often these so-called "flaws" are detectable only by experienced breeders or show judges. Naturally the more perfect animal, in terms of its breed standard, will cost more—even though he seems almost identical to his pet-quality littermate.

If you think you may eventually want to show your dog or raise a litter of puppies, by all means buy the best you can afford. You will save expense and disappointment later on. However, if the puppy is strictly to be a pet for the children, or a companion for you, you can afford to look for a bargain. The pup which is not show material, or the older pup for which there is often less demand, or the grown dog which is not being used for breeding are occasionally available and offer opportunities to save money. Remember that your initial investment may be a bargain, but it takes good food and care— and plenty of both—to raise a healthy, vigorous puppy through its adulthood.

Facing page: *The desired coat of the Pekingese is long, straight and flat; it is well feathered with a thick undercoat. This judge at the 1987 Westminster Dog Show observes a competing Peke.*

The price you pay for your dog is little compared to the love and devotion he will return over the many years he'll be with you. With proper care and affection, your pup should live to a ripe old age; thanks to modern veterinary science and improvements in canine nutrition, dogs today are better maintained and live longer. It is not uncommon to see dogs living well into their teens.

Generally speaking, small dogs live longer than big ones. With love and the proper care any dog will live to its optimum age. Many persons, however, opt for a particular breed because of its proven longevity. This, of course, is purely a personal decision.

MALE OR FEMALE

Let us first disregard the usual generalizations and misconceptions applied to male vs. female dogs and consider the practical concerns. If you intend to show your new dog, a male will likely closer adhere to the

Size variation in the dog family is extreme. The consideration of size must be a high priority when choosing a breed. The amount of housing, exercise, and food required, as well as the animal's lifespan are just some of the factors involved.

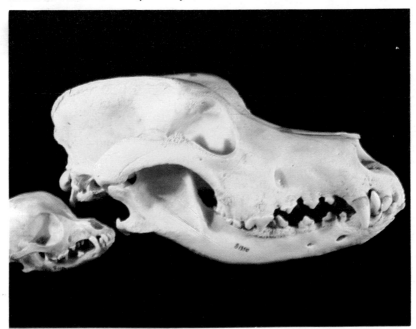

breed standard, though ring competition for males is stiffer. A female chosen to show cannot be spayed and the owner must contend with the bitch's heat period. If it is solely a pet—and pet animals should *not* be bred—castration or spaying is necessary. Neutered pets have longer lifespans and have a decreased risk of cancer. Males are more economical to neuter than are females. You might also consider that females are generally smaller than males, easier to housetrain, may be more family oriented and protective of home and property. Any dog will roam—male or female—castration will not affect roaming in most cases. Males are larger and stronger, proving better guard-dog candidates. Of course, a dog of either sex, if properly trained, can make a charming, reliable, and loving pet. Male vs. female is chiefly a matter of personal preference—go with your first instinct.

ADULT OR PUP

Whether to buy a grown dog or a young puppy is another question. It is surely an undeniable pleasure to watch your dog grow from a lively pup to a mature, dignified dog. If you don't have the time to spend on the more frequent meals, housebreaking, and other training a puppy needs in order to become a dog you can be

Life Expectancy	
Dog's Age in Years	Comparative Human Age in Years
1	15
2	24
3	28
4	32
5	36
6	40
7	44
8	48
9	52
10	56
11	60
12	64
13	68
14	72
15	76
16	80
17	84
18	88
19	92
20	96
21	100

This chart is designed to provide a comparative view of ages between a dog and its human counterpart. Necessarily it is an oversimplification since larger breeds often have shorter lifespans than do average or medium-sized dogs; likewise working dogs may tend to live shorter lives than the easygoing pet dog. These factors, and many others, must be taken into account when considering this chart.

proud of, then choose an older, partly-trained adolescent or a grown dog. If you want a show dog, remember that no one, not even an expert, can predict with one hundred percent accuracy what a puppy will be like when he grows up. The dog may seem to exhibit show potential *most* of the time, but six months is the earliest age for the would-be exhibitor to select a prospect and know that its future is in the show ring.

If you have a small child, it is best to get a puppy big enough to defend itself, one not less than four or five months old.

Older children will enjoy playing with and helping to take care of a baby pup; but at less than four months, a puppy wants to do little else but eat and sleep, and he must be protected from teasing and overtiring. You cannot expect a very young child to understand that a puppy is a fragile living being; to the youngster he is a toy like his

One of the breed's most cherished characteristics is its eyes—deep and expressive and never compromising the breed's age-old dignity and nobility.

Selecting a pup from a litter as charming as this one would certainly be difficult.

stuffed dog. Children, therefore, must learn how to handle and care for their young pets.

We recommend you start with a puppy so that you can raise and train it according to the rules you have established in your own home. While a dog is young, its behavior can be more easily shaped by the owner, whereas an older dog , although trainable, may be a bit set in his ways.

WHAT TO LOOK FOR IN A PUPPY

In choosing a puppy, assuming that it comes from healthy, well-bred parents, look for one that is friendly and outgoing. The biggest pup in the litter is apt to be somewhat coarse as a grown dog, while the appealing "runt of the litter" may turn out to be a timid shadow—or have a Napoleonic complex! If you want a show dog and have no experience in choosing a prospect, study the breed standard and listen carefully to the breeder on the finer points of show conformation. A breeder's prices will be in accord with his puppies' expected worth, and he will be honest with you about each pup's potential because it is to his own advantage. He wants his top-quality show puppies placed in the public eye to reflect glory on him—and to attract future buyers. Why should he sell a potential show champion to someone who just wants a pet?

Now that you have paid your money and made your choice, you are ready to depart with puppy, papers, and instructions. Make sure that you know the youngster's feeding routine, and take along some of his food. For the trip home, place him in a comfortable, sturdy carrier. Do not drive home with a puppy on your lap! If you'll be travelling for a few hours, at the very least bring along a bottle of water from the breeder and a small water dish.

PEDIGREE AND REGISTRATION

Owners of puppies are often misled by sellers with such ruses as leading the owner to believe his dog is something special. The term *pedigree papers* is quite different from the term *registration papers*. A pedigree is nothing more than a statement made by the breeder of the dog;

If you have never been to a dog show, whether you're interested in show dogs or not, by all means—Go! An all-breed dog show will give you hands-on experience with different breeds of dog, the chance to meet their owners and breeders, and the answers to many of your questions.

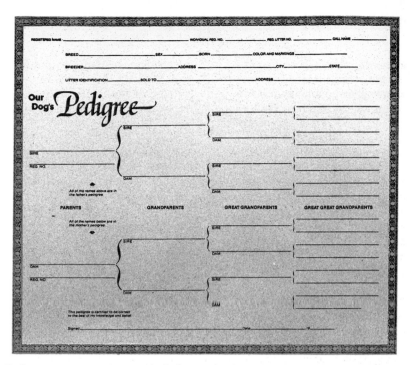

Pedigree papers can trace a dog's lineage back several generations. They do not, however, guarantee that a puppy is purebred, healthy or sound.

and it is written on special pedigree blanks, which are readily available from any pet shop or breed club, with the names of several generations from which the new puppy comes. It records your puppy's ancestry and other important data, such as the pup's date of birth, its breed, its sex, its sire and dam, its breeder's name and address, and so on. If your dog has had purebred champions in his background, then the pedigree papers are valuable as evidence of the good breeding behind your dog; but if the names on the pedigree paper are meaningless, then so is the paper itself. Just because a dog has a pedigree doesn't necessarily mean he is registered with a kennel club.

Registration papers from the American Kennel Club or the United Kennel Club in the United States or The Kennel Club of Great Britain attest to the fact that the mother and father of your puppy were purebred dogs of the breed represented by your puppy and that they were registered with a particular club. Normally every registered dog also has a complete pedigree available. Registration papers, which you receive when you buy a puppy, merely enable you to register your puppy. Usually the breeder has registered only the litter, so it is the new owner's responsibility to register and name an individual pup. The papers should be filled out and sent to the appropriate address printed on the application, along with the fee required for the registration. A certificate of registration will then be sent to you.

Pedigree and registration, by the way, have nothing to do with licensing, which is a local regulation applying to purebred and mongrel alike. Find out what the local ordinance is in your town or city and how it applies to your dog; then buy a license and keep it on your dog's collar for identification.

Whether you are choosing a pet- or show-quality Peke, you can be assured that he will be a delight to own.

The New Family Member

Every Peke has a personality most certainly his own and will share this uniqueness and specialness with his new family.

At long last, the day you have all been waiting for, your new puppy will make its grand entrance into your home. Before you bring your companion to its new residence, however, you must plan carefully for its arrival. Keep in mind that the puppy will need time to adjust to life with a different owner. He may seem a bit apprehensive about the strange surroundings in which he finds himself, having spent the first few weeks of life with his dam and littermates, but in a couple of days, with love and patience on your part, the transition will be complete.

First impressions are important, especially from the puppy's point of view, and these may very well set the pattern of his future relationship with you. You must be consistent in the

The puppy's bed will provide a place of refuge and privacy. Make sure that the puppy's toilet needs have been met before sending him to bed for the night.

way you handle your pet so that he learns what is expected of him. He must come to trust and respect you as his keeper and master. Provide him with proper care and attention, and you will be rewarded with a loyal companion for many years. Considering the needs of your puppy and planning ahead will surely make the change from his former home to his new one easier.

ADVANCE PREPARATION

In preparing for your puppy's arrival, perhaps more important than anything else is to find out from the seller how the pup was maintained. What brand of food was offered and when and how often was the puppy fed? Has

the pup been housebroken; if so, what method was employed? Attempt to continue whatever routine was started by the person from whom you bought your puppy; then, gradually, you can make those changes that suit you and your lifestyle. If, for example, the puppy has been paper trained, plan to stock up on newspaper. Place this newspaper toilet facility in a selected spot so that your puppy learns to use the designated area as his "bathroom." And keep on hand a supply of the dog food to which he is accustomed, as a sudden switch to new food could cause digestive upsets.

Another consideration is sleeping and resting quarters. Be sure to supply a dog bed for your pup, and introduce him to his special cozy corner so that he

This chart lists some of the many items that the dog owner should have on hand before he brings home his new charge.

knows where to retire when he feels like taking a snooze. You'll need to buy a collar (or harness) and leash, a safe chew item (such as Nylabone® or Gumabone®), and a few grooming tools as well. A couple of sturdy feeding dishes, one for food and one for water, will be needed; and it will be necessary, beforehand, to set up a feeding station.

FINDING A VETERINARIAN

An important part of your preparations should include finding a local veterinarian who can provide quality health care in the form of routine check-ups,

noculations, and prompt medical attention in case of illness or an emergency. Find out if the animal you have selected has been vaccinated against canine diseases, and make certain you secure all health certificates at the time of purchase. This information will be valuable to your veterinarian, who will want to know the puppy's complete medical history. Incidentally, don't wait until your puppy becomes sick before you seek the services of a vet; make an appointment for your pup before or soon after he takes up residence with you so that he starts out with a clean bill of health in his new home.

CHILDREN AND PUPPIES

Prepare the young members of the household on pet care. Children should learn not only to love their charges but to respect them and treat them with the consideration one would give all living things. It must be emphasized to youngsters that the puppy has certain needs, just as humans have, and all family members must take an active role in ensuring that these needs are met. Someone must feed the puppy. Someone must walk him a couple of times a day or clean up after him if he is trained to relieve himself on newspaper. Someone must groom his coat, clean his ears, and clip his nails from time to time. Someone

must see to it that the puppy gets sufficient exercise and attention each day.

A child who has a pet to care for learns responsibility; nonetheless, parental guidance is an essential part of his learning experience. Many a child has been known to "love a pet to death," squeezing and hugging the animal in ways which are irritating or even painful. Others have been found guilty of teasing, perhaps unintentionally, and disturbing their pet while the animal is eating or resting. One must teach a child, therefore, when and how to gently stroke and fondle a puppy. In time, the child can learn how to carefully pick up and handle the pup. A dog should always be supported with both hands, *not* lifted by the scruff of the neck. One hand placed under the chest, between the front legs, and the other hand supporting the dog's rear end will be comfortable and will restrain the animal as you hold and carry him. Always demonstrate to children the proper way to lift a dog.

BE A GOOD NEIGHBOR

For the sake of your dog's safety and well being, don't allow him to wander onto the property of others. Keep him confined at all times to your own yard or indoors where he won't become a nuisance. Consider what

The New Family Member

Clockwise from upper right: *pokeweed, jimson weed, foxglove, and yew.* If ingested, any toxic plant can be dangerous to your dog.

As adorable and lovable as they are haughty and bold, the Pekingese have fascinated dog lovers for centuries. Owner, Shirley Schwartz.

ROVER WiLL NOT BE HARMED IF YOU FOLLOW MY INSTRUCTIONS

AMF

Dog theft is not an uncommon event. Dognappers will steal either a purebred or mongrel puppy so all owners must always be wary.

dangers lie ahead for an unleashed dog that has total freedom of the great outdoors, particularly when he is unsupervised by his master. There are cars and trucks to dodge on the streets and highways. There are stray animals with which to wrangle. There are poisons all around, such as car antifreeze in driveways or toxic plants and shrubs, which, if swallowed, could prove fatal. There are dognappers and sadistic people who may steal or bring harm to your beloved pet. In short, there are all sorts of nasty things

waiting to hurt him. Did you know that if your dog consumes rotting garbage, there is the possibility he could go into shock or even die? And are you aware that a dog left to roam in a wooded area or field could become infected with any number of parasites if he plays with or ingests some small prey, such as a rabbit, that might be carrying these parasitic organisms? A thorn from a rosebush imbedded in the dog's foot pad, tar from a newly paved road stuck to his coat, and a wound inflicted by a wild animal all can be avoided if you take the precaution of keeping your dog in a safe enclosure where he will be protected from such dangers. Don't let your dog run loose; he is likely to stray from home and get into all sorts of trouble.

GETTING ACQUAINTED

Plan to bring your new pet home in the morning so that by nightfall he will have had some time to become acquainted with you and his new environment. Avoid introducing the pup to the family around holiday time, since all of the extra excitement will only add to the confusion and frighten him. Let the puppy enter your home on a day when the

Resist the temptation to handle him too much during these first few days. And, if there are other dogs or animals around the house, make certain all are properly introduced. If you observe fighting among the animals, or some other problem, you may have to separate all parties until they learn to accept one another. Remember that neglecting your other pets while

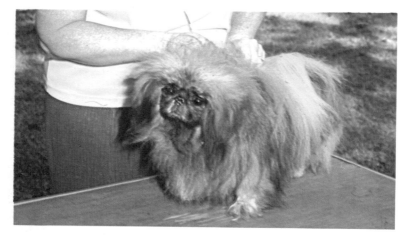

routine is normal. For those people who work during the week, a Saturday morning is an ideal time to bring the puppy to his new home; this way he has the entire weekend to make adjustments before being left alone for a few hours, come Monday morning.

Let the puppy explore, under your watchful eye of course, and let him come to know his new home without stress and fear.

A well-groomed Peke is a source of unabounding pride and joy to his master.

Facing page: *Among the toy dogs, the Pekingese is hailed as the aristocrat—his self-confident, bold way about himself has earned him this distinction.*

showering the new puppy with extra attention will only cause animosity and jealousy. Make an effort to pay special attention to the other animals as well.

On that eventful first night, try not to give in and let the puppy sleep with you; otherwise, this could become a difficult habit to break. Let him cry and whimper, even if it means a night of restlessness for the entire family. Some people have had success with putting a doll or a hot water bottle wrapped in a towel in the puppy's bed as a surrogate mother, while others have placed a ticking alarm clock in the bed to simulate the heartbeat of the pup's dam and littermates. Remember that this furry little fellow is used to the warmth and security of his mother and siblings, so the adjustment to sleeping alone will take time. Select a location away from drafts and away from the feeding station for placement of his dog bed. Keep in mind, also, that the bed should be roomy enough for him to stretch out in; as he grows older, you may need to supply a larger one.

Prior to the pup's arrival, set up his room and partition it the way you would to keep an infant out of a particular area. You may want to keep his bed, his feeding station, and his toilet area all in the same room—in separate locations—or you may want to set the feeding station up in your kitchen, where meals for all family members are served. Whatever you decide, do it ahead of time so you will have that much less to worry about when your puppy finally moves in with you.

Above all else, be patient with your puppy as he adjusts to life in his new home. If you purchase a pup that is not housebroken, you will have to spend time with the dog—just as you would with a small child—until he develops proper toilet habits. Even a housebroken puppy may feel nervous in strange new surroundings and have an occasional accident. Praise and encouragement will elicit far better results than punishment or scolding. Remember that your puppy wants nothing more than to please you, thus he is anxious to learn the behavior that is required of him.

Feeding Requirements

Perhaps more than any other single aspect of your dog's development, proper feeding requires an educated and responsible dog owner. The importance of nutrition on your dog's bone and muscle growth cannot be overemphasized. Soon after your puppy comes to live with you, he will need to be fed. Remember to ask the seller what foods were given to the youngster and stay with that diet for a while. It is important for the puppy to keep eating and to avoid skipping a meal, so entice him with the food to which he is accustomed. If you prefer to switch to some other brand of dog food, each day begin to add small quantities of the new brand to the usual food offering. Make the portions of the new food progressively larger until the pup is weaned from his former diet.

What should you feed the puppy and how often? His diet is really quite simple and relatively inexpensive to prepare. Puppies need to be fed small portions at frequent intervals, since they are growing and their activity level is high. You must ensure that your pup gains weight steadily; with an adult dog, however, growth slows down and weight must be regulated to prevent obesity and a host of other problems. At one time, it was thought that home-cooked meals were the answer, with daily rations of meat,

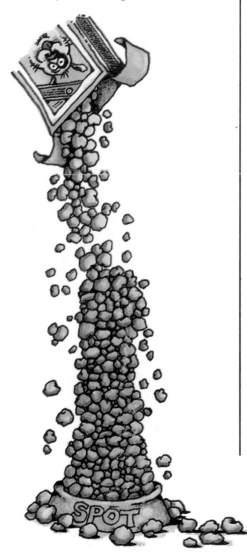

Choosing a quality dog food from your pet shop is easy—deciding how much to feed may not be as straightforward. Feedings must always be carefully monitored.

vegetables, egg yolk, cereal, cheese, brewer's yeast, and vitamin supplements. With all of the nutritionally complete commercial dog food products readily available, these time-consuming preparations really are unnecessary now. A great deal of money and research has resulted in foods that we can serve our dogs with confidence and pride; and most of these commercial foods have been developed along strict guidelines according to the size, weight, and age of your dog. These products are reasonably priced, easy to find, and convenient to store.

THE PUPPY'S MEALS

After a puppy has been fully weaned from its mother until approximately three months of age, it needs to be fed four times a day. In the morning and evening offer kibble (dog meal) soaked in hot water or broth, to which you have added some canned meat-based food or fresh raw meat cut into small chunks. At noon and bedtime feed him a bit of kibble or whole-grain cereal moistened with milk (moistening, by the way, makes the food easier to digest, since dogs don't typically chew their food). From three to six months,

No matter what size your dog is, he will need to chew. A Nylabone® or a similar safe chew toy is highly recommended by countless vets and breeders.

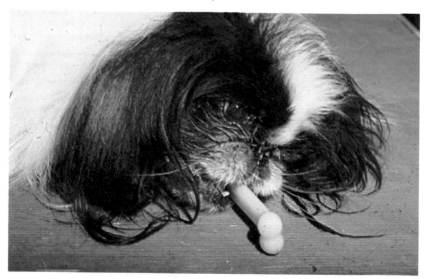

In order for your puppy to grow up healthy and strong, intelligent feeding habits must be adhered to.

offer just three meals—one milk and two meat. At six months, two meals are sufficient; at one year, a single meal can be given, supplemented with a few dry biscuits in the morning and evening. During the colder months, especially if your dog is active, you might want to mix in some wheat germ oil or corn oil or bacon drippings with the meal to add extra calories. Remember to keep a bowl of cool, fresh water on hand always to help your dog regulate its body temperature and to aid in digestion.

From one year on, you may continue feeding the mature dog a single meal (in the evening, perhaps, when you have your supper), or you may prefer to divide this meal in two, offering half in the morning and the other half at night. Keep in mind that while puppies require foods in small chunks, or nuggets, older dogs can handle larger pieces of food at mealtime. Discuss your dog's feeding schedule with your veterinarian; he can make suggestions about the right diet for your particular canine friend.

COMPARISON SHOPPING
With so many fine dog-food products on the market today, there is something for

everyone's pet. You may want to serve dry food "as is" or mix it with warm water or broth. Perhaps you'll choose to combine dry food with fresh or canned preparations. Some canned foods contain all meat, but they are not complete; others are mixtures of meat and grains, which have been fortified with additional nutrients to make them more complete and balanced. There are also various packaged foods that can be served alone or as supplements and that can be left out for a few hours without spoiling. This self-feeding method, which works well for dogs that are not prone to weight problems, allows the animal to serve himself whenever he feels hungry. Many people who work during the day find these dry or semi-moist rations convenient to use, and these foods are great to bring along if you travel with your dog.

Be sure to read the labels carefully before you make your dog-food purchases. Most

Feeder bins are used by many kennel owners as well as pet owners. These devices help to conveniently store and distribute dry foods in a sanitary, efficient way.

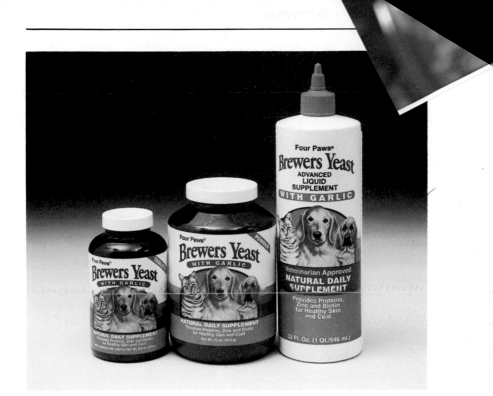

Vitamin/mineral and other food supplements can be formulated for general nutritional value or for particular purposes, such as skin and coat enhancement and/ or flea and tick elimination. Photo courtesy of Four Paws.

reputable pet-food manufacturers list the ingredients and the nutritional content right on the can or package. Instructions are usually included so that you will know how much to feed your dog to keep him thriving and in top condition. A varied, well-balanced diet that supplies the proper amounts of protein, carbohydrate, fat, vitamins, minerals, and water is important to keep your puppy healthy and to guarantee his normal development. Adjustments to the diet can be made, under your veterinarian's supervision, according to the individual puppy, his rate of growth, his activity level, and so on. Liquid or powder vitamin and mineral supplements, or those in tablet form, are available and can be given if you need to feel certain that the diet is balanced.

Pekingese owners seem to agree that their dogs are as unpredictable and entertaining as they are loving and adorable. Pekes surely enjoy all the attention they receive from their antics and waggery.

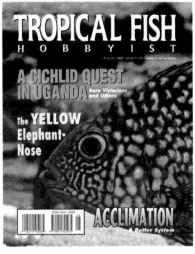

DEVELOPING GOOD EATING HABITS

Try to serve your puppy his meals at the same time each day and in the same location so that he will get used to his daily routine and develop good eating habits. A bit of raw egg, cottage cheese, or table scraps (leftover food from your own meals) can be offered from time to time; but never accustom your dog to eating human "junk food." Cake, candy, chocolate, soda, and other snack foods are for people, not dogs. Besides, these foods provide only "empty" calories that your pet doesn't need if he is to stay healthy. Avoid offering spicy, fried, fatty, or starchy foods; rather, offer leftover meats, vegetables, and gravies. Get in the habit of feeding your puppy or your grown dog his *own* daily meals of dog food. If ever you are in doubt about what foods and how much to serve, consult your veterinarian.

Four Paws Good 'N Plenty Feeder is designed to hold approximately 2 pounds of food. The Good 'N Plenty Waterer holds a generous 3 quarts. Both are designed for easy dismantling and cleaning.

FEEDING GUIDELINES

Some things to bear in mind with regard to your dog's feeding regimen follow.

• Nutritional balance, provided by many commercial dog foods, is vital; avoid feeding a one-sided all-meat diet. Variety in the kinds of meat (beef, lamb, chicken, liver) or cereal grains (wheat, oats, corn) that you offer your dog is of secondary importance compared to the balance or "completeness" of dietary components.

• Always refrigerate opened canned food so that it doesn't spoil. Remember to remove all uneaten portions of canned or moistened food from the feeding dish as soon as the pup has finished his meal. Discard the leftover food immediately and thoroughly wash and dry the feeding dish, as a dirty dish is a breeding ground for harmful germs.

• When offering dry foods, always keep a supply of water on hand for your dog. Water should be made available at all times, even if dry foods are not left out for self-feeding. Each

Feeding your dog is made easy by the use of sturdy non-tip, easy-clean bowls. Pet shops offer the best selection of colors, styles and sizes.

day the water dish should be washed with soap and hot water, rinsed well, and dried; a refill of clean, fresh water should be provided daily.

• Food and water should be served at room temperature, neither too hot nor too cold, so that it is more palatable for your puppy.

• Serve your pup's meals in sturdy hard-plastic, stainless steel, or earthenware containers, ones that won't tip over as the dog gulps his food down. Some bowls and dishes are weighted to prevent spillage, while others fit neatly into holders which offer support. Feeding dishes should be large enough to hold each meal.

• Whenever the nutritional needs of your dog change—that is to say, when it grows older or if it becomes ill, obese, or pregnant; or if it starts to nurse its young—special diets are in order. Always contact your vet for advice on these special dietary requirements.

• Feed your puppy at the same regular intervals each day; reserve treats for special occasions or, perhaps, to reward good behavior during training

sessions.

• Hard foods, such as biscuits and dog meal, should be offered regularly. Chewing on these hard, dry morsels helps the dog keep its teeth clean and its gums conditioned.

• Never overfeed your dog. If given the chance, he will accept

New treats on the block by Nylabone®. These Chooz® crunchy dog bones are delectable and affordable.

and relish every in-between-meal tidbit you offer him. This pampering will only put extra weight on your pet and cause him to be unhealthy in the long run.

• Do not encourage your dog to beg for food from the table while you are eating your meals.

• Food can be effectively used by the owner to train the dog. Doggie treats are practical and often nutritional—choose your chew treats choosily.

FEEDING CHART

Age and No. of Feedings Per Day	Weight in Lbs.	Weight in Kg.	Caloric Requirement kcal M.E./Day
Puppies—Weaning to 3 months Four per day	1–3	.5–1.4	124–334
	3–6	1.4–2.7	334–574
	6–12	2.7–5.4	574–943
	12–20	5.4–9.1	943–1384
	15–30	6.8–13.6	1113–1872
Puppies—3 to 6 months Three per day	3–10	1.4–4.5	334–816
	5–15	2.3–6.8	494–1113
	12–25	5.4–11.3	943–1645
	20–40	9.1–18.2	1384–2352
	30–70	13.6–31.8	1872–3542
Puppies—6 to 12 months Two per day	6–12	2.7–5.4	574–943
	12–25	5.4–11.3	943–1645
	20–50	9.1–22.7	1384–2750
	40–70	18.2–31.8	2352–3542
	70–100	31.8–45.4	3542–4640
Normally Active Adults One or two per day	6–12	2.7–5.4	286–472
	12–25	5.4–11.3	472–823
	25–50	11.3–22.7	823–1375
	50–90	22.7–40.8	1375–2151
	90–175	40.8–79.4	2151–3675

This chart presents general parameters of the dog's caloric requirements, based on weight. The total caloric intake comes from a complete, balanced diet of quality foods. To assist owners, dog food companies generally provide the nutritional information to their product right on the label.

Accommodations

Puppies newly weaned from their mother and siblings should be kept warm at all times. As they get older, they can be acclimated gradually to cooler temperatures. When you purchase your dog, find out from the seller whether he is hardy and can withstand the rigors of outdoor living. Many breeds have been known to adapt well to a surprising number of environments, so long as they are given time to adjust. If your pup is to be an indoor companion, perhaps a dog bed in the corner of the family room will suffice; or you may want to invest in a crate for him to call his "home" whenever he needs to be confined for short intervals. You might plan to partition off a special room, or part of a room, for your pooch; or you may find that a heated garage or finished basement works well as your dog's living quarters. If your breed can tolerate living outside, you may want to buy or build him his own dog house with an attached run. It might be feasible to place his house in your fenced-in backyard. The breed that can live outdoors fares well when given access to some sort of warm, dry shelter during periods of inclement weather. As you begin thinking about where your canine friend will spend most of his time, you'll want to consider his breed, his age, his temperament, his need for exercise, and the money, space, and resources you have available to house him.

A bed for your dog gives him a place to call his own. His bed should be placed in a warm, dry, draft-free area.

69

THE DOG BED

In preparing for your puppy's arrival, it is recommended that a dog bed be waiting for him so that he has a place to sleep and rest. If you have provided him with his own bed or basket, ensure that it is placed in a warm, dry, draft-free spot that is private but at the same time near the center of family activity. Refrain from placing his bed near the feed and water dishes or his toilet area. You may want to give your puppy something with which to snuggle, such as a laundered towel or blanket or an article of old clothing. Some dogs have been known to chew apart their beds and bedding, but you can easily channel this chewing energy into more constructive behavior simply by supplying him with some safe toys or a Nylabone® pacifier for gnawing. Pet shops stock dog beds, among other supplies that you might need for your pup. Select a bed that is roomy, comfortable, and easy to clean, keeping in mind that you may have to replace the smaller bed with a larger one as the puppy grows to adulthood. Remember to clean and disinfect the bed and sleeping area from time to time, as these can become parasitic playgrounds for fleas, lice, mites, and the like.

Beds can have personality. Pet shops offer many different bedding options to the owner willing to explore.

The wire crate is a most effective means to accelerate housebreaking and is the safest way to ensure that the puppy is safe when he cannot be supervised.

THE CRATE

Although many dog lovers may cringe at the mere mention of the word *crate,* thinking of it as a cage or a cruel means of confinement, this handy piece of equipment can be put to good use for puppies and grown dogs alike. Even though you may love your dog to an extraordinary degree, you may not want him to have free reign of the house, particularly when you are not home to supervise him. If used properly, a crate can restrict your dog when it is not convenient to have him underfoot, *i.e.,* when guests are visiting or during your mealtimes.

A surprising number of dog owners, who originally had negative feelings about crating their dogs, have had great success using crates. The crate itself serves as a bed, provided it is furnished with bedding material, or it can be used as an indoor dog house. Not all dogs readily accept crates or being confined in them for short

Four Paws offers a wide range of shampoos for every need: from flea and tick to medicated and many others. All shampoos are pH balanced for a gentle yet effective cleaning.

intervals, so for these dogs, another means of restriction must be found. But for those dogs that do adjust to spending time in these structures, the crate can be useful in many ways. The animal can be confined for a few hours while you are away from home or at work, or you can bring your crated dog along with you in the car when you travel or go on vacation. Crates also prove handy as carriers whenever you have to transport a sick dog to the veterinarian.

Most crates are made of sturdy wire or plastic, and some of the collapsible models can be conveniently stored or folded so that they can be moved easily from room to room or from inside the house to the yard on a warm, sunny day. If you allow your puppy or grown dog to become acquainted with its crate by cleverly propping the door open and leaving some of his favorite toys inside, in no time he will come to regard the crate as his own doggie haven. As with a dog bed, place the crate away from drafts in a dry, warm spot; refrain from placing food and water dishes in it, as these only crowd the space and offer opportunity for spillage.

If you need to confine your puppy so that he can't get into mischief while you're not home, remember to consider the animal's needs at all times. Select a large crate, one in which the dog can stand up and move around comfortably; in fact, bigger is better in this context. Never leave the animal confined for more than a few hours at a time without letting him out to exercise, play, and, if necessary, relieve himself. Never crate a dog for ten hours, for example, unless you keep the door to the crate open so that he can get out for food and water and to stretch a bit. If long intervals of confinement are necessary, consider placing the unlatched crate in a partitioned section of your house or apartment.

Crates have become the answer for many a dog owner faced with the dilemma of either getting rid of a destructive dog or living with him despite his bad habits. People who have neither the time nor the patience to train their dogs, or to modify undesirable behavior patterns, can at least restrain their pets during the times they can't be there to supervise. So long as the crate is used in a humane fashion, whereby a dog is

Available at pet shops today are grooming products that not only groom your dog but also remove any loose hair while massaging your pet. Photo courtesy of Four Paws.

confined for no more than a few hours at any one time, it can figure importantly in a dog owner's life. Show dogs, incidentally, learn at an early age that much time will be spent in and out of crates while they are on the show circuit. Many canine celebrities are kept in their crates until they are called to ringside, and they spend many hours crated to and from the shows.

THE DOG HOUSE

These structures, often made of wood, should be sturdy and offer enough room for your dog to stretch out in when it rests or sleeps. Dog houses that are elevated or situated on a platform protect the animal from cold and dampness that may seep through the ground. For the breeds that are temperature hardy and will live outdoors, a dog house is an excellent option for daytime occupancy. Owners who cannot provide indoor accommodations for their chosen dog should consider a smaller breed since no dog should lead an exclusively outdoor existence.

If you have no option but to accommodate your dog with only an outdoor house, it will be necessary to provide him with a more elaborate house, one that really protects him from the elements. Make sure the dog's house is constructed of waterproof materials. Furnish

The pet trade offers many commercially made dog houses and other outdoor living structures that make great temporary accommodations for your pet.

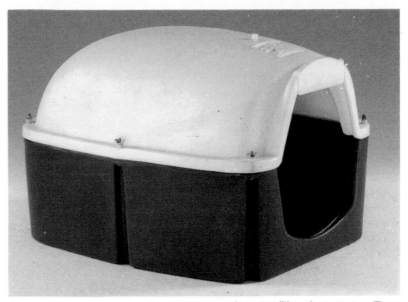

Indoor-outdoor dog houses offer pest-free, sanitary conditions for your dog. These attractive living options can be acquired from pet shops or supply outlets.

him with sufficient bedding to burrow into on a chilly night and provide extra insulation to keep out drafts and wet weather. Add a partition (a kind of room divider which separates the entry area from the main sleeping space) inside his house or attach a swinging door to the entrance to help keep him warm when he is inside his residence. The swinging door facilitates entry to and from the dog house, while at the same time it provides protection, particularly from wind and drafts.

Some fortunate owners whose yards are enclosed by high fencing allow their dogs complete freedom within the boundaries of their property. In these situations, a dog can leave his dog house and get all the exercise he wants. Of course such a large space requires more effort to keep it clean. An alternative to complete backyard freedom is a dog kennel or run which attaches to or surrounds the dog's house. This restricts some forms of movement, such as running, perhaps, but it does provide ample room for walking, climbing, jumping, and stretching. Another option is to fence off part of the yard and place the dog house in the enclosure. If you need to tether your dog to its house, make certain to use a fairly long lead so as not to hamper the animal's need to move and exercise his limbs.

An anchored lead can provide efficient temporary restraint. This is not a viable substitute for a fenced-in yard and no dog should be left unsupervised on such a lead for any length of time.

CLEANLINESS

No matter where your dog lives, either in or out of your home, be sure to keep him in surroundings that are as clean and sanitary as possible. His excrement should be removed and disposed of every day without fail. No dog should be forced to lie in his own feces. If your dog lives in his own house, the floor should be swept occasionally and the bedding should be changed regularly if it becomes soiled. Food and water dishes need to be scrubbed with hot water and detergent and rinsed well to remove all traces of soap. The water dish should be refilled with a supply of fresh water. The dog and his environment must be kept free of parasites (especially fleas and mosquitoes, which can carry disease) with products designed to keep these pests under control. Dog crates need frequent scrubbing, too, as do the floors of kennels and runs. Your pet must be kept clean and comfortable at all times; if you exercise strict sanitary control, you will keep disease and parasite infestation to a minimum.

EXERCISE

A well-balanced diet and regular medical attention from a qualified veterinarian are essential in promoting good health for your dog, but so is daily exercise to keep him fit and mentally alert. Dogs that have been confined all day while their owners are at work or school need special attention. There should be some time set aside each day for play—a romp with a family member, perhaps. Not everyone is lucky enough to let his dog run through an open meadow or along a sandy beach, but even a ten-minute walk in the fresh air will do. Dogs that are house-bound, particularly those that live in apartments, need to be walked out-of-doors after each meal so that they can relieve themselves. Owners can make this daily ritual more pleasant both for themselves and their canine companions by combining the walk with a little "roughhousing," that is to say, a bit of fun and togetherness.

Whenever possible, take a stroll to an empty lot, a playground, or a nearby park. Attach a long lead to your dog's collar, and let him run and jump and tone his body through aerobic activity. This will help him burn calories and will keep him trim, and it will also help relieve tension and stress that may have had a chance to develop while you were away all day. For people who work Monday through Friday,

weekend jaunts can be especially beneficial, since there will be more time to spend with your canine friend. You might want to engage him in a simple game of fetch with a stick or a rubber ball. Even such basic tricks as rolling over, standing on the hindlegs, or jumping up (all of which can be done inside

Four Paws Stain & Odor Remover contains active enzymes to remove tough urine stains and the odor that attracts puppies to the previously soiled area.

the home as well) can provide additional exercise. But if you plan to challenge your dog with a real workout to raise his heart rate, remember not to push him too hard without first warming up with a brisk walk. Don't forget to "cool him down" afterwards with a rhythmic trot until his heart rate returns to normal. Some dog owners jog with their dogs or take them along on bicycle excursions.

At the very least, however, play with your dog every day to keep him in good shape physically and mentally. If you can walk him outdoors, or better

yet run with him in a more vigorous activity, by all means do it. Don't neglect your pet and leave him confined for long periods without attention from you or time for exercise.

EXERCISING FOR YOU AND YOUR DOG

Dogs are like people. They come in three weights: overweight, underweight, and the correct weight. It is fair to say that most dogs are in better shape than most humans who own them. The reason for this is that most dogs accept exercise without objection—

The most popular in flying discs designed especially for dogs is the Nylabone Frisbee®, a toy that outlasts plastic discs by ten times. The molded dog bone on the top makes for easy retrieves by your dog.

people do not! Follow your dog's lead towards exercise and the complete enjoyment of the outdoors—your dog is the ideal work-out partner. There are toys at your local pet shop which are designed just for that purpose: to allow you to play and exercise with your dog. Here are a few recommended exercise toys for you and your dog.

Frisbee® Flying Discs® Most dog owners capitalize on the dog's natural instinct to fetch or retrieve, and the Frisbee® flying disc is standard fare for play. The original Frisbee® is composed of polyethylene plastic, ideal for flying and great for games of catch between two humans. Since humans don't usually chew on their flying discs, there is no need for a "chew-worthy" construction material. Dogs, on the other hand, do chew on their Frisbees® and therefore should not be allowed to play with a standard original Frisbee®. These discs will be destroyed quickly by the dog and the rigid plastic can cause intestinal complications.

Nylon Discs More suitable for playing with dogs are the Frisbee® discs that are constructed from nylon. These durable Frisbee® discs are designed especially for dogs and the nearly indestructible

manufacturing makes them ideal for aggressive chewing dogs. For play with dogs, the nylon discs called Nylabone Frisbee® are guaranteed to last ten times as long as the regular plastic Frisbee®. Owners should

Made of durable and flexible polyurethane, the Gumabone® Frisbees® prove chew-worthy and good-smelling to dogs. These and other Nylabone® discs are available in pet shops and other stores.

carefully consider the size of the nylon Frisbee® they purchase. A rule of thumb is choose the largest disc that your dog can comfortably carry. Nylabone manufactures two

Dogs enjoy toys they can carry around. The Gumaring® is a favorite plaything for many dogs.

The Tug Toy from Gumabone® is a flavorable exercise device that can be enjoyed by dog and owner.

sizes only—toy and large—so the choice should be apparent.

Polyurethane Flexible Floppy Flying Discs The greatest advance in flying discs came with the manufacture of these discs from polyurethane. The polyurethane is so soft that it doesn't hurt you, your dog, or the window it might strike accidentally. The polyurethane Gumadisc® is floppy and soft. It can be folded and fits into your pocket. It is also much tougher than cheap plastics, and most pet shops guarantee that it will last ten times longer than cheap plastic discs.

Making the polyurethane discs even more suited to dog play is the fact that many of the Gumabone® Frisbee® Flexible Fly Discs have the advantage of a dog bone molded on the top. Very often a Frisbee® without the bone molded on the top is difficult for a dog to pick up when it lands on a flat surface. The molded ones enable the dog to grasp it with his mouth or turn it with his paw. Dogs love pawing at the bone and even chew on it occasionally.

This product has one further capacity—it doubles

as a temporary drinking dish while out running, hiking and playing. The Gumabone Frisbee® flyers may also be flavored or scented, besides being annealed, so your dog can find it more easily if it should get lost in woods or tall grass.

Flying discs manufactured by the Nylabone® Company may cost more than some of its imitators, but an owner can be assured that the product will last and not be quickly destroyed.

(100 feet) is more than enough room. You throw the disc to each other, arousing your dog's interest as he tries to catch it.

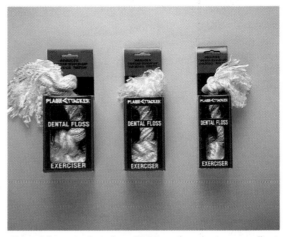

Dental floss devices from Nylabone® serve two excellent purposes: good exercise and clean teeth.

With most flying discs made for dogs comes an instruction booklet on how to use the disc with your canine friend. Basically, you play with the dog and the disc so the dog knows the disc belongs to him. Then you throw it continuously, increasing the distance, so that the dog fetches it and brings it back to you.

The exercise for you comes in when your dog stops fetching it, or when you have a partner. The two of you play catch. You stand as far apart as available space allows—usually 30–35 m

When the disc is dropped or veers off, the dog grabs it and brings it back (hopefully). Obviously you will have to run to catch the disc before your dog does.

There are contests held all over the world where distance, height, and other characteristics are measured competitively. Ask your local pet shop to help you locate a Frisbee® Club near you.

*Frisbee® is a trademark of the Kransco Company, California, and is used for their brand of flying disc.

Tug Toys A tug toy is a hard rubber, cheap plastic, or polyurethane toy which allows a dog and his owner to have a game of tug-o-war. The owner grips one end while the dog grips the other—then they pull. The polyurethane flexible tug toy is the best on the market at the present time. Your pet shop will have one to show you. The polyurethane toys are clear in color and stay soft forever. Cheap plastic tug toys are indisputably dangerous, and the hard-rubber tug toys get brittle too fast and are too stiff for most dogs; however, there *is* a difference in price—just ask the advice of any pet shop operator.

It pays to invest in entertainment toys and exercise devices which are marketed particularly for dogs. These products outlast everyday play things and are much safer for your pet. The Gumaball® is a great example of a dog toy worth the price of admission.

Balls Nobody has to tell you about playing ball with your dog. The reminder you may need is that you should not throw the ball where traffic might interfere with the dog's catching or fetching of it. The ball should not be cheap plastic (a dog's worst enemy as far as toys are concerned) but made of a substantial material. Balls made of nylon are practically indestructible, but they are very hard and must be rolled, never thrown. The same balls made of polyurethane are great—they bounce and are soft. The Nylaballs® and Gumaballs® are scented and flavored, and dogs can easily find them when lost.

Other manufacturers make balls of almost every substance, including plastic, cotton, and wood. Soft balls, baseballs, tennis balls, and so on, have all been used by dog owners who want their dogs to play with them in a game of catch. A strong caveat is that you use only those balls made especially for dogs.

Preventive Dental Care

ALL DOGS NEED TO CHEW

Puppies and young dogs need something with resistance to chew on while their teeth and jaws are developing—to cut the puppy teeth, to induce growth of the permanent teeth under the puppy teeth, to assist in getting rid of the puppy teeth on time, to help the permanent teeth through the gums, to assure

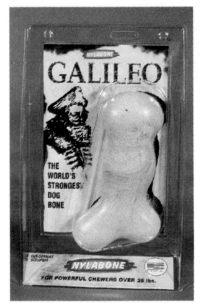

The Galileo™ is the strongest dog bone in the world! Made of extremely tough nylon, it is based upon original sketches by the scientist Galileo. Although designed for powerful chewers, Galileo Bones™ come in all sizes and are welcomed by any dog.

normal jaw development and to settle the permanent teeth solidly in the jaws.

The adult dog's desire to chew stems from the instinct for tooth cleaning, gum massage, and jaw exercise—plus the need to vent periodic doggie tensions. . . . A pacifier if you will!

Dental caries, as they affect the teeth of humans, are virtually unknown in dogs; but tartar (calculus) accumulates on the teeth of dogs, particularly at the gum line, more rapidly than on the teeth of humans. These accumulations, if not removed, bring irritation and then infection, which erode the tooth enamel and ultimately destroy the teeth at the roots. It is important that you take your dog to your local veterinarian for periodic dental examinations.

Tooth and jaw development will normally continue until the dog is more than a year old—but sometimes much longer, depending upon the dog, its chewing exercise, rate of calcium utilization and many other factors, known and unknown, which affect the development of individual dogs. Diseases, like distemper for example, may sometimes arrest development of the teeth and jaws, which may resume months or even years later.

This is why dogs, especially puppies and young dogs, will

often destroy valuable property when their chewing instinct is not diverted from their owners' possessions, particularly during the widely varying critical period for young dogs. Saving your possessions from destruction, assuring proper development of teeth and jaws, providing for "interim" tooth cleaning and gum massage, and channeling doggie tensions into a non-destructive outlet are, therefore, all dependent upon the dog's having something suitable for chewing readily available when his instinct tells him to chew. If your purposes, and those of your dog, are to be accomplished, what you provide for chewing must be desirable from the doggie viewpoint, have the necessary functional qualities, and, above all, be safe.

It is very important that dogs be prohibited from chewing on anything they can break or indigestible things from which they can bite sizeable chunks. Sharp pieces, such as those from a bone which can be broken by a dog, may pierce the intestinal wall and kill. Indigestible things which can be bitten off in chunks, such as toys made of rubber compound or cheap plastic, may cause an intestinal stoppage; if not regurgitated, they are certain to bring painful death unless surgery is promptly performed.

NATURAL CHEW BONES

Strong natural bones, such as 4- to 8-inch lengths of round shin bone from mature beef—either the kind you can get from your butcher or one of the varieties available commercially in pet stores—may serve your dog's teething needs, if his mouth is large enough to handle them effectively, *but,* constant chewing on hard bones wears down a dog's teeth. Natural bones are very abrasive and should be used sparingly.

You may be tempted to give your puppy a smaller bone and he may not be able to break it when you do, but puppies grow rapidly and the power of their jaws constantly increases until maturity. This means that a growing dog may break one of the smaller bones at any time, swallow the pieces and die painfully before you realize what is wrong.

Many people have the mistaken notion that their dog's teeth are like those of wild carnivores or of dogs from antiquity. The teeth of wild carnivorous animals and those found in the fossils of the dog-like creatures of antiquity have far thicker and stronger enamel than those of our dogs today.

All hard natural bones are highly abrasive. If your dog is an avid chewer, natural bones may wear away his teeth

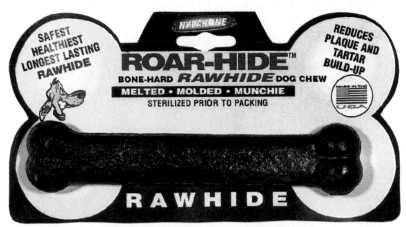

Roar-Hide™ from Nylabone® is the only safe rawhide product that also helps to fight plaque and tartar build-up on dogs' teeth. Roar-Hide™ is molded rawhide that is 86.20 % protein—it's edible and delectable to dogs. Don't confuse Roar-Hide™ with pressed rawhide, which is neither safe nor long-lasting.

prematurely; hence, they then should be taken away from your dog when the teething purposes have been served. The badly worn, and usually painful, teeth of many mature dogs can be traced to excessive chewing on animal bones. Contrary to popular belief, knuckle bones that can be chewed up and swallowed by the dog provide little, if any, useable calcium or other nutrient. They do, however, disturb the digestion of most dogs and might cause them to vomit the nourishing food they really need.

Never give a dog your old shoe to chew on, even if you have removed all the nails or metal parts, such as lace grommets, buckles, metal arches, and so on. Rubber heels are especially dangerous, as the dog can bite off chunks, swallow them, and suffer from intestinal blockage as a result. Additionally, if the rubber should happen to have a nail imbedded in it that you cannot detect, this could pierce or tear the intestinal wall. There is always the possibility, too, that your dog may fail to differentiate between his shoe and yours and chew up a good pair while you're not looking. It is strongly recommended that you refrain from offering old shoes as chew toys, since there are much safer products available.

Rawhide treats are popular choices for dogs. Owners are advised to keep an eye on their dogs whenever they are playing with rawhide.

RAWHIDE CHEWS

The most popular material from which dog chews are made is the hide from cows, horses, and other animals. Most of these chews are made in foreign countries where the quality of the hide is not good enough for making leather. These foreign hides may contain lead, antibiotics, arsenic, or insecticides which might be detrimental to the health of your dog...or even your children. It is not impossible that a small child will start chewing on a piece of rawhide meant for the dog! Rawhide chews do not serve the primary chewing functions very well. They are also a bit messy when wet from mouthing, and most dogs chew them up rather rapidly. They have been considered safe for dogs until recently.

Rawhide is flavorful to dogs. They like it. Currently, some veterinarians have been attributing cases of acute constipation to large pieces of incompletely digested rawhide in the intestine. Basically it is good for them to chew on, but dogs think rawhide is food. They do not play with it nor do they use it as a pacifier to relieve doggie tension. They eat it as they would any other food. This is dangerous, for the hide is very difficult for dogs to digest and swallow, and many dogs choke on large particles of rawhide that become stuck in their throats. *Before you offer your dog rawhide chews, consult your veterinarian.* Vets have a lot of experience with canine chewing devices; ask them what they recommend.

NYLON CHEW DEVICES

The nylon bones, especially those with natural meat and bone flavor added, are probably the most complete, safe, and economical answer to the chewing need. Dogs cannot break them nor bite off sizeable chunks; hence, they are completely safe. And being longer lasting than other things offered for the purpose, they are very economical.

Hard chewing raises little bristle-like projections on the surface of the nylon bones to provide effective interim tooth cleaning and vigorous gum massage, much in the same way your toothbrush does it for you. The little projections are raked off and swallowed in the form of thin shavings, but the chemistry of the nylon is such that they break down in the stomach fluids and pass through without effect.

The toughness of the nylon provides the strong chewing resistance needed for important jaw exercise and effective help for the teething functions; however, there is no tooth wear because nylon is non-abrasive. Being inert, nylon does not

Annealed nylon and polyurethane chew toys are recommended by veterinarians as proven-safe and effective canine chew devices.

Polyurethane bones come in many colors and sizes. The Rainbows collection from Gumabone® adds flair to any dog's dental hygiene program.

support the growth of microorganisms, and it can be washed in soap and water or sterilized by boiling or in an autoclave.

There are a great variety of Nylabone® products available that veterinarians recommend as safe and healthy for your dog or puppy to chew on. These Nylabone® Pooch Pacifiers® usually don't splinter, chip, or break off in large chunks; instead, they are frizzled by the dog's chewing action, and this creates a toothbrush-like surface that cleanses the teeth and massages the gums. At the

same time, these hard-nylon therapeutic devices channel doggie tension and chewing frustation into constructive rather than destructive behavior. The original nylon bone (Nylabone®) is not a toy and dogs use it only when in need of pacification. Keeping a bone in each of your dog's recreation rooms is the best method of providing the requisite pacification. Unfortunately, many nylon chew products have been copied. These inferior quality copies are sold in supermarkets and other chain stores. The really good products are sold only through veterinarians, pet shops, grooming salons and places where the sales people really know something about dogs. The good products have the flavor impregnated *into* the bone. This makes the taste last longer. The smell is undetectable to humans. The artificial bones which have a strong odor are poor-quality bones with the odor sprayed on to impress the dog owner (not the dog)! These heavily scented dog toys may impart the odor to your carpets or furniture if an odor-sprayed bone lies there wet from a dog's chewing on it.

FLOSS OR LOSS!

Most dentists relay that brushing daily is just not enough. In order to prevent unnecessary tooth loss, flossing is essential. For dogs, human dental floss is not the answer—however, canine dental devices are available. The Nylafloss® is a revolutionary product that is designed to save dogs teeth and keep them healthy. Even though your dogs won't believe you, Nylafloss® is not a toy but rather a most effective agent in removing destructive plaque between the teeth and *beneath* the gum line where gum disease begins. Gentle tugging is all that is necessary to activate the Nylafloss®. These 100% inert nylon products are guaranteed

to outlast rawhide chews by ten times and are available for sale at all pet shops.

THE IMPORTANCE OF PREVENTION

In order to get to the root of canine dentistry problems, it is important for owners to realize that no less than 75% of all canine dental health problems, serious enough to require a vet's assistance, and nearly 98% of all canine teeth lost are attributable to periodontal disease. Periodontal disease not only mars the teeth but also the gums and other buccal tissue in the mouth. Severe cases of periodontal disease involve resultant bacterial toxins which are absorbed into the blood

The Nylafloss® cannot cure tooth decay, but it is an optimum decay-prevention device. Make your dog's playtime a healthy time and invest in your pet's future.

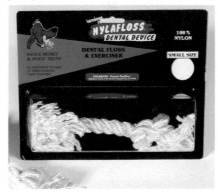

stream and cause permanent damage to the heart and kidneys. In the infected mouth, teeth are loosened; tartar, unsightly and bad smelling, accumulates heavily; and the dog experiences a complete

The Hercules™ by Nylabone® has been designed for the avid chewer. It is made of polyurethane, like some car bumpers. Illustrated is the largest Hercules™ available, but these strongest of bones come in sizes appropriate for all dogs.

loss of appetite. Long-standing periodontitis can also manifest itself in simple symptoms such as diarrhea and vomiting.

Periodontal disease deserves the attention of every dog owner—a dog's teeth are extremely important to his ongoing health. The accumulation of plaque, food matter mixed with saliva attaching itself to the tooth surface, is a sure sign of potential bacteria build-up. As toxic material gathers, the bone surrounding the teeth erodes. If plaque and calculus continue to reside without attention, bacteria-fighting cells will form residual pus at the root of the teeth, dividing the gum from the tooth. The debris is toxic and actually kills the buccal tissue. This is a most undesirable situation, as hardened dental calculus is one of the most direct causative agents of periodontitis.

In actuality, the disease is a result of a number of contributing factors. Old age, a diet comprised solely of soft or semi-soft foods, dental tartar, constant chewing of hair and even coprophagy (the eating of stool) are among the most common contributors.

Just as regular dental visits and brushing are necessary for humans, regular hygienic care and veterinary check-ups can help control tooth problems in canines. Involved and expensive routines can be performed on the affected, neglected mouth and teeth if decay has begun eroding the enamel and infecting the gums. Cleaning, polishing, and scaling are routine to remove calculus build-up.

Owners must claim responsibility for their dog's health, and tooth care is no small aspect of the care required. Daily brushing with a salt/baking soda solution is the best answer, but many owners find this tedious or just too difficult to perform. The simpler and more proven effective way to avoid, reduce, and fight periodontal disease and calculus build-up is giving the dog regular access to a thermoplastic polymer chew device. The Gumabone® products are the only scientifically proven line that offers the desired protection from calculus and tartar build-up.

CANINE DENTAL BREAKTHROUGH

The independent research of Dr. Andrew Duke, D.V.M., reveals that 70% of the dogs that regularly use Gumabone® experience a reduction of calculus build-up. This find is a breakthrough for the dog world, since the Gumabone® has already resided in the toy boxes of many dogs as their favorite play item. Little did owners know previously that their dogs were gaining entertainment and unparalleled dental treatment at the same time. Dr. Duke writes: "There is little debate left that dental calculus is an excellent indicator of periodontal health in the dog, just as it is in humans. "Calculus does not cause gingivitis and periodontitis, but the plaque and bacteria that cause periodontitis are

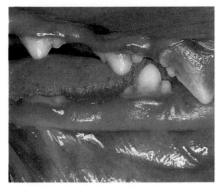

Regular use of the Gumabone® chew products can significantly reduce plaque build-up.

responsible for the mineral precipitation we know as 'calculus.' All veterinarians who have made a study of dogs' oral health have noticed the middle aged dog who actively chews with excellent gingival health. Many of these dogs that chew

Teeth of an infected dog showing little to no plaque accumulation after professional cleaning.

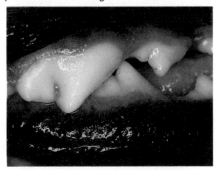

hard substances regularly wear the cusps down and even may expose the pulp cavity faster than secondary dentin can be formed. Often these "excellent chewers" are presented with slab fractures of the premolars or apical abcesses.

"The challenge then becomes to find a substance which is effective in removing calculus and plaque but does not wear the enamel excessively. In an attempt to duplicate the chewstuffs enjoyed by dogs in the wild, researchers have used bovine tracheas to demonstrate the inhibition of plaque and gingivitis. Very little else has been done in veterinary medicine to establish a scientific basis for evaluating chewstuffs.

"In the human field it is generally accepted (incorrectly) that fibrous foodstuffs and diet have no effect on oral health. This is a moot point since the practice of brushing is by far a more efficient technique of preventing plaque accumulation, calculus and periodontal disease. Studies in human subjects failed to find any benefits in eating apples, raw carrots, etc. If people are not allowed to brush, it is difficult to

Dental products are available for helping to fight plaque, reduce tartar build-up and control unpleasant breath in dogs. Photo courtesy of Four Paws.

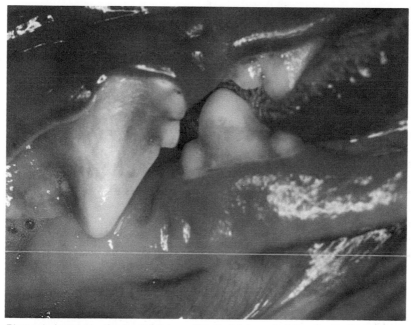

Plaque is formed by the food debris and bacterial deposits left on teeth. Due to the high carbon dioxide and pH levels in the mouth, minerals precipitate quickly on the plaque to form calculus.

conduct clinical trials of more than one week.

"The increased awareness of animals' dental health of recent years has resulted in most veterinary practitioners' recommending some kind of chewstuff to their dog owners. To meet this market demand, there has been a stampede into the market by vendors ready to promote their products. The veterinarian is furnished no scientific data, but is asked to promote rawhide, bounce, and squeaky toys. How would our human colleagues handle this situation? Can Listerine® say that it prevents colds, but not support the claim? Can "Tartar Control Crest®," or "Colgate Tartar Control Formula®" be sold if it is not proven that it does in fact reduce tartar? Of course not.

"To this end, the following study was made.

"*Method:* Twenty dogs of different breeds and age were selected from a veterinary

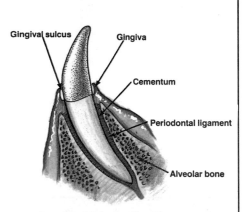

Comparative look at healthy gums (above) *and affected gums* (below) *in a dog's mouth. Instinctively dogs need to massage their gums—and the Gumabone® can satisfy this doggie craving.*

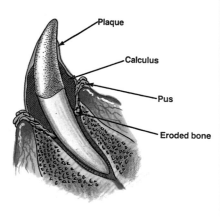

practice's clientele. Although most were from multiple pet households, none were colony dogs. The owners were asked if they would allow their dogs to be anesthetized for two prophylactic cleanings which included root planing, polishing, and gingival debridement necessary to insure good oral hygiene.

"The dogs were divided into two groups of 10. Their teeth were cleaned and their calculus index converted to 0. One group was allowed only their normal dry commercial dog ration for 30 days. The other was allowed to have free choice access to Gumabone® products of the appropriate size.

"After 30 days, photoslides were made of the upper 3rd premolar, upper 4th premolar, and the lower 4th premolar on both sides of the dog's mouth. The dogs were again subjected to a prophylactic cleaning and the group reversed. After the second 30 days, photoslides were again made. A total of six teeth in each mouth were evaluated on each dog. This was 80 slides representing 240 teeth."

Fourteen out of 20 dogs (or 70%) experienced a reduction in calculus build-up by regularly using the Gumabone® product. These products are available in a variety of sizes (for different

Nylabone® and Gumabone® offer a new option for the choosy canine—chicken-flavored bones. Entertainment and pearly white teeth have never been better acquainted.

size dogs) and designed in interesting shapes: bones, balls, knots and rings (and even a tug toy). The entertainment value of the Gumabone® products is but an added advantage to the fighting of tooth decay and periodontitis. The products are ham-flavored and made of a thermoplastic polymer that is designed to outlast by ten times any rawhide, rubber or vinyl chew product, none of which can promise the proven benefit of the Gumabone®.

If your dog is able to chew apart a Gumabone®, it is probable that you provided him with a bone that is too small for him. Replace it with a larger one and the problem should not re-materialize. Economically, the Gumabone® is a smart choice, even without comparing it to the cost of extensive dental care.

Of course, nothing can *substitute* for periodic

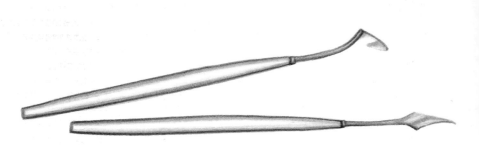

In cases of bad neglect, scaling a dog's teeth can help to save or salvage affected teeth. Your veterinarian can perform this procedure.

professional attention to your dog's teeth and gums, no more than your toothbrush can replace your dentist. Have your dog's teeth cleaned by your veterinarian at least once a year—twice a year is better—and he will be healthier, happier, and a far more pleasant companion.

Gumabones® are available through veterinarians and pet shops.

Products that help eliminate bad breath for your pet are widely available at pet shops. The one shown here is chewable and works with the digestive system to help neutralize your pet's bad breath. Photo courtesy of Four Paws.

Your Pekingese is the aristocrat of dogdom. Be sure to care for him as such, and he will provide you with many wonderful years of loving companionship.

Housebreaking and Training

HOUSEBREAKING

The new addition to your family may already have received some basic house training before his arrival in your home. If he has not, remember that a puppy will want to relieve himself about half a dozen times a day; it is up to you to specify where and when he should "do his business." Housebreaking is your first training concern and should begin the moment you bring the puppy home.

Ideally, puppies should be taken outdoors after meals, as a full stomach will exert pressure on the bladder and colon. What goes into the dog must eventually come out; the period

Four Paws Wee-Wee Pads are scientifically treated to attract puppies when nature calls. The plastic lining prevents damage to floors and carpets.

after his meal is the most natural and appropriate time. When he eliminates, he should be praised, for this will increase the likelihood of the same thing happening after every meal. He should also be encouraged to use the same area and will probably be attracted to it after frequent use.

Some veterinarians maintain that a puppy can learn to urinate and defecate on command, if properly trained. The advantage of this conditioning technique is that your pet will associate the act of elimination with a particular word of your choice rather than with a particular time or place which might not always be convenient or available. So whether you are visiting an unfamiliar place or don't want to go outside with your dog in sub-

zero temperatures, he will still be able to relieve himself when he hears the specific command word. Elimination will occur after this "trigger" phrase or word sets up a conditioned reflex in the dog, who will eliminate anything contained in his bladder or bowel upon hearing it. The shorter the word, the more you can repeat it and imprint it on your dog's memory.

Your chosen command word should be given simultaneously with the sphincter opening events in order to achieve perfect and rapid conditioning. This is why it is important to familiarize yourself with the tell-tale signs preceding your puppy's elimination process. Then you will be prepared to say the word at the crucial moment. There is usually a sense of

Crates assist in house-training the puppy. The dog's natural instinct is never to soil his sleeping area.

urgency on the dog's part; he may follow a sniffing and circling pattern which you will soon recognize. It is important to use the command in his usual area only when you know the puppy can eliminate, i.e., when his stomach or bladder is full. He will soon learn to associate the act with the word. One word of advice, however, if you plan to try out this method: never use the puppy's name or any other word which he might frequently hear about the house—you can imagine the result!

Finally, remember that any training takes time. Such a conditioned response can be obtained with intensive practice with any normal, healthy dog over six weeks of age. Even Pavlov's salivating dogs required fifty repetitions before the desired response was achieved. Patience and persistence will eventually produce results—do not lose heart!

Indoors, sheets of newspapers can be used to cover the specific area where your dog should relieve himself. These should be placed some distance away from his sleeping and feeding area, as a puppy

Begin the training of your Pekingese pups right away. Patience and persistence will produce a well-behaved pet.

Holidays are not the best time to bring your Pekingese pup home. The excitement and visitors may be too much for a puppy to handle. Plan to make your Peke's arrival as relaxed and routine as possible.

The choke collar and walking lead are commonly used in training.

will not urinate or defecate where he eats. When the newspapers are changed, the bottom papers should be placed on top of the new ones in order to reinforce the purpose of the papers by scent as well as by sight. The puppy should be praised during or immediately after he has made use of this particular part of the room. Each positive reinforcement increases the possibility of his using that area again.

When he arrives, it is advisable to limit the puppy to one room, usually the kitchen, as it most likely has a linoleum or easily washable floor surface. Given the run of the house, the sheer size of the place will seem overwhelming and confusing and he might leave his "signature" on your furniture or clothes! There will be time later to familiarize him gradually with his new surroundings.

PATIENCE, PERSISTENCE, AND PRAISE

As with a human baby, you must be patient, tolerant, and understanding of your pet's mistakes, making him feel loved and wanted, not rejected and isolated. You wouldn't hit a baby for soiling his diapers, as you would realize that he was not yet able to control his bowel movements; be as compassionate with your canine infant. Never rub his nose in his excreta. Never indulge in the common practice of punishing him with a rolled-up newspaper. Never hit a puppy with your hand. He will only become "hand-shy" and learn to fear you. Usually the punishment is meted out sometime after the offense and loses its efficacy, as the bewildered dog cannot connect the two events. Moreover, by association, he will soon learn to be afraid of you and anything to do with newspapers—including, perhaps, that area where he is

supposed to relieve himself!

Most puppies are eager to please. Praise, encouragement, and reward (particularly the food variety) will produce far better results than any scolding or physical punishment. Moreover, it is far better to dissuade your puppy from doing certain things, such as chewing on chair legs or other furniture, by making those objects particularly distasteful to him. Some pet shops stock bitter apple sprays or citronella compounds for application to furniture legs. These products are generally safer than old-fashioned home remedies. An owner may soon discover that application of these products may indeed make it seem as if

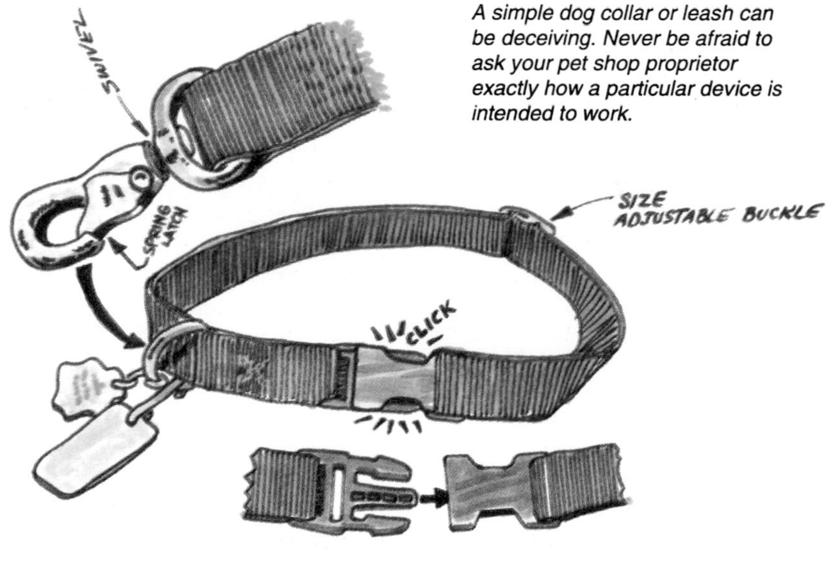

A simple dog collar or leash can be deceiving. Never be afraid to ask your pet shop proprietor exactly how a particular device is intended to work.

SWIVEL

SPRING LATCH

SIZE ADJUSTABLE BUCKLE

CLICK

Though loving and friendly with the whole household, Pekes usually have a "favorite" family member whom they will obey more readily.

the object itself was administering the punishment whenever he attempted to chew it. He probably wouldn't need a second reminder and your furniture will remain undamaged.

Remember that the reason a dog has housebreaking or behavior problems is because his owner has allowed them to develop. This is why you must begin as you intend to continue, letting your dog know what is acceptable and unacceptable behavior. It is also important that you be consistent in your demands; you cannot feed him

from the dining room table one day and then punish him when he begs for food from your dinner guests.

TRAINING

You will want the newest member of your family to be welcomed by everyone; this will not happen if he urinates in every room of the house or barks all night! He needs training in the correct forms of behavior in this new human world. You cannot expect your puppy to become the perfect pet overnight. He needs your help in

The tiny Pekingese has very clean habits, and is easily housebroken.

his socialization process. Training greatly facilitates and enhances the relationship of the dog to his owner and to the rest of society. A successfully trained dog can be taken anywhere and behave well with anyone. Indeed, it is that one crucial word—*training*—which can transform an aggressive animal into a peaceful, well-behaved pet. Now, how does this "transformation" take place?

WHEN AND HOW TO TRAIN

Like housebreaking, training should begin as soon as the puppy enters the house. The formal training sessions should be short but frequent, for example, ten to fifteen minute periods three times a day. These are much more effective than long, tiring sessions of half an hour which might soon become boring. You are building your relationship with your puppy during these times, so make them as enjoyable as possible. It is a good idea to have these sessions *before* the puppy's meal, not after it when he wouldn't feel like exerting himself; the dog will then associate something pleasurable with his training sessions and look forward to them.

A choke collar can be an effective training tool when properly used.

THE COLLAR AND LEASH

Your puppy should become used to a collar and leash as soon as possible. If he is very young, a thin, choke-chain collar can be used, but you will need a larger and heavier one for training when he is a little older. Remember to have his name and address on an identification tag attached to his collar, as you don't want to lose your pet if he should happen to leave your premises and explore the neighborhood!

Let the puppy wear his collar until he is used to how it feels. After a short time he will soon become accustomed to it and you can attach the leash. He might resist your attempts to lead him or simply sit down and refuse to budge. Fight him for a few minutes, tugging on the leash if necessary, then let him relax for the day. He won't be trained until he learns that he must obey the pull under any circumstance, but this will take a few sessions. Remember that a dog's period of concentration is short, so *little* and *often* is the wisest course of action—and patience is the password to success.

GIVING COMMANDS

When you begin giving your puppy simple commands, make them as short as possible and use the same word with the same meaning at all times, for example, "Heel," "Sit," and "Stay." You must be consistent; otherwise your puppy will become confused. The dog's name should prefix all commands to attract his attention. Do not become impatient with him however many times you have to repeat your command.

A good way to introduce the "Come" command is by calling the puppy when his meal is ready. Once this is learned, you can call your pet to you at will, always remembering to praise him for his prompt obedience. This "reward," or positive

Fully retractable leads are available in different strengths (and lengths) to allow owners to match the lead to the size and weight of their dogs. Photo courtesy of Flexi USA, Inc.

A pair of pretty Pekes. Owner, Sheila McClure.

reinforcement, is such a crucial part of training that a Director of the New York Academy of Dog Training constructed his whole teaching program upon the methods of "Love, Praise, and Reward." Incidentally, if you use the command "Come," use it every time. Don't switch to "Come here" or "Come boy," as this will only confuse your dog.

Guaranteed by the manufacturer to stop any dog, any size, any weight from ever pulling again. It's like having power steering for your dog.

It is worth underlining the fact that punishment is an ineffective teaching technique. We have already seen this in housebreaking. For example, if your pup should run away, it would be senseless to beat him when he eventually returns; he would only connect the punishment with his return, not with running away! In addition, it is unwise to call him to you to punish him, as he will soon learn not to respond when you call his name.

SOME SPECIFIC COMMANDS

"Sit" This is one of the easiest and most useful commands for your dog to learn, so it is a good idea to begin with it. The only equipment required is a leash, a collar, and a few tasty tidbits. Take your dog out for some exercise before his meal. After about five minutes, call him to you, praise him when he arrives, and slip his collar on him. Hold the leash tightly in your right hand; this should force the dog's head up and focus his attention on you. As you say "Sit" in a loud, clear voice, with your left hand press steadily on his rump until he is in a sitting position. As soon as he is in the correct position, praise him and give him the tidbit you have in your hand. Now wait a few minutes to let him rest and repeat the routine. Through repetition, the dog soon associates the word with the act. Never make the lesson too long. Eventually your praise will be reward enough for your puppy. Other methods to teach this command exist, but this one, executed with care and moderation, has proven the most effective.

Great for the athletic dog and less-active owner are commercially designed retractable leads which give the dog much more freedom when exercising in an open field or cleared area. Photo courtesy of Flexi USA, Inc.

"Sit-Stay/Stay" To teach your pet to remain in one place or "stay" on your command, first of all order him to the sitting position at your side. Lower your left hand with the flat of your palm in front of his nose and your fingers pointing downwards. Hold the leash high and taut behind his head so that he cannot move. Speak the command "Sit-stay" and, as you are giving it, step in front of him. Repeat the command and tighten the leash so the animal cannot follow you. Walk completely around him, repeating the command and keeping him motionless by holding the leash at arm's length above him to check his movement. When he remains in this position for about fifteen seconds, you can begin the second part of the training. You will have to exchange the leash for a nylon cord or rope about twenty to thirty feet long. Repeat the whole routine from the beginning and be ready to prevent any movement towards you with a sharp "Sit-stay." Move around him in ever-widening circles until you are about fifteen feet away from him. If he still remains seated, you can pat yourself on the back! One useful thing to remember is that the dog makes associations with what you say, how you say it, and what you do while you are saying it. Give this command in a firm, clear tone of voice, perhaps using an admonishing forefinger raised, warning the dog to "stay."

"Heel" When you walk your dog, you should hold the leash firmly in your right hand. The dog should walk on your left so you have the leash crossing your body. This enables you to have greater control over the dog.

Let your dog lead you for the first few moments so that he fully understands that freedom can be his if he goes about it properly.

He already knows that when he wants to go outdoors the leash and collar are necessary, so he has respect for the leash. Now, if he starts to pull in one direction while walking, all you do is *stop walking.* He will walk a few steps and then find that he can't walk any further. He will then turn and look into your face. *This is the crucial point!* Just stand there for a moment and stare right back at him . . . now walk another ten feet and stop again. Again your dog will probably walk to the end of the leash, find he can't go any further, and turn around and look again. If he starts to pull and jerk, just stand there. After he quiets

Grooming is part of the training process. Begin brushing your Peke as a pup and he will easily become accustomed to a regular grooming schedule.

Make sure your Pekingese has a proper-fitting collar and always use a leash when training outdoors.

down, bend down and comfort him, as he may be frightened. Keep up this training until he learns not to outwalk you.

Once the puppy obeys the pull of the leash, half of your training is accomplished. "Heeling" is a necessity for a well-behaved dog, so teach him to walk beside you, head even with your knee. Nothing looks sadder than a big dog taking his helpless owner for a walk. It is annoying to passers-by and other dog owners to have a large dog, however friendly, bear down on them and entangle dogs, people, and packages.

To teach your dog, start off walking briskly, saying "Heel" in a firm voice. Pull back with a sharp jerk if he lunges ahead, and if he lags repeat the command and tug on the leash, not allowing him to drag behind. After the dog has learned to heel at various speeds on leash, you can remove it and practice heeling free, but have it ready to snap on again as soon as he wanders.

"Come" Your dog has already learned to come to you when you call his name. Why? Because you only call him when his food is ready or when you wish to play with him or praise him. Outdoors such a response is more difficult to achieve, if he is happily playing by himself or with other dogs, so he must be trained to come to you when he is called. To teach him to come, let him reach the end of a long lead, then give the command, gently pulling him towards you at the same time. As soon as he associates the word *come* with the action of moving towards you, pull only when he does not respond immediately. As he starts to come, move back to make him learn that he must come from a distance as well as when he is close to you. Soon you may be able to practice without a leash, but if he is slow to come or actively disobedient, go to him and pull him toward you, repeating the command. Always remember to reward his successful completion of a task.

"Down" Teaching the "down" command ideally begins while your dog is still a pup. During puppyhood your dog frequently will lie down, as this position is one of the dog's most natural positions. Invest some time, and keep close watch over your pup. Each time he begins to lie, repeat in a low convincing tone the word "down." If for the first day of training, you concur a majority of the dog's sitting with your commands and continue with reinforcement and moderate praise your pup should conquer the "down" command in no time.

Teaching the "down" command to a mature dog likely will require more effort. Although the lying position is still natural to a dog, his being forced into it is not. Some dogs may react with fear, anger, or confusion. Others may accept the process and prove quick learners. Have your dog sit and face you. If he is responsive and congenial, gently take his paws, and slowly pull them towards you; give the "down" command as he approaches the proper position. Repeat several times: moderate reinforcement of this procedure should prove rewardingly successful.

For the dog that responds with anger or aggression, attach a lead (and a muzzle) and have the dog sit facing you at a close distance. There should be a J-loop formed by the lead. With moderate force, relative to the size and strength of your dog, step on the J-loop, forcing the dog down, while repeating the command "down" in a low forceful tone. When the dog is down, moderate praise should be given. If the dog proves responsive, you may attempt extending his legs to the "down" position—leaving the muzzle on, of course. Daily reinforcement of the training method will soon yield the desired results. The keys to remember are: patience, persistence, and praise.

Behavior Modification

"Problems with the Barking Dog" and "Aggressive Behavior and Dominance" are extracts from the veterinary monograph *Canine Behavior* (a compilation of columns from *Canine Practice,* a journal published by Veterinary Practice Publishing Company).

PROBLEMS WITH THE BARKING DOG

One of the most frequent complaints about canine behavior is barking. Aside from the biting dog, the barking dog is probably the pet peeve of many non-dog owners. I know of at least one city in which owners of dogs that bark excessively, and for which there are complaints on file, are required to take steps to eliminate the barking.

Canine practitioners are drawn into problems with barking when they are asked for their advice in helping an owner come up with a solution or, as a last resort, when they are requested to perform a debarking operation or even euthanasia. In this column I will deal with some of the factors that apparently cause dogs to bark and suggest some corrective approaches.

Barking is, of course, a natural response for many dogs. They have an inherited predisposition to bark as an alarm when other dogs or

The Water Bucket Approach is an effective way to punish a dog for barking without being directly involved in administering the punishment.

people approach their territory. Alarm barking makes many dogs valuable as household watchdogs and is not necessarily undesirable behavior. With a different vocal tone and pattern, dogs bark when they are playing with each other. On occasion dogs have a tendency to bark back at other dogs or join in with other barking dogs.

In addition to inherited barking tendencies, dogs can also learn to bark if the barking is followed, at least sometimes,

Though jealous by nature, Pekingese can easily be trained to share the affection of their master. Photo by Robert Smith.

by a reward. Thus dogs may bark when they wish to come in the house or to get out of a kennel. Some dogs are trained to bark upon hearing the command "speak" for a food reward.

One of the first approaches to take when discussing a barking problem is to determine if the behavior is a manifestation of a natural (inherited) tendency or is learned behavior which has been rewarded in the past.

Can Barking Be Extinguished? Extinction, as a way of eliminating a behavioral problem, may be considered when it is clear that the behavior has been learned and when one can identify the specific rewarding or reinforcing factors that maintain the behavior.

For example, the dog that barks upon hearing the command "speak" is periodically rewarded with food and praise. If a dog is never, ever given food or praise again when it barks after being told to "speak," it will eventually stop this type of barking. This is the process of extinction and it implies that the behavior must be repeated but never again rewarded.

A more practical example of the possible use of extinction would be in dealing with the dog that apparently barks because, at least occasionally, it is allowed in the house. By not allowing the dog in the house

Muzzles may prevent biting, but the root cause of biting must be extracted if the dog is to live as a trusted member of the human family.

until the barking has become very frequent and loud, the owners may have shaped the barking behavior to that which is the most objectionable. If the dog is never allowed in the house again when barking, the barking should eventually be extinguished—at least theoretically.

How Should Punishment Be Used? Sometimes it is not feasible to attempt to extinguish barking even if it seems to be the case that the behavior was learned. This brings up the advisability of punishment. Clients who seek advice in dealing with a barking problem may already have employed some type of punishment such as shouting at the dog or throwing something at it. That this type of punishment is ineffective is attested to by the fact that the client is seeking advice. By shouting at a dog or hitting, a person interferes with what effect the punishment may have on the behavior itself through the arousal of autonomic reactions and escape attempts or submissive responses by the dog.

The Water Bucket Approach I am rather impressed by the ingenuity of some dog owners in coming up with ways to punish a dog for barking without being directly involved in administering the punishment. One such

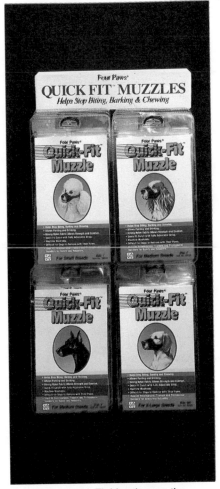

Four Paws Quick Fit Muzzles are the most comfortable and humane muzzles for dogs. Allow dogs to drink water while wearing the muzzles. They are made of nylon and are completely washable.

One fascination of the Pekingese character is that you never quite know exactly what they are thinking. Owner, Elizabeth Nisbet.

Pet gates are used to confine a dog to certain areas of the house. The dog must learn to accept any such restrictions and not attempt to overcome them.

harried dog owner I talked to, who was also a veterinarian, was plagued by his dog's barking in the kennel commencing at about 1:30 a.m. every night. A platform to hold a bucket of water was constructed over the area of the kennel in which the dog usually chose to bark. Through a system of hinges, ropes, and pulleys, a mechanism was devised so that the dog owner could pull a rope from his bedroom window, dumping a bucket of water on the dog when he started to bark. The bucket was suspended such that once it was dumped, it uprighted itself and the owner could fill it again remotely by turning on a garden hose. After two appropriate dunkings, the dog's barking behavior was apparently eliminated.

In advising a client on the type of punishment discussed above, keep in mind one important consideration. From the time the owner is ready to administer punishment for barking, every attempt should be made to punish all undesirable barking from that point on and not to allow excessively long periods of barking to go unpunished. Thus it may be necessary to keep a dog indoors when away unless the dog will be punished for barking when the owner is gone.

Alternative Responses

Barking dogs are, and probably always will be, one of the enduring problems of dog owners. Barking is relatively effortless, and it is such a natural response for many dogs that it is admittedly hard to eliminate with either punishment or a program of conditioning non-barking. In some instances it may be advisable to forget about eliminating barking and to suggest that the problem be dealt with by changing the circumstances which lead to barking. For example, a dog that barks continuously in the backyard while the owners are away may not bark if left in the house while they are gone. But the problem of keeping the dog in the house may be related to inadequate house training or the

Four Paws repellents are excellent training aids to keep dogs out of forbidden areas. Use indoors on furniture and rugs; outdoor formula for flowerbeds, shrubs and garbage cans.

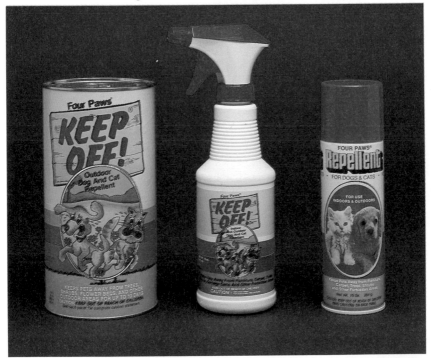

This pretty Pekingese is owned by Mary Gay.

dog's shedding hair or climbing onto the furniture. It may be easier to correct these latter behavioral problems than it is to change the barking behavior.

AGGRESSIVE BEHAVIOR AND DOMINANCE

Aggressiveness can have many causes. Determining what kind of aggression an animal is manifesting is a prerequisite to successful treatment of the behavior. A frequent problem that is presented to the practitioner is one of aggression related to dominance.

Dogs, which are social animals, have a hierarchal system of dominance within their pack. This predisposition to take a dominant or submissive position relative to fellow canines also occurs in relationship to people. Only in unusual situations would a submissive dog threaten a dominant animal, and almost never would it physically assault its superior. The dominant dog, however, frequently threatens submissive individuals to maintain its position. In a household setting, a person may be the object of threats, and when the person backs off, the dog's position is reassured. The aggressive behavior is also reinforced, and when behavior is reinforced it is likely to recur.

Owners must take an active part in shaping their dog's behavior. Providing a sensible chew device can help alleviate an animal's frustration and thereby eliminate some undesirable behavior. Once a dog has chewed the Gumabone® to this extent, it's time to buy a new one.

Case History The following is a typical case history of a dog presented for aggression stemming from dominance.

Max was a two-year-old intact male Cocker Spaniel. He had been acquired by Mr. Smith, one year prior to his owner's marriage, as a puppy. He liked and was well liked by both Mr. and Mrs. Smith. He frequently solicited and received attention from both people. However, several times over the last few months, Max had snapped at Mrs. Smith and repeatedly growled at her. A detailed anamnesis revealed that such incidents usually occurred in situations where the dog wanted his own way or did not want to be bothered. He would growl if asked to move off a chair or if persistently commanded to do a specific task. He growled if Mrs. Smith came between him and a young female Cocker Spaniel acquired a year ago. He also refused to let Mrs. Smith take anything from his possession. Max never showed any of these aggressive behaviors toward Mr. Smith or strangers. Admittedly he did not

Treats can be effective in shaping behavior and establishing a rapport with your pet.

have much opportunity to demonstrate such behaviors toward strangers. A description of the dog's body and facial postures and circumstances under which the aggression occurred did not indicate that this was a case of fear-induced aggression, but rather one of assertion of dominance.

Mrs. Smith's reaction to the aggression was always to retreat, and, hence, the dog was rewarded for his assertiveness. She had never physically disciplined the dog and was afraid to do so. To encourage her to physically take control of the dog would likely have resulted in her being bitten. The dominance-submissive

The Pekingese is a hardy little dog and has stamina much greater than his size. Be sure to keep your Peke away from any poisonous plants when romping outside.

While crates may be used principally for sleeping and traveling, some owners might opt to employ a crate for disciplining a dog, rather like sending a naughty child to his room.

relationship had to be reversed in a more subtle manner.

Instructions to Client Mrs. Smith was instructed to avoid all situations which might evoke any aggressive signs from Max. This was to prevent any further reinforcement of his growling and threats.

Both she and her husband were not to indiscriminately pet or show affection towards the dog. For the time being, if Max solicited attention from Mr. Smith, he was to ignore the dog. Mrs. Smith was to take advantage of Max's desire for attention by giving him a command which he had to obey before she praised and petted him. She was also to take advantage of high motivation levels for other activities whenever such situations arose. Max had to obey a command before she gave him anything—

before she petted him, before she let him out or in, etc.

Mrs. Smith also was to assume total care of the dog and become "the source of all good things in life" for Max. She was to feed him, take him on walks, play with him, etc.

Mrs. Smith also spent 5–10 minutes a day teaching Max simple parlor tricks and obedience responses for coveted food rewards as well as praise. These were entirely fun and play sessions—but within a few days the dog had acquired the habit of quickly responding to commands. And this habit transferred over to the non-game situations.

Results Within a few weeks, Max had ceased to growl and threaten Mrs. Smith in situations that he previously had. He would move out of her way or lie quietly when she would pass by him. She could order him off the furniture and handle the female Cocker Spaniel without eliciting threats from Max.

Mrs. Smith still felt that she would not be able to take the objects from Max's possession. Additional instructions were given to her. She then began placing a series of objects at progressively closer distances to the dog while the dog was in a sit-stay position. After she placed the object on the floor for a short time, she would pick it up. If the dog was still in a sit-stay (which it always was), he received a reward of cheese and verbal praise. Eventually the objects were to be placed and removed from directly in front of the dog. At first she was to use objects that the dog did not care much about and then progressively use more coveted items. This was what she was supposed to do, but before she actually had completed the program she called in excitedly to report that she had taken a piece of stolen food and a household ornament from Max's mouth. And he didn't even object! She said she had calmly told Max to sit. He did. He was so used to doing so, in the game and other situations, that the response was now automatic. She walked over, removed the item from his mouth, and praised him.

Mrs. Smith did resume the systematic presentation of objects and put the dog on an intermittent schedule of food and praise reinforcement during the practice sessions. Mr. Smith again began interacting with Max.

A progress check six months later indicated Max was still an obedient dog and had definitely assumed a submissive position relative to both of his owners. The dominance hierarchy between Max and Mrs. Smith had been reversed *without resorting to any physical punishment.* Mrs. Smith was instructed to reinforce her dominance position by frequently giving Max a command and reinforcing him for the appropriate response.

Summary The essential elements in treatment of such cases are as follows. First, of course, there must be a correct diagnosis of what kind of aggressive behavior is occurring. During the course of treatment, the submissive person(s) should avoid all situations that might evoke an aggressive attitude by the dog. All other family members should totally ignore the dog during the treatment interim. The person most dominated by the dog should take over complete care of the dog in addition to spending 5–10 minutes a day teaching the dog tricks or simple obedience commands (sit-stay is a useful one to gain control of the dog in subsequent circumstances). These should be fun-and-games situations. Food rewards are highly recommended in addition to simple praise.

The person submissive to the dog should take the opportunity to give the dog a command, which must be obeyed, before doing anything pleasant for the dog.

Four Paws offers Bitter Lime in two ways. A pump spray to stop fur biting and a gel to stop chewing of furniture. Both are safe and non-toxic.

It must be emphasized to the owner that no guarantee can be made that the dog will never threaten or be aggressive again. What is being done, as with all other aggression cases, is an attempt to reduce the likelihood, incidence, and intensity of occurrence of the aggressive behavior.

Old discardable shoes should not be included in the dog's toy box. Such items are dangerous to a puppy or an adult dog.

DESTRUCTIVE TENDENCIES

It is ironical but true that a dog's destructive behavior in the home may be proof of his love for his owner. He may be trying to get more attention from his owner or, in other cases, may be expressing his frustration at his owner's absence. An abundance of unused energy may also contribute to a dog's destructive behavior, and therefore the owner should ensure that his dog has, at least, twenty minutes of vigorous exercise a day.

As a dog's destructive tendencies may stem from his desire to get more attention from his owner, the latter should devote specific periods each day to his dog when he is actively interacting with him. Such a period should contain practice obedience techniques during which the owner can reward the dog with his favorite food as well as praise and affection.

Planned departure conditioning is one specific technique which has been used to solve the problem of destructive tendencies in a puppy. It eventually ensures the dog's good behavior during the owner's absence. A series of short departures, which are identical to real departures, should condition the dog to behave well in the owner's absence. How is this to be achieved? Initially, the departures are so short (2–5 minutes) that the dog has no opportunity to be destructive.

The dog is always rewarded for having been good when the owner returns. Gradually the duration of the departures is increased. The departure time is also varied so that the dog does not know when the owner is going to return. Since a different kind of behavior is now expected, it is best if a new stimulus or "atmosphere" is introduced into the training sessions to permit the dog to distinguish these departures as different from previous departures when he was destructive.

This new stimulus could be the sound of the radio or television. The association which the dog will develop is that whenever the "signal" or "stimulus" is on, the owner will return in an unknown period of time and, if the dog has not been destructive, he will be rewarded. As with the daily owner-dog interaction, the food reward is especially useful.

If the dog misbehaves during his owner's absence, the owner should speak sternly to him and isolate him from social contact for at least thirty minutes. (Puppies hate to be ignored.)

Then the owner should conduct another departure of a shorter time and generously reward good behavior when he returns. The owner should progress slowly enough in the program so that once the departure has been initiated, the dog is never given an opportunity to make a mistake.

If planned departures are working satisfactorily, the departure time

There is a wide variety of collars and harnesses available to the dog owner. Talk with your pet shop proprietor to determine which one best satisfies your needs.

may gradually be extended to several hours. To reduce the dog's anxiety when left alone, he should be given a "safety valve" such as the indestructible Nylabone® to play with and chew on.

Health Care

From the moment you purchase your puppy, the most important person in both your lives becomes your veterinarian. His professional advice and treatment will ensure the good health of your pet. The vet is the first person to call when illness or accidents occur. Do *not* try to be your own veterinarian or apply human remedies to canine diseases. However, just as you would keep a first aid kit handy for minor injuries sustained by members of your family at home, so you should keep a similar kit prepared for your pet.

First aid for your dog would consist of stopping any bleeding, cleaning the wound, and preventing infection. Thus your kit might contain medicated powder, gauze bandages, and adhesive tape to be used in case of cuts. If the cut is deep and bleeding profusely, the bandage should be applied very tightly to help in the formation of a clot. A tight bandage should not be kept in place longer than necessary, so take your pet to the veterinarian immediately.

Walking or running on a cut pad prevents the cut from healing. Proper suturing of the cut and regular changing of the bandages should have your pet's wound healed in a week to ten

Bandaging a minor cut on the paw pad is one of many basic first-aid techniques that the dog owner should learn. Thoroughly clean the injury with peroxide and apply an antibiotic. Then place the injured pad in sterile gauze, secure with first-aid tape, and replace daily.

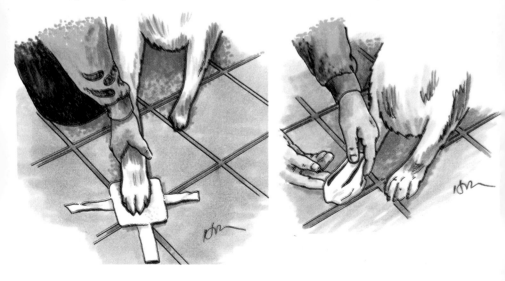

days. A minor cut should be covered with a light bandage, for you want as much air as possible to reach the wound. Do not apply wads of cotton to a wound, as they will stick to the area and may cause contamination.

You should also keep some hydrogen peroxide available, as it is useful in cleaning wounds and is also one of the best and simplest emetics known. Cotton applicator swabs are useful for applying ointment or removing debris from the eyes. A pair of tweezers should also be kept handy for removing foreign bodies from the dog's neck, head or body.

Nearly everything a dog might contract in the way of sickness has basically the same set of symptoms: loss of appetite, diarrhea, dull eyes, dull coat, warm and/or runny nose, and a high temperature. Therefore, it is most important to take his temperature at the first sign of illness. To do this, you will need a rectal thermometer which should be lubricated with petroleum jelly. Carefully insert it into the rectum, holding it in place for at least two minutes. It must be held firmly; otherwise there is the danger of its being sucked up into the rectum or slipping out, thus giving an inaccurate reading. The normal temperature for a dog is between 101° and 102.5°F. If your pet is

Four Paws Crystal Eye is a safe product for the removal of ugly tear stains.

seriously ill or injured in an accident, your veterinarian will advise you what to do before he arrives.

SWALLOWING FOREIGN OBJECTS

Most of us have had experience with a child swallowing a foreign object. Usually it is a small coin; occasionally it may be a fruit pit or something more dangerous. Dogs, *as a general rule,* will not swallow anything which isn't edible. There are, however, many dogs that swallow pebbles or small shiny objects such as pins, coins, and bits of cloth and plastic. This is especially true of dogs that are offered so-called "chew toys."

Chew toys are available in many sizes, shapes, colors and materials. Some even have whistles which sound when the dog's owner plays with it or when the dog chomps on it quickly. Most dogs attack the whistle first, doing everything possible to make it stop squeaking. Obviously, if the whistle is made of metal, a dog

The contents of a full ashtray if consumed by the curious dog may induce nicotine poisoning. Pet owners must dog-proof their home for the safety of their animals.

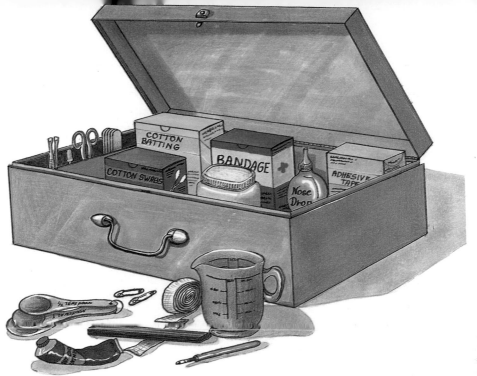

When emergencies occur, being prepared pays off. A first-aid kit should be accessible and always well stocked with medical accessories and supplies.

can injure its mouth, teeth, or tongue. Therefore, *never* buy a "squeak toy" made with a metal whistle.

Other chew toys are made of vinyl, a cheap plastic which is soft to the touch and pliable. Most of the cute little toys that are figures of animals or people are made of this cheap plastic. They are sometimes hand-painted in countries where the cost of such labor is low. Not only is the paint used dangerous to dogs, because of the lead content, but the vinyl tears easily and is usually destroyed by the dog during the first hour. Small bits of vinyl may be ingested and cause blockage of the intestines. You are, therefore, reminded of these things before you buy anything vinyl for your dog!

Very inexpensive dog toys, usually found in supermarkets and other low-price venues, may be made of polyethylene. These are to be avoided completely, as this cheap plastic is, for some odd reason, attractive to dogs. Dogs destroy the toy in minutes and sometimes swallow the indigestible bits and pieces that come off. Most pet shops carry only safe toys.

WHAT TOYS ARE SAFE FOR DOGS?

Hard Rubber Toys made of hard rubber are usually safe for dogs, providing the toy is made of 100% hard rubber and not a compound of rubber and other materials. The rubber must be "virgin" and not re-ground from old tires, tubes, and other scrap rubber products. The main problem with rubber, even 100% virgin rubber, is that it oxidizes quickly, especially when subjected to the ultraviolet rays of the sun and a dog's saliva. The rubber then tends to be brittle, to crack, to dust off, and to be extremely dangerous to dogs that like swallowing things.

Nylon Toys Toys made of nylon could well be the safest of all toys, *providing the nylon is annealed.* Nylon that is not annealed is very fragile, and if you smash it against a hard surface, it might shatter like glass. The same is true when the weather is cold and the nylon drops below freezing. Thus far there is only one line of dog toys that is made of annealed virgin nylon—Nylabone®. These toys not only are annealed but they are flavored and scented. The flavors and scents, such as hambone, are undetectable by humans, but dogs seem to find them attractive.

Some nylon bones have the

The Plaque Attacker® is a Dental Ball™, not just a plaything, designed to reduce plaque and tartar by use of its revolutionary "dental tips."

138

flavor sprayed on them or molded into them. These cheaper bones are easy to detect—just smell them. If you discern an odor, you know they are poorly made. The main problem with the nylon toys that have an odor is that they are not annealed and they "smell up" the house or car. The dog's saliva dilutes the odor of the bone, and when he drops it on your rug, this odor attaches itself to the rug and is quite difficult to remove.

The Puppy Bone® by Nylabone® is multi-purpose: designed for teething, chew-pacification, teeth-cleaning and the elimination of behavioral problems before they become habitual.

Gumabone® is available in different sizes and shapes. These are probably the most popular of all chew toys because dogs love them.

Annealed nylon may be the best there is, but it is not 100% safe. The Nylabone® dog chews are really meant to be Pooch Pacifiers®. This trade name indicates the effect intended for the dog, which is to relieve the tension in your excited puppy or anxious adult dog. Instead of chewing up the furniture or some other object, he chews up his Nylabone® instead. Many dogs ignore the Nylabone® for weeks, suddenly attacking it when they have to relieve their doggie tensions.

The Nylabone® is designed for the most aggressive chewers. Even so, owners should be wary that some dogs may have jaws strong enough to chomp off a piece of Nylabone®, but this is extremely rare. *One word of caution:* the Nylabone® should be replaced when the dog has chewed down the knuckle. Most dogs slowly scrape off small slivers of nylon which pass harmlessly through their digestive tract. The resultant frizzled bone actually becomes a toothbrush.

One of the great characteristics of nylon bones is that they can be boiled and sterilized. If a dog loses interest in his Nylabone®, or it is too hard for him to chew due to his age and the condition of his teeth, you can cook it in some chicken or beef broth, allowing it to boil for 30 minutes. Let it cool down normally. It will then be perfectly sterile and re-flavored for the next dog. *Don't try this with plastic bones, as they will melt and ruin your pot.*

Polyurethane Toys Because polyurethane bones such as the Gumabone® are constructed of

Plaque Attacker™ Dental Bones from Gumabone® are designed for maximum tartar reduction for the aggressive chewer.

the strongest *flexible* materials known, some dogs (and their owners) actually prefer them to the traditional nylon bones. There are several brands on the market: ignore the ones which have scents that you can discern. Some of the scented polyurethane bones have an unbearable odor after the scent has rubbed off the bone and onto your rug or car seat. Again, look for the better-quality polyurethane toy. Gumabone® is a flexible material, the same as used for making artificial hearts and the bumpers on automobiles, thus it is strong and stable. It is not as strong as Nylabone®, but many dogs like it because it is soft.

If your dog is soft-mouthed and a less aggressive, more playful chewer, he will love the great taste and fun feel of the Gumabone® products.

The most popular of the Gumabone® products made in polyurethane are the tug toys, knots, balls, and Frisbee® flying discs. These items are almost clear in color, have the decided advantage of lasting a long time, and are useful in providing exercise for both a dog and his master or mistress.

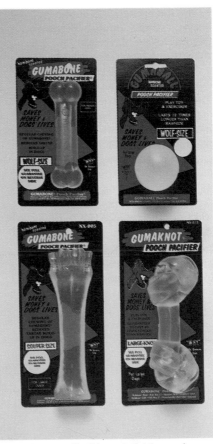

Made of a more flexible material than nylon, Gumabone® devices often are more appealling to dogs.

Gumabone® has also introduced new spiral-shaped dental devices under the name Plaque Attacker®. These unique products are fast becoming standards for all aggressive chewers. The Plaque Attacker Dental Device® comes in four fun sizes and each is designed to maximize gum and teeth massage through its upraised "dental tips," which pimple the surface of the toy. Similarly, the Plaque Attacker Dental Ball® ensures a reduction in plaque and tartar. This one-of-a-kind product provides hours of fun for a dog. It bounces erratically and proves to be the most exciting of all polyurethane toys. All Plaque Attacker® products are patented and scented with hambone to make them even more enticing for the dog. Clinical findings

The Plaque Attacker™ Dental Ball® is a unique and challenging toy for dogs big and small.

support the assertion that a significant reduction in calculus accompanies use of the Gumbone® products.

Whatever dog toy you buy, be sure it is high quality. Pet shops and certain supermarkets, as a rule, always carry the better-quality toys. Of course there may be exceptions, but you are best advised to ask your local pet shop operator—or even your veterinarian—what toys are suitable for *your* dog.

In conclusion, if your dog is a swallower of foreign objects, don't give him anything cheap to chew on. If he swallows a coin, you can hardly blame the Treasury! Unless your dog is carefully supervised, use only the largest size Nylabone® and Gumabone®, and replace them as soon as the dog chews down the knuckles. *Do not let the dog take the Nylabone® outdoors.* First of all he can hide and bury it, digging it up when his tensions rise. Then, too, all nylon becomes more brittle when it freezes, even Nylabone®.

IF YOUR PET SWALLOWS POISON

A poisoned dog must be treated instantly; any delay could cause his death. Different poisons act in different ways and require different treatments. If you know the dog has swallowed an acid, alkali, gasoline, or kerosene, do not induce vomiting. Give milk to dilute the poison and rush him to the vet. If you can find the bottle or container of poison, check the label to see if there is a recommended antidote. If not, try to induce vomiting by giving him a mixture of hydrogen peroxide and water. Mix the regular drugstore strength of hydrogen peroxide (3%) with an equal part of water, but do not attempt to

Four Paws offers three pleasantly scented colognes that can be used in between baths to freshen up pets.

pour it down your dog's throat, as that could cause inhalation pneumonia. Instead, simply pull the dog's lips away from the side of his mouth, making a pocket for depositing the liquid. Use at least a tablespoonful of the mixture for every ten pounds of your dog's weight. He will vomit in about two minutes. When his stomach has settled, give him a teaspoonful of Epsom salts in a little water to empty the intestine quickly. The hydrogen peroxide, on ingestion, becomes oxygen and water and

is harmless to your dog; it is the best antidote for phosphorus, which is often used in rat poisons. After you have administered this emergency treatment to your pet and his stomach and bowels have been emptied, rush him to your veterinarian for further care.

DANGER IN THE HOME
There are numerous household products that can prove fatal if ingested by your pet. These include rat poison,

Wasps can be harmful to dogs and humans alike. Paper wasps often build their nests close to the ground, where a dog may happen to visit.

antifreeze, boric acid, hand soap, detergents, insecticides, mothballs, household cleansers, bleaches, de-icers, polishes and disinfectants, paint and varnish removers, acetone, turpentine, and even health and beauty aids if ingested in large enough quantities. A word to the wise should be sufficient: what you would keep locked away from your two-year-old child should also be kept hidden from your pet.

There is another danger lurking within the home among the household plants, which are almost all poisonous, even if swallowed in small quantities. There are hundreds of poisonous plants around us, among which are: ivy leaves, cyclamen, lily of the valley, rhododendrons, tulip bulbs, azalea, wisteria, poinsettia leaves, mistletoe, daffodils, delphiniums, foxglove leaves, the jimson weed—we cannot name them all. Rhubarb leaves, for example, either raw or cooked, can cause death or violent convulsions. Peach, elderberry, and cherry trees can cause cyanide poisoning if their bark is consumed.

There are also many insects that can be poisonous to dogs

such as spiders, bees, wasps, and some flies. A few toads and frogs exude a fluid that can make a dog foam at the mouth—and even kill him—if he bites too hard!

There have been cases of dogs suffering nicotine poisoning by consuming the contents of full ashtrays which thoughtless smokers have left on the coffee table. Also, do not leave nails, staples, pins, or other sharp objects lying around. Likewise, don't let your puppy play with plastic bags which could suffocate him. Unplug, remove, or cover any electrical cords or wires near your dog. Chewing live wires could lead to severe

mouth burns or death. Remember that an ounce of prevention is worth a pound of cure: keep all potentially dangerous objects out of your pet's reach.

VEHICLE TRAVEL SAFETY

A dog should never be left alone in a car. It takes only a few minutes for the heat to become unbearable in the summer, and to drop to freezing in the winter.

A dog traveling in a car or truck should be well behaved. An undisciplined dog can be deadly in a moving vehicle. The dog should be trained to lie on the back seat of the vehicle. Allowing your dog to stick its head out of

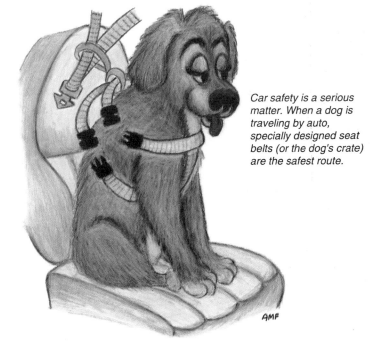

Car safety is a serious matter. When a dog is traveling by auto, specially designed seat belts (or the dog's crate) are the safest route.

Four Paws Pet Safety Sitter is designed to protect pets from injury by securing them in place and preventing them from disturbing drivers and passengers.

the window is unwise. The dog may jump or it may get something in its eye. Some manufacturers sell seat belts and car seats designed for dogs.

Traveling with your dog in the back of your pick-up truck is an unacceptable notion and dangerous to all involved.

PROTECT YOURSELF FIRST

In almost all first aid situations, the dog is in pain. He may indeed be in shock and not appear to be suffering, until you move him. Then he may bite your hand or resist being helped at all. So if you want to help your dog, help yourself first by tying his mouth closed. To do this, use a piece of strong cloth four inches wide and three feet long, depending on the size of the dog. Make a loop in the middle of the strip and slip it over his nose with the knot under his chin and over the bony part of his nose. Pull it tight and bring the ends back around his head behind the ears and tie it tightly, ending with a bow knot for quick, easy release. Now you can handle the dog safely. As a dog perspires through his tongue, do not leave the "emergency muzzle" on any longer than necessary.

ADMINISTERING MEDICINE

When you are giving liquid medicine to your dog, it is a good idea to pull the lips away from the side of the mouth, form a lip pocket, and let the liquid trickle past the tongue. Remain at his side, never in front of the dog, as he may cough and spray you with the liquid. Moreover, you must never pour liquid medicine while the victim's tongue is drawn out, as inhalation pneumonia could be the disastrous result.

Medicine in pill form is best administered by forcing the dog's mouth open, holding his head back, and placing the capsule as far back on his tongue as you can reach. To do this: put the palm of your hand over the dog's muzzle (his foreface) with your fingers on one side of his jaw, your thumb on the other. Press his lips hard against his teeth while using your other hand to pull down his lower jaw. With your two fingers, try to put the pill as far back on the dog's tongue as you can reach. Keep his mouth and nostrils closed and he should be forced to swallow the medicine. As the dog will not be feeling well, stroke his neck to comfort him and to help him swallow his medicine more easily. Do keep an eye on him for a few moments afterward, however, to make certain that he does not spit it out.

IN CASE OF AN ACCIDENT

It is often difficult for you to assess the dog's injuries after a road accident. He may appear normal, but there might be

Choose from a variety of ear care products from Four Paws from cleaners to remedies for proper ear hygiene.

internal hemorrhaging. A vital organ could be damaged or ribs broken. Keep the dog as quiet and warm as possible; cover him with blankets or your coat to let his own body heat build up. Signs of shock are a rapid and weak pulse, glassy-eyed appearance, subnormal temperature, and slow capillary refill time. To determine the last symptom, press firmly against the dog's gums until they turn white. Release and count the number of seconds until the gums return to their normal color. If it is more than 2–3 seconds, the dog may be going into shock. Failure to return to the reddish pink color indicates that the dog may be in serious trouble and needs immediate assistance.

If artificial respiration is required, first open the dog's mouth and check for obstructions; extend his tongue and examine the pharynx. Clear his mouth of mucus and blood and hold the mouth slightly open. Mouth-to-mouth resuscitation involves holding the dog's tongue to the bottom of his mouth with one hand and sealing his nostrils with the other while you blow into his mouth. Watch for his chest to rise with each inflation. Repeat every 5–6 seconds, the equivalent of 10–12 breaths a minute.

If the veterinarian cannot come to you, try to improvise a stretcher to take the dog to him. To carry a puppy, wrap him in a blanket that has been folded into several thicknesses. If he is in shock, it is better to pick him up by holding one hand under his chest, the other under the hindquarters. This will keep him stretched out.

It is always better to roll an injured dog than to try and lift him. If you find him lying beside the road after a car accident, apply a muzzle even if you have to use someone's necktie to make one. Send someone for a blanket and roll him gently onto it. Two people, one on each side, can make a stretcher out of the blanket and move the dog easily.

If no blanket is available and the injured dog must be moved, try to keep him as flat as possible. So many dogs' backs are broken in car accidents that one must first consider that possibility. However, if he can move his hind legs or tail, his spine is probably not broken. Get medical assistance for him immediately.

It should be mentioned that unfortunate car accidents, which can maim or kill your dog, can be avoided if he is confined at all times either indoors or, if out-of-doors, in a fenced-in yard or some other protective enclosure. *Never* allow your dog to roam free; even a well-trained dog may, for some unknown reason,

VACCINATION SCHEDULE

Age	Vaccination
6-8 weeks	Initial canine distemper, canine hepatitis, tracheobronchitis, canine parvovirus, as well as initial leptospirosis vaccination.
10-12 weeks	Second vaccination for all given at 6-8 weeks. Initial rabies and initial Lyme disease to be given at this time.
14-16 weeks	Third vaccination for all given at 6-8 and 10-12 weeks.Re-vaccinate annually, hereafter. Second rabies and second Lyme disease to be given at this time, and then re-vaccinated annually.

Vaccination schedules should be confirmed with your vet.

dart into the street—and the result could be tragic.

If you need to walk your dog, leash him first so that he will be protected from moving vehicles.

PROTECTING YOUR PET

It is important to watch for any tell-tale signs of illness so that you can spare your pet any unnecessary suffering. Your dog's eyes, for example, should normally be bright and alert, so if the haw is bloodshot or partially covers the eye, it may be a sign of illness or irritation. If your dog has matter in the corners of his eyes, bathe them with a mild eye wash; obtain ointment or eye drops from your veterinarian to treat a chronic condition.

If your dog seems to have something wrong with his ears which causes him to scratch at them or shake his head, cautiously probe the ear with a cotton swab. An accumulation of wax will probably work itself out. Dirt or dried blood, however, is indicative of ear mites or infection and should be treated immediately. Sore ears in the summer, due to insect bites, should be washed with mild soap and water, then covered with a soothing ointment and wrapped in gauze if necessary. Keep your

Mosquitoes are the vectors of disease; although males like this one do not bite, females can transmit heartworm and other diseases to dogs.

pet away from insects until his ears heal, even if this means confining him indoors.

INOCULATIONS

Periodic check-ups by your veterinarian throughout your puppy's life are good health insurance. The person from whom your puppy was purchased should tell you what inoculations your puppy has had and when the next visit to the vet is necessary. You must make certain that your puppy has been vaccinated against the following infectious canine diseases:

distemper, canine hepatitis, leptospirosis, rabies, parvovirus, and parainfluenza. Annual "boosters" thereafter provide inexpensive protection for your dog against such serious diseases. Puppies should also be checked for worms at an early age.

DISTEMPER

Young dogs are most susceptible to distemper, although it may affect dogs of all ages. Some signs of the disease are loss of appetite, depression, chills, and fever, as well as a watery discharge from the eyes and nose. Unless treated promptly, the disease goes into advanced stages with infections of the lungs, intestines, and nervous system. Dogs that recover may be impaired with paralysis, convulsions, a twitch, or some other defect, usually spastic in nature. Early inoculations in puppyhood should be followed by an annual booster to help protect against this disease.

CANINE HEPATITIS

The signs of hepatitis are drowsiness, loss of appetite, high temperature, and great thirst. These signs may be accompanied by swellings of the head, neck, and abdomen. Vomiting may also occur. This disease strikes quickly, and death may occur in only a few hours. An annual booster shot is

needed after the initial series of puppy shots.

LEPTOSPIROSIS

Infection caused by either of two serovars, *canicola* or *copehageni,* is usually begun by the dog's licking substances contaminated by the urine or feces of infected animals. Brown rats are the main carriers of *copehageni*. The signs are weakness, vomiting, and a

Biting bugs not only have a painful bite but also carry blood parasites.

yellowish discoloration of the jaws, teeth, and tongue, caused by an inflammation of the kidneys. A veterinarian can administer the bacterins to protect your dog from this disease. The frequency of the doses is determined by the risk factor involved.

RABIES

This disease of the dog's central nervous system spreads by infectious saliva, which is transmitted by the bite of an infected animal. Of the two main classes of signs, the first is "furious rabies," in which the dog shows a period of melancholy or depression, then irritation, and finally paralysis. The first period can be from a few hours to several days, and during this time the dog is cross and will change his position often, lose his appetite, begin to lick, and bite or swallow foreign objects. During this phase the dog is spasmodically wild and has impulses to run away. The dog acts fearless and bites everything in sight. If he is caged or confined, he will fight at the bars and possibly break teeth or fracture his jaw. His bark becomes a peculiar howl. In the final stage, the animal's lower jaw becomes paralyzed and

Heartworm life cycle: a carrier mosquito bites a dog and deposits microfilariae, which travel through the dog's bloodstream, lodging in the heart to reproduce. The carrier dog is later bitten by an uninfected mosquito, which becomes infected, and bites and infects another dog...

hangs down. He then walks with a stagger, and saliva drips from his mouth. About four to eight days after the onset of paralysis, the dog dies.

The second class of symptoms is referred to as "dumb rabies" and is characterized by the dog's walking in a bearlike manner with his head down. The lower jaw is paralyzed and the dog is unable to bite. It appears as if he has a bone caught in his throat.

If a dog is bitten by a rabid animal, he probably can be saved if he is taken to a veterinarian in time for a series of injections. After the signs appear, however, no cure is possible. The local health department must be notified in the case of a rabid dog, for he is a danger to all who come near him. As with the other shots each year, an annual rabies inoculation is very important. In many areas, the administration of rabies vaccines for dogs is required by law.

PARVOVIRUS

This relatively new virus is a contagious disease that has spread in almost epidemic proportions throughout certain sections of the United States. It has also appeared in Australia, Canada, and Europe. Canine parvovirus attacks the intestinal tract, white blood cells, and heart

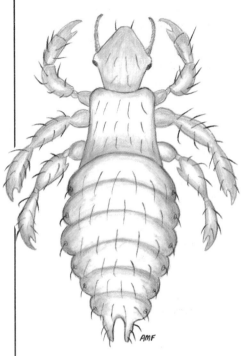

Lice are not a common problem in dogs and usually only infest dogs that are poorly cared for. Proper care of your dog will prevent lice infestation.

muscle. It is believed to spread through dog-to-dog contact, and the specific course of infection seems to come from fecal matter of infected dogs. Overcoming parvovirus is difficult, for it is capable of existing in the environment for many months under varying conditions and temperatures, and it can be transmitted from place to place

streaked. Because of the vomiting and severe diarrhea, the dog that has contracted the disease will dehydrate quickly. Depression and loss of appetite, as well as a rise in temperature, can accompany the other symptoms. Death caused by this disease usually occurs within 48 to 72 hours following the appearance of the symptoms. Puppies are hardest hit, and the virus is fatal to 75 percent of puppies that contract it. Death in puppies can be within two days of the onset of the illness.

A series of shots administered by a veterinarian is the best preventive measure for canine parvovirus. It is also important to disinfect the area where the dog is housed by using one part sodium hypochlorite solution (household bleach) to 30 parts of water and to keep the dog from coming into contact with the fecal matter of other dogs.

Four Paws Protector Flea & Tick Spray offers a quick kill and will repel fleas for up to 14 days. Super Fly Repellent repels flies and mosquitoes, which are known to transmit heartworm.

on the hair and feet of infected dogs, as well as on the clothes and shoes of people.

Vomiting and severe diarrhea, which will appear within five to seven days after the animal has been exposed to the virus, are the initial signs of this disease. At the onset of illness, feces will be light gray or yellow-gray in color, and the urine might be blood-

LYME DISEASE

Known as a bacterial infection, Lyme disease is transmitted by ticks infected with

a spirochete known as *Borrelia burgdorferi*. The disease is most often acquired by the parasitic bite of an infected deer tick, *Ixodes dammini*. While the range of symptoms is broad, common warning signs include: rash beginning at the bite and soon extending in a bullseye-targetlike fashion; chills, fever, lack of balance, lethargy, and stiffness; swelling and pain, especially in the joints, possibly leading to arthritis or arthritic conditions; heart problems, weak limbs, facial paralysis, and lack of tactile sensation.

Concerned dog owners, especially those living in the United States, should contact a veterinarian to discuss Lyme disease. A vaccination has been developed and is routinely administered to puppies twice before the 16th week, and then repeated annually.

PARAINFLUENZA

Parainfluenza, or infectious canine tracheobronchitis, is commonly known as "kennel cough." It is highly contagious, affects the upper respiratory system, and is spread through direct or indirect contact with already diseased dogs. It will readily infect dogs of all ages that have not been vaccinated or that were previously infected. While this condition is definitely one of the serious diseases in dogs, it is self-limiting, usually lasting only two to four weeks. The symptoms are high fever and intense, harsh coughing that brings up mucus. As long as

The fraternity of internal parasites and their eggs: whipworms, hookworms, roundworms and tapeworms.

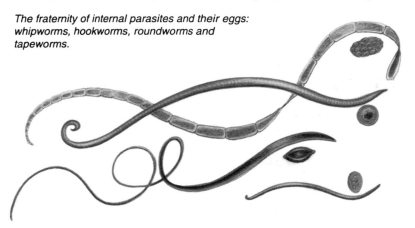

your pet sees your veterinarian immediately, the chances for his complete recovery are excellent.

EXTERNAL PARASITES

A parasite is an animal that lives in or on an organism of another species, known as the host, without contributing to the well-being of the host. The majority of dogs' skin problems are parasitic in nature and an estimated 90% of puppies are born with parasites.

Ticks can cause serious problems to dogs where the latter have access to woods, fields, and vegetation in which large numbers of native mammals live. Ticks are usually found clinging to vegetation and attach themselves to animals passing by. They have eight legs and a heavy shield or shell-like covering on their upper surface. Only by keeping dogs away from tick-infested areas can ticks on dogs be prevented.

The flea is the single most common cause of skin and coat problems in dogs. There are 11,000 kinds of fleas which can transmit specific disorders like tapeworm and heartworm or transport smaller parasites onto your dog. The common tapeworm, for example, requires the flea as an intermediate host for completion of its life cycle.

A female flea can lay hundreds of eggs and these will become adults in less than three weeks. Depending on the temperature and the amount of moisture, large numbers of fleas can attack dogs. The ears of dogs, in particular, can play host to hundreds of fleas.

Fleas can lurk in crevices and cracks, carpets, and bedding for months, so frequent cleaning of your dog's environment is absolutely essential. If he is infected by other dogs, then have him bathed and "dipped," which means that he will be put into water containing a chemical that kills fleas. Your veterinarian will advise which dip to use, and your dog must be bathed for at least twenty minutes.

INTERNAL PARASITES

Four common internal parasites that may infect a dog are: roundworms, hookworms, whipworms, and tapeworms. The first three can be diagnosed by laboratory examination of the dog's stool, and tapeworms can be seen in the stool or attached to the hair around the anus. When a veterinarian determines what type of worm or worms are present, he then can advise the best treatment.

Roundworms, the dog's most common intestinal parasite, have a life cycle which permits complete eradication by worming twice, ten days apart. The first worming will remove all adults and the second will destroy all subsequently hatched eggs before they, in turn, can produce more parasites.

A dog in good physical condition is less susceptible to worm infestation than a weak dog. Proper sanitation and a nutritious diet help in preventing worms. One of the best preventive measures is to have clean, dry bedding for the dog, as this diminishes the possibility of reinfection due to flea or tick bites.

Heartworm infestation in dogs is passed by mosquitoes. Dogs with this disease tire easily, have difficulty in breathing, and lose weight despite a hearty appetite. Administration of preventive medicine throughout the spring, summer, and fall months is advised. A veterinarian must first take a blood sample from the dog to test for the presence of the disease, and if the dog is heartworm-free, pills or liquid medicine can be prescribed to protect against any infestation.

CANINE SENIOR CITIZENS

The processes of aging and gradual degenerative changes start far earlier in a dog than often observed, usually at about seven years of age. Your pet will become less active, will have a poorer appetite with increased thirst, there will be frequent periods of constipation and less than normal passage of urine. His skin and coat might become dull and dry and his hair will become thin and fall out. There is a tendency towards obesity in old age, which should be avoided by maintaining a regular exercise program. Remember, also, that your pet will be less able to cope with extreme heat, cold, fatigue, and change in routine.

There is the possibility of loss or impairment of hearing or eyesight. He may become bad-tempered more often than in the past. Visits to the vet should be more regular. Care of the teeth is also important in the aging dog. Indeed, the mouth can be a barometer of nutritional health. Degenerating gums, heavy tartar on the teeth, loose teeth, and sore lips are common. The worst of all diseases in old age, however, is neglect. Good care in early life will have its effect on your dog's later years; the nutrition and general health care of his first few years can determine his lifespan and the quality of his life. It is worth bearing in mind that the older, compared to the younger, animal needs more protein of good biological value, more vitamins A, B-complex, D and E, more calcium and iron, less fat and fewer carbohydrates.

The Dog Show World

Quality in the sense of "show quality" is determined by various factors such as the dog's health, physical condition, temperament, ability to move, and appearance. Breeders trying to breed show dogs are attempting to produce animals which come as close as possible to the word description of perfection as set out in the breed standard.

Keep in mind that dog show terminology varies from one place to another and even from one time to another. If you plan to show your dog, it always makes sense to check with your local or national breed club or with the national dog registry for the most complete, most up-to-date information regarding dog show regulations. In Great Britain, for example, match shows are known as limit shows. Age limit also differs, as dogs less than six months old may not be shown in Britain. Additionally, Britain has no point system for dogs, rather the dogs compete for championship certificates (C.C.s). Thus, point shows are known as championship shows in Great Britain.

MATCH SHOWS

One of the best ways to see if your puppy has championship potential is to attend a match show which is usually organized by the local kennel club or breed specialty club. Such shows provide a useful learning experience for the amateur and they offer you the opportunity to see how well your dog measures up to others being shown. There you can mingle with owners and professional handlers and pick up basic guidelines in showmanship, performance, and procedure. You can learn a great deal merely by closely observing the professional handlers performing in the ring.

The age limit is usually reduced to two months at match shows so that puppies can have four months of training before they compete in the regular shows when they reach six months. This time also helps them to overcome any "crowd nervousness." As class categories are the same as those included at a regular show, much experience can be gained in this informal atmosphere. Entry fees are low and paid at the door.

Before you go to a show, your dog should be trained to gait at a trot beside you, with head up and in a straight line. In the ring you will have to gait

Facing page: The most prestigious dog show in America is the Westminster Kennel Club Show held annually in Madison Square Garden, New York City.

around the edge with other dogs and then individually up and down the center runner. In addition, the dog must stand for examination by the judge, who will look at him closely and feel his head and body structure. He should be taught to stand squarely, hind feet slightly back and head up. He must hold the pose when you place his feet, and he must show a lively interest when you "bait" him, i.e., tempt him with a piece of boiled liver or a small squeak toy.

If your puppy receives praise and words of encouragement from the judges and other knowledgeable people, then you can begin to dream of Westminster or Crufts. It is always useful to visit such prestigious shows to see the best examples of all the various breeds.

After you have taken some handling lessons yourself, or employed a professional handler, the next step is participation in the point shows where you can earn points toward your dog's championship.

POINT SHOWS

Unlike match shows where your dog was judged on ring behavior, at point shows he will be judged on conformation to his breed standard. It is advisable to write to your national dog registry for information on how to register your dog and apply to dog shows. Below are the names and addresses of registries in the United States, Canada, Great Britain, and Australia.

The American Kennel Club
51 Madison Avenue
New York, NY 10010

The Canadian Kennel Club
111 Eglinton Avenue
East Toronto, Ontario M6S 4V7
Canada

The Kennel Club
1 Clarges Street Piccadilly,
London, W1Y 8AB, England

The Australian Kennel Club
Royal Show Grounds
Ascot Vale, Victoria, Australia.

Your local kennel club can provide you with the names and addresses of the show-giving superintendents (or show secretaries) near you, who will be staging the club's dog show for them, and where you must write for an official entry form. The forms will be mailed in a pamphlet called the "premium list" which will include the names of the judges for each breed, a list of the prizes and trophies, the names and addresses of the show-giving club, where the show will be held, as well as the rules and required procedure. Make certain that you fill in the form clearly and carefully and

Ch. St. Aubrey Dragonora of Elsdon, owned by Mrs. Anna E. Snellin. Photo by John Ashbey.

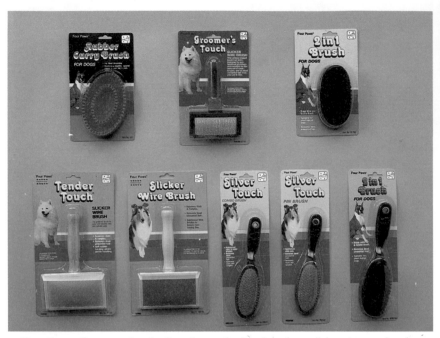

Four Paws offers an extensive line of grooming brushes, from slickers to curry brushes to pin brushes. These are sure to suit the grooming needs of every dog.

mail it in plenty of time.

Before then, however, you will have to decide in which classes your dog should compete. In the United States these are: Puppy, Novice, Bred-by-Exhibitor, American-bred and Open.

Puppy Classes are for dogs six months of age and over but under twelve months which are not champions. The age of a dog shall be calculated up to and inclusive of the first day of the show.

The *Novice Class* is for dogs six months of age and over, whelped in the United States or Canada, which have not, prior to the official closing date for entries, won three first prizes in the Novice Class, a first prize in Bred-by-Exhibitor, American-bred or Open Class or one or more points toward championship. In Britain, of course, dogs competing in the Novice Class must have been whelped in Britain.

The *Bred-by-Exhibitor Class*

is for dogs whelped in the U.S.A. or, if individually registered in the American Kennel Club Stud Book, for dogs in Canada that are six months of age and over. They must not be champions (although they may be in Britain), and must be owned wholly or in part by the person or the spouse of the person who was the breeder or one of the breeders of record. Dogs in this class must be handled by an owner or by a member of the immediate family of the owner. (This is not the case, however, in Britain.) Members of an immediate family for this purpose are: husband, wife, father, mother, son, daughter, brother and sister. This class has been referred to as the "breeder's showcase" as it is the one where the breeders can be justly proud of their achievements. The

American-bred Class is for all dogs (except champions) six months of age or over, whelped in the U.S.A. by reason of a mating that took place in the U.S.A.

The *Open Class* is for any dog six months of age or over, except in a member specialty club show held only for American-bred dogs, in which

The Shed 'N Blade is a tool used by groomers and handlers to eliminate dead, unwanted hair and allow for a healthy and vibrant coat.

The Pekingese is exhibited in the Toy Group, competing against such breeds as the Pomeranian and the Papillon. Photo by Robert Smith.

case the class is for American-bred dogs only.

In the United States and Canada, one does not enter the *Winners Class.* One earns the right to compete in it by winning first prize in one of the above classes. Winners Dog and Winners Bitch are the awards which carry points toward championship with them. Also

designated by the judge are the Reserve Winners Dog and the Reserve Winners Bitch (in Britain these are designated Reserve C.C. Dog and Reserve C.C. Bitch) but they do not receive any points. This award means simply that the dog or bitch receiving it are standing "in reserve" should the Winners Dog or Winners Bitch be disallowed through any technicality in the official show rules and regulations.

The dog and bitch then compete against each other for Best of Winners, and they also vie with the champions in the Specials Class for Best of Breed and for Best of Opposite Sex to Best of Breed. In Britain, the Reserve C.C. winners compete against each other for Best of Breed, not Best of Winners.

Best of Breed is the highest-placing dog in a given breed, and that winner then represents the particular breed in Group competition. Groups include: Sporting Dogs, Herding Dogs, Hounds, Working Dogs, Terriers, Toys, and Non-sporting Dogs. The judge of each Group selects first, second, third, and fourth place among the Best of Breed winners within specific Groups. First-place winners in each Group then compete for Best in Show.

A scale of points is printed in each dog-show catalog, and the number of points awarded in a breed depends on the number of dogs shown in competition. A win of three or more points at a show is called a "major." To attain championship, a dog must win a total of fifteen points under at least three different judges, and included in those fifteen points must be two majors (each under a different judge). A dog that accumulates fifteen points and no majors does not qualify for championship. A dog must win in keen competition. (This is the case in the United States but not in Great Britain. As there is no point system in Britain, it doesn't matter how many dogs are shown in competition. Championship Certificates are awarded at the discretion of the judge, however few dogs are competing.)

OBEDIENCE AND FIELD TRIALS

It should be mentioned that obedience trials, in which any purebred dog may compete, are often held in conjunction with conformation shows. Dogs are judged on performance rather than on how well they measure up to their breed standard. Many dogs that have already earned their championship in the conformation ring also compete for obedience trial degrees.

Two training accessories especially common with obedience trial enthusiasts are the hurdle (below) and the dumbbell (facing page). To see dogs performing with these and other field accessories, attend an obedience competition. Remember that training requires consistency and commitment, but the rewards are well worth the effort.

Practice stacking your Pekingese at home. The tail should be set high; lying well over back to either side with long, profuse, straight feathering.

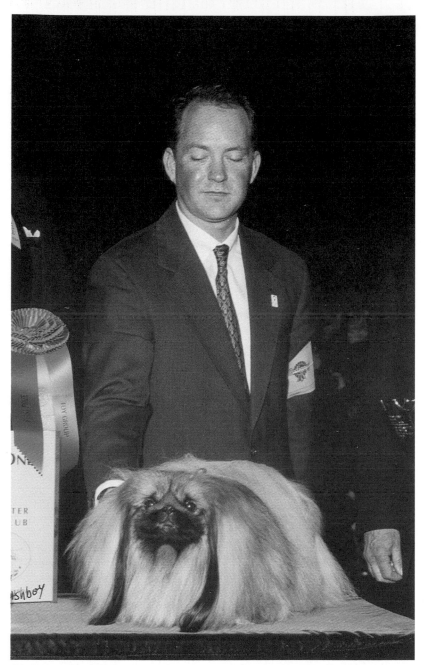

Ch. Briarcourt's Damien Gable winning Group 1 placement at the Westminster Kennel Club Dog Show, 1994. Owner, Nancy H. Shapland.

Some breeds, particularly hunting dogs and some of the hounds, also compete in field trials.

There are three classes in obedience: Novice, Open, and Utility. Tracking tests also are held. The respective degrees earned are: C.D., C.D.X., U.D., and T.D. These are: Companion Dog, Companion Dog Excellent, Utility Dog, and Tracking Dog. To earn a C.D., both the dog and his handler must perform six exercises together to the satisfaction of three different judges. Judges score the teams on a scale of zero to 200 points, and a score of 170 points or higher earns a dog a "leg" toward his obedience degree. A dog must achieve three "legs" for a C.D. Exercises in this Novice Class are: heel on lead and figure eight, stand for examination by a judge, heel off lead, long sit (sitting for a required number of minutes), long down (being down for several minutes), and recall (returning to his owner when called). After a dog gets his C.D., he then may try for his C.D.X. in Open obedience where he must jump over obstacles, retrieve items, and do more difficult exercises in three different trials. To achieve a U.D. title, a dog must do directed retrieving, jumping, and scent discrimination. To obtain a tracking degree, a dog competes in field trials where he "tracks" or follows a scent.

PRE-SHOW PREPARATIONS

As a very basic guide, the following list has been compiled to help you with your preparations for your first point show: the identification ticket sent by the show superintendent, a grooming table, a sturdy tack box in which to carry your dog's grooming tools, a leash to fasten him to the bench or stall and another show lead, your first aid kit, packaged "dog treats," and a supply of food and water for man and beast. Take the largest thermos you can find and a water dish. Remember to feed your dog after the show, not before, and make certain that he exercises and relieves himself before he enters the ring. Many experts think that an exercise pen is mandatory to eliminate the risk of exposing your dog to any diseases in the common exercise ground at shows, but before you bring one along, check the show rules to see if these are allowed. Moreover, exercise pens are useful as places where your dog can stretch out or rest during your travels or at a motel.

Even take time to think about what you are going to wear on the big day; sports clothes and

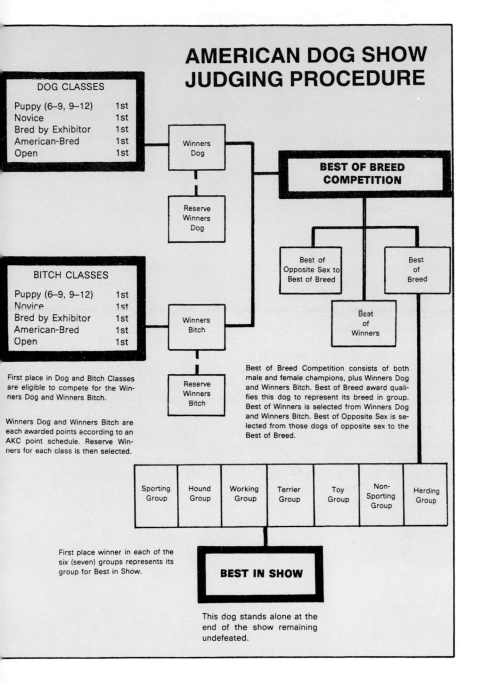

AMERICAN DOG SHOW JUDGING PROCEDURE

DOG CLASSES

Puppy (6–9, 9–12)	1st
Novice	1st
Bred by Exhibitor	1st
American-Bred	1st
Open	1st

Winners Dog

Reserve Winners Dog

BEST OF BREED COMPETITION

Best of Opposite Sex to Best of Breed

Best of Breed

Best of Winners

BITCH CLASSES

Puppy (6–9, 9–12)	1st
Novice	1st
Bred by Exhibitor	1st
American-Bred	1st
Open	1st

Winners Bitch

Reserve Winners Bitch

First place in Dog and Bitch Classes are eligible to compete for the Winners Dog and Winners Bitch.

Winners Dog and Winners Bitch are each awarded points according to an AKC point schedule. Reserve Winners for each class is then selected.

Best of Breed Competition consists of both male and female champions, plus Winners Dog and Winners Bitch. Best of Breed award qualifies this dog to represent its breed in group. Best of Winners is selected from Winners Dog and Winners Bitch. Best of Opposite Sex is selected from those dogs of opposite sex to the Best of Breed.

Sporting Group	Hound Group	Working Group	Terrier Group	Toy Group	Non-Sporting Group	Herding Group

First place winner in each of the six (seven) groups represents its group for Best in Show.

BEST IN SHOW

This dog stands alone at the end of the show remaining undefeated.

The expression of the Pekingese should suggest the breed's Chinese origin in its quaintness and individuality.

low-heeled, comfortable shoes are the best. You certainly do not want to wear anything that would distract the judge's attention from your dog; you should merely provide an attractive background for him.

Although your knees may be trembling, try to appear self-confident as you gait (move) and set up the dog. The judging routine usually begins when the judge asks that the dogs be gaited in a circle around the ring while he observes their style, topline, head and tail carriage, reach and drive, and general balance. Avoid going too close to the dog in front of you. Make certain that the judge has an unrestricted view of your dog by keeping him on the inside of the circle, between you and the judge.

DOG SHOW ETIQUETTE

There are a few "golden rules" to be followed at dog shows which are worth mentioning at this stage. First of all, you are responsible for the behavior of your dog at all times. Keep your dog with you until the showing and keep him under control at all times. Constant vigilance is necessary as thefts have been known at dog shows, as well as poisoning and physical abuse of the animals by jealous exhibitors. You do not want your dog to become involved in a dog fight or taken for a walk by an irresponsible child or one too young to discipline him. In other words, you must not let your dog out of your sight.

Another golden rule is to be punctual; do not be late for your class. Remember that in the ring

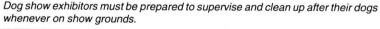

Dog show exhibitors must be prepared to supervise and clean up after their dogs whenever on show grounds.

Squeaky toys and fuzzy animals are excellent tools to bait a dog in the show ring. Be sure not to distract your dog when the judge is examining him.

you must not communicate with the judge or fellow competitors. Watch the judge carefully and follow his instructions. Bear in mind that the ring is not the place to discipline or train your dog; it is too late at this stage! Whatever the judge's decision, accept it with good grace whether you win or lose. *Never* argue with a judge. Finally, remember to praise your dog for his efforts. It has been a long day for him as well.

"DOUBLE HANDLING"

Only one person should be handling your dog; there should not be other "handlers" in the audience who hope to influence his performance by the well-timed whistle, the "spontaneous" applause, or the secret signal. Such tactics are unsportsmanlike as they often distract the attention of other dogs. This so-called "double handling" is frowned upon by the American Kennel Club as a desperate measure resorted to by a desperate owner. Moreover, to try to prompt a win or stir up interest in your dog by bringing along your own cheering section is a futile gesture as a judge is concentrating on what he is doing and is not influenced by such subversive strategy. These people seem to be declaring that their dog cannot win by its own merits under normal conditions but needs some extra assistance.

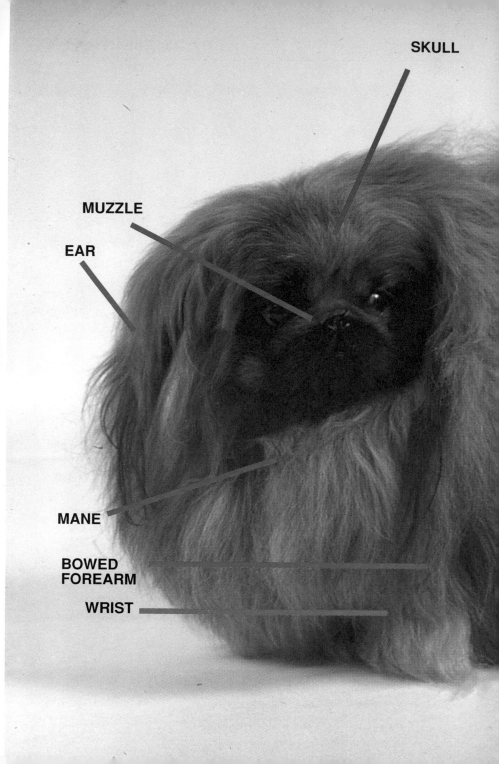

SKULL

MUZZLE

EAR

MANE

BOWED
FOREARM

WRIST

Topographical Anatomy of the Pekingese

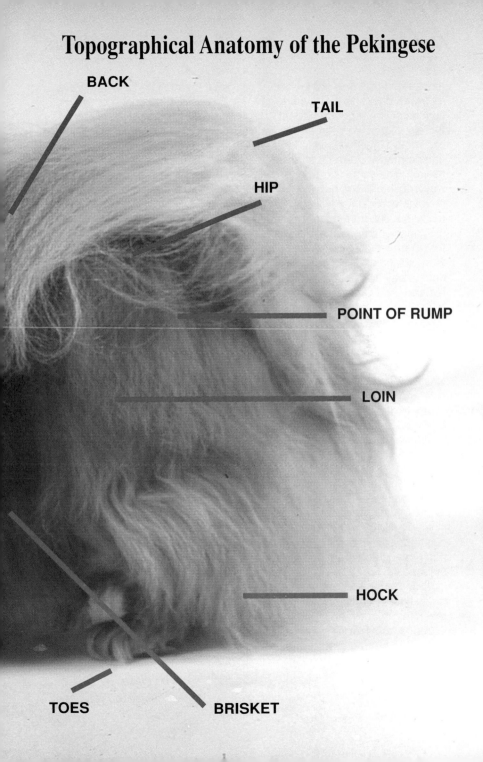

BACK

TAIL

HIP

POINT OF RUMP

LOIN

HOCK

TOES

BRISKET

Owner Concerns

By Chris Walkowicz

If something's worth doing at all, it's worth doing right. Behind the scenes of every gourmet feast, there's a lot of work, time and expense. Someone has to handle messy clean-up chores as well. The same is true of any worthwhile effort: a prize-winning novel, a community play, a good marriage, children, pets.

Conscientious owners know that there's more to raising a dog than picking one out, feeding it once a day and petting it if they feel the urge. Just as a fancy restaurant includes fine linens, flowers on the table and an attractive ambiance with the sustenance, being a top-quality dog owner means more than tossing a bone in the backyard now and then.

STRAYS

Although some people still have the mistaken idea that "a dog must be free," most are discovering that the world isn't what it once was. Loose dogs enjoying their "freedom" face all kinds of traumas: shotguns, poison, traps, oncoming trucks, dog pounds and the resulting euthanasia.

A dog without a home can rarely find a handout or even a rabbit to run down anymore. Garbage forays don't go far enough to fill an empty stomach, and they anger the person who is left to pick up the mess. Cars take their tolls on the highways. To combat these and other problems, good owners are taking steps to make sure their dogs remain welcome in society.

When a breeder is first contacted by a prospective buyer, the question is not simply, "Do you have a fenced yard?" but "Do you have a pen or a fenced yard—or do you plan to walk your dog on leash?" No option. If "none of the above" is the answer, it's bye-bye, buyer.

Children who are uncontrolled and unrestricted are obnoxious, cause damage and are a danger to themselves. Responsible people know that when they tell their children "No," it really is for their own good and that of others. It's not just a power ploy to deny them a privilege. Although it is difficult, there are reasons parents deny complete freedom to children, and there are reasons to deny it to dogs.

Dogs will be dogs. Loose animals are, at the least, a pain in the posterior and, at worst, a threat to themselves and others. Stray dogs bite, poop, scare kids, chase people, strew garbage, ruin lawns and gardens, kill other animals and produce unwanted litters.

OVERPOPULATION

The number of once-upon-a-time pets humanely euthanized annually in pounds and shelters is mind-boggling. These and the additional number of animals who die in agony—starvation, abuse, disease, trauma or road kills—were murdered by irresponsible owners and breeders as surely as if they aimed a gun and pulled the trigger. If animals were considered as living creatures instead of property by the court systems, many owners could be charged with negligence in their pets' deaths.

Neutering (spaying and castrating) means fewer animals, and fewer animals enable us to decrease the horrible statistics. Not only do we ascertain that none of our dog's pups become part of the canine carnage, but neutering also lowers the percentage of cancers and diseases of the reproductive system.

There are already plenty of dogs in the world without creating more. Anyone who wants one can find one immediately. It's only when people want specifics (i.e., a Pointer with great hunting ability; a Saint Bernard with lines that are hip-certified and show longevity; a Dachshund pup with the potential to go Best in Show) that someone needs to supply a demand.

It is true that a mixed-breed dog can make a great pet. Any dog, even one whose background is unknown, might turn into your best pal. But you're taking your chances. There are already thousands of those to go around—no need to create more. Only someone who cares enough to obtain the knowledge to produce canines with specific physical characteristics, temperament and instincts has a right to add to the already-bulging and suffering canine population. Therefore, ethical breeders now sell companion pups with a spay/neuter clause, which requires the dog to be neutered at puberty or by the age of one year. Many also use the Limited Registration option with the American Kennel Club. This allows the dog itself to be registered and shown in obedience and instinct tests, but in case of a "mistake," none of its progeny can be registered.

Dog breeding, done properly, is an expensive proposition. It is also time-consuming, extra work, occasionally heartbreaking and often frustrating. Add all of these problems to the fact that a neutered pet is a healthier one, many pet—and even some show—owners now choose a sexless life for their dog.

LICENSING

Dog licenses are not another means to extract more money from your pocket for the local government, but rather they are

The flowing mane of the Pekingese has made him known as the "Lion Dog." Owner, Diane Renchan.

insurance for your dog. A dog license just might save your pet from euthanasia. Animal control officers compare the dog license to our own driver's licenses. It's an I.D. That tag hanging from his collar can be traced to the owner, which means a lost pet might be saved from the gas chamber. Licenses also contribute toward the care of the unwanted, forgotten and forlorn ex-pets who will pay the price for "freedom."

THEFT AND LOSS

It's terrifying when a dog owner first looks outdoors and sees the empty yard with the gate swinging open. When someone realizes his pet is gone, the heart takes a plummeting ride to the pit of the stomach.

Sometimes, no matter what precautions are taken, accidents happen—a child leaves a gate open or a well-behaved dog finds a rabbit on the other side of the fence too attractive to resist.

Owners should take action immediately to assure the pet's return. Don't wait a few hours to see if he'll come home. It may be too late.

To find a lost dog:

1. POSTERS—Have hundreds printed at a jiffy printer, preferably with a photo, and post every one. Someone who sees one poster may not retain the memory, but someone who sees 20 will remember. Describe the dog, always keeping in mind the fable of the blind men and the elephant. To a large man, a medium-sized dog may appear to be small; to a child, it may seem to be an elephant. In addition, a lost dog usually loses weight. It's better to print a lower estimate of his size and describe the breed, even if it's a well-known breed. Remember if the dog is gone for more than a few hours, a well-groomed animal can quickly become disheveled and appear unkempt.

2. SPREAD THE WORD—Tell the mail carrier (who's always on the alert for stray dogs). Call the neighbors and schools (kids enjoy helping and love dogs). Call the police, veterinarians, pounds, shelters and humane societies not only in your county but in the surrounding counties. Dogs travel many miles in search of the cat they spied . . . or home. Not all dogs have the homing instinct of Lassie. As soon as possible, visit animal organizations with your posters. Don't take their word that there is no such purebred on the premises. Most people wouldn't recognize one if it bit them—and then it would probably be too late.

3. ADVERTISE—Call the papers and the radio stations. Offer a reward (which should also be printed on the posters). Make it high enough to make it worthwhile for someone to return the dog, but low enough that it does not invite extortionists.

4. SEARCH—Never stop searching. Use an answering machine or have someone stay by the phone to answer any reports of the dog being sighted. Dogs have been found as long as six months after their loss.

5. HUMANE TRAP—Set a familiar object (a blanket or a crate with a favorite toy) on your porch or in your garage, along with bowls of food and water. If he does come home while you're out searching, he'll have a reason to stay.

6. PREVENTION—Fences, kennel runs and walking on leash. If the dog is a jumper or climber, make the fence higher or plant shrubs around to increase the distance and top the run. I.D. your dog with tags and a tattoo. Take photos, both *haute coiffure* and *au naturel.*

7. BE PREPARED—A lost dog is often terrified. Even those who are normally friendly can panic when called by a stranger, or even by someone they've known and loved all their lives. Use a lure: food, a kennelmate, an open car door, a bitch in season for a stud dog, a favorite toy or sound (like food pans, or a gunshot for a hunting dog).

Too often, also, dognappers are lured by a winsome face,

easy prey, or the potential easy money flashed by a purebred. The dognapper's booty is sometimes sold to people who are unaware of the circumstances. Sometimes, however, they're sold to people who fake papers and resell the dog. Worse yet, they might be sold to dog fighters (as bait or fighters) or laboratories (for experiments). Stolen dogs are difficult, if not impossible, to trace unless they can be positively identified.

TATTOO IDENTIFICATION

To prevent a much-loved family pet from ending his days in fear and agony, the best method of prevention is tattooing. Many dog clubs and veterinarians provide tattoo identification. By law, no laboratory may use a dog bearing a tattoo. Although some owners tattoo on the inside of the ear, most choose the inside of the rear thigh. An ear can be easily cut off.

Most American owners use their social security number, which is usually put on the inside of the dog's right hind thigh. Some use the dog's registration number, which goes on the inside of the left rear thigh. The area is first shaved and numbed. There is no pain, although a few dogs do not like the buzzing sound.

The Pekingese body should be short, heavy in front with a broad chest. The coat is long and straight, with the profuse mane extending beyond the shoulders and forming a cape around the neck. Owner, Diane Renchan.

NO DOGS!

In Europe, dogs accompany their masters everywhere—to stores, buses and even in restaurants. Because the dogs are accustomed to public acceptance, they're well behaved and sit or lie quietly. Or is it because the pets are well behaved that they are accepted?

In the United States, however, "No Dogs"! signs are popping up like weeds—all over and too many. Because of bratty canines and careless owners, landlords demand a no-pets clause in leases. Parks restrict certain areas for pets if they're allowed at all. Many motels and hotels no longer admit anyone with a dog.

Many cities have a poop-scoop ordinance. Owners are required to clean up after their dogs or pay a fine. For too long, people have had the mistaken notion that their bad habits are not offensive to others, or even if they are, that's tough luck. These people claim, "It's our right to leave doggy doo-doo (drive carelessly, be sloppy drunk, blow smoke in your face or you fill in the blank). We aren't hurting anyone." Wrong. It's our right to own dogs but not to turn parks, sidewalks and public places into doggy latrines. Now we know our bad habits can be not only offensive but harmful to others, and we've got to straighten up and fly right, or we'll be flying solo.

If we want to continue this special bond between dogs and people, we must scoop poop, walk dogs on leash and train them to behave in public. It's no longer a good idea but a necessity that we attend classes and practice good manners. That demands confining pets and curtailing barking. It means no destruction of motel rooms, no jumping up when uninvited and no disgusting piles left behind— in other words, cleaning up our act.

RESCUE

Dog fanciers have recognized the need to spread good will beyond the home boundaries. There are too many strays, abuse cases and abandoned animals. Dogs in these situations need help, and they can't supply it themselves. Their so-called owners won't supply it.

Local and national clubs have organized rescue associations to aid in placing these needy dogs. Members volunteer to investigate situations, check out shelters and even to house a victim temporarily. Because of conditions where the animals may have suffered physically as well as mentally, many dogs need TLC and veterinary treatment before a new home is sought. Usually the dog is neutered before placement.

Occasionally, there is a waiting list for "orphans of the storm." Other times, a dog must be maintained and made well again before being adopted. All prospective homes are thoroughly screened so that the tragedy does not reoccur.

Medical care, boarding, adoption fees, transportation and routine expenses all mean that breed rescue programs need funds. Some samaritans foot the bills themselves. Clubs hold fundraising occasions which include bake sales, garage sales, recycling, tattoo clinics, auctions, matches, dog washes and dips and a rescue "check-off" included with the check for annual dues. Recipients of rescued dogs often respond and are, in some cases, required to make donations.

When these dogs are once again sound, they are placed in good homes. In this way, club members feel they are giving something back to the breed they love so much.

Breeders can assist in assuring that their pups won't someday be in need of rescue by including return clauses in their contracts. The breeder should always have first option to take the dog back if he needs to be placed. Follow up on pups with inquiries to see how they're doing, requests for photos to fill the breeder's scrapbook, and suggestions of training classes. Offering your assistance to groom or handle the dog and your availability to answer questions will help the new owner make it through tough times and offer assurance that one of your pups won't become a victim of our throw-away society.

PETS AND HEALTH: A FRIEND INDEED
By Diana Schellenberg
Excerpted from the December 1993 issue of the HARVARD HEALTH LETTER, ©1993, President and Fellows of Harvard College.

"I think I could turn and live with animals," Walt Whitman wrote, "they are so placid and self-contained." And as T. S. Eliot pointed out, animals are "such agreeable friends—they ask no questions, they pass no criticisms." Apparently the majority of Americans agree with the poets: 58% of households in the United States now include at least one pet. A 1992 survey sponsored by the American Veterinary Medical Association showed that cats, with a population of around 60 million, have surpassed dogs as America's favorite companion animal—a shift that probably comes as no surprise to cats, who have always acted as though they were number one. What with the cats and around

The Pekingese muzzle should be wrinkled, very short and broad, not overshot nor pointed. Owner, Diane Renchan.

52 million dogs, 12 million birds, and 5 million horses, Americans are sharing their daily lives with nearly 130 million of these creatures. In addition, around 8% of households keep fish and at least 4% have more unusual pets such as ferrets, gerbils, rabbits, or reptiles.

Most people who have companion animals consider them members of the family. Unlike humans in the household who have their ups and downs, most pets behave in fairly predictable ways and many offer unconditional affection. Dogs and cats typically spend most of their time in the house, and many sleep on their owners' beds. One measure of the value of their company is the billions of dollars that Americans spend each year on pet food, accessories, and veterinary care. And everyone has read about the elaborate markers that grieving pet owners erect to memorialize their departed companions.

Baby talk

People enjoy their animals, and being with them stirs a sense of security and of being needed. Pets, regardless of their age, fill the role of an infant or young child in the household, according to researcher Alan Beck, who heads the Center for Applied Ethology and Human-Animal Interaction at the Purdue University School of Veterinary Medicine. He and psychiatrist Aaron Katcher did pioneering studies of the connection between humans and animals during the 1970s and 1980s, when both were at the University of Pennsylvania.

Drs. Beck and Katcher found that people talk to their pets as if they were young infants. They move close to the animal's head, use a higher-pitched voice, and speak more softly and slowly than usual. They insert pauses as if the animal were answering back. Their facial expressions also soften, which may be one reason why people are perceived as more attractive and more approachable when they are with a pet.

Warm fuzzies

Only during the past few decades have scientists become interested in the beneficial effects that pets may have on human health. One way to assess the effect is to measure the short-term physiological impact of contact with an animal. So far, experiments using children and college students have found that watching or petting and talking with an animal can lower blood pressure and heart rate.

Short-term studies have also demonstrated that interacting with animals can reduce mental distress. For college students in a laboratory setting, petting a friendly dog lowered not only their blood pressure and heart rate but also their anxiety level, as measured by a standard test. Researchers found that patients who watched fish in an aquarium while they waited to have oral surgery did just as well as those who underwent hypnosis to reduce anxiety and discomfort during the surgery. These results help explain why aquariums are so popular in dental and medical waiting rooms.

Most epidemiologic studies comparing people with and without pets have suggested that those who share their lives with animals have higher morale and lower rates of depression. Such studies do not tell us, however, whether pet owning leads to better psychological health or whether it's healthier people who acquire pets in the first place.

Heartfelt support

A large Australian study reported in 1992 did not answer this question but did indicate that pet owners have fewer risk factors for heart disease than people without such companions. The researchers assessed common predictors of cardiovascular problems in 5,741 people who attended a free screening clinic in Melbourne. Overall, the 13.6% who owned pets had lower systolic blood pressure and lower total cholesterol and triglyceride levels than non-owners. These differences were significant despite variations in participants' smoking habits, diet, body height and weight, and socioeconomic status. It did not appear to matter if pets had four legs, wings, or scales: all pet owners benefited whether or not they had pets that needed regular exercise.

Although the association between pet ownership and an apparent reduction in cardiovascular risk is an interesting finding, it does not demonstrate that pets can guard their masters against heart disease or any other illness. This kind of evidence can be gained only from *prospective* studies, where researchers, in anticipation of possible patterns or correlations, design research to analyze ongoing events. In this instance, researchers would need to track the health status of many pet owners and non-owners over a long period of time.

So far, the largest prospective investigation of the effect of pet owning was done by epidemiologist Judith Siegel of the University of California, Los Angeles. For one year Dr. Siegel monitored stressful life

The large, dark, round, and lustrous eyes of the Pekingese quaintly portray his sincere loyalty and devotion.

events, use of physician services, and the psychological well-being of 938 people who were covered by Medicare and enrolled in a health maintenance organization. The 37% of participants who owned pets made fewer visits to the doctor than people without animal companions. This was true regardless of the chronic health problems they had at the beginning of the study period, or of their sex, age, race, education, income, employment status, and degree of social support from other people.

When family members or friends became severely ill or died, pets seemed to be a "stress buffer" for their bereaved human companions. People without pets made more physician visits as stressful events accumulated in their lives, but pet owners—especially those with dogs—did not follow this pattern. Reporting her findings in the *Journal of Personality and Social Psychology,* Dr. Siegel speculated that elderly people sometimes go to the doctor because they need companionship, or because loneliness exacerbates their health concerns.

Pets, particularly dogs, appear at least partially to satisfy the need for company. About 25% of people in Dr.

Siegel's study said that their pets made them feel secure, and 21% said they felt loved by their animals. These findings, coupled with results from smaller inquiries, suggest that the social and psychological support that people gain from pets may reduce their need for the attention of health care providers.

Animal companionship may also be a boon to people recovering from an acute illness. A prospective study of 92 people admitted to a coronary care unit for confirmed or suspected myocardial infarction found that those with animals were more likely to be alive one year later than those without pets.

The dark underbelly

The benefits of pet owning seem so obvious—especially after a brisk walk with a lively dog or an evening curled up with a purring puss—that it is tempting to brush aside the negative aspects of living with animals. Unfortunately, problems can arise from allergies, bites, or infections.

Roughly 1.5% of the general population and 25% of patients being treated for allergies are sensitive to dogs or cats. When doctors recommend that the offending animal be removed from the home, pet-owning patients often resist. Recent research suggests that people who are allergic to cats may be able to coexist with them if they wash the cat once a week, accustom the animal to spending more time outdoors, eliminate carpeting, use air filters, and follow a rigorous housecleaning schedule. (Researchers, however, do not report what sort of protective gear pet owners should don for the weekly bath.)

Animal bites pose an even more obvious health problem. Bites account for 1% of all visits to hospital emergency rooms, although about 80% of these injuries are minor. Many bites need not have occurred in the first place. Children should be taught how to approach and handle pets, read their warning signals, and avoid high-risk situations. Dog owners must do their part by training their dogs and by keeping potentially dangerous animals leashed or fenced.

Infectious diseases can be spread when a bite deposits organisms from the animal's mouth into a wound. These infections range from the annoying to the potentially deadly, such as rabies. Any bite that breaks the skin calls for prompt medical attention. Fortunately, taking a few simple measures can reduce the risk.

The difficulty of balancing the benefits and risks of sharing one's life with an animal may be illustrated most poignantly by the pet owner with AIDS, who needs a loving companion but whose impaired immune system is particularly vulnerable to certain infections. Volunteer organizations help AIDS patients keep their pets by offering food deliveries, in-home pet care, foster care, and adoption services when the need arises.

Prescription pets

In the therapeutic arena, there is a growing appreciation for the roles that companion animals can play in institutions and in the world at large. Dogs have long been used as a source of support for troubled children and for psychiatric patients, and today many volunteers take their pets to visit local nursing homes. Assistance dogs serve as surrogate eyes, ears, or legs for thousands of people with disabilities.

For most people pets are neither a panacea nor a plague. Responsible pet ownership entails a commitment to the animal and a promise to train it properly and to provide it with adequate care. The return on this investment can be considerable: a loving companion, an antidote to stress, and perhaps a reason for regular exercise, all wrapped up in fur or feathers.

Breeding

As the owner of a purebred dog, you may have considered breeding your pet at one time or another. If your dog is a beloved family pet, and not a show dog, you should *not* breed your dog. Breeding is not a hobby for pet owners, but rather a demanding, complicated vocation that is not to be dabbled with. Many people have thought of breeding as an easy-money opportunity: buy two dogs and let them do the work. The rule of thumb is: if you're making money by breeding dogs, you're doing something wrong!

Consider the time and money involved just to get your bitch into breeding condition and then to sustain her throughout pregnancy and afterwards while she tends her young. You will be obligated to house, feed, groom, and housebreak the puppies until good homes can be found for them; and, lest we forget, there will be periodic trips to the vet for check-ups, wormings, and inoculations. Common sense should tell you that it is indeed cruel to bring unwanted or unplanned puppies into an already crowded canine world; only negligent pet owners allow this to happen. Recognizing the number of dogs, purebred and mixed breeds, pet-, show- and breeding-quality, that are put to sleep annually, responsible breeders require that all pet animals be neutered. This

condition most often is incorporated into the selling contract. The motives of good breeders are clear: avoid the manufacturing and mass-producing of average and below-average dogs; control the overblown canine population; concentrate on the improvement of purebred bloodlines. Breeding is a noble calling and unless you can improve the breed, you should not consider breeding your animal. Despite all of the obvious virtues of breeding texts, no book could ever prepare a person for breeding. What a heart-breaking and tragic experience to lose an entire litter because a good-intentioned pet owner wasn't aware of potential genetic complications, didn't recognize a breech birth, or couldn't identify the signals of a struggling bitch! Possibly the dam could be lost as well!

Before you take any step towards mating your bitch, think carefully about why you want her to give birth to a litter of puppies. If you feel she will be deprived in some way if she is not bred, if you think your children will learn from the experience, if you have the mistaken notion that you will make money from this great undertaking, think again. A dog can lead a perfectly happy, healthy, normal life without having been mated; in fact, spaying a female and neuterin a male helps them become better, longer-lived pets, as they are not so anxious to search for a mate in an effort to relieve their sexual tensions and have a diminished risk of cancer. As for giving the children a lesson in sex education, this is hardly a valid reason for breeding your dog. And on an economic level, it takes not only years of hard work (researching pedigrees and bloodlines, studying genetics, among other things), but it takes plenty of capital (money, equipment, facilities) to make a decent profit from dog breeding. Why most dedicated breeders are lucky just to break even. If you have only a casual interest in dog breeding, it is best to leave this pastime to those who are more experienced in such matters, those who consider it a serious hobby and a real vocation. If you have bought a breeder– or show-quality canine, one that may be capable of producing champions, and if you are just starting out with this

Breeding dogs requires more than book knowledge. In dogs, breech presentation is not uncommon and the breeder must be prepared to handle this situation and guide the puppy so that neither the pup nor the bitch is injured.

breeding venture, seek advice from the seller of your dog, from other veteran breeders, and from your veterinarian before you begin.

The following sections on reproduction are intended for academic value only. This is not a "How-to" chapter on breeding, nor a step-by-step approach for the novice for getting started. Hopefully the reader will understand the depth and complexity of breeding as well as the expected ethical and moral obligations of persons who

choose to do so—and never attempt it.

THE FEMALE "IN SEASON"

A bitch may come into season (also known as "heat" or estrus) once or several times a year, depending on the particular breed and the individual dog. Her first seasonal period, that is to say, the time when she is capable of being fertilized by a male dog, may occur as early as six months with some breeds. If you own a female and your intention is *not* to breed her, by

Ideally the puppy will be delivered in the normal head-first position.

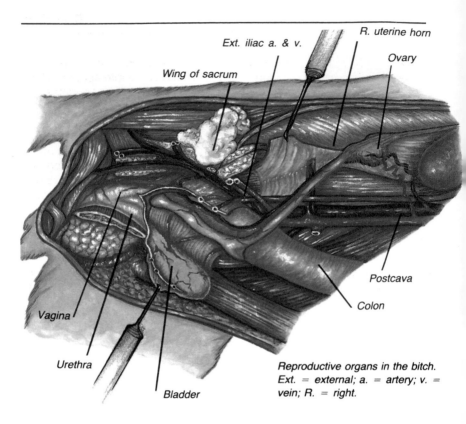

Reproductive organs in the bitch.
Ext. = external; a. = artery; v. = vein; R. = right.

The reproductive system of the female dog consists of a highly specialized system of organs situated to the rear of the animal.

all means discuss with the vet the possibility of having her spayed: this means before she reaches sexual maturity.

The first sign of the female's being in season is a thin red discharge, which may increase for about a week; it then changes color to a thin yellowish stain, which lasts about another week. Simultaneously, there is a swelling of the vulva, the exterior portion of the female's reproductive tract; the soft, flabby vulva indicates her readiness to mate. Around this second week or so ovulation occurs, and this is the crucial period for her to be bred, if this is what you have in mind for her. It is during this middle phase of the heat cycle when conception can take place. Just remember that there is great variation from bitch to bitch with regard to how often they come into heat, how long the heat cycles last, how long the period of ovulation lasts, and how much time elapses between heat cycles. Generally, after the third week of heat, the vulval swelling decreases and the estrus period ceases for several months.

It should be mentioned that the female will probably lose her puppy coat, or at least shed part of it, about three months after she has come into season. This is the time when her puppies would have been weaned, had she been mated, and females generally drop coat at this time.

With female dogs, there are few, if any, behavioral changes during estrus. A bitch may dart out of an open door to greet all available male dogs that show an interest in her, and she may occasionally raise her tail and

Each egg within the female is surrounded by a wall that normally takes many sperm to penetrate. In this way, it is more likely that only the strongest sperm will fertilize the egg. A fertile female in season usually has a number of eggs, known as gametes.

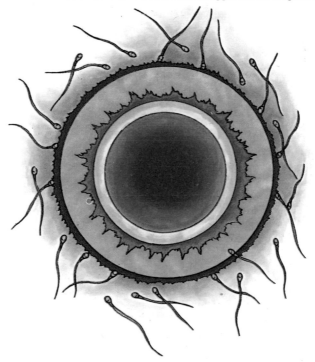

assume a mating stance, particularly if you pet her lower back; but these signs are not as dramatic as those of the sexually mature male. He himself does not experience heat cycles; rather, he is attracted to the female during all phases of her seasonal period. He usually becomes more aggressive and tends to fight with other males, especially over females in heat. He tends to mark his territory with urine to attract females and at the same time to warn other competitive males. It is not uncommon to see him mount various objects, and people, in an effort to satisfy his mature sexual urges.

If you are a homeowner and you have an absolutely climb-proof and dig-proof run within your yard, it may be safe to leave your bitch in season there. But then again it may not be a wise idea, as there have been cases of males mating with females right through chain-link fencing! Just to be on the safe side, shut her indoors during her heat periods and don't let her outdoors until you are certain the estrus period is over. Never leave a bitch in heat outdoors, unsupervised, even for a minute so that she can defecate or urinate. If you want to prevent the neighborhood dogs from hanging around your doorstep, as they inevitably will do when

they discover your female is in season, take her some distance away from the house before you let her do her business. Otherwise, these canine suitors will be attracted to her by the arousing odor of her urine, and they will know instinctively that she isn't far from her scented "calling card." If you need to walk your bitch, take her in the car to a nearby park or field for a chance to stretch her legs. Remember that after about three weeks, and this varies from dog to dog, you can let her outdoors again with no worry that she can have puppies until the next heat period.

If you are seriously considering breeding your dog, first talk to as many experienced breeders as possible and read up on the subject in specific books and articles. Only when you are fully aware of the demands and responsibilities of breeding should you make your final decision. It must be stated here that there is no shortage of fine dogs in need of good homes, nor is there likely to be in the foreseeable future. So, if

Facing page: The male reproductive system includes the penis and testicles. When not excited, the penis is withdrawn into the dog's body.

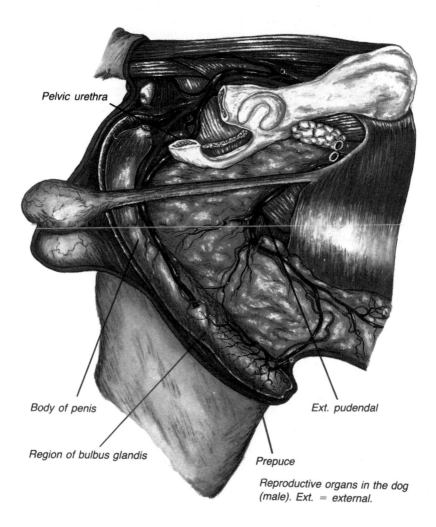

Pelvic urethra

Body of penis

Region of bulbus glandis

Ext. pudendal

Prepuce

Reproductive organs in the dog
(male). Ext. = external.

PERPETUAL WHELPING CHART

	1	2	3	4	5	6	7	8	9	10	11	12	13	14	15	16	17	18	19	20	21	22	23	24	25	26	27	28	29	30	31
Bred—Jan.	1	2	3	4	5	6	7	8	9	10	11	12	13	14	15	16	17	18	19	20	21	22	23	24	25	26	27	28	29	30	31
Due—March	5	6	7	8	9	10	11	12	13	14	15	16	17	18	19	20	21	22	23	24	25	26	27	April 1	2	3	4				
Bred—Feb.	1	2	3	4	5	6	7	8	9	10	11	12	13	14	15	16	17	18	19	20	21	22	23	24	25	26	27	28			
Due—April	5	6	7	8	9	10	11	12	13	14	15	16	17	18	19	20	21	22	23	24	25	26	27	28	29	30	May 1	2			
Bred—Mar.	1	2	3	4	5	6	7	8	9	10	11	12	13	14	15	16	17	18	19	20	21	22	23	24	25	26	27	28	29	30	31
Due—May	3	4	5	6	7	8	9	10	11	12	13	14	15	16	17	18	19	20	21	22	23	24	25	26	27	28	29	30	31	June 1	2
Bred—Apr.	1	2	3	4	5	6	7	8	9	10	11	12	13	14	15	16	17	18	19	20	21	22	23	24	25	26	27	28	29	30	
Due—June	3	4	5	6	7	8	9	10	11	12	13	14	15	16	17	18	19	20	21	22	23	24	25	26	27	28	29	30	July 1	2	
Bred—May	1	2	3	4	5	6	7	8	9	10	11	12	13	14	15	16	17	18	19	20	21	22	23	24	25	26	27	28	29	30	31
Due—July	3	4	5	6	7	8	9	10	11	12	13	14	15	16	17	18	19	20	21	22	23	24	25	26	27	28	29	30	31	August 1	2
Bred—June	1	2	3	4	5	6	7	8	9	10	11	12	13	14	15	16	17	18	19	20	21	22	23	24	25	26	27	28	29	30	
Due—August	3	4	5	6	7	8	9	10	11	12	13	14	15	16	17	18	19	20	21	22	23	24	25	26	27	28	29	30	31	Sept. 1	
Bred—July	1	2	3	4	5	6	7	8	9	10	11	12	13	14	15	16	17	18	19	20	21	22	23	24	25	26	27	28	29	30	31
Due—September	2	3	4	5	6	7	8	9	10	11	12	13	14	15	16	17	18	19	20	21	22	23	24	25	26	27	28	29	30	Oct. 1	2
Bred—Aug.	1	2	3	4	5	6	7	8	9	10	11	12	13	14	15	16	17	18	19	20	21	22	23	24	25	26	27	28	29	30	31
Due—October	3	4	5	6	7	8	9	10	11	12	13	14	15	16	17	18	19	20	21	22	23	24	25	26	27	28	29	30	31	Nov. 1	2
Bred—Sept.	1	2	3	4	5	6	7	8	9	10	11	12	13	14	15	16	17	18	19	20	21	22	23	24	25	26	27	28	29	30	
Due—November	3	4	5	6	7	8	9	10	11	12	13	14	15	16	17	18	19	20	21	22	23	24	25	26	27	28	29	30	Dec. 1	2	
Bred—Oct.	1	2	3	4	5	6	7	8	9	10	11	12	13	14	15	16	17	18	19	20	21	22	23	24	25	26	27	28	29	30	31
Due—December	3	4	5	6	7	8	9	10	11	12	13	14	15	16	17	18	19	20	21	22	23	24	25	26	27	28	29	30	31	Jan. 1	2
Bred—Nov.	1	2	3	4	5	6	7	8	9	10	11	12	13	14	15	16	17	18	19	20	21	22	23	24	25	26	27	28	29	30	
Due—January	3	4	5	6	7	8	9	10	11	12	13	14	15	16	17	18	19	20	21	22	23	24	25	26	27	28	29	30	31	Feb. 1	
Bred—Dec.	1	2	3	4	5	6	7	8	9	10	11	12	13	14	15	16	17	18	19	20	21	22	23	24	25	26	27	28	29	30	31
Due—February	2	3	4	5	6	7	8	9	10	11	12	13	14	15	16	17	18	19	20	21	22	23	24	25	26	27	28	March 1	2	3	4

your object in breeding is merely to produce more dogs, you are strongly encouraged to reconsider your objective.

WHEN TO BREED

It is usually best to breed a bitch when she comes into her second or third season. Plan in advance the time of year which is best for you, taking into account your own schedule of activities (vacations, business trips, social engagements, and so on). Make sure you will be able to set aside plenty of time to assist with whelping of the newborn pups and caring for the dam and her litter for the next few weeks. At the very least, it probably will take an hour or so each day just to feed and clean up after the brood—but undoubtedly you will find it takes

much longer if you stop to admire and play with the youngsters periodically! Refrain from selling the litter until it is at least six weeks old, keeping in mind that a litter of pups takes up a fair amount of space by then. It will be your responsibility to provide for them until they have been weaned from their mother, properly socialized, housebroken, and ready to go to new homes (unless you plan to keep them all). Hopefully, as strongly recommended, you will have already lined up buyers for the pups in advance of their arrival into this world.

CHOOSING THE STUD

You can plan to breed your female about six-and-one-half months after the start of her last season, although a variation of a

Whelping box prepared with "pig rails," bars on either side of the box to prevent the bitch from rolling on the puppies.

month or two either way is not unusual. Do some research into the various bloodlines within your breed and then choose a stud dog and make arrangements well in advance. If you are breeding for show stock, which will command higher prices than pet-quality animals, a mate should be chosen very carefully. He should complement any deficiencies (bad traits) that your female may have, and he should have a good show record or be the sire of show winners, if he is old enough to have proven himself. If possible, the bitch and stud should have several ancestors in common within the last two or three generations, as such combinations have been known, generally, to "click" best.

The owner of a stud dog usually charges a stud fee for use of the animal's services. This does not always guarantee a litter, but if she fails to conceive, chances are you may be able to breed your female to that stud again. In some instances the owner of the stud will agree to take a "first pick of the litter" in place of a fee. You should, of course, settle all details beforehand, including the possibility of a single puppy surviving, deciding the age at which the pup is to be taken, and so forth.

Each puppy is delivered in a separate membranous sac. This sac must be removed by the bitch without delay—if not, the breeder must come immediately to the assistance of the pup.

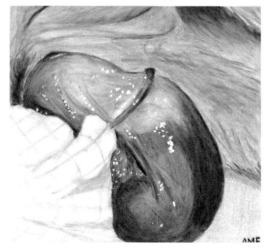

If you plan to raise a litter that will be sold exclusively as pets, and if you merely plan to make use of an available male (not a top stud dog), the most important selection point involves temperament. Make sure the dog is friendly, as well as healthy, because a bad disposition can be passed on to his puppies—and this is the worst of all traits in a dog destined to be a pet. If you are breeding pet-quality dogs, a "stud fee puppy," not necessarily the choice of the litter, is the usual payment. Don't breed indiscriminately; be sure you will be able to find good homes for each of the pups, or be sure you have the facilities to keep them yourself, *before* you plan to mate your dog.

PREPARATION FOR BREEDING

Before you breed your female, make sure she is in good health. She should be neither too thin nor too fat. Any skin disease *must* be cured first so that it is not passed on to the puppies. If she has worms, she should be wormed before being bred or within three weeks after the mating. It is generally considered a good idea to revaccinate her against distemper and hepatitis before the puppies are born.

The female will probably be ready to breed twelve days after the first colored discharge appears. You can usually make arrangements to board her with the owner of the stud for a few days, to insure her being there at the proper time; or you can take her to be mated and bring her home the same day if you live near enough to the stud's owner. If the bitch still appears receptive she may be bred again two days later, just to make certain the mating was successful. However, some females never

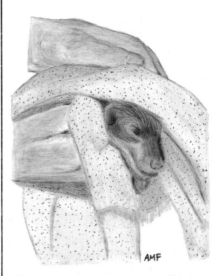

Newborn pups are very susceptible to chills, so the breeder must dry the puppy off thoroughly and place it in a temperature-controlled puppy box.

show signs of willingness, so it helps to have an experienced breeder on hand. In fact, you both may have to assist with the mating by holding the animals against each other to ensure the "tie" is not broken, that is, to make certain copulation takes place.

Usually the second day after the discharge changes color is the proper time to mate the bitch, and she may be bred for about three days following this time. For an additional week or so, she may have some discharge and attract other dogs by her odor; but she should not be bred.

Once she has been bred, keep her far from all other male dogs, as they have the capacity to impregnate her again and sire some of her puppies. This could prove disastrous where purebred puppies.

THE FEMALE IN WHELP

You can expect the puppies nine weeks from the day of the mating, although 61 days is as common as 63. Gestation, that period when the pups are developing inside their mother, varies among individual bitches. During this time the female should receive normal care and exercise. If she was overweight at the start, don't increase her food right away; excess weight at whelping time can be a problem with some dogs. If she is on the thin side, however, supplement her meal or meals with a portion of milk and biscuit at noontime. This will help build her up and put weight on her.

You may want to add a mineral and vitamin supplement to her diet, on the advice of your veterinarian, since she will need an extra supply not only for herself but for the puppies growing inside her. As the mother's appetite increases, feed her more. During the last two weeks of pregnancy, the pups grow enormously and the mother will have little room for food and less of an appetite. She should be tempted with meat, liver, and milk, however.

As the female in whelp grows heavier, cut out violent exercise and jumping from her usual routine. Although a dog used to such activities will often play with the children or run around voluntarily,

"Pooping" the puppies, or rubbing the bowels and genitals to stimulate elimination, may be necessary if the bitch doesn't tend to this herself.

restrain her for her own sake.

A sign that whelping is imminent is the loss of hair around her breasts. This is nature's way of "clearing a path" so that the puppies will be able to find their source of nourishment. As parturition draws near, the breasts will have swelled with

The breeder must actively partake in cleaning the pup after feedings. Hands-on contact serves as the initial step in socialization—accustoming the pup to his human family.

milk and the nipples will have enlarged and darkened to a rosy pink. If the hair in the breast region does not shed for some reason, you can easily cut it short with a pair of scissors or comb it out so that it does not mat and become a hindrance to the suckling pups later on.

PREPARING FOR THE PUPPIES

Prepare a whelping box a few days before the puppies are due, and allow the mother to sleep there overnight or to spend some time in it during the day to become accustomed to it. This way she is less likely to try to have her pups under the front porch or in the middle of your bed. A variety of places will serve, such as the corner of your cellar or garage (provided these places are warm and dry). An unused room, such as a dimly lit spare bedroom, can also serve as the place for delivery. If the weather is warm, a large outdoor dog house will do, as long as it is well protected from rain, drafts, and the cold—and enclosed by fencing or a run. A whelping box serves to separate mother and puppies from visitors and other distractions. The walls should be high enough to restrain the puppies yet low enough to allow the mother to take a short respite from her brood after she has fed them. Four feet square is minimum size (for most dogs) and six-to-eight-inch high walls will keep the pups in until they begin to climb; then side walls should be built up so that the young ones cannot wander away from their nest. As the puppies grow, they really need more

over the whole area will make excellent bedding and be absorbent enough to keep the surface warm and dry. These should be removed daily and replaced with another thick layer. An old quilt or washable blanket makes better footing for the nursing puppies than slippery newspaper during the first week; this is also softer for the mother to lie on.

Be prepared for the actual

Bottle-feeding may be necessary with particularly large litters or with a bitch who has become overly stressed or neglectful or whose milk has gone bad.

room anyway, so double the space with a very low partition down the middle of the box, and soon you will find them naturally housebreaking themselves. Puppies rarely relieve themselves where they sleep. Layers of newspapers spread

whelping several days in advance. Usually the mother will tear up papers, refuse food, and become restless. These may be false alarms; the real test is her temperature, which will drop to below 100°F (38°C) about twelve hours before whelping. Take her temperature with a rectal thermometer, morning and evening, and usher her to her whelping box when her temperature goes down. Keep a close watch on her and make sure she stays safely indoors (or outdoors in a safe enclosure); if she is let outside, unleashed, or allowed to roam freely, she could wander off and start to go into labor. It is possible that she could whelp anywhere, and this could be unfortunate if she needs your assistance.

WHELPING

Usually little help is needed from you, but it is wise to stay close to be sure that the mother's lack of experience (if this is her first time) does not cause an unnecessary complication. Be ready to help when the first puppy arrives, for it could smother if she does not break the amniotic membrane enclosing it. She should tear open the sac and start licking the puppy, drying and stimulating it. Check to see that all fluids have

Using simple genetic rules, an owner can predict to some degree the traits that the offspring of a given mating can exhibit. The six possible ways in which a pair of determiners can unite are illustrated on this Mendelian expectation chart. Ratios apply to expectancy over large numbers, except in lines 1, 2, and 6 where exact expectancy is realized in every litter.

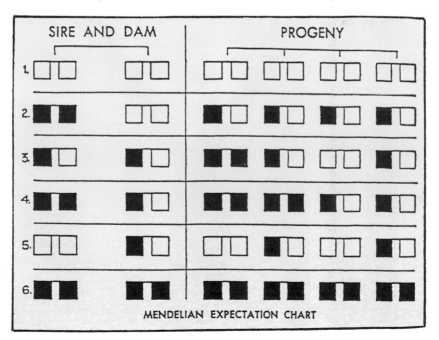

MENDELIAN EXPECTATION CHART

been cleared from the pup's nostrils and mouth after the mother has licked her youngster clean; otherwise the pup may have difficulty breathing. If the mother fails to tear open the sac and stimulate the newborn's breathing, you can do this yourself by tearing the sack with your hands and then gently rubbing the infant with a soft, rough towel. The afterbirth attached to the puppy by the long umbilical cord, should follow the birth of each puppy. Watch to be sure that each afterbirth is expelled, for the retention of this material can cause infection. In her instinct for cleanliness the mother will probably eat the afterbirth after severing the umbilical cord. One or two meals of this will not hurt her; they stimulate her milk supply, as well as labor, for remaining pups. However, eating too many afterbirths can make her lose appetite for the food she needs to feed her pups and regain her strength. So remove the rest of

Prior to birth, the developing pups are housed in the horns of the uterus.

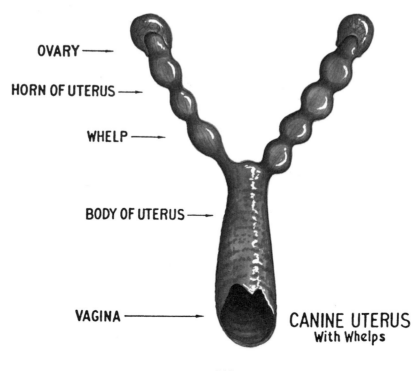

OVARY

HORN OF UTERUS

WHELP

BODY OF UTERUS

VAGINA

CANINE UTERUS
With Whelps

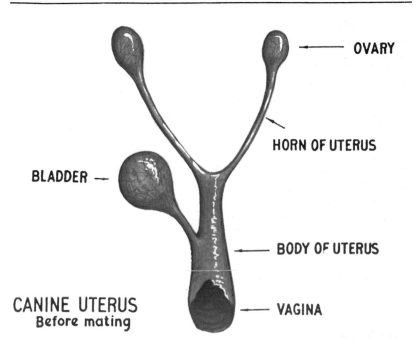

OVARY

HORN OF UTERUS

BLADDER —

BODY OF UTERUS

CANINE UTERUS
Before mating

VAGINA

The canine uterus is quite different from the human uterus. Besides the difference in shape, the canine uterus is designed to house an average of five to eight offspring.

them, along with the wet newspapers, and keep the box dry and clean.

If the mother does not bite the cord or bites it too close to the puppy's body, take over the job to prevent an umbilical hernia. Tearing is recommended, but you can cut the cord, about two inches from the body, with a sawing motion with scissors that have been sterilized in alcohol. Then dip the end of the cut cord in a shallow dish of iodine; the cord will dry up and fall off in a few days.

The puppies should follow each other at intervals of not more than half an hour. If more time goes past and you are sure there are still pups to come, taking the mother for a brisk walk outside may start labor again. If she is actively straining without producing a puppy, the youngster may be presented backward, a so-called "breech" birth. Careful assistance with a well-lubricated finger to feel for the puppy or to ease it back may help, but never attempt to pull it out by force. This could cause serious damage, so seek the services of an expert—your veterinarian or an experienced breeder.

Even the best planned breeding can bear unexpected problems and complications. Therefore, do not rely solely on textbook knowledge of breeding and genetics. Experienced breeders and veterinarians will generally lend their words of wisdom—take full advantage of their generosity. Mere trial and error is no basis for any responsible breeding program.

If *anything* seems wrong during labor or parturition, waste no time in calling your veterinarian, who will examine the bitch and, if necessary, give her hormones to stimulate the birth of the remaining puppies.

You may want his experience in whelping the litter even if all goes well. He will probably prefer to have the puppies born at his hospital rather than getting up in the middle of the night to come to your home. The mother would, no doubt, prefer to stay at home; but you can be sure she will get the best of care in a veterinary hospital. If the puppies are born at home, and all goes as it should, watch the mother carefully afterward. Within a day or two of the birth, it is wise to have the veterinarian check her and the pups to ensure that all is well.

Be sure each puppy finds a teat and starts nursing right away, as these first few meals supply colostral antibodies to help him fight disease. As soon

Cells reproduce by a process called mitosis, in which the cells divide, forming two identical cells.

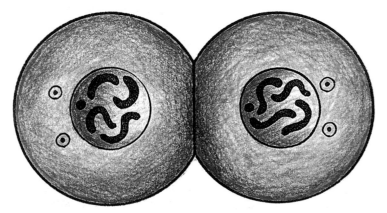

PUPPY GROWTH AND BREEDER RESPONSIBILITY

AGE	REQUIRED CARE/EXPECTED DEVELOPMENT
WEEKS 1–2	Helpless; dam must provide constant care; owner must ensure warmth and cleanliness; puppy nurses, crawls, needs stimulation for elimination; sleeps 90% of time.
WEEKS 3–4	Owner sustains optimum environment; puppy is alert, laps from bowl, takes first steps; defecates on its own; baby teeth emerge; barks, wags tail.
WEEKS 4–5	Ambles, growls, and bites; play and interaction increase; human contact limited but essential; learning begins.
WEEKS 5–6	Weaning; human socialization vital; pack order apparent; sex play; explores and sleeps less.
WEEKS 6–8	Two to three daily meals; puppy accustomed to human family; breeder initiates housetraining; first veterinary visit; wary of the unknown.

as he is dry, hold each puppy to a nipple for a good meal without competition. Then he may join his littermates in the whelping box, out of his mother's way while she continues giving birth. Keep a supply of puppy formula on hand for emergency feedings or later weaning. An alternative formula of evaporated milk, corn syrup, and a little water with egg yolk can be warmed and fed if necessary. A pet nurser kit is also a good thing to have on hand; these are available at local pet shops. A supplementary feeding often helps weak pups (those that may have difficulty nursing) over the hump. Keep track of birth weights and weekly readings thereafter; this will furnish an accurate record of the pups' growth and health, and the information will be valuable to your veterinarian.

RAISING THE PUPPIES

After all the puppies have been born, take the mother outside for a walk and drink of water, and then return her to take care of her brood. She will probably not want to stay away for more than a minute or two for the first few weeks. Be sure to keep water available at all times and feed her milk or broth frequently, as she needs nourishment to produce milk. Encourage her to eat, with her favorite foods, until she seeks them of her own accord. She will soon develop a ravenous appetite and should have at least two large meals a day, with dry food available in addition. Your veterinarian can guide you on the finer points of nutrition as they apply to nursing dams.

Prepare a warm place to put the puppies after they are born to keep them dry and to help them to a good start in life. An electric heating pad, heat lamp or hot water bottle covered with flannel can be placed in the bottom of a cardboard box and near the mother so that she can see her puppies. She will usually allow you to help her care for the youngsters, but don't take them out of her sight. Let her handle things if your interference seems to make her nervous.

Be sure that all the puppies are getting enough to eat. If the mother sits or stands instead of lying still to nurse, the probable

While in the womb, each pup is encased in an individual protective sac.

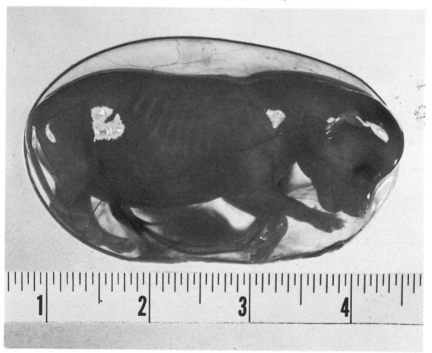

cause is scratching from the puppies' nails. You can remedy this by clipping them, as you would the bitch's, with a pet nail clipper. Manicure scissors also do for these tiny claws. Some breeders advise disposing of the smaller or weaker pups in a large litter, as the mother has trouble handling more than six or seven. You can help her out by preparing an extra puppy box or basket furnished with a heating pad and/or heating lamp and some bedding material. Leave half the litter with the mother and the other half in the extra box, changing off at two-hour intervals at first. Later you may exchange them less frequently, leaving them all together except during the day. Try supplementary feedings, too. As soon as their eyes open, at about two weeks, they will lap from a small dish.

A puppy nurser kit is considered standard equipment by many breeders. These kits are available at your local pet shop.

WEANING THE PUPPIES

Normally the puppies should be completely weaned at five weeks, although you can start to feed them at three weeks. They will find it easier to lap semi-solid food than to drink milk at first, so mix baby cereal with whole or evaporated milk, warmed to body temperature, and offer it to the puppies in a saucer. Until they learn to lap it, it is best to feed one or two at a time because they are more likely to walk into it than to eat it. Hold the saucer at their chin level, and let them gather around, keeping paws off the dish. Cleaning with a damp sponge afterward prevents most of the cereal from sticking to the pups if the mother doesn't clean them up. Once they have gotten the idea, broth or babies' meat soup may be alternated with milk, and you can start them on finely chopped meat. At about four weeks, they will eat four meals a day and soon do without their mother entirely. Start them on canned dog food, or leave dry puppy food with them in a dish for self-feeding. Don't leave the water dish with them all the time; at this age everything is a play toy and they will use it as a wading pool. They can drink all they need if it is offered several times a day, after meals. As the puppies grow up, the mother will go into their "pen" only to nurse them, first sitting up and then standing. To dry up her milk supply completely, keep the mother away for longer periods; after a few days of part-time nursing she can stay away for even longer periods, and then permanently. The little milk left will be resorbed by her body.

The puppies may be put outside during the day, unless it is too cold or rainy, as soon as their eyes are open. They will benefit from the sunlight. A rubber mat or newspapers underneath will protect them from cold or dampness. As they mature, the pups can be let out for longer intervals, although you must provide them with a shelter at night or in bad weather. By now, cleaning up after the matured youngsters is a man-sized job, so put them out at least during the day and make your task easier. If you enclose them in a run or kennel, remember to clean it *daily*, as various parasites and other infectious organisms may be lurking if the quarters are kept dirty.

You can expect the pups to need at least one worming before they are ready to go to new homes. Before the pups are three weeks old, take a stool sample from each to your veterinarian. The vet can determine, by analyzing the stool, if any of the pups have worms—and if so, what kind of worms are present. If one puppy is infected, then all should be wormed as a preventive measure. Follow the veterinarian's advice; this also applies to vaccinations. You will want to vaccinate the pups at the earliest possible age. This way, the pups destined for new homes will be protected against some of the more debilitating canine diseases.

THE DECISION TO SPAY OR NEUTER

If you decide not to use your male or female for breeding, or if you are obligated to have the animal altered based on an agreement made between you and the seller, make the necessary arrangements with your veterinarian as soon as possible. The surgery involved for both males and females is relatively simple and painless: males will be castrated and females will have their ovaries and uterus removed. In both

REASONS TO SPAY/NEUTER DOGS

• Reduces dog's need to roam.
• Reduces and/or eliminates certain reproductive cancers.
• Disburdens female dog of heat cycle and discomforts which accompany.
• Lessens dominance and mounting activity.
• Increases general lifespan of dog.
• Eliminates owner's concern of unwanted puppies, runaway stud dogs, stained furniture, nervous, and aggressive mood swings in pets.
• Relieves community of homeless dogs and property damage.

cases, the operation does not alter their personalities; you will, however, notice that males will be less likely to roam, to get into fights with other male dogs, and to mount objects and people.

Your veterinarian can best determine at what age neutering or spaying should be done. With a young female dog, the operation may be somewhat more involved, and as a result be more costly; however, in the long run you will be glad you made the decision to have this done for your pet. After a night or two at the veterinarian's or an animal hospital, your bitch can be safely returned to your home. Her stitches will heal in a short time, and when they are removed, you will hardly notice her souvenir scar of the routine operation. Once she has been spayed, she no longer will be capable of

having a litter of puppies.

Check with your city or town or with the local humane society for special programs that are available for pet owners. In many municipalities you can have your pet altered for just a small fee; the low price is meant to encourage pet owners to take advantage of this important means of birth control for their dogs. Pet adoption agencies and other animal welfare organizations can house only so many animals at one time, given the money, space, and other resources they have available. This is why pet owners are urged to have their pets altered, so that puppies resulting from accidental breedings won't end up being put to sleep as so many others have that are lost, stray, unwanted, or abandoned.

Traveling With Your Pet

Most pets can be trained to become very good travellers provided you begin that training when your pet is still very young. Unfortunately, your puppy's first ride in the car is likely to be to the veterinarian's where, after a frightening, abrupt introduction to the noisy, jolting automobile, he is stabbed by horrible long needles. Is there any wonder that, in the future, he will run for cover whenever he hears you jingling your car keys?

TRIPS BY CAR

Familiarize your pet with your car by taking him to a nearby park or an open area where he can run about and enjoy himself. Thus, you will have associated the car with something pleasant. Throw a dog biscuit or favorite toy into his crate, which you have placed on the back seat of the car, in an effort to preoccupy him. Never allow your dog to ride uncrated, as there is nothing more dangerous than a playful pup jumping on his owner as he is driving. Your puppy should also keep his head inside a moving car as dust and debris could irritate his eyes and nostrils.

When you park your car and leave your pet inside, make certain that the windows are open at least two inches; dogs are particularly susceptible to heat exhaustion and the temperature in a parked car in the height of summer can reach over 120°F. Try to find a shady spot to park your car and return as soon as possible, as unscrupulous dognappers do exist who might pounce on your unsupervised pet. Of course, you must NEVER put your pet in the trunk of your car.

LONG TRIPS

When you prepare for a lengthy trip, make certain that you pack a few essential items for your canine companion: a blanket, a thermos of water, pet food, his food and water dishes, favorite toys, and any necessary medicine.

Do not give your pet a heavy meal before the trip but do ensure that he has a plentiful water supply. This will mean that you will have to break your journey several times so that he can relieve himself, but the rests and exercise will probably do you both good.

Most hotel chains in the United States welcome well-behaved pets but it is always wise to ask about their policy ahead of time when you make your reservation.

With early training and a little common sense, you and your pet will make excellent travelling companions *and* benefit from each other's company along the way.

BOARDING YOUR DOG

It may be necessary one day, however, to board your dog while you are on an extended vacation or business trip. In the United States, kennels which are members of the American Boarding Kennels Association should provide very good care for your pet. The A.B.K.A. is a nationwide non-profit organization established to promote high standards and professionalism in the pet-boarding industry.

Make certain to visit the kennels for an inspection before you board your dog. Examine the facilities, check the cleanliness of the stalls and exercise runs, talk to the owners about any special dietary or medical requirements your dog may have, look at the dogs staying there, and find out if there is a veterinarian on call. Also make your reservation well in advance, particularly if you plan to be away in the busy summer months or during the sometimes hectic holidays.

You can help your pet feel less homesick by taking his bed or favorite toy along. Finally, remember to leave an address or telephone number where you can be reached in case of an emergency.

Always include the dog's favorite toys in his crate whenever you travel by car.

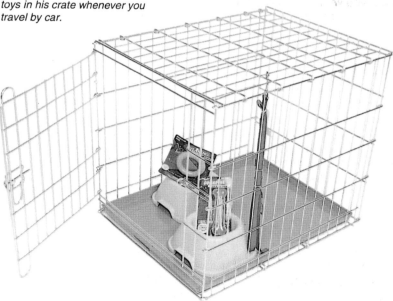

Dog Books from

H-1016, 224 pp
135 photos

H-969, 224 pp
62 color photos

H-1061, 608 pp
Black/white photos

TS-101, 192 p
Over 100 pho

TW-102, 256 pp
Over 200 color

TW-113, 256 pp
200 color photos

H-962, 255 pp
Nearly 100 photos

SK-044, 64 pp
Over 50 color
photos

PS-872, 240 pp
178 color illustrations

H-1095, 272 pp
Over 160 color illustrations

All-Breed Dog Books From T.F.H.

The ATLAS of **DOG BREEDS** of the World **T.F.H.**

NEW!
FOURTH EDITION
TWO VOLUMES

BONNIE WILCOX, DVM,
—and—
CHRIS WALKOWICZ

OVER 1100 FULL-COLOR PHOTOS

The most comprehensive fully illustrated volume on dogs ever published—*EVERY* photo in full color

VOLUME 2

H-1091, 2 Vols., 912 pp
Over 1100 color photos

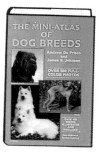

H-1106, 544 pp
Over 400 color photos

TS-175, 896 pp
Over 1300 color photos

The T.F.H. all-breed dog books are the most comprehensive and colorful of all dogs books available. The most famous of these recent publications, *The Atlas of Dog Breeds of the World,* written by Dr. Bonnie Wilcox and Chris Walkowicz, is now available as a two-volume set. Now in its fourth edition, the *Atlas* remains one of the most sought-after gift books and reference works in the dog world.

A very successful spinoff of the *Atlas* is *The Mini-Atlas of Dog Breeds,* written by Andrew De Prisco and James B. Johnson. This compact but comprehensive book has been praised and recommended by most national dog publications for its utility and reader-friendliness. The true field guide for dog lovers.

Canine Lexicon by the authors of the *Mini-Atlas* is an up-to-date encyclopedic dictionary for the dog person. It is the most complete single volume on the dog ever published covering more breeds than any other book as well as other relevant topics, including health, showing, training, breeding, anatomy, veterinary terms, and much more. No dog book before has ever offered this many stunning color photographs of all breeds, dog sports, and topics (over 1300 in full color).

221

Index

Off the
Beaten Path®

**maritime
provinces**

Help Us Keep This Guide Up to Date

Every effort has been made by the author and editors to make this guide as accurate and useful as possible. However, many changes can occur after a guide is published—establishments close, phone numbers change, hiking trails are rerouted, facilities come under new management, etc.

We would love to hear from you concerning your experiences with this guide and how you feel it could be improved and be kept up to date. While we may not be able to respond to all comments and suggestions, we'll take them to heart, and we'll make certain to share them with the author. Please send your comments and suggestions to the following address:

The Globe Pequot Press
Reader Response/Editorial Department
P.O. Box 480
Guilford, CT 06437

Or you may e-mail us at: editorial@GlobePequot.com

Thanks for your input, and happy travels!

INSIDERS'GUIDE®

OFF THE BEATEN PATH® SERIES

Off the Beaten Path®

SIXTH EDITION

maritime provinces

A GUIDE TO UNIQUE PLACES

TRUDY FONG

INSIDERS'GUIDE®

GUILFORD, CONNECTICUT
AN IMPRINT OF THE GLOBE PEQUOT PRESS

INSIDERS' GUIDE®

Text design by Linda Loiewski
Maps by Equator Graphics © Morris Book Publishing, LLC
Illustrations by Carole Drong
Illustration of Grand Falls Gorge on page 27 from slide courtesy of New Brunswick Tourism Department. Illustration of *Bluenose II* on page 113 from slide courtesy of Nova Scotia Department of Tourism and Culture. All other illustrations from photos by Greg Fong.
Spot photography throughout © Andre Jenny / Alamy

ISSN 1542-5533
ISBN 978-0-7627-4417-6

Manufactured in the United States of America
Sixth Edition/First Printing

To Greg, companion of all

my significant voyages—

"The only railroad romance that ever lasted."

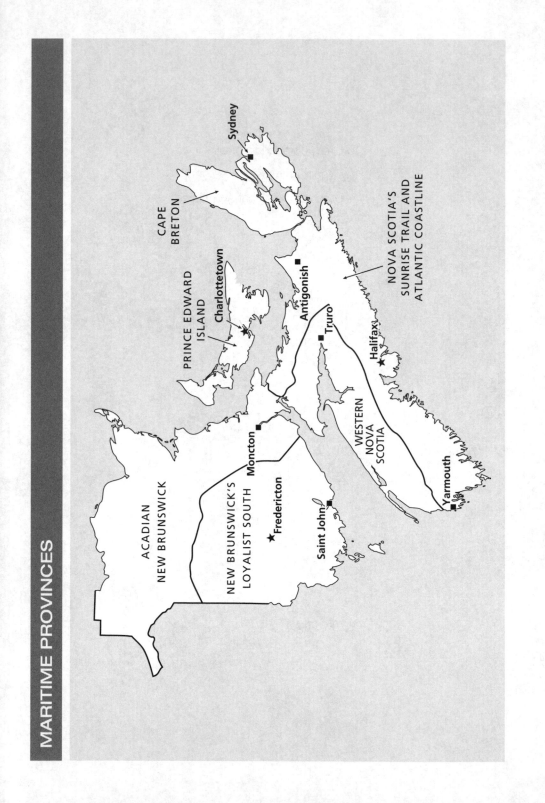

MARITIME PROVINCES

Sydney

CAPE
BRETON

NOVA SCOTIA'S
SUNRISE TRAIL AND
ATLANTIC COASTLINE

PRINCE EDWARD
ISLAND

Charlottetown

Antigonish

Truro

Halifax

WESTERN
NOVA
SCOTIA

Yarmouth

ACADIAN
NEW BRUNSWICK

NEW BRUNSWICK'S
LOYALIST SOUTH

Moncton

Fredericton

Saint John

Contents

Acknowledgments

The following people have been wonderfully enthusiastic and informative and have inspired me with their special love of the Maritimes. I wish to thank them: Randy Brooks, Carol Horne, and Diane Rioux.

All but two of the renderings in this book are drawn from photographs shot by my husband, photographer Greg Fong. The Nova Scotia Department of Tourism and Culture supplied the shot of the *Bluenose II,* and the Grand Falls Gorge illustration is from a shot supplied by the New Brunswick Tourism Department.

Introduction

My first real experience of travel in the Maritimes came as a result of a job on VIA Rail, the passenger-train service, which at that time left twice daily for Montreal from Halifax. I had graduated from college and was at loose ends when I took the job.

There were many opportunities to become familiar with the lay of the land as the train trundled by farms and woodlands, lakes and rivers. And with every stop the cultural and linguistic fabric would subtly change. Then as now, what struck me is the region's tremendous diversity, the vastness of the land, and the tiny communities that live in relative isolation from one another. Perhaps it is this isolation that has created fiercely independent peoples who are nevertheless able to extend exceptionally warm welcomes to outsiders. While exchange rates fluctuate and prices change, businesses close, and new spots open, there is an enduring quality about the Maritimes that keeps visitors coming back year after year.

Prices in this book are in Canadian dollars. If you are coming from another country, you will want to know the value of your currency compared with the Canadian dollar. To calculate conversions quickly, divide any Canadian price by the rate posted for your currency on that day.

Canada uses metric measurements for weight, distance, and temperature. In this book I've listed measures according to the U.S. standards and provided their metric equivalents in parentheses. Take note that all road signs in Canada are in kilometers, not miles. Posted speed limits of 100, often shown without a "km," translate to 62 miles per hour.

Dressing for weather conditions in the Maritimes means packing layers. Carry a windbreaker, which is good in fog or mist, conditions that occur in the Maritimes about as often as the tides. A warm sweater is a good item to pack even in the summer months, because Maritime temperatures often drop significantly at night. Sunblock is also a must. The cool sea breeze or overcast skies can fool you into thinking that the sun is not very strong, but even a hazy day at the beach can result in a severe burn if you don't take precautions.

I include several good hikes in each province. These were selected for the natural wonders that you may discover along the trails more than for their ease. That said, a good pair of walking shoes or, better still, hiking boots is a must. Hats are also a good idea, as is bug repellent in the countryside, particularly in the spring.

Most museum admission prices in the Maritimes are quite reasonable, because many of these sites are government operated. If you plan to visit several national parks, it may be more economical to buy a season-pass sticker for a flat fee rather than paying for each entry.

In some remote areas accommodations are quite limited, so I have listed several places you can call to reserve a room ahead of time to avoid a last-minute search. In a number of places I refer to Heritage properties. These are buildings or areas that various government bodies have determined to have significant historical connections. Having survived the plow and wrecking ball thus far, they have been designated by the government for future protection. Heritage properties are taxed at special rates, and the owners are assisted in restoration so that the sites may be preserved for future generations. The "Heritage" designation means that the property is preserved as much as possible in its original state. Scenic Heritage Roads on Prince Edward Island are old clay roads that appear exactly as they did one hundred years ago and offer the traveler an abundance of scenic beauty.

Every trip has to start somewhere. That said, my travel throughout the Maritimes seems to have happened consistently in a clockwise direction. Therefore, if your entry point into the Maritimes is not the same as the one at the beginning of this guidebook, merely search through the index for your starting point and follow the route clockwise from that point onward.

The Maritimes are full of hidden treasures—for the gourmet, the photography buff, or the artist. This book is intended as a compass, to help you make your own personal discovery of the wonders that Canada's east coast has to offer. *Bon voyage!*

Rates for accommodations (before taxes, per night):
Under $70	Standard
$70–$150	Moderate
$151 and above	Deluxe

New Brunswick's Loyalist South

The first province you reach when entering the Maritimes by land is New Brunswick, with its vast, unpopulated interior full of rich timberlands and salmon rivers.

The first characteristic that will strike you is that the bulk of the population is distributed around the rim of the province. Next, you will notice that the province retains many native Indian place names. But certain areas, like the northwestern interior and the gulf coast, have a preponderance of French names, while the Fundy Coast and the Saint John River Valley feature many names of British origin.

These are clues to the character of New Brunswick. Overlaid on a land inhabited by people of the Maliseet and Mi'K-maq (formerly spelled Micmac) tribes for thousands of years, today the province's linguistic fabric resembles that of Canada as a whole more closely than any other province: Roughly 34 percent of the population is French-speaking, with the remainder using English in their day-to-day communication.

New Brunswick is really two places in one: the French New Brunswick of the northwest and the north and east coasts, and the British Empire Loyalist New Brunswick of the Saint John River Valley and the Fundy shore. It is because of these two distinct characters, rather than any particular geographical

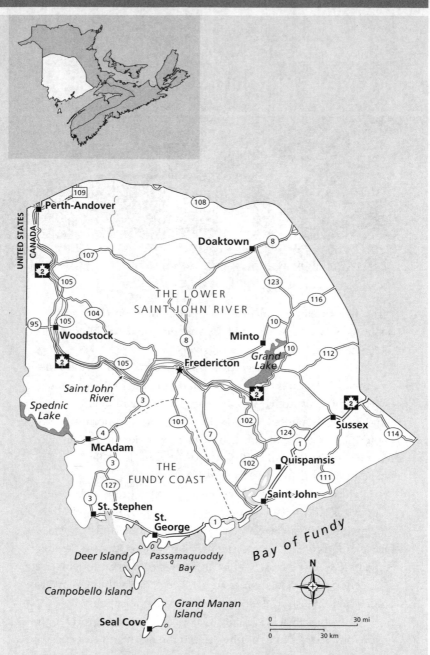

reason, that we discuss New Brunswick in two separate chapters. The first, the Loyalist South, begins at the Maine–New Brunswick border, where Yankees and British Loyalists have lived cheek by jowl for two centuries.

The Fundy Coast

If you enter New Brunswick from Calais, Maine, you're struck by the fact that the national border runs right smack dab through the middle of town. In fact, Calais and *St. Stephen* natives have had such congenial relations that they refused to fight each other during the War of 1812. They still seem to form one community.

Upgrades in the New Brunswick highway system (now featuring large sections of twinned [divided] highway) have caused changes in exit numbers for certain areas. Repeat visitors to New Brunswick will want an up-to-date map to avoid confusion. The development of new highway and New Brunswick's growing popularity has caused a hotel-room shortage. Book rooms well in advance, or book early in the day. You can book rooms en route by calling (800) 561-0123.

If you want to wind down after the rigors of crossing the border, or even if you just need a quick endorphin rush, why not visit St. Stephen's *Chocolate Museum* at 73 Milltown Road? Housed in a former chocolate factory, the museum tells the fascinating story of this town's most famous industry, and Canada's oldest candy company. In existence since 1873, the Ganong Bros. Chocolate Company was the first company to introduce the heart-shaped chocolate box to North America in 1932. This wasn't their only innovation in the

TRUDY'S FAVORITES

Ministers Island

Rossmount Inn,
St. Andrews by-the-Sea

Roosevelt Cottage,
Campobello Island

Grand Manan Island

Machias Seal Island

City Market,
Saint John

Beaverbrook Art Gallery,
Fredericton

Legislative Assembly Building,
Fredericton

Harvest Jazz and Blues Festival,
Fredericton

Kings Landing Historical Settlement,
Fredericton

World's Longest Covered Bridge,
Hartland

marketplace: They also were the inventors of the original five-cent chocolate bar, in 1910. For decades, this has been one of the town's biggest employers. At the museum you can learn how chocolates are hand-dipped, how their antique candy-making machinery was used, and other interesting facts about the industry. The same building houses **Ganong Chocolatier,** a re-creation of an old-fashioned candy store. You could also join the Heritage Chocolate Walk from mid-June to mid-October. It includes a tour of the museum plus an outdoor walk past homes and buildings that relate to the history of the town of St. Stephen and Ganongs. Everyone receives sample chocolates at the museum, but Chocolate Walk participants also get treats from the Ganong Chocolatier! The museum is open all summer Monday to Saturday from 9:00 A.M. until 6:30 P.M., and Sundays from 1:00 to 5:00 P.M. In September, it closes at 5:00 P.M. and doesn't open Sundays. During the spring and fall, the museum opens Monday to Friday from 9:00 A.M.

agarrisontown

St. Andrews's strategic location on the New Brunswick–Maine border made it a garrison town of long standing. A fort once stood above the town on Barracks Hill. While some documents identify the fort as Fort Tipperary, today the earthen rampart and few cannons that remain are generally referred to as Barracks Hill.

Although neither New Brunswick nor Maine wanted any part of the hostilities, the War of 1812 necessitated the construction of further fortifications, including batteries and blockhouses rimming the coastline, to serve as protection against marauding American privateers. Today only St. Andrews Blockhouse National Historic Site on Joe's Point Road (888–773–8888) remains.

to 5:00 P.M. Admission rates vary, depending on whether you take the Heritage Chocolate Walk or not. To confirm tour times, call (506) 466–7406.

After St. Stephen, continue along the TransCanada Highway (TCH) Route 1 to **St. Andrews by-the-Sea.** The signs will indicate St. Andrews long before anything much appears: The town is there, hidden behind trees. Watch carefully for the sign indicating Provincial Highway 127. Turn right here and drive toward the shore.

You will soon see a small sign pointing left and indicating **Ministers Island,** where you can visit the former **Estate of Sir William Van Horne,** the builder of the Canadian Pacific Railway. Note: If you would rather bypass Ministers Island and head directly to St. Andrews, simply continue east on Highway 127 (in the direction of Saint John).

To get to Ministers Island take the left turn, then turn right onto Mowat Drive, and take another left onto Bar Road. This will lead you to a barricaded bit of shoreline. In this area of the Bay of Fundy, the tides change the water

Carriage at Van Horne Estate

level by about 25 feet (7.6 m). At high tide, the island is inaccessible by car, but at low tide a sandbar serves as the tail end of Bar Road.

A small sign indicates the times when guides will lead small contingents of cars to the island. Without a guide, a barricade will prevent you from entering even during low tide.

When you first arrive on Ministers Island, you will see a small stone building, then a windmill and one of the largest barns in Canada. It was here that Van Horne kept his prized herd of Dutch cattle and his Thoroughbred horses.

Van Horne had his country house built on the other side of the island using sandstone cut from the shore. Its massive rooms are full of mahogany paneling and post-and-beam supports. The drawing room alone is as large as the average modern bungalow. There are fifty rooms in the house; seventeen of these were bedrooms. In the billiards room is a 6-by-12-foot (1.8-by-3.6 m) billiards table crafted for Van Horne in London.

Van Horne was an avid and skilled painter. Some of his finest paintings hang in the National Art Gallery in Ottawa. He created them at night in a huge circular stone bathhouse overlooking Passamaquoddy Bay. The property included several heated greenhouses. Even when Van Horne lived in Montreal, the dairy products and fruit from his estate were sent via Bar Road to a waiting train, to be delivered the next morning to him.

Sadly, after 1941 the property remained empty for many years until it was sold to a succession of speculators, all of whose plans to turn it into a lodge fell through. More than 600 pieces of Van Horne's original mahogany furniture were auctioned off by one group of investors just three days before the province declared it a protected historic site. Even though today the building is emptied of nearly all its furnishings, it is still an amazing place and well worth a visit. Call (506) 529–5081 to inquire about tour times. A small admission is charged.

After leaving Ministers Island, return to Highway 127 and drive east (in the direction of Saint John) for a few minutes. To your left will be a sign indicating the **Rossmount Inn,** a Provincial Heritage building. Even if you don't stay here, plan to drop by to eat something so that you can soak up some of the Old World atmosphere inside.

There are so many pieces of pure Anglophile magic here that you'll swear you are in a manor house in England. In the front hallway, rich with mahogany paneling, banisters, and stairway and carpeted with Persian rugs, is a chair used by the King of Belgium during the Queen of England's coronation in 1952. The tables in the dining room are decked out in the finest English bone china and silverware, while the lamps are Tiffany. Reservations can be made by calling (506) 529–3351 or faxing (506) 529–1920. Rates for nonsmoking rooms are moderate.

trivia

The fronds of the ostrich fern, which is native to New Brunswick, are commonly called "fiddleheads" when they appear in the spring and are a much-loved delicacy.

This part of New Brunswick has long been the haunt of Ivy League types and their yachts. Franklin D. Roosevelt learned to sail in this area. The waters of the bay are quite calm, and each island is unique and appealing.

Continuing along Highway 127, you will find exquisitely preserved St. Andrews by-the-Sea. Still oozing with charm, St. Andrews was founded by United Empire Loyalists from nearby Maine in 1783. It was laid out in a grid pattern common in New England towns of that era.

Streets were named after royal personages to leave no doubt about the political stripe of the town's founders. There are King, Queen, Princess Royal, and Prince of Wales Streets. Prosperity came from selling lumber and wooden ships to Mother England and fish to the West Indies.

Some of the old houses were actually disassembled in their original locations in Castine, Maine, moved by barge in 1783, and reassembled here.

Downtown St. Andrews offers marvelous possibilities for puttering and sight-seeing. Some of its quaint historic houses date back to the province's early days. Of note is **Sheriff Andrews House,** an authentic Loyalist home built in 1820 by Elisha Andrews, the sheriff of Charlotte County. Situated on the corner of King and Queen Streets, the mint-condition home was taken over by the province in the late 1980s and meticulously restored. It features nine period-furnished rooms depicting domestic life in the old seaport. Rooms have working fireplaces, and one of its most appealing features is the huge stone hearth in the basement, typical of Loyalist houses of the time. The basement "keeping room" also contains beehive ovens and a pantry. The cooking fireplace is kept going all summer long for visitors, who are invited by the cos-tumed guides to enjoy some refreshments while exploring the house. Guides also demonstrate early cooking and hand-work techniques. The house is open mid-June to late September, Monday to Saturday from 9:30 A.M. to 4:30 P.M., and Sunday from 1:00 to 4:30 P.M. Admission is free. For information, call (506) 529–5080.

New Brunswick has seventy-odd "kissing bridges," or covered wooden bridges, that span the many woodland rivers, particularly on old logging roads. Although picturesque, they can be quite tricky to find without detailed direc-tions. The best approach is to work in a visit to a couple of covered bridges en route to somewhere else, with a slight detour onto a secondary road that will take you near a bridge.

Bridges were covered to keep them from wearing out too soon. Uncov-ered wooden bridges last an average of ten years; covered ones last eight times as long. Because of the romantic opportunities they offered they came to be called kissing bridges. Crossing the bridges by horse and buggy or horse-drawn sleigh (in winter the bridge flooring was covered with snow so that sleighs could pass through) must have taken some time. If the horse was experienced and reliable, a romantic young couple could leave the driving to their four-legged friend and take advantage of the momentary privacy and darkness afforded by the covered bridges.

Among these bridges is the so-called **Covered Bridge Number Four,** which spans the Digdeguash River, near McCann. You can reach it by turning off Route 127 onto Route 760 at Rollingham.

The next stop is **Deer Island,** reached by the Deer Island L'Etete Ferry, off Route 1 at St. George. Take Route 772. Departures are frequent, and the ferry is free. Crossing takes about twenty-five minutes and is quite pleasant, especially

TOP ANNUAL EVENTS

Times for these events vary, unless specified. For full details, contact the **New Brunswick Department of Tourism** at (800) 561–0123.

Acadian National Day,
Acadian Pioneer Village and Saint John (August 15)

Summer Music Festival,
Fredericton (mid-August)

Harvest Jazz and Blues Festival,
Fredericton (second week of September)

Atlantic Balloon Fiesta,
Sussex (mid-September)

on a sunny day when a cool breeze is blowing across the calm waters of Passamaquoddy Bay. The ferry lands at Lambert's Cove.

Follow the shore road until you reach the Eastport/Campobello Ferry dock just before **Deer Island Point Park.** If you have timed the tides right, enter the park to get a close-up view of **Old Sow,** the biggest natural tidal whirlpool in the Western Hemisphere, just offshore, opposite the Deer Island Point Park campground, to the right of the dock.

You must be on-site three hours before high tide to see Old Sow do its thing. If you are too early, relax and await the forces of nature at the picnic area here at the park.

The ferry ride from Deer Island to **Campobello Island** takes forty-five minutes. It's privately run, so a modest fee is charged for both the car and passengers. Campobello is beautifully located on the Bay of Fundy. It's easy to see how it grew into a summer retreat for yachtsmen and Harvard grads. Here you will find **Roosevelt Cottage,** one of a complex of several cottages that now are often used for conferences and meetings. Clustered next to one another facing Lubec, Maine, across the water, the cottages and surrounding acreage are part of **Roosevelt Campobello International Park.**

President Franklin D. Roosevelt spent many summers here. This is where he learned how to sail before he contracted polio at age thirty-nine. Everything in the house has been kept just as it was the last time Eleanor Roosevelt visited the cottage, right down to two massive megaphones left standing in the entrance to the dining room. (They were used to call the children in to eat.) Along with other memorabilia, you can see the flags presented to Roosevelt when he won the presidency. They now flank his desk.

Be sure to visit the house to the right of Roosevelt Cottage, which is part of the same complex. Graced with a roomy wraparound sunporch made from

Roosevelt Cottage, Campobello Island

logs, its living room's oval-shaped picture window treats visitors to a perfectly composed view of Lubec across the water. For details on Roosevelt Campobello International Park, call (506) 752–2922. Admission is free. Donations are welcome.

Also on the island you will find **Herring Cove Provincial Park.** It has a beach where you can enjoy the bracing water of the Bay of Fundy. The park also encompasses an active beaver pond and some breathtaking cliffs overlooking the sea. For information on Herring Cove Provincial Park, call (506) 752–7010. The park is on Route 774.

Before you leave Campobello Island, take advantage of the handy **Campobello Welcome Centre,** which can book accommodations for you in other parts of the province at no charge. It is recommended that those planning to go on to nearby Grand Manan Island take the time to book a room while still on Campobello. Campobello Island's tourist information center is just inside the Canadian border, next to Canadian customs, just a stone's throw from the bridge to Lubec. It is open mid-May to mid-October. For information, call (506) 752–7043.

If you are in the mood to visit a remote, unspoiled place, **Grand Manan Island** is the ticket, but you can't easily get there from Campobello. The best route is via the ferry, which leaves from Blacks Harbor, southwest of Saint John. Fares are sold on a round-trip basis, and vary depending on the type of vehicle and number of passengers. It will cost you roughly $52 for a vehicle and two adults, round-trip. For complete fare details and sailing times, consult the Coastal Transport Web site at www.coastaltransport.ca/.

At the junction of Routes 785 and 776 on the mainland, take a right. Within five minutes you'll approach the ferry. Plan to take your car, since Grand Manan is quite large. The trip is roughly one and a half hours, and on breezy days you'll need either your sea legs or an antiseasickness pill or both, because the seas can be much rougher than landlubbers expect of a bay. (On the ferry are pictures of the vessel being tossed so wildly by the seas that one end or the other is completely out of the water.)

The ferry docks in **North Head.** If you get there before noon on Saturday, you can visit the island's farmers' market, which is about 0.5 mile (1 km) from the ferry dock. For details and information on the Grand Manan Island ferry, call (506) 662–3724. Ferries sail up to seven times a day from both the island and the mainland during high season.

When you plan to leave the island, you can reserve a spot on the next morning's ferry, taking some of the uncertainty out of departure times. Apart from this small change, little else has been altered since I first visited Grand Manan, except that the island now has a few stop signs, and once a year, for a half hour during the Rotary Days Festival at the beginning of August, Grand Harbour has its own traffic jam.

At that time of year, with so many former residents returning to visit family and such a small number of inns, you will have a very hard time chancing upon accommodations, so reserve ahead. Also remember that August is prime whale-watching time; romance is in the water, and mating activity takes place.

North Head is also the best place to look at the remains of the phenomenon that caused the island to come into being in the first place. Around 380,000 years ago, the ground folded up and formed the island out of massive igneous rock. At North Head you can still see where the folding happened if you take the hike that begins at North Head's pier. It is marked by an understated sign announcing HOLE IN THE WALL and indicating a pathway. This path leads to a rocky stretch of coast where the highlight is a rock formation with a massive hole in it. The hike is roughly 2 miles (3 km) long and takes about an hour round-trip.

Turning left off the ferry dock, proceed down Route 776. You will almost immediately spot a number of pretty little houses that have been converted to bed-and-breakfast establishments. The *Compass Rose* offers a good view of the wharf and tiny North Head fleet.

The Compass Rose includes two adjacent Heritage houses with a sunroom dining room that stretches from one house to the other and faces the harbor, giving a lovely view. Their top room has a fireplace and king-size bed.

Guests are served a traditional English breakfast. During lunch and suppertime, the Compass Rose features fresh local seafood specialties like lobster Newburg, pan-fried lobster, and the chef's own pasta stuffed with lobster. The menu also features scallops either pan-fried with ginger or in coquilles St.-Jacques. Make reservations to avoid disappointment.

Rates are standard to moderate. For reservations call or fax at (506) 662–8570 or visit www.compassroseinn.com. It is open from the end of May to the beginning of October.

Note the local paintings on the walls of this establishment; many are framed in sea-weathered old planks and bits of driftwood. This type of framing is very characteristic of Grand Manan's artists. One such frame trims a lobster still life at Compass Rose, which was painted for the previous owner as partial payment for a room.

Since Grand Manan is such a picturesque island, complete with quaint fishing communities, stunning sea vistas, lighthouses, and a bird sanctuary, it is a magnet for artists.

The poshest digs on Grand Manan are in North Head at the *Manan Island Inn Ocean Side,* which has a three-and-a-half-star Canada Select rating. Rates are moderate. Call ahead to reserve a room at (506) 662–8624.

The **Shorecrest Lodge,** in the same community as Compass Rose, trails the aforementioned spa by only a star, has similar rates, and includes breakfast. This waterfront property is wheelchair accessible and also has accommodations for the visually impaired. For information, contact Mr. and Mrs. Andrew Normandeau at Shorecrest Lodge, North Head, Grand Manan, NB E0G 2M0. Call (506) 662–3216, or visit their Web site at www.shorecrestlodge.com.

This area of North America's east coast is located on the migratory path of many species of birds, and the island's isolation has ensured their continued presence here. One of the neighboring islands is **Machias Seal Island,** a bird sanctuary. The island is home to puffins (which look like small penguins in casual attire), razorbill auks, arctic terns, and other birds.

From mid-June through the first week of August, you can take a guided tour to the island and watch the puffins being their adorable selves from an arm's length away, since you will be concealed inside blinds. You can arrange this trip through your place of lodging, but be sure to do so well in advance, because only a limited number of people are allowed on the island per day.

There are five lighthouses on Grand Manan, pictures of which show up on scenic calendars with impressive regularity. It's easy to see why: Every corner of Grand Manan seems like a promontory at the end of the known universe, and land's end seems to be around every corner. Check out **Swallowtail Lighthouse** in particular if you want to get a feel for the rugged isolation.

If this is still not far enough away from the crowds, you can take a short (and free) ferry ride to **White Head Island.** Ferries departing Ingalls Head run every hour from 7:00 A.M. to 4:30 P.M., but the schedule for the ten-car ferry is not cast in stone. The 7:00 A.M. crossing is "on demand," and it's a good idea to let them know the day before if you want to get started that early. In the late afternoon there is about a three-hour gap after the 4:30 P.M. crossing. If demand exists, one more ferry sails around 7:00 P.M. The crossing takes twenty minutes. The boats also wait until the mainland ferry docks in case there will be more passengers.

trivia

In 1885, in response to the danger of disease transmission by new immigrants, Saint John became the location of the first quarantine station. At the time, immigrants who were ill could potentially spread dangerous diseases, such as smallpox, typhus, cholera, and influenza.

White Head is a great place for hiking and biking and has a lighthouse, and two completely beautiful and empty beaches for that Robinson Crusoe experience.

Grand Manan has two provincial parks, both along Route 776. The park in Castalia includes a picnic and rest area. Farther along Route 776, take the second left turn after the community of Grand Harbor to visit **Anchorage**

Getting a Good Look at Puffins

Grand Manan Island offers the ideal opportunity to get a rare look at the common *Atlantic puffin.* Many of these adorable creatures are found on Machias Seal Island, which is about 10 miles (16 km) from Grand Manan.

Puffins are sometimes referred to as "bottlenoses" or "sea parrots" because of their colorful beaks. They are compactly built at about 12 inches (30 cm) tall, with three webbed front toes. The birds are happy campers in the Bay of Fundy, where they feed by diving for marine organisms. Getting a good look at a puffin is a challenge since they live along isolated seacoasts and on islands in the northern oceans, where they nest in colonies of as many as 50,000. This is quite a hopeful sign, because the common Atlantic puffin was once threatened with extinction in this region and in the United States. Puffins from colonies in Canada were used to reestablish breeding colonies in Maine. The common Atlantic puffin is one of three species in the world.

Machias Seal Island has roughly 1,000 nesting pairs of puffins (along with thousands of pairs of arctic terns, hundreds of common terns, and razorbill auks). The puffins usually nest in burrows or caves, and each female lays a single white egg.

Sea Watch Tours operates the only Canadian tour vessels that are permitted to land on Machias Seal Island. When I visited the island with Sea Watch, I was glad that my boots had a good tread because we had to walk across some slippery seaweed-covered rocks to get onto the narrow island. Once ashore, our group was greeted by a warden of the Canadian Wildlife Service, who led us to a series of enclosed blinds, permitting us to hide from the birds. The puffins came within 3 feet (0.9 meters) of us. Bring an extra roll or two of film. The pictures you'll get will be incredible.

You can arrange a tour with Sea Watch by calling (506) 662–8552, or by e-mail at seawatch@nbnet.nb.ca.

Bear in mind that access to the island is very limited. Only twenty-five people a day are permitted to land, six days a week. There are several Machias Seal Island tour possibilities. Note that viewing the puffins on the island itself costs $75, whereas going around the island in a 16-foot skiff is $55 for ages twelve and older, $35 for younger children. (Plan ahead, if possible. While most of the shore spaces are booked by late April, there are still a few spaces left for shore access in late July and August.) Tours to Machias Seal Island run from mid-June until mid-August. Whale-watching and birding tours ($50 per adult and $30 for children under twelve) operate from mid-July until the end of September.

Provincial Park. Here you can hike, recreate, or take advantage of the camping facilities, including fully serviced sites. The park includes a migratory bird sanctuary. For information on both parks, call (506) 662–7022.

Anchorage Provincial Park is just a stone's throw from *Seal Cove,* which is reached by taking the left turn off Route 776 after the park. Seal Cove, at the southern tip of the island, is a photographer's dream. Once in the village turn left and follow the signs to the breakwater to get some beautiful shots. (Plan to arrive with lots of film as there isn't much chance of stocking up in Seal Cove.) Viewed from the water's edge, Seal Cove is dotted with well-tended neatly shingled and painted herring-smoking facilities. They look like a new cottage development. To the left of the smokehouses is a pleasant beach for strolling, beachcombing, or swimming.

At Seal Cove you can join a group of whale watchers with **Sea Watch Tours,** a company operating from the southernmost pier in the village. To get there, stop next to the two churches of the community and turn onto the road directly opposite. Follow this lane to take you up to the last pier on the cove. To book ahead with Sea Watch, call (506) 662–8552.

The Lower Saint John River

Back on the mainland, take Provincial Highway 776 until you reach the turnoff for the TransCanada Highway (TCH) Route 1, headed east to Saint John. If you wish, you can take a small detour onto Highway 790 at Lepreau. Continue until you reach the Little Lepreau Road. Take a slight detour to see the covered bridge that spans the Little Lepreau River, overlooking a mill pond. This road is closed to traffic but is wonderfully scenic.

Saint John is a good place for antiques hunting, because this is where the Loyalists did their shipbuilding. If you are eager to look at some pieces, emulate the locals and scan the newspaper for auction notices.

In the days of wooden ships, mahogany was prized because its density made it ideal as a ballast in the hull of the ships. Shipbuilders would discard their mahogany "scraps," which craftsmen quickly gathered up to use in the making of furniture.

You might want to stay at a Heritage inn in Saint John to enjoy many old-fashioned antique niceties in a charming inn that happens to be run by one of the province's finest chefs. The **Dufferin Inn and San Martello Dining Room** are operated by Axel and Margaret Begner, who ran a hotel and restaurant in Germany for a decade. Axel, a European-trained master chef and pastry chef, has been cooking for decades. The restaurant is the sort recommended by other chefs—with dishes like Bay of Fundy Cake, done with crab, scallops, salmon, and lobster; and

trivia

In 1896, while visiting Canada's first mental asylum, in Saint John, New Brunswick, Harry Houdini (the famous escape artist) obtained his first straight-jacket and formulated his idea for freeing himself from it.

Grand Marnier crème brûlée, you can be certain that you won't be bored with the selection.

The Begners came to Canada years ago and renovated and restored the home of J. B. M. Baxter, a former premier and chief justice of the province. Be sure to visit the inn's library, where you will find a wealth of information on Saint John. Environmentally friendly and fully renovated, the inn also offers the occasional organic cooking class for groups or individuals. I recommend calling ahead for information or booking.

To get to the inn, travel to **Saint John** west on Route 109. Turn left onto Market Place just after crossing the bridge. Take a right turn onto Saint John Street, and continue along this street for 5 blocks, by which time the road will be called Dufferin Row. The inn is at 357 Dufferin Row. Room rates are moderate. For a reservation, call (506) 635–5968 or e-mail duffinn@nb.aibn.com.

The Dufferin Inn is just down the street from the **Carleton Martello Tower,** a stone battery built during the War of 1812.

Martello towers originated in the Mediterranean, where they were used as watchtowers. One such tower in Corsica allowed so stiff a resistance to its British attackers in 1793 and 1794 that the idea of using these lookouts for coastal defense caught on in a big way. During the Napoleonic Wars, the British built more than a hundred Martello towers.

The flat roof of the Carleton tower was meant to hold two twenty-four-pounder guns and two twenty-four-pounder carronades. It never was armed for the War of 1812—by the time the tower was finished, the war was over. Some guns were installed in 1866, when a group of Irish-American Fenians threatened to capture British North America in a quest for Irish independence. Inside this particular tower you will see a barracks restored to the 1866 period and the powder magazine to its 1840s appearance. From June to mid-October, the tower is open daily from 9:00 A.M. to 5:00 P.M. A small admission is charged. For more information call (506) 636–4011 in season.

While in Saint John you may want to visit the **City Market.** The building was constructed by famous shipbuilders, who also built one of the world's fastest sailing ships, the Marco Polo. The market has had a charter since 1785 (along with Saint John itself) and is the oldest farmers' market in Canada.

The City Market is a large open space, made possible by the post-and-beam ceiling. Take a picture of this ceiling, then hold it upside down to see how the builders solved the problem of supporting a roof this size without a lot of braces: It's actually the upside-down hull of an old-time sailing ship!

The entrance to the market on Germain Street includes a glassed-in foyer and a spot for eating. The City Market is located at the corner of Charlotte and

Germain Streets. It is open year-round, Monday to Thursday from 7:30 A.M. 6:00 P.M., Friday until 7:00 P.M., and Saturday until 5:00 P.M. Closed Sunday. Admission is free.

If you proceed just past this market, you will soon come upon a park and then the old Loyalist graveyard, with markers dating back to the 1780s. The buildings along these streets and in the vicinity of Market Square are largely older buildings with intricate brickwork. You can hail a horse-drawn carriage to check out the downtown core if you want a different perspective. If you want to stay in downtown Saint John, you might want to check out the classy **Chipman Hill Suites,** which covers ten buildings, including the beautiful former home of a local physician and city mayor at 71 Sydney Street. Each of its ten suites includes a kitchenette. One phone number connects you to all ten of the properties: (506) 693–1171.

Just twenty minutes' drive outside of town, at the **Irving Nature Park,** you'll see harbor seals frolic at a location where more than 240 different species of birds have been spotted. To get there, take exit 119 A-B off Route 1 onto Bleury Street, turn right onto Sand Cove Road, and drive 1.2 miles (2 km) to the park. For details, call (506) 653–7367. Bring binoculars, sturdy hiking boots, and plenty of insect repellent. Admission is free, but remember that the park closes at dusk. Exercise caution on some trails along the ocean side; the occasional rough wave can give you quite a soaking.

Now turn inland along the river valley to Welsford, on Route 7. Adjacent to Route 7, on Cochran Road, about 1 mile (1.6 km) south of the community, you can admire a covered bridge over the Nerepis River. Then return to Route 101 north.

Inland on Route 101 you can see three more covered bridges without too much trouble. Exit Route 101 in Hoyt and turn onto Hoyt Station Road. There you will see **Back Creek Bridge Number Two** (Hoyt's Station).

Farther along Route 101, turn off onto Mill Settlement Road until you reach North Mill Settlement Road—here you will find spanning the South Oromocto River another bridge called the **South Oromocto Number Two Bridge** (Mill Settlement).

Continuing on Mill Settlement Road, you will come across Boyne Road. At this point, turn right and continue until you reach the **South Oromocto Number Three Bridge,** also called the Bell Bridge. From Boyne Road, return to Route 101 and proceed toward Fredericton.

Once you've puttered around historic **Fredericton,** walked under the city's elms, and had a look at the Victorian and Queen Anne homes, you will not find it at all surprising that many places here display the British flag. The United Empire Loyalists who came to New Brunswick left the same sort of indelible British stamp found in former outposts of the empire like Belize, Malaysia's west coast, and India.

Fredericton is a wonderful city for strolling around, particularly because driving in the downtown is quite tricky. Many of the streets are one-way—with no prior indication until you come to an intersection and find youself facing the wrong way down a one-way street.

When you arrive in Fredericton, drop in first at the city hall tourist office, which is right downtown on Queen Street (next to the water). Here you can get a three-day tourist parking pass, available to any out-of-province vehicle. This entitles you to park in the lot behind City Hall or at any meter without paying a cent—or getting a ticket.

Turn left when you leave city hall to visit Fredericton's former British officer's quarters (dating from 1840), which are now the *York-Sunbury Historical Society Museum.* Between these onetime officer's quarters and the guardhouse is a parade ground in typical Colonial British style, around which "soldiers" in period costume march in traditional fashion during the summer months. If you wish to witness the changing of the guard, visit just before 11:00 A.M. or 7:00 P.M. Tuesday through Saturday in July and August. The officer's square also hosts free evening concerts on Tuesday and Thursday during the summer months.

A visit to the museum reveals unexpected treasures. It has an interesting upstairs display on the city's role in the World Wars (complete with realistic World War I trench), and displays of uniforms dating from the British military's presence from 1785 until 1869. Displays of artifacts from the early Loyalist pioneer days in the area round out the regimental ornamentation and war memorabilia.

trivia

"Only in Canada, you say?" is the typical television ad for Red Rose Tea. It is in fact a very typical Canadian tea, and the flagship product of T. H. Estabrooks Company of Saint John. By 1900, Red Rose Tea—a blending of teas from at least three different plantations—had won adherents from all over Canada and abroad, and it sold in excess of two million pounds annually.

On the other side of the upstairs, the rooms have been restored to the era of Confederation. It was the residence briefly of Julianna and Rex (Alexander) Ewing. He was the last British officer in charge of this garrison, from 1867 until 1869. His wife, Julianna, wrote dozens of now-classic children's novels, admired by many writers of that era including Tennyson, Ruskin, and Jean Ingelow. Her hugely successful books (selling in the hundreds of thousands) strongly influenced later children's writers such as Frances Hodgson Burnett, Rudyard Kipling, and particularly E. Nesbit. When you visit their living quarters at the museum, it is as if she never left: Clothes are left laid out on the bed awaiting their owner's return, small watercolors dot the walls, her writing desk is still at the ready, and some of her correspondence is on view. A book she began while in Fredericton became the enduring children's classic entitled *Brownies and Other Stories*. This provided the characters who inspired Lord Baden Powell in the naming of the junior wing of Girl Guides.

Downstairs, at the back of the museum, is enshrined the infamous taxidermied frog, which was reputed to be the largest in the world. Several postings on the wall outline the controversial frog and questions surrounding its authenticity. Reportedly, this already-huge frog jumped into the life and heart of his owner, Fred Coleman, in 1885. The frog purportedly remained Coleman's pet for eight years until his untimely death due to misadventure. During this time, Coleman, who was a hotelkeeper and, I suspect, a character of the P. T. Barnum variety of huckster and promoter, must have recognized the crowd-pleasing potential of his supposedly beloved pet, who he claimed subsisted on a diet of whisky, honey, and june bugs. Pictures on the wall attest to the alleged loving relationship between man and amphibian, with all the tenderness of a carnival sideshow act. Whether anyone ever saw the frog in action is impossible to establish, and even the old photographs are no help in determining if the alleged giant frog was alive at the time that he was purportedly exchanging loving glances with his master. Nevertheless, a giant frog sits here for your close scrutiny, and I leave it for you to decide if Coleman was Dr. Doolittle or a "Flim-Flam Man" of the highest order. In summer, the museum is open daily from 10:00 A.M. to 5:00 P.M.; in the spring and fall they open Tuesday to Saturday from 1:00 to 4:00 P.M. A small admission is charged.

Just beyond the parade ground is a lighthouse that's now a gift shop down on St. Anne Point. It has a large wooden deck where people can relax and enjoy the river views. In front of this is a charming riverfront walkway, ***Waterloo Row.*** On warm summer nights people stroll along the river while the odd houseboat and its occupants look on from offshore. A number of speedboats tie up here, giving access to the downtown for people up- and downriver.

Proceeding in the same direction, away from city hall, you will eventually come to a must-see attraction: the ***Beaverbrook Art Gallery,*** which has a huge painting by Salvador Dalí and several of his smaller works. The gallery has quite an extensive collection of art, including a number of paintings by Cornelius Krieghoff, J. M. Turner, John Constable, and Thomas Gainsborough. There are some works by the Group of Seven, Canada's most famous group of artists.

You will also find a number of Graham Sutherland studies of Winston Churchill. Commissioned by the British House of Lords and House of Commons, Sutherland's definitive portrait was presented to Churchill as an eightieth birthday gift. Both Sir Winston Churchill and Lady Churchill hated the portrait. After its presentation, it was never allowed to be seen again. Within a year Lady Churchill reportedly destroyed it. The gallery is at 703 Queen Street. Call (506) 458–8545 or (506) 458–0970. The gallery is open daily June 1 to September 30 from 9:00 A.M. to 6:00 P.M. Monday to Friday, 10:00 A.M. to 5:00 P.M. Saturday, and noon to 5:00 P.M. on Sunday. A small admission is charged.

trivia

The father of nature photography was George T. Taylor of Fredericton, who began work in 1856, thirteen years after Canada's first photo studio was established. Many of his photographs show remote corners of New Brunswick.

The art gallery is named for William Maxwell Aitken, who became Lord Beaverbrook. He was born in Ontario but grew up in Newcastle (now Miramichi). He served in Britain as the minister of aircraft production during World War II, but he is chiefly known as a press baron and famous for the empire he created from the *Daily Express* newspaper. The name Beaverbrook is forever connected to the Fleet Street newspapers in England.

One other building you must get a look at before leaving Queen Street is the **Legislative Assembly Building,** the seat of the provincial government, which is across the street from the gallery. This particular Colonial sandstone building dates from 1882, when it was constructed to replace an earlier edifice destroyed by fire. The whole structure, including its fittings and furnishings, cost $120,000 in the currency of the 1880s. (At that time, a typical annual salary was $300.) It is constructed in the Second Empire style, with a mansard roof and corner towers.

There is no mistaking just which empire mattered when this was built. Perched like some daring stuntman in the exact center of the facade is a statue of Britannia with her trident. Other Colonial reminders are inside: Portraits of King George III and Queen Charlotte flank the throne in the chamber. (The province was named after George III—when New Brunswick was separated from Nova Scotia in 1784, it was named for his family's ancestral seat, Brunswick in Germany.) Admission is free.

In this area of New Brunswick, the British Loyalists almost completely supplanted the Acadian settlers, and there is no stronger evidence of this than the city's old architecture.

If you're looking for a nice place to eat in downtown Fredericton, there are two possibilities along Queen Street, a stroll much favored by visitors. Try **The Regency Rose Cafe** at 608/610 Queen Street for excellent seafood crepes, as well as salads and soups. Or, visit the **M&T Deli** at 602 Queen Street for deli sandwiches and bagels. This friendly spot will even supply the picnic basket and blanket if you want to take your lunch to the park across the street.

Two blocks farther away from the water and a block east is ***Christ Church Cathedral,*** on Church Street. To get there on foot, follow Queen Street as it rounds the point for another block or so past the legislature building.

The outside masonry is in mint condition, so the cathedral sparkles like new. This is an impressive Gothic church, a copy of St. Mary's at Snettisham, England. The cornerstone was laid in 1845, with construction completed in eight years. This was the first entirely new cathedral foundation on British soil since the time of the Norman Conquest in 1066.

In July and August, you may join a free guided tour of the cathedral Monday to Friday from 9:00 A.M. to 6:00 P.M., Saturday from 10:00 A.M. to 5:00 P.M.; Sunday visits are limited to the afternoon, from 1:00 to 5:00 P.M. For details call (506) 450–8500.

A huge shot of adrenalin rocks the city of Fredericton in late summer when the ***Harvest Jazz and Blues Festival*** kicks off, just a week after the two local universities resume classes. This timing enables organizers to call on eight hundred eager volunteers who staff the event, which bills itself as the largest of its kind in Atlantic Canada. Now well into its second decade, it boasts a strong emphasis on the Acadian-Cajun connection and has attracted Grammy winners and East Coast Music Award winners among their 350 musicians and performers. Artists are drawn from as far away as Texas, Louisiana, Mississippi, and Virginia, and there are also renowned New Brunswick and other Canadian performers. Perhaps the most well-known of this region's performers is Theresa Malenfant, who has a huge following in Europe, as well as in Canada. The festival unfolds in a series of event tents erected at community spaces along the city's riverside, as well as other venues downtown. As well, many of the festival performers go on to gigs in the city's clubs and restaurants, so to avoid missing a favorite performer, it's worth following the schedule closely and keeping up with other events around town by reading the local paper, the *Daily Gleaner.*

My experience of Fredericton has been that quite often all the stars align perfectly in September, such that tropical air masses push up the Atlantic coastline, giving perfect festival weather. Imagine this: a soothing breeze blowing across you from the riverside, daytime temperatures ranging from about 22°C to 26°C (that's about 72°F to 79°F) but cooling off enough at night for comfortable sleep, and the charming downtown core pulsating with life in the most upbeat mood imaginable. Shows start early in the afternoons in the tents and other venues such as theaters, bars, clubs, and market squares, with some performances free. Ticketed events cost from $10 to $25, and "Afterburner" shows go on until the wee hours. (A steady flow of cabs will ensure that you won't have to walk too far to retire from a long day's partying.)

As well, many up-and-coming performers pull into town to play minor gigs outside of the festival line-up, to boost their exposure and their chances of landing a festival gig further down the road. The downtown core is dotted with eateries and clubs, thanks to the town's high percentage of university students. And since it's the provincial capital, there is a good mix for a variety of tastes and budgets.

The festival runs for the better part of a week in mid-September, just as the leaves are starting to turn. It makes for a perfect Indian summer break and if you are looking for a terrific way to bring summer to a close, I give this festival my highest recommendation. Tickets are sold for individual shows, while day passes and festival passes are also available. You can check out the festival line-up, and even purchase tickets, online at www.harvestjazzand blues.com. Or call (506) 454–2583 for details. If you are planning to make a special trip to take in all or part of the festival, I recommend that you go online and buy your tickets in advance to ensure you don't miss out.

On the spur of the moment, I dropped into *Racines Restaurant* for a bite to eat. Located at 536 Queen Street, deep in the heart of the festival activity, it tempted me with a sign promising a daily special of profiteroles with lobster in lemon butter. (Seafood is their avowed specialty.) It was reasonably priced, made a great presentation on the plate, and tasted delicious. To reserve a table, call (506) 474–1915.

A pleasant stand of virgin forest can be found at *Odell Park*, just outside the downtown core. Take Smythe Road headed away from the water and turn left just after Dundonald Street. You will then be at one end of the park, wedged between it and the Fredericton Exhibition Grounds. The park is quite extensive (388 acres, or 175 hectares), so plan to spend at least a full morning or afternoon roaming around here. The park also contains a picnic area and a children's zoo.

There are beaches in the vicinity, including one at Killarney Lake, 5 miles (8 km) from Fredericton on the Killarney Road. Fairly close by, a covered bridge spans the Keswick River, at Stone Ridge. It is roughly 4.5 miles (7.2 km) off Route 104 on the Morehouse Road, going north from Fredericton.

If you are staying in Fredericton overnight, consider checking in at the *Carriage House Inn,* which is located on University Avenue, 2 blocks from the Beaverbrook Art Gallery and the legislative building. The former home of a mayor and lumber baron, the cozy inn is a lovely mahogany-accented Victorian. Rates are moderate. Breakfast is included, and laundry facilities or services are available on-site. Pets are welcome, and the inn has nonsmoking rooms. (You can still light up on the lovely porch.) For reservations call (800) 267–6068 or (506) 452–9924.

A twenty-minute drive outside Fredericton is the large hydroelectric **Mactaquac Dam,** the building of which flooded a sizable chunk of woodland in 1968. From the town, get on the TCH Route 2 headed west, and turn off onto Provincial Highway 105 at the Mactaquac turnoff.

There is a beautiful provincial park here with a good golf course and a warm beach along the edge of the lake created by the dam. The cost per vehicle entering the park is only $3.50 for the day. As you dip your toes into the lake, consider this: The entire area was once a forest, now submerged under the water. The buildings that used to be where the lake is now were moved to an area twenty minutes away: They became **Kings Landing Historical Settlement.**

To get there from Mactaquac, return to Highway 105 and drive for a minute or two until you reach the turnoff for TCH Route 2. Head west in the direction of MacAdam. Fifteen minutes later a series of signs will direct you to Kings Landing.

The settlement is authentic right down to the cow pies in the field. More than one hundred costumed residents and seventy authentically restored buildings re-create a United Empire Loyalist settlement dating back to the first century following the American War of Independence.

These living-history lessons are always lots of fun, but Kings Landing is also quite historically accurate. The assistant curator told me that when the houses were moved to their new locations, they were even oriented in exactly the same way as they were on their previous site. If a house was built on a sloping hill with a kitchen in the basement, with one side of the lower floor exposed, that was exactly how it was set up on its new location.

Visitors leave their cars at the reception-center building and then walk along a dirt road to the old-time settlement, so no sign of the modern world is evident. A horse-drawn cart helps with the commute to the village; you'll see youngsters in costume hitching a ride on this cart, or weeding the gardens and doing other chores.

trivia

New Brunswick is home to 10 percent of the world's covered bridges.

These young people are participants in a program that allows them to stay at the settlement for five days, living life exactly as it was lived in the early nineteenth century. The program, called Visiting Cousins, accepts kids from nine to fourteen years old and costs $330 a session. Family Kin is for children twelve to fifteen who have visited previously. Seniors can also get into the act in the $575 Elderhostel program. Day programs allow short-term visitors to spend their time learning crafts and doing nineteenth-century chores. If you want to take historic authenticity to its fullest extent, you can have a genuine Victorian wedding, using a rented reproduction wedding dress (or have your own made to order by expert staff). The cost of these weddings runs less than $2,000, but you need to do some advance planning, including finding clergy or a justice of the peace who will do the deed. For details on any of these living-history holidays, contact the staff well in advance.

At the blacksmith shop you can watch a skilled craftsman turning out tools to be used in the settlement's other enterprises—hooks for holding logs at the sawmill, for example.

The cooper I watched making wooden buckets has it down to a science, slowly carving out the perfect curve in each slat so that a group of them will result in a round, airtight bucket. Eight hours of work will give you a bucket worth forty cents, he notes—"A good day's pay."

The settlement includes a sawmill with the largest functioning waterwheel in Canada. I watched a log being maneuvered into position for cutting, a process that took a good half hour.

If you are interested in sampling some of the early settlers' homestyle cooking, drop by the **King's Head Inn** for lunch. (There are also benches outside.) After lunch, hitch a ride on the horse-drawn cart outside the door of the inn back to the reception center.

For more details on the various programs, or to make a reservation at the King's Head Inn, call (506) 363–4999 or fax (506) 363–4989; write to Kings Landing Historical Settlement, Prince William, NB E0H 1S0; or visit www.kings landing.nb.ca. Admission is $14 per adult or $34 for a family.

Just after this settlement is **Lake George Park,** about 7 miles (11 km) off Route 2 west on Route 259, or 8 miles (13 km) north of Harvey on Route 636. There is a lovely beach here.

Whether you find yourself in Prince William, Kings Landing, or Lake George, when you want to resume your travels, return to the TCH via Route 2 and drive northwest to Pokiok. It is about 13 miles (21 km) north of Prince William. From here you can cross the Saint John River (it's quite narrow at this point), turn right at the fork in the road at the end of the crossing, and proceed to Nackawic and then Millville, about 9.5 miles (15 km) farther on.

Turn left onto Route 104, then left onto Route 585. To see the **Nackawic Siding Covered Bridge** that straddles the Nackawic River here, take the exit to Nortondale, just north of the main road. Then return to Route 585 and in about a half hour you will come to **Woodstock,** which is at most a twenty-minute drive from the Canada–U.S. border. Woodstock is a pretty little town for stretching your legs (and for shopping when the currency exchange rate favors it). Communities that straddle the border in this area are at the mercy of changing fiscal policies and monetary fluctuations, so businesspeople on both sides of the border find themselves suffering periodic downturns due to the drop in their neighbor's dollar.

To view yet another covered bridge, turn back onto Route 2 and head south toward Meductic. Just before Meductic you will see a sign for Benton. Turn right here and continue until you reach the Benton Village Road. Here, the covered *Benton Bridge* crosses the Eel River, which also serves as the county line for a while along its meandering path.

Now return to Route 2 and head north past Woodstock to *Hartland.* As if you haven't already seen enough of covered bridges, now you come to the granddaddy of them all, the *world's longest covered bridge,* at 1,282 feet (391 m) in length. Imagine the possibilities for clandestine romantic interludes presented by a kissing bridge that took a horse a good quarter hour to traverse. The bridge remains a popular site to this day, long after automotive breakdowns and drive-in movies replaced it as a lovers' hot spot. To the east of Hartland you will come to the Becaguimec River System and a collection of yet more picturesque covered bridges.

Places to Stay in New Brunswick's Loyalist South

FREDERICTON

Carriage House Inn
University Avenue
(800) 267–6068
(506) 452–9924
fax (506) 458–0799
Victorian charmer.
Moderate.

GRAND MANAN

Compass Rose
North Head
(506) 662–8570
fax (506) 662–8570
Two charming seaside houses.
Standard to moderate.

Manan Island Inn
Ocean Side North Head
(506) 662–8624
Walking distance to whale-watching.
Moderate.

Shorecrest Lodge
North Head
(506) 662–3216
Bird-watcher's paradise.
Moderate.

SAINT JOHN

Chipman Hill Suites
71 Sydney Street
(506) 693–1171
Also other locations in town.
Moderate.

Dufferin Inn
357 Dufferin Row
(506) 635–5968
fax (506) 674–2396
For gourmets and antiques lovers.
Moderate.

ST. ANDREWS BY-THE-SEA

The Algonquin
184 Adolphus Street
(506) 529–8823
(800) 441–1414
fax (506) 529–4194
Set in an Old World–style castle.
Deluxe.

Rossmount Inn
Highway 127
(506) 529–3351
fax (506) 529–1920
Steeped in Old World atmosphere, with lots of mahogany.
Moderate.

Places to Eat in New Brunswick's Loyalist South

FREDERICTON

M&T Deli
602 Queen Street
(506) 458–9068
Good sandwiches.

Racines Restaurant
536 Queen Street
(506) 474–1915
Delicious continental cuisine.

The Regency Rose Cafe
608/10 Queen Street
(506) 455–2233
Great seafood crepes, excellent salads.

GRAND MANAN

Compass Rose
North Head
(506) 662–8570
fax (506) 662–8570
Great seafood, lobster.

PRINCE WILLIAM

King's Head Inn
TCH Route 2, exit 253
Kings Landing Historical
Settlement
(506) 363–4999
Set in re-creation village.

SAINT JOHN

Dufferin Inn
357 Dufferin Row
(506) 635–5968
fax (506) 674–2396
Authentic gourmet
experience.

**Grannan's Seafood
Restaurant and Oyster Bar**
1 Market Square
(506) 648–2323
Located on the Saint John
waterfront; excellent steak.

Il Fornello Restaurant
33 Canterbury Street
(506) 658–6027
Generous portions of
delicious Italian in romantic
atmosphere.

ST. ANDREWS BY-THE-SEA

Rossmount Inn
Highway 127
(506) 529–3351
fax (506) 529–1920
Victorian touches in
charming dining room.

ST. GEORGE

**Granite Town Hotel and
Country Inn**
79 Main Street
(506) 755–6415
Great fresh salmon.

Acadian New Brunswick

The Upper Saint John River

As you drive inland along the Saint John River Valley, you will gradually enter the land that has been home to the Acadians for more than 300 years, despite massive population upheavals. One historian noted that because of the great distance from the French capital at Port Royal, the Acadian French, who lived in these parts long before the British takeover in 1755, had no real force of law, and yet they managed to maintain societal order purely through their sense of community.

Uprooted in 1755 from their homes, they were determined to return to this independent way of life, so much so that many Acadians deposited along the eastern seaboard spent years finding their way back to Acadia, only to discover that their lands had been taken over by the English. They then settled informally along the coast and in the northern interior of New Brunswick.

Without external structure or governmental endorsement, they managed to keep their language, traditions, and culture intact. They remained loyal to their identity even though the boundaries of Acadia could never be shown on a map.

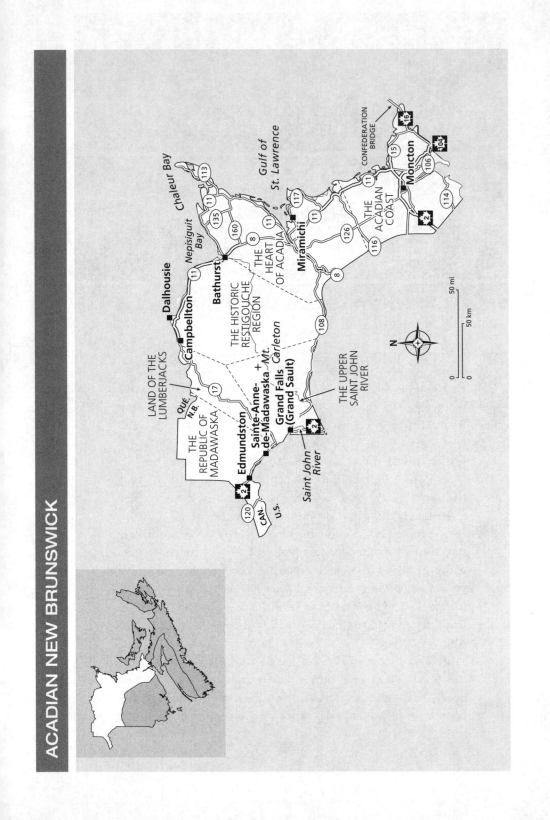

ACADIAN NEW BRUNSWICK

The first major stop along Route 2 in Acadian New Brunswick is *Grand Falls,* noted for a set of gorges and a series of falls that, step by step, descend a total of about 1 mile (1.6 km). If the weather has been dry, Grand Falls is not quite as spectacular as in rainy seasons. But periodically the people who run the electrical generating station situated at the falls let a backlog of water go, so be sure to check when the gates are due to be released if you want to see the falls in their full glory. A pontoon boat offers an interesting alternative for viewing the falls close up. Trips depart from the Falls and Gorge campground, which also offers a combination

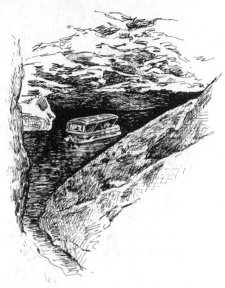

Grand Falls Gorge

camping/boat rate. You get one night at a campsite and the boat tour for a fee of $45 per couple or $50 per family. To book ahead (which is highly recommended), call (877) 475–7769. The campgrounds are open from mid-June to mid-September.

The massive rock face through which the water flows is, in itself, quite something to see. At night it is illuminated with colored lights, making for a surreal spectacle.

An interpretive center at the power station has a scale model where tour guides explain exactly how the generator functions. Called the *Malabeam Reception Centre,* it is named for a young Malecite Indian maiden. According

TRUDY'S FAVORITES

Waterfall at Grand Falls

New Brunswick Botanical Garden,
Saint-Jacques

Forestry Museum,
Kedgwick

Acadian Historical Village,
Rivière du Nord

Miscou Lighthouse,
Miscou Island

Cap-Pelé Beach,
Shediac

Hopewell Cape

Sackville Waterfowl Park,
Sackville

to Indian legend, the young girl was captured by Mohawks. Forced to head an expedition of Mohawks who intended to attack her village, the girl instead led all of them to their doom over the gorges of Grand Falls. The center, off Front Street, which doubles as a tourist office and reception, houses an interpretive display of the dam. Teamed with this, and a 1.2-mile (2-km) pathway away, is the Centennial Park on Chapel Street. Along with the usual amenities of a municipal park (free admission), you will have the opportunity to enter *La Rochelle Visitor Centre,* which leads to a series of 253 steps down the side of the falls. A small admission is charged. The most scenic part of the trail lies at the bottom of a deep 0.9-mile (1.5-km) gorge carved out by the falls. Bug repellent is a good idea, and footing can be slippery in damp weather.

trivia

In 1982 Grand Falls was officially declared bilingual and given a name in both English and French. Its French name is Grand Sault.

The *Baie de Chaleur*—Chaleur Bay— means "Bay of Warmth" in English.

The three-pointed hats worn by the Loyalists were called "tricornes."

This is a region of fertile farmland. The biggest crop here is the potato, which New Brunswick produces in greater abundance than any other province in Canada. Grand Falls holds an annual potato festival at the beginning of July and crowns a Miss Potato to preside over the festivities.

If you think that a small center like Grand Falls doesn't have nightlife, then think again. Indeed, the town is noted for it in the region. The main drag in town is particularly wide, since it was used at one time for military parades. Once those spectacles ended, the wide street was turned into a divided boulevard with a park running down the middle, complete with gazebo and a few old pieces of military hardware. On hot summer nights all Grand Falls seems to show up, walking or driving down this street. In winter, however, it's cold in Grand Falls, and there are no real nightlife hot spots to warm lingering travelers.

If you are staying in the neighborhood for any length of time and are feeling a bit restless, drive from Route 2 to Route 108 and then on to *New Denmark.* (Note, however, that you must follow the signs for Plaster Rock, since New Denmark does not figure prominently on the maps.) This is a trek of 10 miles (16 km) on secondary roads, but the scenery, provided by the lush potato farmlands and the distant hills, is well worth the time and effort.

This is the site of Canada's first Danish community. The area was settled by Danes in 1872. They had been assured that it was good farmland, but they discovered after they arrived that it was woodland that had to be cleared by manual labor. The small *New Denmark Memorial Museum* recounts their story and displays a collection of century-old dolls and porcelain from Copenhagen. Next door you will find *Immigrant House,* which depicts the life of the early settlers. For information call (506) 553–6724. Admission is free, and donations are welcome. The museum is open Monday to Saturday from 9:00 A.M. until 5:00 P.M. and from 2:00 until 5:00 P.M. Sunday.

The Republic of Madawaska

About 34 miles (57 km) northwest of Grand Falls on Route 2 is *Edmundston,* the commercial hub for this neck of the woods. Across the Upper Saint John River is Madawaska, Maine. The residents of these communities cross the border the way other people cross the street. The flow of workers in lumbering and related industries has caused the area to develop a distinctive character of its own, regardless of which side of the border its occupants live on. This is the *Republique de Madawaska,* named for the river that flows from across the Quebec border and into the Upper Saint John River.

Here the Upper Saint John serves as a border between Canada and the United States. Not many people today realize that during the nineteenth century, there was considerable wrangling about where the border actually fell. When it came to this particular area, the line was moved around so much that in 1827, a man by the name of John Baker erected a flag in protest and declared the land the American Republic of Madawaska.

The name has stuck, and the memory of John Baker lives on in the form of Baker Brook and Lac Baker, wedged in the tiny strip of land between Maine and Quebec. As for John Baker, he was sent to jail for treason. Today you can visit a park at *Lac Baker,* which has picnic facilities, a nice beach, and lots of water sports.

This area has become a major gateway to New Brunswick from Quebec, Maine, and upstate New York. It is lush agricultural land that can get quite hot in summer. Combine these—a flow of visitors from all over the region and excellent growing conditions—and you have the ideal location for a botanical garden.

In *Saint-Jacques,* just off TCH Route 2 and only 6 miles (10 km) south of the Quebec border (and ten minutes' drive north of Edmundston) is the *New Brunswick Botanical Garden,* opened in 1993. Over a meticulously groomed seventeen-acre (seven-hectare) site is a garden planned by the expert consultants to the Montreal Botanical Garden, including noted landscape architect Michel Marceau.

TOP ANNUAL EVENTS

Times for these events vary, unless specified. For full details, contact the **New Brunswick Department of Tourism** at (800) 561–0123.

Shediac Canada Day Celebrations, Shediac (July 1)

Irish Festival on the Miramichi, Miramichi (mid-July)

Festival Western de Saint-Quentin, Saint-Quentin (mid-July)

Sand Sculpture Competition, Parlee Beach, Shediac (mid-July)

Lamèque International Festival of Baroque Music, Lamèque (late July)

Miramichi Folksong Festival, Miramichi (early August)

The site now consists of eight separate gardens and two arboretums, or tree gardens. Hidden under the shrubbery are small outdoor speakers, which broadcast classical music deemed appropriate for each specific garden. For example, Mozart sonatas for piano complement the rose garden; perennials invite up-tempo works by Handel, Bach, and Vivaldi; and the lake and gazebo areas have more tranquil compositions by the same musical greats.

There are more than 30,000 annuals and 850 rosebushes of more than fifty varieties. A total of 80,000 plants are divided into the Rose Garden, the Garden of Annuals, the Garden of Perennials, the Garden of Economic Plants, the Alpine Garden, the Shade Garden, the Garden of Rhododendrons, and the Flowery Brook. Trees are arranged into the Arboretum of Coniferous Trees and Deciduous Shrubs and the Arboretum of Deciduous Trees and Coniferous Shrubs. Nature has been coaxed into submission here: Boulders were rearranged and water pumped in to create a miniature waterfall in the style of Grand Falls, complete with gorges. There are also several ponds.

Avid gardeners take note: Although the greenhouses are closed to the public, they'll be opened to gardeners who make the request to look around. A snack bar and gift shop are on-site. A modest admission is charged. Open year-round. For information call (506) 737–5383.

The parking lot for the botanical garden is directly behind the *Antique Automobile Museum.* Along with other unusual cars, here you can get a look at the Bricklin, a failed automobile design that enjoyed a brief heyday in the 1970s when New Brunswick's premier, Richard Hatfield, threw his support behind a would-be entrepreneur who briefly established his factory in the province. Open year-round. Admission is $3.75 for adults and $3.00 for children ages six to eighteen. For details call (506) 735–2637.

This area is part of a provincial park called ***Les Jardins de La Republique,*** which has the usual recreational and camping facilities and a supervised heated pool. Nearby is ***Petit-Témis Interprovincial Park,*** which you can access from the botanical garden. This linear park is a cycle path 80 miles (130 km) long that takes bicyclists into Quebec, along the shores of Lake Temiscouata and the bank of the Madawaska River. The trail reaches the town of Cabano and then continues on to Rivière du Loup.

If you've driven as far north as Saint-Jacques, you're going to have to return to the outskirts of Edmundston via Route 2 and continue on this same stretch of highway to Saint-Léonard. Then you can get onto Trunk 17 and head to Kedgwick. (From Saint-Jacques to the Saint-Léonard exit is 32 miles [56 km]—not that much of a detour to enjoy the beautiful botanical garden and cycle path.)

Land of the Lumberjacks

Almost as soon as you leave Saint-Léonard, you'll be surrounded by dense forest, the trees so much alike that they appear to have been cloned from the same original seedling. In fact, these trees were planted at the same time after the area had been intensively logged.

The first large community after Saint-Léonard is ***Saint-Quentin.*** When a railway was built between Saint-Léonard and Campbellton, this little community sprang up. It was originally named Five Fingers, after a brook of the same name. After a logging company operating there caused the community to swell in size, it became Anderson Siding, named for the head of the Canadian National Railroad. (The "Siding" part of the name was common to any area where sawmills operated.) In 1919 the town was renamed again, this time to commemorate the Canadian victory in Saint-Quentin, France, during World War I.

The town's location in the middle of densely wooded New Brunswick seems incongruous with its chief claim to fame: Saint-Quentin is home to the biggest annual Western festival in eastern Canada. Apparently, you can't get more country-and-western than Saint-Quentin; even the streetlights are festooned with cowboy boots as the town puts its best foot forward for its shindig, culminating in a weekend-long rodeo including cowboys from the United States, western Canada, Quebec, and Ontario. Held the second week in July, it also features concerts, a powwow, and a parade. Free camping is available for serious cowboys, but reserve early. To get an idea of the east-turned-west, you can check out their Web site at www.festivalwesternnb.com. Take your French–English phrase book with you.

Mount Carleton Mini-Excursion

I'm recommending this trip only to outdoor types who also have a car with a powerful engine, fully functioning radiator, and reliable brakes. This is a lengthy, arduous drive through wilderness, with no handy service stations in sight. If your radiator overheats, it's a long, lonely walk back. Just after Saint-Quentin, fill your gas tank and check your oil, and then turn onto Highway 180 and drive 27 miles (43 km) to the entrance of **Mount Carleton Provincial Park.**

Mount Carleton Provincial Park is the province's largest and wildest park, encompassing 43,000 acres (17,427 hectares) and Mount Carleton, the highest mountain in the Maritimes. The park includes stands of spruce, fir, and yellow birch; wild blueberries; mountain cranberries; and lots of wildlife.

Stop at the entrance to get extensive maps and information about camping and hiking opportunities along the 36 miles (60 km) of trails. Most of the hikes take between two and four hours and form loops that culminate in mountain peaks. The Mount Bailey Trail is the easiest of the lot, the Mount Carleton Trail takes you to the top of the highest peak and includes access to a backcountry camp, and Sagamook Trail is the most scenic.

Note: While the trails provide gradual ascent, there are points where you will be above the tree line and you'll need a warm windbreaker. Pack a whistle (in case you get lost), high-energy snacks, matches, a first-aid kit, a compass, and plenty of water. It is also a good idea to pack a couple of Sterno canisters to quickly heat up some food.

You will see spectacular scenery: sweeping vistas of mountain peaks, beaver ponds, and beautiful Nictau Lake. The trailhead of the most scenic trail, the Sagamook, is conveniently located near **Mount Carleton Lodge,** where you can refresh yourself and soothe your feet. If you decide to stay the night, the lodge has cabins and canoes to rent. Prices are standard. To reserve a cabin call (506) 235–6040.

There are a number of campsites as well, some more rustic than others. Phone (506) 235–0793 for details. There are no reservations for campsites; it's a first-come, first-served basis. Serviced sites are $11.00 weekdays to $14.00 on the weekend. Wilderness sites are only $9.00, but they have no showers or flush toilets. Caution: The park's wildlife includes bears, who will be attracted to the scent of any food left carelessly lying around. If you don't want a sleepless night, keep all foodstuffs locked in your cooler, inside your vehicle.

When you've finished visiting Mount Carleton, you can backtrack to Saint-Quentin via Highway 180 and then rejoin Trunk 17E, turning in the direction of Campbellton.

An interesting outdoor excursion possibility is located near Saint-Quentin. Leave Trunk 17 at the exit for Kedgwick River and take the smaller Collector Highway 265. It is here that you will find the rustic cabins of the **Centre Echo-**

Restigouche. The facilities are of excellent quality, with some of the cabins large enough to accommodate up to eight people. For details on ecoadventure packages that the facility offers, or for reservations, call (506) 284–2022. Rates are moderate.

If you don't detour to the Kedgwick River, you'll continue along Trunk 17 to *Kedgwick.* After you pass through what appears to be almost all of this community, you will see a sign marked MUSÉE FORESTIER. This is the *Forestry Museum,* formerly known as the Heritage Lumbercamp. It provides a detailed look into the lives of lumberjacks before the introduction of modern tree-harvesting methods.

The complex includes a number of log cabins built under the direction of old-time loggers. The tour of the complex begins with a short film in which lumberjacks and storytellers recount their experiences in the woods from the nineteenth century to the 1960s. You will quickly see that the life of a lumberjack was extraordinarily hard. Your understanding of the logging industry will be enhanced by the old tools and other artifacts that have been donated to the complex by people who worked in the industry.

Before you leave the camp, be sure to look at the original 1937 snowmobile, the manufacture of which launched industrial giant Bombardier. It's a fascinating machine, fully enclosed and constructed of wood. And glance at the wall of the museum's main reception building. A forty-pound (nineteen-kg) salmon is mounted here, a fitting example of why the area is a favorite among anglers and outdoorsmen. A small admission is charged. For information, call (506) 284–3138.

To resume your drive, continue east on Trunk 17.

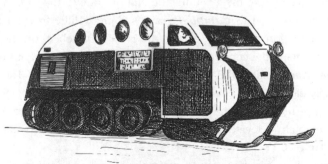

1937 Snowmobile at Kedgwick Forestry Museum

Life of a Lumberjack

The life of a lumberjack, or logger, was often complicated by the rules of the forestry companies. For example, they issued the men cleated boots for working in the woods. "If a logger decided to quit," said one old-timer, "then he had to walk 30 miles [48 km] through the woods without his work boots."

Beds were made of soft tree branches, collected fresh every Sunday. The loggers were sometimes crammed so tightly into the bunkhouse that they had to sleep two in a bed. To make sure there were no complaints about the food, the men were obliged to remain silent at the table.

Work was especially hazardous at the time of the log drives downriver. To loosen up the logs, they sometimes blasted them with dynamite. Drivers also rode on top of the logs, poking at trapped ones with sticks. Every year, loggers died while driving logs downriver. Some drowned and some were too close when the dynamite went off.

A particularly tough job was held by the person who manned the lookout towers, deep in the woods. In the area of Kedgwick, there were three lookouts who would immediately notify others of any sign of fire. Each lookout tower was manned by a single person, who stayed there alone twelve months of the year.

If you are interested in knowing more about the old-time logging camps, I suggest you see the award-winning feature film *Mon Oncle Antoine,* made by a noted Quebec cinematographer.

The Historic Restigouche Region

Just before you reach Campbellton, you will see a turnoff for Matapédia, Quebec. After this point be on the lookout for Atholville and one of the province's most popular ski slopes: *Sugarloaf.* Even if you are here in the summer, this slope is noteworthy: You can take the chairlift to the top and then slide down on a luge course made of cement. The view from the top of Sugarloaf is quite spectacular, well worth the $3.50 for the chairlift ride to the top.

Now continue on to *Campbellton.* It's a pretty little town, a gateway to Quebec. Just before the bridge across the river to Quebec, on the right-hand side, is a fountain, the centerpiece of which is a statue of a giant salmon, *Restigouche Sam,* promoted as "the largest salmon in the world." The fountain is surprisingly elegant, considering that it is dominated by a 28-foot (8.5-m) metal fish that appears to be in the throes of being reeled in by a giant angler.

The fountain is located on Salmon Street. You can guess what the town's claim to fame is.

Campbellton has managed to maintain its rail connection, though many other communities in the region have lost theirs. The passenger service passes through six times a week, with its next stop Matapédia in Quebec. Railway lore abounds about the train from Halifax to Montreal and the many times that it literally was "frozen in its tracks." (You knew that expression had to come from somewhere!)

Just down from the giant salmon fountain at 1 Ritchie Street is a lighthouse that has been turned into a youth hostel run by Hostelling International called **Campbellton Youth Hostel.** The lighthouse is small and not that interesting, but the hostel offers a rare opportunity to spend the night in a lighthouse. The doors are closed every day from noon until 4:00 P.M. For reservations call (506) 759–7044 or e-mail hihostels@campbellton.org.

Restigouche Sam

Just to the left of the tourist information center and to the right of the giant salmon fountain as you face the river is Andrew Street. The **Galerie Restigouche,** easily found by looking for the rather large statues at the front, houses a collection of regional, national, and international exhibitions year-round. To get to the gallery, drive 8 blocks up Andrew Street from the harbor. The gallery is on your right. For information call (506) 753–5750.

Campbellton was once the site of a native village. Over the centuries the Restigouche natives were gradually pushed farther north. Today the Restigouche Nations are on the other side of the water, in Quebec.

Few people realize it, but the final battle in which the English gained control of Canada from the French was fought just off these shores in 1760.

thelegendof sugarloaf

Indian legend has it that Sugarloaf was once a giant beaver, which was turned into the mountain by the Mi'Kmaq god Glooscap. The beaver had angered the god by building a dam that prevented the salmon from swimming upriver to spawn. In anger, Glooscap destroyed the dam and turned the beaver into a ski hill. While he was at it, he cut the other beavers down to size, turning them into the small creatures they are today, as opposed to the mythic giants they once were.

After the Battle of the Plains of Abraham in 1759, when Quebec City fell, the navies of the two countries met just outside Campbellton (then Restigouche) at a point about 3 miles (5 km) east along Route 132, on the Quebec side of the border. It is now a national historic site designated by a humble marker that belies its significance. As you drive there you pass through native lands at Pointe-à-la-Croix. These are the Restigouche Mi'Kmaq who used to live on the New Brunswick side of the bay.

fiddleheadfans

Since the late 1700s, fiddleheads have been a popular source of food for New Brunswick's Mi'K-maq and Maliseet natives. About forty-seven tons of the elegantly curled edible wild ferns are picked and commercially processed here each year for sale in local and international markets. Nutritionally similar to asparagus, fiddleheads are loaded with vitamins A and C, niacin, and riboflavin, and are high in potassium and low in sodium, making them ideal for low-salt diets.

It is a short drive from Campbellton to *Dalhousie.* Follow either TCH Route 11, which bypasses Dalhousie, or Highway 134, which takes a more meandering route into Dalhousie and then back out to River Charlo, where it connects to Route 11 again. From this point they become one road, following the coast along *Chaleur Bay.*

If you want to putter around the area of Dalhousie, try the **Chaleur Phantom,** which offers both nature cruises and scenic cruises, depending on the time of day. The 50-foot (13.2-m) boat is also available for private charters. It operates from late May to the first week in October.

The morning nature cruises offer close-up looks at seals, eagles' nests, the occasional whale, and a multitude of bird life, including black cormorants. The afternoon cruise involves sight-seeing, such as trips to the Bon Ami Rocks and possibly some points on the Quebec side, and Heron Island, which is now the home of thousands of birds (and was at one time the home of nineteen human families).

The cruise itineraries vary, so it's best to ask if your particular trip will take you to the sites you want to see. Tickets are $17 for adults. Tickets for children are half price. For details or to reserve a trip, call (506) 684–4722.

Just outside Dalhousie is a beach with the longest natural sandbar in North America. Blue herons fish inside it. Locals call it the *Eel River Sandbar* or Eel River Beach, but it's marked on the provincial highway map as Charlo, which apparently has another beach that runs into the sandbar. To reach it you must get on Highway 380. This minor road connects to Highway 134 in a rather confusing way, so be sure you are headed east. Incidentally, as you drive from Dalhousie to Eel River Sandbar via Highway 134, you will be passing through a native community.

The day I dropped in to check out the Eel River Sandbar, the beach was the meeting place of 3,500 Boy Scouts from all over the region. (Apparently there are a lot of Scout camps in the vicinity.) A madhouse, you say? Near the food concession, perhaps, but the beach is sufficiently long that at the other end there was no sign of a crowd.

The beach is a bit on the pebbly side, so beach sandals will come in handy. Several other pleasant beaches are along this coast. Most of them are not visible from the road, however, so you need to be armed with a map. Unlike Nova Scotia, where roads follow the coast and lighthouses and beaches are self-evident, roads in New Brunswick are almost always a bit of a way from the shore.

One beach that is not so hidden away is at Jacquet River Campground on Highway 134. The beach is accessible through a small provincial park, entrance to which costs $1.00 per vehicle. ***Fenderson Beach*** is behind the campground, down a small hill. The water here is quite shallow and therefore warm enough for even the fussiest swimmers. From this point, on a clear day, you can see across the water to Quebec. The stretch of land up and down the coast from this point appears as unbroken wilderness. This cozy little campground has 31 sites and costs $16 and up for a semi-serviced site.

stuckonthevia railline

During our youth, both my husband and I worked on the VIA Rail service, which ran from Halifax to Montreal. On one of its midwinter runs, the train became stuck between Matapédia and Campbellton for three days, because the track was so buried in deep snow. Once supplies and fuel ran out, passengers were kept warm with blankets and fed takeout that was brought in by snowmobile from nearby Matapédia. The train often came up against other obstacles, such as moose on the tracks.

The next major urban center is ***Bathurst,*** which you can reach by either TCH Route 11 or Highway 134, the more scenic of the two, which also passes several more beaches, but you won't get much of a look at them from the road. Be sure to visit the ***Nicolas Denys Monument*** on Main Street, overlooking Bathurst Harbor.

This Nicolas Denys was quite a busy chap. In the 1650s he established a fur-trading post in the then-virgin territory of Cape Breton (see Cape Breton chapter). When you visit Cape Breton, you'll see a small museum dedicated to and named for Denys along the side of the St. Peter's Canal. In Miscou you'll pick up Denys's traces, and here, somewhere in Bathurst's Gowan Brae Golf and Country Club, he is believed to be buried.

After his exploits in Cape Breton, this native of Tours, France, was made governor of the entire gulf region of New France, from Cape Breton to the Gaspé Region of Quebec. Denys wrote one of the first classic works on the people of Acadia a century before the Expulsion, which uprooted them from their homes in Nova Scotia and left them scattered throughout the eastern seaboard and Louisiana.

Because of the instrumental role he played in bringing over settlers, Denys is credited with giving the region its distinctive Acadian flavor, with its mixed population of fishermen, fur traders, and farmers who were expert in farming the marshlands. (Many of the latter came from an area of France with the same kinds of marshlands, farmed for centuries by their ancestors.) In 1654 Denys and his wife set up housekeeping at Pointe-aux-Pères, at a site that later became the golf course. He died there in 1688.

If you continue along the Acadian Coastal Route, also known as Highway 134, you will come to *Daly Point Reserve,* just on the other side of Bathurst. This consists of 3.75 miles (6 km) of walking trails leading through more than one hundred acres (forty hectares) of salt marsh, forest, and old farmland that is gradually reverting to its wild state. It is a great spot for nature lovers. Thousands of Canada geese stop by here during their fall migration, and the ringlet butterfly, found in only four salt marshes in the world, can be seen here.

There are five trails and two paths, with the latter requiring more stable footwear. Scenery varies from a large gulch, which you cross on a footbridge, to twisting woodland paths, to the tamer boardwalks of the salt marsh trails. Bring plenty of bug repellent.

You won't get out of this region without hearing references to the phantom ship. (Recall that the tour boat in Dalhousie is called the Phantom.) For centuries people have claimed to see a ship on fire, far offshore. Skeptics argue that it is an optical illusion. The rest claim that it's the ghost of a ship lost long ago in battle.

The Heart of Acadia

From the Daly Point Reserve, continue on Trunk 11 until you reach the outskirts of Caraquet. The drive should take about an hour; the road follows the coast quite closely until after Grande-Anse. When you reach a small community called Rivière du Nord, a sign on the right-hand side of the road will indicate the *Acadian Historical Village.*

This is far more than just a historic re-creation of an Acadian village. Many of the fifty buildings are actual restored Acadian homesteads from the 1800s, gathered into one village along with artifacts of bygone days and some carefully constructed replicas. There are also a blacksmith shop dating from 1865, a school from 1869, and a reproduction of a Neguac cobbler's shop, circa 1875, where moccasins were the specialty.

The wonderful thing about this site is that all contact with the modern world has been kept at a minimum so that history is a living thing. Here the costumed guides illustrate life as it was lived by Acadian settlers from 1780 to 1890. A close look at period clothing reveals the skills of bygone days: Buttons made of wood or bone fasten hand-loomed clothes dyed the color of berries. You'll see the home of a Scottish administrator whose powerful position in the commu nity gave him the poshest accommodations. He even had a grandfather clock and other imported furniture. Most of the other villagers lived in rough-hewn houses the size of a modern family's single-car garage, with rugged plank floors and simple furniture made by the occupants.

farming the marshlands

Early Acadian settlers were experts in cultivating marshes. They built dikes and reclaimed land from the sea on their coastal settlements.

Like farmers of the Dutch lowlands, the Acadians kept their feet dry by wearing wooden clogs, called *sabots* in French. The name was once linked in France to a group of insurrectionists, hence the origin of the word *sabotage*.

Acadian marshlands are fertile places, and today Acadian entre-preneurs export their coastal wetland's abundant peat moss to gardeners worldwide.

A boat awaits repair in front of one dwelling, while the lady next door sweeps her steps with a broom made by whittling a young birch trunk. Else-where in the village you can watch as men split cedar to make roof shingles. Throughout the summer, activities follow the pattern traditionally followed in an Acadian village: There are gatherings or working "bees" of various sorts, and occasionally visitors can see a whole milling "frolic" taking place.

Milling frolics, like barn raisings, were the early settlers' way of turning a tedious task into a fun event so that as many participants could be roped into the job as possible. A parade with all the equipment usually started the day. Next, the homespun cloth, often close to 50 yards long, would be soaked in soft lye soap and water in troughs made from hollowed-out tree trunks. Using long wooden pestles, the cloth was then beaten by a half-dozen men until soft-ened. The men would sing songs to maintain the rhythm. Since the cloth was usually made from wool or flax, it was very coarse until it was softened and, essentially, preshrunk in a milling frolic. The payoff for all the hard work was a big feast prepared by the women and a party that lasted well after midnight. Milling frolics were still held in the early part of the twentieth century.

On the Acadian National Holiday, which falls on August 15, the staff re-creates a turning point in the history of the Acadian people: It is 1884. Actors, including one playing Rogersville founder Father Richard, debate the future of Acadia. (Father Richard instigated a number of "National Conventions" between 1881 and 1905 that helped to establish a common voice for the Acadians.) Finally, after much discussion, they agree on the priest's suggestion and choose a flag, an anthem, and a patron saint, strengthening their identity and creating a rallying point for cultural pride. Admission to the village is $15 for adults and $10 for children six to eighteen years of age; children under six enter free; families pay $36. If you want to take historic re-creation seriously, you can now stay at the village in the *Chateau Albert,* modeled after a Caraquet hotel, which was built in 1907 but burned down in 1955. In 2000, the exact replica was built using the original blueprints that survived the fire. Details like wide pine-board halls, exposed wooden beams, and claw-foot tubs add to the authentic feel. The hotel has fifteen spacious guest rooms. But, in keeping with its historic theme, there are no television sets or fax machines. However, they do have Acadian-style musical entertainment during authentic suppers.

Packages are available from the end of June until the last week of August. To make a reservation call (506) 726–2600, or visit www.villagehistorique acadien.com.

Caraquet seems to be a mecca for Quebecois tourists in search of the picturesque. You will find hints of the Quebec urban landscape that seem quite out of place here, including a club with exotic dancers, and Quebec-style restaurants.

Check out the *Crêpes Bretonne* restaurant, in nearby *Paquetville* (the birthplace of noted Acadian folksinger Edith Butler). This village is reached by turning onto Highway 325 directly after the Acadian Historical Village, before Caraquet. Paquetville is near the junction of Highways 135, 325, and 340. To get to Paquetville after leaving the Acadian Village, turn west on Highway 325, then south onto Highway 135 for a short distance, to the main intersection at the center of town. Here you will find New Brunswick's largest church, St.-Augustin, and nearby, Crêpes Bretonne, at 1805 Ruc du Parc (Park Street). The food served is typical of the Brittany-style crepe places in Quebec City: meat or seafood and vegetables, served up in a cream sauce and then rolled in a thin French "pancake."

From Paquetville you can go on to Caraquet, where you may stay for the night. Or you can drive on to the junction with Highway 355, where you must turn left at the intersection and then right at Junction 217 to go in the direction of *Shippagan* via Highway 113.

There is an excellent natural harbor in Shippagan, which on the map looks almost like a collection of islands. In fact, the land is so low-lying that much of

Rappie Pie (*Pâté à la Râpure*)

Why not try rappie pie when visiting Acadian communities or **La Paneterie,** a snack bar at Le Pays de la Sagouine? This soul-satisfying variation of a chicken pot pie is featured on menus in French as pâté à la râpure. In case you want to make it at home, the following is a good all-purpose recipe.

10 pounds potatoes, peeled

1 chicken, 3 to 4 pounds

1 teaspoon dry thyme

½ teaspoon ground, dry bay leaves

½ teaspoon poultry seasoning

2 tablespoons salt

1 tablespoon pepper

1 medium onion, chopped

8 strips of cooked bacon, finely chopped

1. Place the peeled potatoes in a bowl and cover with cold water (so they retain their color) until needed.
2. Rinse the chicken and simmer it in a pot of water, along with all the seasonings.
3. After 1½ to 2 hours, the meat will fall away from the bone. Remove the meat and cut into pieces. Leave the water and the chicken bones to simmer until needed. This will be your chicken stock.
4. Grate the potatoes ten at a time. Then squeeze them in a cloth bag until all moisture and starch are removed, and set aside this liquid. Remove from the bag, and cover the grated potatoes with a wet cloth.
5. Measure the liquid squeezed from the potatoes. This will be the amount of chicken stock required. Discard the liquid.
6. Strain the chicken stock; add water if necessary to reach the amount of stock needed. Place squeezed potatoes into a large pan. Add the stock and stir slowly to remove all lumps. The potatoes will look like jelly.
7. Cover the bottom of a well-greased lasagna-style pan with half the potatoes. Then arrange the chicken pieces, chopped onion, and 2 chopped slices of bacon. Cover with the remaining potato mash and top with the remaining bacon. Bake at 400°F (182°C) for 1½ to 2 hours, or until crust forms on top.

the area is covered in peat moss—so much so that they even have a peat moss festival, Le Festival de Tourbe, the fourth week of July, during which time they crown a peat moss queen and throw a big party. Peat moss is a big industry now, due to the growth of home gardening. You'll be able to tell when you're in peat moss territory, because the area seems unusually flat and boglike.

At the tail end of Shippagan you will come to a causeway that will bring you to **Île Lamèque.** This is quite a picturesque island, popular with Quebecois because the region boasts several beaches with relatively warm water, due to their location in the shallow, narrow Chaleur Bay instead of right out on the gulf.

Once you get there, stay on Highway 113 and drive along the northern side of the island. Soon you will see a small coastal village in which the church of *Ste.-Cécile* hosts the annual *Lamèque International Festival of Baroque Music.* Despite its remote location, the festival features authentic period instruments and musicians from all over the world. Constructed in 1913, Ste.-Cécile is noted not only for its wonderful accoustics, but also for its "naive" interior decor, executed in vibrant colors, the intensely painted handiwork of two artists.

A unique event for Canada, the festival confines its musical programming to works of the Baroque period (1600–1750). It offers concerts, brunch, conferences, and even boat tours at prices ranging from $10 to $35. An award winner as the best cultural event in New Brunswick, it's a bargain. One of the highlights includes performances on a spectacular Casavant organ. You can check out concert details by visiting http://festivalbaroque.acadie.net. Keep your French–English dictionary handy. I am convinced that one of the reasons this festival is an inside secret is that very little information is available in English. The French-language twin of CBC, La Société Radio-Canada, records and rebroadcasts these performances nationally.

Because the area's accommodations could easily get filled to the limit during the concert series, reserve a room in advance if at all possible. The closest accommodations to the concert are found in the neighborhood of Lamèque. Try *L'Auberge des Compagnons* at 11 Main Street. It has sixteen rooms and is right downtown, close to the beach, and fifteen minutes by car from most of the musical performances. Reserve by phone at (506) 344–7762, or by e-mail at auberge@nbnet.nb.ca. Breakfasts are included in the price. Rates are deluxe.

The village where you will find Ste.-Cécile is called Petite Rivière de l'Île. It ends just a short distance from the connection to *Miscou Island.*

Miscou is now connected by a bridge, which makes this summer paradise slightly more accessible. Still, its relative isolation lends it a bit of a Robinson Crusoe effect. The island is beautiful, as unspoiled as anyone could want. There are five beaches here.

The best one is located by taking the marked turnoff to *Miscou Island Camping,* just before the road turns abruptly right and leads to the lighthouse. The beach is accessed by a privately run campground. The parking fee entitles you to day use of the campground's facilities. The rate for overnight camping, with all hookups, is $20 and up. There are no lifeguards, and the big waves and strong current are quite hazardous. The water is warm and the beach is well worth the drive to the island.

Be sure to visit *Miscou Lighthouse,* the oldest functioning wooden lighthouse in the Maritimes. It overlooks a pristine natural setting, with miles of sandy shore. For a small fee you can climb to the top.

Once there, look out toward the flatland to see the site of a Russian pilot's crash landing back in 1939. He was attempting to make the first solo transpolar flight from Moscow to New York when he ran into difficulty. He attempted to land on what appeared to be a good makeshift tarmac, but it turned out to be a peat bog, unfrozen, and the plane was destroyed. He did, however, officially make it across the polar ice cap—alive and without too much wear and tear on his body.

This is the most incredible place I have ever seen for beachcombing. The beach in front of the lighthouse is covered in driftwood of all sorts—so much so that you won't want to swim here. Try the beach at the campground to take a dip.

Slightly fewer than 900 people live on Miscou Island. The French spoken on Miscou and Lamèque dates back to the era of the first Europeans in Canada, so you will have a chance to brush up on your Balzac.

Miscou's remote location has always been its biggest selling point. In the era of New France, it was favored as the ideal location for the illegal fur trade, since it was so far away from Port Royal.

Its proximity to a rich fishing area drew French fishermen here as far back as the early 1600s. Among the early entrepreneurs to invest time and effort in the island was Nicolas Denys, who had a post here before moving on to Cape Breton and then becoming governor.

Miscou is, unfortunately, only a summer paradise. In the winter it is blanketed by heavy snow, lashed by the bracing winds of the gulf. You'll notice that few trees attain much height.

After returning to Île Lamèque, take Route 113 until you reach exit 217. This is a fork in the road: Haut Pokemouche lies to the north. Turn left, heading south toward Pokemouche, and follow Highway 11 until you reach *Miramichi,* comprising the former communities of Chatham, Newcastle, and Nelson-Miramichi.

In the midst of all this Acadian culture you will suddenly come upon an area of considerable Irish settlement, so much so that Miramichi is the site of an *Irish Festival on the Miramichi.* Held in mid-July, this is the first and largest Irish festival in Canada. It features traditional music, culture, and entertainers from Ireland. Some recent innovations include a "cyberpub," where a local pub links to a pub in Ireland. Nighttime admission is $14. The main festival venue is the Lord Beaverbrook Arena, directly under the Miramichi water tower. Festival details can be found by visiting www.canadasirishfest.com.

After Miramichi you have the option of taking Route 11 south as far as Kouchibouguac National Park or driving along the coast on a pretty stretch of highway called Route 117. The reward of this latter course is an unsullied stretch of coast culminating in *Pointe-Sapin,* where you can snuggle up with nature. If you wish, you can camp or enjoy solitary stretches of beach here.

Pointe-Sapin is a charming Acadian village. The residents hold the Festival du Bon Pecheur (Festival of the Good Fisherman) each mid- to late July, purely as a local thing.

The village is at the northern, coastal entrance to *Kouchibouguac National Park.* The protected dunes of the shoreline stretch like a long arm the length of the park. Along with watching rare birds along the grassy dunes of Kouchibouguac, you can hike on any of ten trails; rent canoes, bikes, or paddleboats; or swim in lagoons holding the warmest salt water north of Virginia.

Much of the shoreline of this park is protected wilderness hosting a variety of rare flora and fauna, including the piping plover. There is an active beaver dam in the park, which always makes for fascinating viewing, and along the coast you can spot harbor and gray seals. For details call (506) 876–2443.

After leaving the national park, you will be traveling south on Route 11 until you reach exit 42. Turn into a small town called *Sainte-Anne-de-Kent,* along a smaller highway, Rural Route 505. This village offers a unique opportunity to mix shopping, learning, and grooming at a combination museum and specialist soap shop. (Say that twice rapidly!) *The Olivier Soapery and Soap Museum of Canada* is a provincially run museum that demonstrates the traditional art of soap making and displays objects from history that were dedicated to personal grooming products and their manufacture.

They also manufacture their own line of mild biodegradable skin solutions, created from pure essential oil extracts of plants and flowers. Some of the shampoos, milk baths, therapeutic oils, and creams are specifically designed to treat skin disorders. And, of course, some are just to pamper yourself, naturally. They make great gifts for the people who stayed home on this trip. The museum is open from May to September daily from 10:00 A.M. to 8:00

P.M. They hold demonstrations five times a day. During winter months, the museum is open from 9:00 A.M. to 5:00 P.M.

After the museum, return to Route 11 by backtracking to exit 42 and continue south to Bouctouche.

The Acadian Coast

Bouctouche is the birthplace of two of New Brunswick's most famous natives: billionaire K. C. Irving and writer Antonine Maillet. Maillet's play *La Sagouine* (*The Cleaning Woman*) won the highest acclaim possible in the French-speaking world, but its biggest impact by far is the fact that audiences have been unable to separate fact from fiction and are convinced that *la sagouine* is a real person. So, on the nearby *Île-aux-Puces,* reached by boardwalk and footbridge, you can enter an entire alternate universe devoted to her, entitled **Le Pays de la Sagouine** or the Land of the Cleaning Lady. Think of this as a 3-D play where you get to participate. By the time you've finished a meal of Acadian *poutine râpées, pâtés à la viande, poutines à trou,* and *poulet fricot,* and listened to some typical Acadian music and old-time storytelling in local French, you will have a hard time distinguishing fact from fiction yourself. Prices are moderate. For details, call (800) 561–9188 or (506) 743–1400.

Farther south along Route 11, in **Shediac,** the thing to do is visit **Cap-Pelé Beach.** The water is consistently wonderful here, and the sand goes on forever. All summer long it's a good bet for a swim because it is situated along a very narrow and shallow stretch of the Northumberland Strait, which causes the water to be warm.

Shediac has also laid claim to the title of "World's Lobster Capital," and while I've heard that before, only in Shediac will you have the opportunity to climb all over a gigantic lobster sculpture, situated along the village's main drag, overlooking a small inlet.

If you feel the need for an urban break, turn inland again on Route 15 west to **Moncton,** a surprisingly cosmopolitan and thoroughly pleasant little city, where the population is almost evenly divided between French and English speakers and bilingualism is a way of life. As a result, many nationwide services have gravitated to the area, adding to the dynamic feel of this cozy place.

Whether you are in Shediac or Moncton, you now must make a crucial decision: whether to explore the rest of New Brunswick's Fundy Coast, head for Prince Edward Island, or go on to Nova Scotia. Here are the three possible routes:

    1. If you are sticking to New Brunswick, then point your Pontiac south from Moncton along Route 114 until you reach **Hopewell Cape,** where the Petitcodiac River widens out to Shepody Bay. This is the site of the

Flowerpot Rocks, which give a nature walk an added appeal. Actually chunks of land created by erosion resulting from the action of the Bay of Fundy's tides, these sandstone rocks tower above you at a height of four stories when the tide is out. At high tide, though, the site is unimpressive, and you'll wonder what all the fuss is about. This is the fate of sight-seers along the Bay of Fundy—everything depends on the tides. The average difference between high and low tide is 36 feet (11 meters). When tides are low, you'll get a one-time chance to walk on the ocean floor.

Hopewell Rocks Park is now triple its original size and has several large parking lots at the entrance. Nearby is a modern shop and dining complex, where you can get a decent meal for roughly $10 to $15 a plate. The setting is very nice, and while outside seating on the viewing decks may be very breezy, the inside tables still offer a good view of the Bay of Fundy. The complex includes an interpretive center with displays of the ecology of the area and a multimedia exhibit. The souvenir shop here has a wide selection of gift items.

When you are ready for your hike among the Flowerpot Rocks, a shuttle will take you to the starting point, where you will descend a series of stairs to the ocean floor. After you're finished, take advantage of the hoses provided to scrub down your muddy footwear (as much as possible). This is a good place to take rubber boots with good tread or, failing that, the kind of Velcro-strapped sandals favored by kayakers. Admission to the park is $8.00 for adults, $6.75 for seniors, $5.75 for children ages five to eighteen, and $20.00 for a family.

The most dramatic way to see the Flowerpot Rocks is by kayak with a naturalist guide from *Baymount Outdoor Adventures.* The two-man kayaks are extremely stable and handle much more easily than canoes, so they can be used even by novices.

Kayaking around the rocks takes some forethought and timing, since the Flowerpots are flooded roughly two hours before and after high tide. Tours are timed to coincide with the tide's peak, so call ahead to book a spot. For $55 per person, Baymount provides the seaworthy with basic instruction, the use of sea kayaks, and a three-hour guided tour. To book a kayak and instruction, call (506) 734–2660.

For about two weeks, starting at the end of July, between one and two million semipalmated sandpipers make their way here to double their weight before a marathon five-day flight. Hopewell Cape is their one stop on an annual journey from the Arctic to Suriname, a country on the northern coast of South America. They shift around every few

A Visit to Sackville Waterfowl Park

There are now 160 different species of birds in the *Sackville Waterfowl Park.* Part of the park is built on an old rail line that has been torn up and replaced by gravel trails. Boardwalks crisscross the old Acadian pastureland. Remaining are apple trees, now hundreds of years old, and basket willows, which early settlers used for weaving household goods.

The wild snapdragons growing here were used to make an ointment for bee stings and mosquito bites. In a thicket of the shrub spirea, so dense the locals call it "hard hack," we find yellow warblers hiding out.

Unfortunately, decades ago European settlers brought purple loosestrife to this country, and it has been crowding out other plants ever since. Park workers periodically tried to eradicate the loosestrife by hand. Eventually they decided to use a newer tactic of releasing several hundred mating pairs of a small weevil, which feed off the weed.

Much of the water in the park is covered by duckweed, which feeds almost all of the species of ducks that live here. The park's residents include mallards, green-wing and blue-wing teals, gadwalls, wigeons, ring-necked ducks, and pied-billed grebes.

The area is also visited by osprey. To encourage a mating pair to set up house, the park constructed an "osprey tower," which looks like a telephone pole rising out of the water, with a platform on top.

Amid the reeds you may see a muskrat. From a cluster of bulrushes comes a high-pitched squeak. It's from a bird called the sora rail, completely camouflaged by the bulrushes when its beak points skyward. Once it drops its beak, it looks like a small chicken.

Although the area is marshland, we weren't plagued by mosquitoes. A large number of tree swallows have been established in the park to keep the bug population down.

days, but with some luck and good timing you may get a look at the dramatic sight of a mass migration. Says kayaking guide Richard Faulkner, "It's nature. So we don't promote and advertise and guarantee, because the birds may have a different plan that day."

During a recent migration, kayakers were surrounded by hundreds of thousands of the gray-and-white birds—a flock so thick that the bright yellow boats were invisible to one another, even at distances as close as 30 feet (9 meters).

Bear in mind that the tides here can take you by surprise. The change in water height can be sufficient to leave you stranded if you are not careful. Plan ahead by consulting a tide table (widely available in New Brunswick).

After Hopewell Cape you can return to Route 114 and drive to Riverside-Albert, where the highway joins Route 915 and continues on to Alma, where you can experience *Fundy National Park,* on the Bay of Fundy. There is an outdoor pool here filled with water that is pumped in from the bay and heated. While you swim you can catch some stunning views of the bay, but the area is otherwise quite isolated. Admission to the swimming pool is $2.95 for adults, $1.45 for children, or $7.40 for a family. Season passes are available to campers. From here you can continue through the park on another stretch of Provincial Highway 114 until you reach TCH Route 2 a few miles outside Sussex. For details call (506) 887–6000, or fax (506) 887–6008.

If you happen to be in Sussex and the vicinity in the early fall, you will notice a large number of hot-air balloons overhead; balloonists hold a festival here annually. After Sussex you can return to Saint John via Route 1; now you will have done a complete circumnavigation of New Brunswick.

2. To get to Prince Edward Island from Shediac, take Provincial Highway 15 until you connect to the TCH 16, just a short distance from the link to P.E.I. The road is well marked.

3. If you are headed toward Nova Scotia, be sure to stop first in *Sackville,* New Brunswick, for a visit to the *Sackville Waterfowl Park.* Sackville is right in the middle of the migratory path of millions of birds, particularly ducks. For years the early Acadian settlers tried to turn the Tantramar Marshes into farmland, draining it for the purpose, but to no avail. Eventually the town decided to flood an area and allow the ducks their way. The result is the fifty-five-acre (twenty-five-hectare) park, which has earned the town its reputation as the "Bird-Watching Capital of Atlantic Canada."

Extending right up into the community, the park provides an amazing close-up of airborne wildlife. The park is crisscrossed with boardwalks, giving easy access to the wetlands. Guides are available to take visitors on a tour and explain the intricacies of the ecosystem, which includes rare species of wildflowers and birds. Summertime-only guided tours begin at the Sackville Visitor Centre, which is on Mallard Drive (the first left after you take exit 504 to Sackville off the TCH) and is clearly visible from the TCH, which runs parallel to Mallard Drive. A small admission is charged.

Sackville itself is a great town for aimless puttering: It is the home of Mount Allison University, which includes a well-recognized art college. Over the years it has become a magnet for artists, and the community's gift shops provide many good art-collecting opportunities for out-of-town visitors.

Located just five minutes from the Nova Scotia border and just exiting the TCH 2, in *Aulac, Fort Beauséjour* would win my vote for the perfect location for a paintball game or historical reenactment. Its pentagon-shaped grassworks and bastions are perched high atop a grassy hill overlooking the diked marshlands that stretch along the borderland between Nova Scotia and New Brunswick.

The fort was built by the French in 1751, and the intention was to counterbalance a fort built by the British one year before. Four years

Paddling among the Flowerpots

Baymount Outdoor Adventures tour guide Richard Faulkner takes groups to the Flowerpots twice a day in the summer, to coincide with the times when the rocks are flooded.

I take off with a group early in the morning, while the air is still and cool, a faint mist rising above the chocolate water of Shepody Bay. Because the sun has not yet heated the water, there is little breeze and no discernable current to contend with. Still shrouded in fog, the early-morning Flowerpots seem to hover in a cloud. Up close, the purple-hued, iron-oxide-tinged rocks look as if handfuls of granite were thrown at wet clay, which hardened into a wall.

These are called "conglomerate rocks," made of rock fragments that over eons have been compressed together. The conglomerate rock came from the Appalachian Mountain range 250 million years ago: First, the earth's plates shifted, creating vertical fractures in the rock. Then, water from melting glaciers eroded and caused the separation of some rock from the mainland. The Flowerpots themselves weren't carved out until the last ice age, about ten thousand years ago. They were eroded by the tides of the Bay of Fundy, which sculpted them at the base to look like elegantly formed pottery.

One of the first big rocks is Lover's Arch, through which kayaks easily pass. We continue to weave in and out of the rocks, for a total distance of roughly 1 mile (1.6 km). In the distance a peregrine falcon swoops down over and over again, apparently in search of small shore birds.

After close to an hour, we round the point. From here we see Shepody Mountain and Grindstone Island, 7 nautical miles (11.3 km) away.

Later, as the water moves roughly 450 feet (137.1 m) offshore, tiny mud shrimp burrow into the silt-covered floor of the bay. These are the food of the semi-palmated sandpiper, a small gray-and-white shorebird that makes the upper Bay of Fundy its one stop on its migration from the Arctic to Suriname, on the northern coast of South America.

later, the uneasy stalemate between Fort Beauséjour and Fort Lawrence came to an end with a two-week siege, culminating in the fall of Beauséjour. It was June 1755. Shortly after, the order was given to deport the Acadians.

Inside the grassworks are tunnels called casemates. From this vantage point it is easy to imagine life as it was lived by the Acadians in the mid-1700s, using farming methods they brought from their ancestral homeland. Specially designed drainage conduits made of rough-hewn wood, called *aboiteaux,* were built to keep salt water out of the low, flat, and fertile marshlands, eliminating the need to clear forests in order to plant crops. Three years after a stretch of land was diked, it would be ready for farming.

The community around Beauséjour built their own church and installed a bell brought from France in 1734, only to have the church burn down. They built another, which was destroyed during the fall of the fortress to the British in 1755. The bell eventually found its way into an Anglican church, where it tolled for them until the mid-1900s, when its true identity was discovered. By that time, a local doctor and avid history buff had been collecting artifacts about the area surrounding the fort, which had been renamed Fort Cumberland. The bell was donated to this collection, and now hangs in the museum reception building. This structure also houses quill baskets made by the natives who lived nearby at the time, ancient firearms, and tools from the eighteenth century. The museum has also designed a fun-for-the-whole-family scavenger hunt that encourages kids to explore the artifacts and fortifications. On a good day, it's a great spot for a picnic overlooking the freshwater marshes.

Take note that one casemate has been made wheelchair accessible, and an all-terrain wheelchair is available for loan. A small admission is charged. The national historic site is open daily from the beginning of June until mid-October. For details, call (506) 364–5080.

Places to Stay in Acadian New Brunswick

BATHURST

Bathurst Le Chateau
80 Main Street
(506) 546–6691
Excellent setting overlooking
the bay.
Moderate.

CARAQUET

Chateau Albert
14311 Route 11
Acadian Historical Village
(506) 726–2600
Time travel included in price.
Moderate.

GRAND FALLS

Best Western Près du Lac
TCH Route 2
(506) 473–1300
Good pit stop with
paddleboats, laudromat,
and indoor pool.
Standard.

HOPEWELL CAPE

**Hopewell Rocks Motel
and Inn**
Route 114
(at the entrance to Hopewell
Rocks Park)
(506) 734–2975
Stunning setting.
Standard.

KEDGWICK

Centre Echo Restigouche
Route 17
(506) 284–2022
Nature in surround-sound
(pack repellent).
Moderate.

LAMÈQUE

**L'Auberge des
Compagnons**
11 Main Street
(506) 344–7766
auberge@nbnet.nb.ca
Romantic ambience.
Deluxe.

MIRAMICHI

**Rodd Miramichi River
Lodge**
1809 Water Street
(800) 565–7633
In the heart of anglers'
paradise.
Moderate.

SACKVILLE

Marshlands Inn
55 Bridge Street
(1 mile from TCH)
(800) 561–1266
(506) 536–0170
Historic.
Moderate.

Places to Eat in Acadian New Brunswick

All feature fresh Atlantic
seafood in addition to the
usual fare.

BOUCTOUCHE

**Auberge Le Vieux
Presbytère de
Bouctouche**
157 Chemin du Couvent
(506) 743–5568
Delicious regional cuisine;
excellent wine list.

HOPEWELL CAPE

The Log Cabin Restaurant
Route 114
(at the entrance to
Hopewell Rocks Park)
(506) 734–2110
Spectacular view.

MIRAMICHI

P. J. Billington's
1 Jane Street
(506) 622–0302
At the water's edge.

MONCTON

Cy's Restaurant
170 Main Street
(506) 857–0032
In charming heart of town.

Wharf Village Restaurant
exit 488 off TCH 2 or
Route 126
(506) 859–1812
Noted for good seafood.

PAQUETVILLE

Crêpes Bretonne
1805 Rue du Parc
(near Highways 135 and 325)
(506) 764–5344
Authentic Brittany-style
creperie.

SHEDIAC

**Fisherman's Paradise
Restaurant**
Main Street
(off exit 37 on Route 15)
(506) 532–6811
Lobster heaven. Any closer
to the water and you'd have
to swim.

Prince Edward Island

The original settlers on Prince Edward Island (P.E.I.) were from Ireland, Scotland, or Brittany. Initial European settlements of French Acadians were followed by waves of Irish farmers and Scots. All of them have come to think of P.E.I. as the center of the universe—so much so that anywhere else is referred to, vaguely, as "away," and people from anyplace out of the province are said to "come from away." And Prince Edward Island is simply referred to as "The Island." Even when those words are spoken aloud, you can tell they are in capital letters. A lot has changed for the visitor to Prince Edward Island over the past few years. The Island's section of the Trans-Canada Trail, known locally as the Confederation Trail, is complete. The Confederation Bridge makes shorter visits or even day trips possible, whereas before visitors might have to factor in a half day's wait for a spot on the ferry. If you take day trips into account and plan to target areas farther afield, you can still enjoy the quaint countryside and outdoor lifestyle of this picturesque province.

The key to getting off the beaten path in Prince Edward Island is to concentrate your travel at the two end points of The Island, thereby avoiding the outrageously popular tourist attractions clustered around the home of famous author Lucy

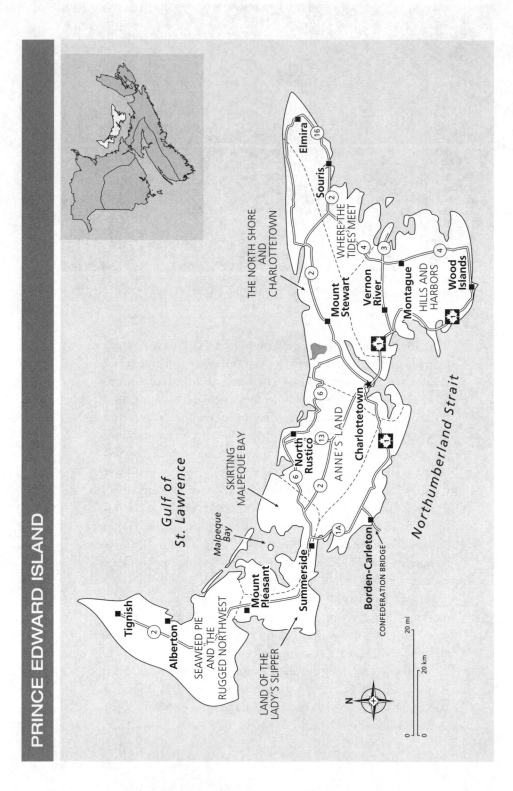

PRINCE EDWARD ISLAND

Gulf of
St. Lawrence

Northumberland Strait

Tignish
Alberton
SEAWEED PIE AND THE RUGGED NORTHWEST
LAND OF THE LADY'S SLIPPER
Mount Pleasant
Summerside
Malpeque Bay
SKIRTING MALPEQUE BAY
North Rustico
ANNE'S LAND
Charlottetown
Borden-Carleton
CONFEDERATION BRIDGE
THE NORTH SHORE AND CHARLOTTETOWN
Mount Stewart
Vernon River
WHERE THE TIDES' MEET
Souris
Elmira
Montague
HILLS AND HARBORS
Wood Islands

N

20 mi
20 km
0
0

Maud Montgomery and the sites related to her fictional heroine of *Anne of Green Gables*. First published in 1908, the book that made this red-haired orphan famous is in its hundredth printing and has now been translated into dozens of languages. It holds cult status in Japan, where its place on the school curriculum and the spunky character of its heroine have guaranteed its supremacy in the hearts of young Japanese women. Thousands of Japanese make an annual summer pilgrimage to the Cavendish area of P.E.I.

Cavendish Beach is undoubtedly spectacular, but if you are looking for Anne, you may find her hard to spot among the legions of Japanese honeymooners, the bus-tour groups, and the visitors to Ripley's Believe It or Not! Museum and the many amusement parks. Since The Island has forty beaches to choose from, a good strategy is to aim for one of the less-frequented beaches. But if you are determined to visit Cavendish, try to get there before school closes at the end of June or, alternatively, go near the end of August. To ensure that you'll be able to find lodgings at this popular spot, book ahead by calling (888) 268–6667. You can also book online at www.gov.pe.ca/visitors guide/reservation/index.php3.

Cavendish no longer allows dogs, since they consider their primary mandate habitat preservation and dogs can present a hazard to the wildlife of the third most visited national park, which is also one of the three smallest. Also note that national park daily entry fees are $17.30 for a single family in a vehicle, so if you are planning to visit several national parks during your holiday, you might want to get a season pass for $87.15.

A little farther along, however, and you are in the countryside that spawned the heartwarming series of Anne books that made The Island famous. Take

TRUDY'S FAVORITES

Victoria by-the-Sea

Cap-Egmont Bottle Houses,
Cap-Egmont

Mill River Golf Course,
Woodstock

The Dunes Studio Gallery,
Brackley Beach

Dalvay by-the-Sea,
Grand Tracadie

Confederation Centre of the Arts,
Charlottetown

Elmira Railway Museum and Confederation Trail,
Elmira

Basin Head,
(museum and beach)

trivia

The interior chamber of a lobster trap is often called a "bedroom" or "parlor."

In 1813, P.E.I.'s lieutenant governor devised a solution to a chronic coin shortage by permitting the use of Spanish silver coins, which had the centers punched out. The "holey money" was to be accepted at face value. They were pulled from circulation quickly, however, because of rampant counterfeiting.

particular note of the Scenic Heritage Roads, which dot the various counties of P.E.I. These are characterized by the deep-red clay (not so scenic in spring thaw or after several days of rain) and the pastoral countryside that has remained unchanged by the modern world. It is a constantly changing canvas: at times, all deep green and red clay; later in the summer, fields of purple and white potato flowers, ripening corn, and yellow hay.

If you fly over The Island, you'll be struck by the impression that you are looking at a diagonally pieced crazy quilt, boasting many shades of green and topstitched in the deep-red clay.

If you are traveling to Prince Edward Island from New Brunswick, you will be taking the *Confederation Bridge,* one of the engineering marvels of the world, currently the longest bridge to traverse ice-covered salt water and the longest span in the Western Hemisphere. Fares are $39.00 per car and $44.50 for recreational vehicles. A free shuttle bus transports pedestrians and cyclists at regular intervals. Major credit cards are accepted at the toll booths. The crossing takes ten minutes. Tolls cover a round trip to and from the island and are paid upon departure from the island.

From the town of Borden-Carleton it is only a short drive to the attractions in the western end of the province, while the east is quite accessible from Wood Islands, which is still served by ferry from Nova Scotia.

Since the entire distance from one tip of P.E.I. to the other is only 180 miles (288 km), and the landscape is either flat or gently rolling, it is the perfect place to take a bicycle tour. This can last a few hours on a rented bike or for the entire holiday on your own trusty steed.

Life Is a Speed Trap

The Confederation Bridge has made The Island so marvelously accessible, and is so straight and direct, that the temptation arises to imagine oneself being catapulted across the Northumberland Strait at considerable velocity. A word to the wise: The 8-mile (12.9-km) crossing has a heavily monitored 50-mph (80-kph) speed limit, and I have never failed to witness someone getting ticketed either coming or going.

TOP ANNUAL EVENTS

Victoria Playhouse Summer Festival,
Victoria by-the-Sea
(end of June to end of August);
(800) 925–2025
www.victoriaplayhouse.com

P.E.I. Bluegrass and Old-Time Music Festival,
Rollo Bay (second week in July);
(902) 569–4501

Souris Regatta,
Souris (second week in July);
(902) 687–2157 or (902) 687–3835

Rollo Bay Fiddle Festival,
Rollo Bay (third weekend in July);
(902) 687–2584 or (902) 687–3464

Rendez-Vous Rustico,
Rustico (fourth weekend in July);
(902) 963–3252

Bluegrass Festival,
Orwell Corner Historic Village
(fourth Sunday in August);
(902) 651–8510

70-Mile Coastal Yard Sale,
Wood Islands and vicinity
(last weekend in September);
(902) 962–3242

Added to this are the many country bed-and-breakfast inns and farm vacations that make slow-paced travel particularly appealing. Most important, you're never very far from a rest stop, a scenic view, or the next village.

When The Island railway closed, the abandoned rail lines were converted to combination bike paths and hiking trails, which are used by snowmobilers in the winter. The many train stations left behind serve as rest areas for outdoor enthusiasts. With the opening of the Confederation Trail and P.E.I.'s reputation as the ultimate bike-holiday locale, the number of bike-rental companies has grown to over two dozen. This means that you can take day trips from several locations on the trail or select from a wide range of departure points, without having to bring your own bike. The shared-use walking and bike trail runs from one tip of the province to the other, with additional branch routes bringing the total length to 219 miles (350 km). There is even a link to the Confederation Bridge in Borden-Carleton. (You can't bike on the bridge, but a free shuttle will take you and your bike across.)

The same thing that makes cycling so wonderful in P.E.I. makes giving road directions a hazardous business. The Island consists of farmland from one end to the other, dotted with little communities, so the entire province is covered with a spider's web of roads. Since it is crescent-shaped and as narrow as 4 miles (6.4 km) across at one point, there are a half dozen ways to get anywhere—great for cyclists. If you don't like where you are, you can always take the next left and traverse the width of the entire province in less than twenty minutes.

We recommend one of two strategies for getting off the beaten path in P.E.I. Either follow the route we have mapped out in a clockwise direction from Borden-Carleton, with it located at six o'clock on the dial; or follow the same route in reverse from the Wood Islands ferry landing, on the southeastern end of the province. If there is something you want to bypass, simply detour onto one of the many rural routes that crisscross the province.

Land of the Lady's Slipper

Once in Borden-Carleton, if you so much as blink, you risk missing a charming little fishing village just fifteen minutes from the ferry landing. Therefore, even though I've mapped out a tour of The Island's western end first, I am going to suggest that you make one small detour east as soon as you arrive.

Victoria by-the-Sea, established along a British Colonial–style grid pattern, is quite compact, which makes for pleasant strolling. Just park your car and drift around among the quaint little nooks and crannies, cafes, and a theater (*The Victoria Playhouse,* which presents popular theater nightly all summer). You would be pleasantly surprised at the caliber of the entertainment that turns up in this tiny seaside village theater. To check its season's offerings, visit www.victoriaplayhouse.com. Summer performances are seven nights a week at 8:00 P.M.; on Sunday there is also a 2:00 P.M. matinee.

The *Studio Gallery,* on a lane to your right as you walk up from the shore, displays the work of a number of local artists, in etchings, oils, and acrylics—some representational, some surrealistic. There are also pottery, antiques, craft and quilt shops, and other appealing stores. You can't miss anything by simply wandering around this tiny village. The wharf has been spruced up to house a restaurant and shops.

trivia

Cars were banned from Prince Edward Island early in the 1900s as a "menace to life and property." While people drive cars all over the island now, strictly speaking, they are against the law.

The little harbor's lighthouse is also home to the *Victoria Seaport Museum,* where you can chat with the students who run the museum and catch up on the local scene. This is the second-oldest lighthouse on P.E.I., and photographs of some of its most reliable keepers are displayed here—one man put in fifty years on the job. The lighthouse exhibits navigational aids from the 1920s, including a kerosene lamp used in the range light for many years. You can climb to the top to see the modern light or just check out the harbor from the second floor. Admission is free, though donations are welcome.

The village boasts several beaches as well as a lobster pound, meaning a good supply of fresh lobster at the local eating establishments. You can also watch chocolates being made at *Island Chocolates.* The shop sells a variety of locally produced and specialty jams. Island Chocolates also offers its own brand of cocoa and specially blended coffees and teas designed to go well with chocolate. It also has *Titanic*-shaped chocolates and even chocolate-scented candles, which owners Ron and Linda Gilbert promote as "a calorie-free experience." Call (902) 658–2320.

The village's foremost accommodations are in an inn dating back to 1900. The *Orient Hotel* on Main Street is one of the last two original hotels operating in P.E.I. (The establishment is now part of a network of Heritage inns in Atlantic Canada.) There are six guest rooms (all with private bath) and cable television. Cycle tourists take note: There is storage for bicycles. For a reservation, call (800) 565–6743 or (902) 658–2503. A full breakfast is included in the room rates. Prices are moderate. Visit www.theorienthotel.com or contact by e-mail at stay@theorienthotel.com.

After enjoying Victoria, turn west and backtrack the fifteen minutes toward Borden-Carleton and the western end of The Island.

If you want to skip Victoria by-the-Sea or leave it to the end of your stay on The Island, then turn west immediately after leaving the ferry. Turning west will take you briefly to *Summerside* and from there to the small fishing villages and cozy beaches of the western end of the island.

In the nineteenth century the economic mainstay of Summerside was its shipbuilding industry. You can relive some of that era at *Spinnakers' Landing,*

Summerside's Fur Industry

The silver-fox fur industry in Summerside began to boom in the late 1800s and reached its peak in the 1920s. Breeding pairs of the top-quality foxes were even traded for houses; one pair fetched an outstanding $35,000 on the open market. At its height the industry constituted one-sixth of The Island's economic base, bringing wealth to many Summerside furriers.

The Island was the site of the first successful fur farm in the world, beginning in the 1870s with the capture of a pair of wild black foxes. A little more than a decade later, experimentation finally resulted in a successful breeding program. The results of these early studies form the basis of all current fur-farming methods in the world. The industry continues to this day with just over sixty fur farmers on the island.

which offers an opportunity to explore an interpretive center showing the ship-building techniques of the early 1800s. The harborside shops stock a variety of crafts and gift items. Harbor cruises can be booked on the spot. In front of the shops is a play area that includes a jungle gym in the shape of a boat. Spin-nakers' Landing has become a venue for free concerts several times a week over the summer. There is also a bike rental location set up here during the summer.

Eighty percent of North America's cultured mussels come from Prince Edward Island. If you just can't wait to tuck into a plate of them, visit **Flex Mussels,** located in the Spinnakers' Landing complex in a tiny cedar-shingled building that is only open in the summer. The chef is a genius with a crustacean, and offers twenty-four distinct preparations of mussels, everything from Mussels Parisienne (made with Pernod, white wine, and basil), Mussels Peking (dressed up with black beans and Chinese barbecued duck), and Wild Turkey (with roasted corn, kumquats, and bourbon). They are open starting June 1 from 11:00 A.M. until 9:30 P.M., until September, when they start to close early. The whole operation shuts down in mid-September.

trivia

Prince Edward Island has dropped the provincial sales tax on clothing and footwear, cutting their cost by 10 percent. If you're itching to replenish your wardrobe, this can give added appeal to the commute across the bridge.

Also along Summerside's shore you will find the **College of Piping** at 619 Water Street East. This is a place for people who want to learn to play the bagpipes like a real Highlander—or at least look like one. In addition to crash courses in piping, the college gives frequent free concerts and demonstrations of Highland dance by the little ones. You can also deck yourself out in full Highland tartan at the Celtic Gift and Highland Supply Outlet. To obtain a course calendar and events schedule, write to the college at 619 Water Street East, Summerside, PE C1N 4H8. Call (877) BAGPIPE (224–7473), or visit www.collegeofpiping.com.

Summerside streets are graced with stately old homes that recall a time of wealth and ease. These date back not only to the years when it was the center of The Island's shipbuilding trade, but also to when it was the focus of the lucrative silver-fox industry. That era is depicted in charcoal drawings, photographs, and folk art at the **International Fox Museum and Hall of Fame,** 286 Fitzroy Street, 3 blocks back from the harbor. For details about the museum, call (902) 436–2400. Admission is free, but donations are accepted.

Fifteen minutes' drive west on Route 11 from Summerside will take you to **Mont-Carmel,** site of **Le Village de l'Acadie,** 1 mile (1.6 km) past Our Lady of Mont-Carmel Church. The route is marked by a logo depicting the lady's slipper, a typical island flower, for which Lady Slipper Drive (Route 11) is named. If you chance upon one of these flowers, don't pick it—it would take thirteen years for a new flower to grow in its place!

The first European settlers on The Island were Acadians, settlers from France's Atlantic coast. While many were exiled shortly after the British won possession of The Island, a number escaped into the woods with the help of native peoples and then quietly reestablished normal lives. The Acadian presence is still significant, with 17 percent of the Island residents descendants from these first European settlers.

In the center of the Le Village de l'Acadie complex is an open-air "theater," painted with massive murals depicting scenes from the early life of the Acadians. Among them is the story of Evangeline, the now-famous Acadian heroine who was separated from her husband on her wedding day. The real Evangeline became a nun in Philadelphia and was reunited with her husband on his deathbed, many years later. The village is open in June Monday to Friday 9:30 A.M. to 5:00 P.M. and Sunday 1:00 to 4:00 P.M., and in July and August daily 9:30 A.M. to 7:00 P.M. Admission is $4.50 for adults, $3.50 for students, and $12.50 per family. Call (902) 432–2880.

The restaurant ***Étoile de Mer*** serves traditional Acadian fare. This includes such hits as *pâté à la râpure,* a potato pie popular throughout Acadian regions; and Quebecois specialties like *poutine.* During the summer the restaurant has a dinner theater. Call (902) 854–2227 for hours and reservations.

Just 3 miles (5 km) farther west down Route 11 (Lady Slipper Drive) from Mont-Carmel, you will come to Cap-Egmont, home of the ***Cap-Egmont Bottle Houses,*** the masterpiece of a stellar attempt at recycling.

Cap-Egmont Bottle House

You must not pass up the chance to consider at length the single-mindedness of someone who collects and then cements together 25,000 glass bottles to form buildings. Originally the work of the late Edouard T. Arsenault, a retired fisherman, the structures include a spectacular little chapel complete with altar and pews, a six-gabled house, and a spacious tavern.

The original inspiration for the project came from a bottle house on Vancouver Island, but that climate was far more benign during the winter. Much of the original complex had to be restored because of the impact of The Island's severe winters on the unique building materials. Two of the three structures have undergone major repairs. Arsenault's family is carrying on his tradition and keeping the kids busy at the same time. Using more than 2,000 bottles, grandson Etienne added his own giant bottle to the site.

Hobbyists in particular will love this place, if for no other reason than to reassure themselves that they have yet to get truly carried away with their obsession. The three bottle houses and the gardens, which at their peak feature more than fifty varieties of flowers, are open daily from 10:00 A.M. to 6:00 P.M. In July and August hours extend from 9:00 A.M. to 8:00 P.M. every day. A small admission is charged. Admission for groups can be arranged by calling (902) 854–2987. In the off-season, phone (902) 854–2254. There is also a gift shop on site with a variety of P.E.I. memorabilia. Some unique souvenirs include blown-glass articles and ornaments made from recycled bottles.

Seaweed Pie and the Rugged Northwest

Continuing along this sparsely populated stretch of shoreline will take you to the black-and-white **West Point Lighthouse,** located in **Cedar Dunes Provincial Park.** This is the only functioning lighthouse in Canada that also serves as an inn. Built in 1875 and operated by the Canadian Coast Guard, this is one of The Island's tallest lighthouses, measuring 69 feet (21 m). It now includes a museum and gift shop. The museum holds maps, tools, logbooks, and a collection of other artifacts that recount the story of The Island's lighthouses and the era of sailing. Here you can read about the fascinating characters who ran the light, among them Lighthouse Willie.

There are nine rooms for overnight guests, including one in the lighthouse tower. All guest rooms have private baths, and two have whirlpool baths. The rooms have been decorated to re-create the era of the lightkeepers, with old-fashioned touches and handmade quilts. Considering the incomparable view and the opportunity to fall asleep to the hypnotic lapping of the waves, you

Lighthouse Willie

Lighthouse Willie held the job of lighthouse keeper from 1875 to 1925, never missing one night of work in fifty years. He was the father of eight children and ran a farm 1.5 miles (2 km) away. During the summer the family came to stay at the West Point Lighthouse, and his wife brought a beautiful organ there for entertainment. After passing through many family hands, that organ has been restored to its original lighthouse location.

really ought to call ahead for reservations; call (800) 764–6854 or (902) 859–3605. Rates are moderate. Write for more information to West Point Lighthouse, O'Leary, RR2, PE C0B 1V0, or visit www.westpointlighthouse.com. The lighthouse is located on Route 14. The inn and lighthouse are open from the third weekend in May (the Victoria Day weekend) until the end of September.

This site offers even more. The 1.5-mile (2-km) long white-sand beach at Cedar Dunes Provincial Park is quite lovely and well enough off the beaten path to offer a quiet respite from civilization. The *Cedar Bog* contains a fragile ecosystem that you can explore through guided nature trails and the interpretive program. There is a provincial government campground here, and they loan out recreational equipment.

While visiting the park and lighthouse, you can also satisfy your urge for souvenir collecting at the *West Point Lighthouse Craft Guild,* located to the right of the lighthouse. The shop features work by several local artisans and is open from June through September.

This end of the province has wonderfully pristine fishing villages and presents a wealth of photographic opportunities. The coastal villages, which are particularly appealing, are clustered along the western end, where Irish moss is a big source of income. Fishermen harvest this seaweed, which is then processed for its carrageenan, a substance used in the making of ice cream and other food products. Depending on which way the wind is blowing, you will see the moss being harvested either by boats that skirt the shoreline, by men raking it by hand, or by men using horses to gather it up.

At *Miminegash,* at the intersection of Route 14 and Route 152, you can learn all about the industry in the *Irish Moss Interpretive Centre,* which is fronted by the *Seaweed Pie Cafe.* The interpretive center is open from 10:00 A.M. to 7:00 P.M. daily. Admission is charged. Stop by and have seaweed pie. I'm serious. Eating seaweed pie is like getting your ears pierced: Regardless of how you feel about it at the moment, you'll be happy with the results. More accurately called Irish moss pie, it is something like a custard or cream pie with a graham-cracker crust and a fruit topping. Since the custard is made from the same substance that is used in the manufacture of ice cream, it's really not bad at all. Take note: Unlike the interpretive center, the Seaweed Pie Cafe is open Monday to Saturday from 11:00 A.M. to 7:00 P.M., Sunday from noon to 8:00 P.M. (902–882–4313). If you get out of your car and walk along the coast north of Miminegash, you'll notice men riding along this shoreline on horseback, pulling what looks like a primitive plow. These are Irish-moss harvesters who have switched from the usual method of harvesting on foot. Using horses overcomes the rougher waves and terrain of this end of The Island.

wouldyou believe?

The gathering of Irish moss is a surprisingly lucrative career. One man waiting to unload his truck at the "plant" mentioned that his truckload took four days to gather and was worth $1,800.

The image of The Island is one of pastoral splendor and potato fields, so the terrain at the far western tip of the province is more rugged than most people expect.

If you continue north on Route 14 after Miminegash, you will soon come to a village called **Skinners Pond,** childhood home of folk singing legend Stompin' Tom Connors. Although he was born in Saint John, New Brunswick, he was adopted into the Aylward family of Skinners Pond, P.E.I., where he lived until he started hitchhiking across Canada at age fifteen. Eventually he wrote and recorded twenty albums chronicling this country's common man and his life experience. Stompin' Tom received the Order of Canada, and despite his scanty early education he now holds an Honorary Doctorate of Law degree from St. Thomas University.

His childhood home in Skinners Pond is marked by a guitar-trimmed sign outside the tiny school he attended before hitting the road.

Continue north to the rock reef of The Island's northern tip and the historic **North Cape Lighthouse** at **North Cape.** A wide rock reef extends along the shoreline for 1 mile (1.6 km) offshore; on warm days people will wade around in the shallow water as far back as they can get, trying to take pictures.

You will not be able to enter this functioning lighthouse, but it's still worth dropping by for the view. Just as you drive up to the lighthouse, you may notice the whirligigs to your left. They mark the location of the **Atlantic Wind Test Site.** The twirling structures dotting the heath are gigantic wind turbines that are being tested and evaluated for use in harvesting the wind's energy.

The interpretive center at the North Cape Lighthouse includes a video explaining the work of the wind-power laboratory. Guides will answer questions, but the actual lab is closed to the public. Admission to the center is $2.00, which includes an aquarium where you can see local aquatic species like lobsters and mussels. The center is open from 10:00 A.M. to 6:00 P.M. from mid-May to mid-October. In July and August hours extend from 9:00 A.M. to 8:00 P.M. Upstairs, the **Wind and Reef** restaurant serves delicious (and very fresh) seafood. It is open from late May until the second weekend in October. Sunday to Friday, it's open from 11:30 A.M. to 10:00 P.M., Saturday from 11:30 A.M. to midnight. For a reservation call (902) 882–3535.

From here turn south again, but this time take the left fork onto Route 12, where you will come to some utterly unspoiled fishing villages, including Kildare Capes, Judes Point, Tignish, and Anglo Tignish, as well as the wonderfully uncrowded beaches of Fisherman's Haven and Jacques Cartier Provincial Park. Fisherman's Haven, between Tignish Shore and Kildare Capes, has picnicking facilities.

There are a fine beach and accommodations at **Jacques Cartier Provincial Park.** On a blazing hot day in August, you'll see perhaps a dozen people at this lovely spot. The water is quite warm here, and the atmosphere is low-key.

While in **Tignish** visit the **Parish Church of St. Simon and St. Jude,** which has a large pipe organ dating back to 1882. Its pipes are up to 16 feet (5 m) tall. The church is a large brick building located at the corner of Maple and Church Streets, near the intersection with the highway.

Its chief historical significance lies in the fact that the organ is a product of the first French Canadian school of organ construction. It is the largest of four tracker-action organs built by the famous Louis Mitchell of Montreal. These pipe organs with huge bellows were operated by a team of two men who pumped air during the performance. Control of the organ was achieved with foot pedals. Many of these organs were either altered to electropneumatic instruments or destroyed as modernity and technology cut a swath through tradition. This is the only one of its kind outside Quebec that is still intact. Only after most of these large pipe organs were gone from the face of the earth did musicologists, recalling the era of Bach, begin yearning for a return to a purer form of organ music.

The sound of the pipes is greatly enhanced by the neo-Gothic vaults of the church. Legends abound about the arrival of the organ in such an out-of-the-way community. One such story holds that it arrived by accident, and it was only when it was uncrated on the church lawn that a decision was made to keep it. Its assembly cost $2,400 at the time. Today it is considered priceless because of its historical significance, but its projected replacement cost is estimated at roughly $100,000.

You can indulge your passion for sublime music if you happen to be in the neighborhood on a Sunday. There are occasional concerts at other times as well. Because there is not always someone available at the church, you can check concert times by calling the parish house at (902) 882–2049.

Just behind this church is a bed-and-breakfast that was once a convent. It is now called the *Tignish Heritage Inn.* There is lots of space for travelers. Although this one-time nun's cloister was built in 1868, it has been considerably revamped; seventeen rooms have their own private bath and shower.

The convent was built so that nuns from Montreal could come and teach in the area. It became a residence for the nuns and was the site of instruction until 1966. It was then used purely as a residence for the sisters until it closed its doors in 1991. When it was taken over in 1993 by a nonprofit group called Tignish Initiatives, careful attention was paid to the preservation of the original structure. Organizers received a 1994 Architectural Preservation Award from the board of governors of the Prince Edward Island Museum and Heritage Foundation. Rates are moderate, with a continental breakfast included. For information or to reserve a spot, call (902) 882–2491 or write to P.O. Box 398, Tignish, PE C0B 2B0.

Just south of Jacques Cartier Provincial Park is *Alberton,* the one-time western terminus of The Island's defunct railway, now reborn as the Confederation Trail. From here you can take a deep-sea fishing trip for a reasonable fee. There are numerous boats for hire on The Island. In Alberton try *Andrew's Mist Deep-Sea Fishing,* which is government-inspected. It is operated by Captain Craig Avery. Equipment is supplied free; you get to keep your cleaned, filleted, and bagged catch. For more information call (902) 853–2307.

trivia

In World War I Canadian soldiers fought alongside the British. The first Allied pilot to shoot down one of Germany's bombers was Wendell W. Rogers, a native of Alberton, P.E.I.

Apart from potatoes and fictional heroines, the rolling green farmland and deep-red soil of P.E.I. have also given birth to a number of excellent golf courses. These are affordable, accessible, and a big hit with visitors and residents alike.

A number of championships have been held on The Island's golf courses. According to *Golf Digest,* the most challenging course in Atlantic Canada is the *Mill River Golf Course.* It was the site of the 1994 Canadian Women's Championship. It was also a stop for the 1997 Canadian Pro Tour, Prince Edward Island Montclair classic. Mill River Golf Course is ranked among the top one hundred public and resort courses in Canada. You can reach it from Alberton by turning south on Route 12 and exiting to Highway 136 south.

Bounded by beautiful stands of hardwoods and spruce, this course features a series of spring-fed ponds down the eighth fairway. Golfers who goof and get their ball in the water are invited to take a drink of the spring water. You can book ahead at (800) 235–8909 or (902) 859–8873.

Mill River Golf Course is near a Scenic Heritage Road. When you exit the golf course onto Highway 136 east, travel to Fortune Cove. Here you can take the clay Heritage Road by turning right and driving southeast until you reach Highway 142. At this junction, turn left and drive east.

You can't be on Prince Edward Island without paying homage to the potato, which grows so well in The Island's rich red soil. If you are interested enough in the Garden Province's sustaining crop, turn right instead of left at the Highway 142 junction and drive for about twenty minutes down Highway 142 until you reach *O'Leary,* home of the ***Prince Edward Island Potato Museum.*** It holds a unique collection of antique farm machinery, a community museum, and an authentic one-room school, as well as interactive displays and a sculpture of a giant potato. Admission is $5.00 per person, $12.00 for a family. Visit its Web site at www.peipotatomuseum.com

Skirting Malpeque Bay

At the time of the European settlement of Prince Edward Island, the Mi'Kmaq of the area were nomadic, hunting game and fishing over a wide range. They settled for only short periods of time in any one area, as the seasons dictated. The white settlers, on the other hand, set about clearing the land and divided it up into lots for farming, establishing a system of ownership completely foreign to the Mi'Kmaq. As more land was cleared and fences built, the population of wild animals diminished. The Mi'Kmaq way of life was imperiled.

Finally, Sir James Montgomery, a wealthy British landlord, gave them the use of *Lennox Island* rent-free. By 1800 a missionary had persuaded some of them to live year-round on the island. Seventy years later, after much petitioning of the government and several attempts to resolve the land issue, Lennox Island was purchased for the Mi'Kmaqs. It lies just north of Route 12. You can visit the Band Council Complex on Lennox Island to get an idea of the history of the fifty or so families who still make Lennox Island their home. This band was the first in Canada to convert to Christianity. These indigenous people have just started giving a mixture of light to in-depth exposures to their culture, including traditional food, craft demonstrations, and adventure tourism and eco-tourism information. The area features showers and facilities for weary hikers. Admission is $2.00. It is open year-round; summer hours are Monday to Saturday from 10:00 A.M. to 6:00 P.M. On Sundays, it opens at noon. Off-season hours are by appointment. For details, call (866) 831–2702 or (902) 831–2702.

Lennox Island also offers a twenty-four-hour sea kayaking adventure that includes a paddle to a secluded beach, where you set up camp and eat a delicious dinner. Afterward, the beach is yours! The next day you explore the shallow waters and natural scenery of the gulf and bay side of Hog Island. Guides provide the kayaking instruction and safety and comfort gear as well as a delicious breakfast and dinner (including P.E.I. jams, bread, cheeses, and local oysters, mussels, or lobster). Tours depart and return at noon. Advance booking is advised. Contact Mi'kmaq Kayak Adventures at (877) 500–3131 or (902) 831–3131. Cost is $370. There is also a small craft shop.

If you continue driving east on Route 12 along Malpeque Bay, you will see an exit to a secondary road, Route 167. Take this exit and you will soon reach a beautiful, pastoral little village called **Tyne Valley,** population 200.

Here you will find **The Doctor's Inn and Organic Market Garden,** operated by Paul and Jean Offer. The "inn" part of the place is a bed-and-breakfast establishment, making use of the charming former home of the village doctor, built in 1860.

For the environmentally conscious, the Offers provide a number of activities, from gardening to gourmet meals. One of their most popular features is a five-hour workshop on the cultivation and use of organic herbs, the intricacies of organic gardening, composting, and safe and effective insect control.

Nonguests may dine by reservation, with meals a mix of health-conscious, international, and classical cuisine. Although the menu choices are limited, the restaurant has been recommended in a number of national publications. Paul and Jean Offer say, "The gardens provide most of the items for our dinners and also guarantee the freshness we have become noted for." They are open year-round. It's a small place, so try to book ahead by calling (902) 831–3057, or check the Web site at www.peisland.com/doctorsinn. Rates are standard.

If you aren't up to a five-hour workshop, opt for a free informal tour of the two-acre market garden. Organized tours are set for 1:00 P.M. Sunday and Wednesday, from late June to September. If you roam around in the garden, take note of the red "balls" on the fruit trees; these are highly effective sticky insect traps that eliminate the need for bug spray.

While in this charming little hamlet, be sure to check out **Shoreline Sweaters Lobster Pattern,** just a minute's drive farther down Route 12. This is the birthplace of P.E.I.'s answer to the Fair Isle sweater: The copyrighted motif features stylized lobsters on pure Island-spun handcrafted wool.

The results are charming and subtle. Designer Lesley Dubey has often had to point out the lobsters in the complex motif, variations of which are found in cardigans, crew necks, and shawl-collar pullovers. "Once people realize it's really a little lobster, they really like it more than if it was a big lobster sprawled across their back or chest."

The cardigans are graced with pewter buttons decorated with little lobsters. Other creations include sweaters with lady's-slipper and lupine designs.

The shop also sells other craft items, including weavings, baskets, and their own wildflower honey. Dubey says, "We keep bees and have customers who spend summers here, then come and get a supply to take home." The nectars are gathered by "overwintered" bees, which make their honey from the profusion of wildflowers that make Tyne Valley particularly idyllic. Call (902) 831–2950.

Leaving Tyne Valley via Route 12, you will be skirting *Malpeque Bay,* with its many fishing communities. If you continue along Blue Heron Drive, you will soon find yourself at the far eastern end of the bay, at a fork in the road and the village of *Kensington.* From here you have the option of visiting gardens or large-scale models of castles, or backtracking and visiting both. There are also a fine beach and campground at the mouth of Malpeque Bay.

If you take Route 101 to Burlington and then turn right onto Route 234, you will come to *Woodleigh Replicas and Gardens.* Large-scale replicas of castles provide hours of fun in the middle of the countryside. Walk amid small versions of York Minster Cathedral, Scotland's Dunvegan Castle, and the Tower of London and never get out of breath. These replicas reach the height of an NBA basketball star and cover a thirty-three-acre (thirteen-hectare) country garden setting. Some of the little castles have interesting replicas inside. The Tower of London portion, for example, which comprises several of the towers where the famous and infamous were kept in dungeons, also houses a set of "crown jewels." The chopping block where two of Henry VIII's wives lost their heads is reproduced outside.

Colonel Ernest Johnstone, the gentleman who built these replicas as a retirement project, passed away in his eighties, just five years after he completed the "Temple of Flora," which opens on the gardens. Woodleigh is now more than forty-five years old and sufficiently successful that it has spawned the creation of another family venture: The *Kensington Towers and Water Gardens,* in nearby Kensington. Admission to Woodleigh Replicas is $8.50 for adults, $8.00 for seniors, $7.00 for youths, and $4.50 for schoolchildren. Call (902) 836–3401.

Just in front of Woodleigh, you will see a marking for a Scenic Heritage Road. This is Millman Road, which is a handy shortcut to Route 20, also known as Blue Heron Drive.

Farther along Blue Heron Drive, you'll come to Malpeque itself and then to *Cabot Beach Provincial Park.* The park has small beaches and is far enough off the tourist trail that it is a pleasant spot for camping. Its two quiet campgrounds are far from the madding crowd that congregates during the tourist high season at Cavendish. These red-sand beaches are opposite each other across a sheltered bay and offer warm water and an unhurried rest only a few miles north of Summerside. The beaches—indeed, the entire shoreline— have a shelf of hard clay upon which bathers can walk from beach to beach, pausing along the way at sheltered spots where the water is bathtub-warm.

This was the location for the filming of the popular Canadian television series *Emily of New Moon.* Part of the filming required a schoolhouse, so the former Fanning School, built in 1794 and named after Governor Fanning, was restored and moved to Cabot Beach. Unique because it was a two-story school-house, the building remains in Cabot Beach's day-use area. It's open daily 10:00 A.M. to sunset during the summer.

Because they are both small campgrounds, it is advisable to book in advance, especially during the high season. For information call (902) 836–4142 for Twin Shores, (902) 836–8945 for Cabot Beach.

Anne's Land

Past Darnley Basin and headed east you will soon come to **Park Corner,** still on Route 20. Several sites in this village recall The Island's famous author, but in a sedate way as compared with the tourist draw near Lucy Maud Mont-gomery's fabled home in Cavendish. These sites are less hectic alternatives if you happen to be an Anne fan.

The first one that you will come to is the **Anne of Green Gables Museum at Silver Bush.** Silver Bush (so named by Montgomery) was the home of the writer's aunt and was built in 1872. The place remains much as it was in Montgomery's time. Because the author was married in the parlor, young Japanese couples often arrange with the owner to tie the knot here, but otherwise the house is not a slick, professionally assembled museum but, rather, a cozy old home. There is a little tearoom for visitors as well as wagon rides on-site. When you peek at the lovely old bedsteads and furnishings, it isn't hard to understand why Montgomery said her ideal home would be an exact duplicate of this.

The farmhouse overlooks the pond for which she coined the name "The Lake of Shining Waters." A small admission is charged. Open daily in July and August from 9:00 A.M. to 5:30 P.M., it closes a half hour earlier in June and September. October hours are 10:00 A.M. to 4:00 P.M. For details, or to ask about group rates, call (800) 665–2663. You can also visit the Anne of Green Gables Society at www.annesociety.org.

After you leave this museum, the little pond will be on your left. Just after passing over a little stream, you will come to the next Anne site.

The *Lucy Maud Montgomery Heritage Museum* was the home of Montgomery's grandfather, an Island senator. Still owned by the family, the house has been turned into an "attraction." It holds many family heirlooms and is largely unchanged since the time of the author's frequent visits, which she wrote about in her journals. Admission is charged. Call (902) 886–2807 or (902) 886–2752 for more information.

Just after passing Park Corner and continuing along Route 20, you will come to *French River,* a picturesque fishing community overlooking New London Bay. Apart from the photographic possibilities, you are directly across the water from Prince Edward Island National Park, which comprises several seemingly endless beaches, and the majority of the sites relating to Anne of Green Gables.

A small village called *Stanley Bridge* is a good place to stay if you want to visit the Cavendish area. Located at the junction of Routes 6, 224, and 254, the village is a mere 5 miles (8 km) west of Cavendish. Here you will find the cottages and country inn of *Stanley Bridge Country Resort.*

worthseeing

Certainly not off the beaten path is a visit to the birthplace of **Lucy Maud Montgomery,** beloved author of the *Anne of Green Gables* books. The cozy white-and-green Victorian house overlooks New London Harbour. The period decor and furnishings include memorabilia and scrapbooks from the author's life. Her wedding dress is also on display. She is so esteemed by the Japanese that thousands make a pilgrimage to this cultural icon's birthplace annually. The house is found at the intersection of Routes 6 and 20. Open daily from mid-May to Thanksgiving. A small admission is charged.

All the cottages as well as a completely renovated motel have been constructed from lumber cut from the owners' woodlot, with rustic pine walls and floors and cathedral ceilings in an open-beam country style. Offering such amenities as hot tubs and two playgrounds for children, owners warn visitors to book as far ahead as January for weeklong stays. Rates are moderate to deluxe. Write to the resort at Route 6, PE C0B 1M0. For information call (902) 886–2882; for reservations, call (800) 361–2882.

In the resort complex you will find *Stanley Bridge Antiques, Gifts & Gallery,* a good bet for locally made quilts as well as reproduction tin lighting, pewter, hand-forged iron, and other collectibles that can help to create a country-style decor in a house.

P.E.I.'s Scenic Heritage Drives

So-called **Scenic Heritage Roads** dot the province and are a good opportunity to experience the old Prince Edward Island. The clay roads are generally covered with a canopy of trees casting shade across the unspoiled beauty of farmlands that ramble down to the water. You'll have views of old farmhouses and barns, paint fading and cracking off, and herds of grazing dairy cows. Some fields are carefully laid out in row after row of potato plants. It's like time travel. This is the land that Lucy Maud Montgomery wrote about so lovingly in Anne of Green Gables.

These roads are best traveled after a brief spell of rain, when they're not too wet to turn into mud yet not so dry as to be a dust bowl.

Near Mill River Resort, along Route 136, you will find a scenic drive called the John Joe Road or the Hackney Road. It is bordered by fields of grain and potatoes alternated with woodland to create a habitat much beloved by the gray partridge and the ruffed grouse.

It runs about 1.5 miles (2.2 km) south from Route 136 until it meets Kelly Road, also known as Route 142. Before 1912 this was a cart track that led to a homestead in the woods. Near its southern end you will find traces of an old stagecoach route.

On this end of The Island, the eatery with the reputation for the freshest fish is the **New London Seafood Restaurant.** Situated right on the wharf in New London, it gives new meaning to the phrase "catch of the day." It's a huge place, with a seating capacity of one hundred. Two full walls of windows yield a spectacular view of the bay, featuring the comings and goings of the local fishing fleet and pleasure boats. Owners Linda and Roger Cole run this family-style restaurant.

This area is noted for its Island blue cultured mussels as well as Malpeque oysters, which are exported worldwide. The chowders in this end of the country are delicious and reasonably priced. The restaurant also has a traditional lobster dinner. These dinners include potato salad, either seafood chowder or mussels, rolls, and homemade pie. Lobsters also find their way into sandwiches and salad rolls. The restaurant is open from early June until early October. To reserve, phone (902) 886–3000.

Two antiques shops are also in the neighborhood. On Route 238, off Route 6, you will find **Linden Cove Antiques.** The shop specializes in high-quality mahogany, walnut, and oak furniture and tableware.

If you are interested in looking at or buying a painting by a local or regional artist, an excellent selection can be found at **The Dunes Studio Gallery,** overlooking Brackley Beach on Route 15 just 11 miles (18 km) north of Charlottetown. The gallery features a wide selection of art from seventy contributing artisans, and the original building consists of virtually all windows and a spiral staircase leading to marvelous views of its lush water gardens. Always a delight architecturally, this contemporary masterpiece has now been expanded so that it can include a larger selection of chic household goods and furniture suitable for modernist and eclectic bohemian tastes alike. Many of these are designed and created under the owner's direction while he winters in Bali. Be sure to check out the wonderful collection of glass by Glassroots and artist Susan Higgins. The new annex at the Dunes also markets unique artwork collected in Indonesia.

The works of many prominent provincial artists, as well as some regional and other Canadian artists, are well represented here. Works include The Island's most high-end paintings, pottery, crafts, sculptures, photographs, and prints. The Dunes has a cafe, a roof garden, a fourth-floor lookout, and a private dining room that can seat up to one hundred. It opens for the summer in early May until mid-October; hours are 9:00 A.M. until 5:00 P.M., plus evenings in the summer. The on-site cafe has great fare available from June to September. To confirm hours, call (902) 672–2586.

The Dunes Studio Gallery carries other island delights as well, including marvelous soaps made locally by Moonsnail Soapworks. My personal favorite is a soap called Spiced Almond Swirl, which gives off the delicious aroma of a cinnamon cookie. Moonsnail Soaps (all twenty-five varieties) are also sold in Charlottetown at **Luna Eclectic Crafts and Gifts,** a trendy shop a stone's throw from the Confederation Centre of the Arts at 138 Richmond Street, and at **Moonsnail Soapworks and Nature Store,** opposite the Delta Hotel at 85 Water Street. Both affiliated shops have great economical, easy-to-pack gifts to take back home.

The North Shore and Charlottetown

To bypass the most heavily visited end of Prince Edward Island National Park near Cavendish but still sample The Island's best beaches, continue east along the coastal route until you reach **Dalvay by-the-Sea.** This is a small, intimate, and charming establishment at the far eastern end of the park, a short drive from the park's eastern gateway. Dalvay overlooks Tracadie Bay and is reached by a left turn after Grand Tracadie.

At the end of the nineteenth century people from other parts of the country discovered Prince Edward Island's unique charms and the opportunity it offered to get away from it all. Some wealthy families built large summer homes here. Dalvay by-the-Sea, built in 1895, is the most notable of these homes. It was originally the home of a U.S. citizen and president of Standard Oil Company, born in Scotland, who found in Dalvay the perfect home away from home. He therefore named it for his birthplace. The home eventually changed hands several times and became a hotel.

Along with the calm atmosphere and lovely vista, Dalvay boasts an excellent restaurant. Executive chef Andrew Morrison was named P.E.I.'s chef of the year for 2006, and is also the manager of the province's Competitive Culinary Team. (Teams of this sort compete internationally for Olympic-style honors.) His signature dish is pumpkinseed-crusted Atlantic salmon with cumin and chili. The Heritage hotel's pastry chef, Megan Burge, creates her own brand of temptation in the form of sticky date pudding with warm toffee sauce.

There are also canoes and croquet sets, big old-fashioned bathtubs, and the massive stone hearths of half a dozen fireplaces at Dalvay.

Fans of the television show *The Road to Avonlea* will recognize the Dalvay, on which it is depicted as the White Sands Hotel. This Victorian hotel is unquestionably one of the most elegant country inns on all the east coast of Canada. Reserve rooms by writing to D. Thompson, Box 8, Little York, PE C0A 1P0 or by calling (902) 672–2048. Rates are deluxe.

From Dalvay you have the choice of cutting across the province to Charlottetown or continuing east to the more remote fishing villages and beaches of the far eastern end of The Island. Traveling from Dalvay to Charlottetown is a simple matter. Get onto Route 6 and drive in the direction of Bedford. Just after Bedford turn right onto Route 2 and continue on into Charlottetown.

Charlottetown may be the provincial capital, but it is a far cry from a big city. Its streets were so narrow in the early part of this century that when cars came on the scene, they were banned from the entire province in 1913. This law was not repealed until 1919.

Charlottetown is a relaxed little place that played a starring role in the founding of Canada, since it was the site of the first conference on Confederation in 1864. (P.E.I. opted out of joining when Confederation took place in 1867, joining later, in 1873.)

A good point of departure for your Charlottetown meanderings is **Founder's Hall,** the lobby of which has been taken over by the provincial department of tourism, great for booking tickets or rooms or walking tours of the city's pretty downtown core. Founder's Hall also has an Internet cafe for checking e-mail. Founder's Hall features a time-travel tunnel that leads visitors through the history of Confederation from 1864 until the present day. Located at 6 Prince Street, it is also a stone's throw from the Lower Prince Street Wharf, which is the departure point for the ***Harbour Hippo.*** This amphibious vehicle is an unusual way to discover the discreet charms of Charlottetown's bourgeoisie, followed by a scenic cruise around Charlottetown harbor.

The town is a good starting point for a cycle tour of the province. For rentals and advice, visit Gordon MacQueen at 430 Queen Street, Charlottetown, PE C1A 4E8. As the proprietor of *MacQueen's Bike Shop,* he can also arrange for on-road service. For reservations or a brochure, call (800) WOW–CUBA (969–2822) or (902) 368–2453. The shop and touring company has a detailed Web site that outlines a variety of bike touring resources on The Island for either the independent cycle tourist or for groups desiring more support. In the off-season, the shop's experienced guides offer trips to other exotic locales like Cuba and Sicily. Visit www.macqueens.com.

While in Charlottetown you can engage in a little time travel by visiting *Beaconsfield Historic House,* which is in the city's poshest neighborhood. This museum overlooks the harbor and the lieutenant governor's residence, *Government House.* Beaconsville is located at 2 Kent Street; you may find yourself driving around in circles if you don't hang a right after Richmond Street, thereby avoiding several one-way streets.

The home was built by a shipbuilder in 1877 at a cost of $50,000, at a time when decent annual salaries averaged $300. The three-and-a-half-story home features a double drawing room, nine decorative fireplaces, gaslight, and central heating. Faced with financial ruin after five short years, the original owner moved on.

Some of the original owner's creditors took it over, and when they couldn't sell it, they moved in. The new residents, the Cundalls, were a sober and dour lot. None of them married, and in 1916, when the last of them died, the home was turned into a "home for friendless young women," where they could get training in "useful arts." By 1935 it had become a student nurses' residence.

Beaconsfield Historic House

Charlottetown's Historic Homes

Charlottetown's many Georgian, Queen Anne Revival, and Victorian buildings add to the town's charm. Among the more interesting houses are:

Beaconsfield Historic House, at 2 Kent Street (902–366–6603). This three-and-a-half-story house was built in 1877.

Government House, on the grounds of Victoria Park, at the corner of Pond Road and Park Roadway (no phone number available). Built in 1834, Government House is the home of the lieutenant governor, who acts as a representative of the queen. The house is open to the public only during the annual New Year's levee.

Province House, at the corner of Richmond and Saint George Streets (902–566–7626). It is here that you will find the provincial government, when it is in session. The house's Confederation Chamber is where in 1864 the Fathers of Confederation discussed the possibility of the British North American colonies joining together to form the Dominion of Canada. Three years later Nova Scotia, New Brunswick, Ontario, and Quebec did join together, but P.E.I. did not.

Ardgowan National Historic Site, at 2 Palmers Lane (902–566–7050). When the delegates were finished at Province House, they gathered for a grand reception at the home of fellow politician William Henry Pope at what is now known as Ardgowan National Historic Site. The home's Victorian-style grounds have been restored to illustrate the style of the 1860s.

In the mid-1970s Beaconsfield became the headquarters of the Prince Edward Island Museum and Heritage Foundation. The home is restored to the era when it was a private home, with period furniture and careful renovations. Even the little nursery is laid out as if the children had just been called away to supper.

Take a moment to look over the floor in the main hallway, made of painstakingly hand-laid tiles in an intricate mosaic pattern. The base of the spiral staircase has an original classic Greco-Roman statue lamp, converted from gas to electric. If you climb the stairs to the top, you can enter "the belvedere," an elegant enclosed lookout that offers beautiful views. Admission is charged.

Every Friday during the summer there is an excellent *ceilidh,* or Gaelic party, at the *Irish Hall,* at 582 North River Road, featuring traditional Celtic song and dance by The Island's best traditional performers. This is a bargain at only $8.00 admission for adults, $3.00 for children younger than twelve. Music plays from 8:00 P.M. to 10:30 P.M. For details call (902) 892–2367.

Charlottetown is such a charming place that you could easily spend days just soaking up the relaxed but trendy atmosphere of the well-tended downtown core. A great way to experience it is by staying in the Nationally Designated Historical District, at **The Great George.** This is actually a series of thirteen Heritage buildings converted into a four-and-a-half-star boutique hotel and fronting on Great George Street and a neighboring street. Beautifully restored, with lots of elegant touches, Island antiques, and artwork, the bedrooms feature working gas fireplaces and Jacuzzi or claw-foot tubs, among other amenities. It is also possible to rent out an entire building, containing several bedrooms and its own kitchen, making it a great home away from home for a small group or large family on holiday, for example. Another building in the complex is the restored Pavilion Hotel, which hosted delegates at the 1864 Charlottetown Conference. Every evening drinks are served in the cozy Pavilion lobby. Scrumptious complimentary "Season's Best" breakfasts and quiet verandahs complete the experience. Since each of the fifty-four bedrooms are unique in character, it's a good idea to check out detailed descriptions of each at www.thegreatgeorge.com. The main lobby, at 58 Great George Street, is less than five minutes' walk from the Confederation Centre of the Arts. Packages are available that include dining at **Off Broadway**, an affiliated restaurant. Prices are deluxe. To reserve, call (800) 361–1118 or (902) 829–0606.

Also in Charlottetown is the much-loved **Confederation Centre of the Arts.** In 2005, the production of *Anne of Green Gables* completed its fortieth year of successful performances. It is the must-see show of The Island, quite possibly of the Maritimes.

Here you can also take in a free show of the young performers-in-training, at the outdoor amphitheater at noon in the summer. Other performances take place at 5:00 P.M. The Young Company presents shows attended by more than 1,000 spectators at times. Seating is on steplike benches and on the ground, so bring a pillow, blanket, or chair if you wish. Many of the young people in these shows end up with careers in the performing arts, so it's a good opportunity to see them in their fledgling roles. For details, call (800) 565–0278 within the Maritimes or (902) 566–1267; or write to 145 Richmond Street, Charlottetown, PE C1A 1J1.

The Confederation Centre of the Arts also houses the largest art gallery and museum east of Montreal, with more than 15,000 works in the permanent collection. To find the complex, head to downtown Charlottetown via Queen Street. From there turn left onto Richmond Street, a block before the harbor. It is wheelchair accessible.

Charlottetown's lovely **Victoria Park** is only a short walk away from the heart of downtown. It features a beautiful boardwalk along the riverside, some interior footpaths (of deep red clay), and a nice set of public tennis courts. The poshest houses are found in this end of town, among them **The Shipwright**

Inn. This is an award-winning five-star bed-and-breakfast established in a Heritage house, located on tree-shaded Fitzroy Street. This was originally a home built in 1865 by James Phillips Douse, a local shipbuilder. The house is timber framed in a manner typical of Island homes of that era, sometimes referred to as a Maritime Vernacular Cottage or The Green Gables style. Rates are deluxe. Reservations can be made by calling (888) 306–9966 or (902) 368–1905.

If you decided to pass up Charlottetown for more rural delights, or if you wanted to save the capital until you've worked your way fully around the island, exit Dalvay onto Route 6, but then turn left onto Route 2. (You will still take this route if you head east from Charlottetown.)

Following Route 2, you will steadily drive uphill until you come to *Mount Stewart.*

Mount Stewart is the perfect spot for sampling a bit of the Confederation Trail, the multiuse railroad bed turned trail stretching from one tip of The Island to the other. The trails are 10 feet (3 m) wide and are surfaced with stone dust. They accommodate walkers, bicycles, and even wheelchairs. Along this segment of the trail, three bridges span rivers and estuaries and skirt the north shore's pristine St. Peters Bay.

At Mount Stewart you can rent bikes or, to ease bike-touring stress, take advantage of a shuttle service operated by *Trailside Adventures.*

Trailside Adventures also operates an outdoor adventure shop, a small cafe, and overnight accommodations in a Heritage-style inn. Guidebooks and maps are also on sale here. You can find them on Route 22, off Route 2. The street address is 109 Main Street, Mount Stewart. Trailside Adventures is open from June to mid-September and off-season by appointment, according to owner Doug Deacon. He advises that since cycle tours are so weather dependent, summertime cyclists should make their arrangements when they arrive. On a recent night every room in Deacon's inn was rented to a cyclist. Deacon can make rental deals for his guests, or shuttle luggage to other inns, and connect you to a canoe rental off-site, so a number of adventures await. For details or reservations call (888) 704–6595 or (902) 676–3130, or visit www.trailside.ca.

The *Trailside Inn and Cafe* has also become a venue for live musical performances by many noted Canadian artists. Check the Trailside Inn's Web site for dates and times.

Still on Route 2, in the midst of Mount Stewart, you will come to St. Peters Road. Take a right turn onto this road and drive another 2 miles (3.2 km) to the small community of *St. Andrews,* where you'll see a sign designating the *Bishop MacEachern National Historic Site.* This is where you will find the "Little Church that's Been to Town and Back," a historic chapel built in 1803.

St. Andrews Chapel was built by the Scottish settlers who had immigrated in 1772. It was the first major church on The Island, but by 1862 it was aban-

St. Andrews Chapel

doned in favor of a larger building. Two years later the congregation embarked on a strange undertaking. With the help of 500 men and fifty teams of horses, the old church was placed on runners and hoisted onto a frozen river to be transported down to Charlottetown. As the little church approached the thin ice of the channel, disaster struck. The building crashed through the ice. With considerable effort the church was dragged out of the water and landed on Pownal Street. There it served as a girls' school for more than one hundred years.

The church was returned to the village in 1990, following a fire that destroyed some additions but left much of the original structure intact. To achieve this second move, the building was cut into four pieces and mounted on a flatbed truck. Now back in its former home, the fully restored church is a fine example of eighteenth-century Georgian architecture, which at the time of the church's original construction was much in use by the early settlers from England and Scotland.

The round-headed windows on the building were discovered during the restoration and refurbishing that followed the near-destruction of the little church by fire in 1987.

The church is designated the Bishop MacEachern National Historic Site because it shares its site with the mausoleum of the revered Bishop MacEachern, who oversaw its original construction in 1803. As a young priest Father MacEachern proved his mettle by ministering to a flock that spread as far afield as New Brunswick. To cover his vast territory on the rudimentary roads, he resorted to snowshoes, skates, horseback, and, finally, a vehicle that combined the features of carriage, boat, and sled. This unusual conveyance can still be found at *St. Joseph's Convent* in Charlottetown.

The Friends of St. Andrews is a community group that administers the restored church. Concerts are held here from time to time, so it is a good idea to ask about upcoming events at the reception desk.

Retrace your steps 2 miles along St. Peters Road and rejoin Route 2 headed east, which will take you along the north shore.

Although the eastern end of the province is not geared up for large numbers of tourists, there are some nice campgrounds and charming lodges and inns, close to deep-sea-fishing opportunities and golf courses. Two places come to mind; they both have standard to moderate rates (the higher prices are for suites with kitchens or for cottages) and offer golf packages. One is *Greenwich Gate Lodge,* in the community of Greenwich, on the north shore of the island on Route 2, overlooking St. Peters Bay. You can reach them at (877) 961–3496, or check out their Web site, www.greenwichgate.com. Six golf courses are in easy reach from Greenwich (roughly fifteen to twenty-five minutes' drive to the greens). This includes the wonderful Links at Crowbush Cove, Canada's only five-star public golf course.

The other nice place to stay in this end of The Island is the *Rollo Bay Inn,* which is on the southern coast, two and a half miles (4 km) west of Souris, at the juncture of Route 330 and Route 2. Since The Island is fairly narrow at this point, that's not as far away from the golf courses as you'd think (twenty minutes to a half hour in the car will get you to the Links at Crowbush Cove). The Rollo Bay Inn is only two minutes' drive to the Rollo Bay Greens (a nine-hole course), and is a prime location to enjoy the Rollo Bay Fiddle Festival, held the third weekend in July. Fiddlers come from all over the region for this fun event. Reserve a room at Rollo Bay Inn by calling (877) 687–3550. You can also check out their features online at www.peisland.com/rollobayinn.

Along with quiet walks through the fields and woods, you have the opportunity in this area to go on a deep-sea-fishing charter. Just after St. Peters Bay, a few miles up the coast, is a cozy little harbor, *Naufrage,* which is French for "shipwreck." It is a rustic harbor, complete with picturesque cliffs and lighthouse, a tiny river flowing through the middle of the cove, and a sandy beach.

There are a number of options for fishing in this end of The Island. At *North Lake* are several charter operations: One is *MacNeill's Tuna and Deep-Sea Fishing* at (902) 357–2858.

Some tours charge as little as $25 per person and half price for kids for a simple deep-sea excursion. Paying for a tuna-fishing trip can be a bit like buying a lottery ticket. A full eight-hour tuna-boat charter can run $750. But, if you land a bluefin tuna on MacNeill's boat, you don't pay a cent. Then again, let's see you pack a tuna into your suitcase.

If you decide to use North Lake as your point of departure for a fishing expedition, you may prefer to stay in St. Peters Bay.

Where the Tides Meet

Continuing along the coast on Route 16, turn left at East Point and drive a short distance to the easternmost point of The Island and the 64-foot (19.5-m) *East Point Lighthouse.* Energetic visitors who opt to climb to the top will be rewarded with a view of the swirling tides as the waves from the Northumberland Strait meet and crash against the surf of the Gulf of Saint Lawrence. Ask the guides for the lowdown on what to look for before you take the climb.

The building that originally held the fog alarm and radio equipment has now been turned into a small shop featuring an excellent selection of regional books and Island-made crafts, including Island-made woolen garments using wool from local sheep. The small canteen makes a good bird-watching pit stop. You can indulge in a cup of coffee and then stretch out and watch cormorants dive for fish while seals loll about the shore.

The coastline here has been so heavily eroded by the action of the waves that the lighthouse has been moved twice, including after the shipwreck of a British warship. This lighthouse was built in 1867 and is one of the oldest on The Island. Admission is charged. For details call (902) 357–2106.

After viewing the lighthouse, head back to East Point. Take a left turn onto Route 16 southbound.

At South Lake is the junction of Route 16A. At this point turn right to drive to *Elmira* to visit the *Elmira Railway Museum.*

The museum is located next to the end point of the *Confederation Trail,* converted from the railroad line when train service was shut down on The Island. The portion in this area was the section chosen for the pilot project. All along this beautiful nature trail are rest stops in converted train stations. The rustic entranceway to the trail is just to your right as you approach the Elmira Railway Museum's reception center. You can rent bicycles at the museum.

The museum is set in the eastern terminus of the railway. Finished in 1912, it was the last station built. It has telegraph equipment that is still in working condition; there are also fare books, schedules, and artifacts from days gone by. The station office looks exactly as it must have looked when the railway was still being run in the British Colonial tradition: Gentlemen and ladies had separate waiting rooms because, the guide explains, "The men would spit into the spittoons and curse and shock the ladies." After Canadian National took over, separate waiting rooms became a thing of the past, and ladies were free to be as shocked as they pleased. A small admission is charged.

From here turn back onto Route 16A, then right onto Route 16, and continue driving south toward *Basin Head.* This is a great spot for photography buffs and bird-watchers. The area boasts the *Basin Head Fisheries Museum* (902–357–7233), constructed on a headland overlooking one of The Island's

Touring P.E.I. on Two Wheels

Why is bicycling so popular on Prince Edward Island? Because it is almost impossible to find a more ideal place for this mode of travel. On the Confederation Trail, the original railway builders avoided the high cost of cutting through hills and valleys by winding the track around such annoyances instead. The result is a really smooth trail ride that yields abundant natural beauty and a stunning view around every corner. And all you need are a moderate level of skill and muscle power, unless you are trying to set speed records.

Distances from one community or amenity to the next are short. Every few miles, cyclists will discover a coffee shop, tearoom, antiques shop, bed-and-breakfast, or even a bicycle repair shop. Traffic is nonexistent. The climate is mild, which is ideal for outdoor activity. And, more important than anything for lazy cyclists such as myself, it's not very hilly. When it comes to biking, you can't beat P.E.I.

finest white-sand beaches. The sand here is so pure that it squeaks when you walk on it. The main beach is popular; however, a five-minute walk south, along the beach, takes you to miles of blissfully secluded sands.

The museum depicts the transition of Prince Edward Island's inshore fishery. By now you will have noticed the large number of "farmed mussels" on The Island; aquaculture has grown into a thriving segment of P.E.I.'s fishery. Here you can also tour a one-time fish cannery that now houses a coastal exhibit.

The museum is open from mid-June to late September. In July and August it is open daily from 9:00 A.M. to 5:00 P.M. In other months, times vary. A small admission is charged.

After Basin Head you will head south in the direction of *Souris.* If time allows and you feel like a country walk, you can take in a Heritage Scenic Road—one of The Island's prettiest—by making a small detour. To do this, when you reach Little Harbour, turn right off Route 16 onto Route 303, also known as the New Harmony Road. From there continue to Greenvale.

A small clay road connects Greenvale Road to the Tarantum Road (also known as Route 304) for a distance of about 1 mile (1.6 km). Sunlight peeks through a lush canopy, created by a mixture of hardwoods and softwoods, and falls on the brilliant green of thick vegetation and the hardened clay of the old road. On the eastern side of this road, the Provincial Department of Energy and Forestry operates a demonstration woodlot that is open to the public.

During Prohibition years the isolation of the canopied road made it a favorite haunt of rum runners, who used the area to stash illegal cargo.

Souris is also the ferry terminal for the boat to the Magdalen Islands, so the town always has a flow of visitors passing through during the summer. Incidentally, the name Souris comes from the French word for "mouse." In the early to mid-1700s, plagues of field mice overran the settlement, giving the place its unusual name.

A nice place to stay in Souris is *The Matthew House Inn,* which features Victorian art and furniture, and several fireplaces (nice for cozy breakfasts). The spacious Victorian inn was once the home of Uriah Matthew, a partner in Matthew, McLean, and Company, which operated the village's general store, the harbor wharf, and a fleet of thirty fishing boats as well as a lobster company and shipping operation that sent goods as far afield as the West Indies. The charming redecorated inn was acquired in 1995 by the Olivieri family, who blended its nostalgic contents with their own antiques and artwork brought from their home in Rome, Italy. Their street address is 15 Breakwater Street, Souris, PE C0A 2B0. Rates are moderate to deluxe.

You can't miss the inn if you look for the Magdalen Islands Ferry, which is a stone's throw away. Call (902) 687–3461 for reservations.

Just outside Souris, on Route 2, is Rollo Bay. Each summer, on the third weekend in July, lovers of traditional fiddle music can have a great time at the *Rollo Bay Fiddle Festival,* which features talent from all over North America. The big attraction is fiddle music, including traditional Celtic violin strathbanes, jigs, and reels played in open-air settings. There are also old-time dances. For a detailed itinerary, call (902) 687–2584 or visit their Web site at www.rollobay fiddlefest.ca.

Railway Fever and the Story of Confederation

As tiny as The Island is, the railway boom of the last century played an important role in P.E.I. history. Remember that although there was a conference on confederation in Prince Edward Island in 1864, Islanders decided not to join the union of Nova Scotia, New Brunswick, Ontario, and Quebec in 1867. They feared that their voice would be overwhelmed by the much greater numbers of voters elsewhere.

By 1870, however, "railway fever" hit The Island in a big way. Islanders were convinced that a railroad would bring new factories, easier access to markets for farmers, and prosperity to every doorstep. Soon all the villages wanted to be connected to the main line, and the rails zigzagged across The Island like topstitching on a crazy quilt.

In short order the railway ran up an unmanageable debt. The Island government was unable to pay its lenders, mostly British banks, and by 1872 a series of railway scandals had toppled it. The Canadian Confederation offered to take over the debt and provide railway service under its administration. In exchange P.E.I. would become part of Canada—hence the name Confederation Trail.

Just south of Rollo Bay, you'll come to a fork in the road that leads to *Bay Fortune.* Turn onto Route 310. Here you will find *The Inn at Bay Fortune,* one of the best restaurants on The Island. It was the location for Canadian Television's Life Network cooking show **The Inn Chef.** The Inn at Bay Fortune, and its sister accommodations, *The Inn at Spry Point,* have won a solid reputation as two of the most exciting places to eat in eastern Canada. One couple per

Island Blue Mussels and Sweet Potato Chowder

Courtesy of the Inn at Bay Fortune

5 pounds Island blue mussels
4 tablespoons water
4 tablespoons (½ stick) butter
1 large onion, chopped (about 2 cups)
4 cloves garlic, chopped
2 cups milk
1 cup heavy cream

1 teaspoon Bay Fortune Seasoning (see recipe next page)
1 teaspoon salt
1 teaspoon Tabasco sauce
2 medium carrots, peeled and grated
2 medium sweet potatoes, peeled and grated

1. Place mussels and water in a pot with a tight-fitting lid. Steam the mussels over high heat for 10 to 12 minutes, until the shells open. Discard any mussels that didn't open. Remove meat from shells and set meat aside. Reserve some shells to use in presentation. Strain and reserve remaining liquid.

2. In a large pot, melt the butter, and sauté onions over high heat for about 10 minutes. Stir frequently, turning the heat down slightly every few minutes to prevent burning. Add garlic and continue cooking until onions are golden brown. Add the remaining ingredients and 1 cup of the reserved mussel broth.

3. Bring mixture to a boil, reduce heat to low, cover pot, and let simmer gently for 30 minutes. Stir frequently to prevent scorching on the bottom of the pot.

4. While the soup is simmering, make the spicy butter (see recipe next page). After 30 minutes, check the soup vegetables for doneness. If soft, remove the pot from the heat. If the vegetables are still slightly al dente, simmer a few minutes longer, or until done.

5. Puree soup thoroughly in a blender, and strain through a fine mesh strainer. If necessary, adjust consistency of the soup with remaining mussel liquid. The soup should be pleasantly thick, but not goopy.

6. Return soup to the pot and heat it, stirring frequently, until it is almost at serving temperature. Add the reserved mussel meat and heat, stirring, for a few minutes until heated through. Serve chowder immediately, with spicy butter swirled around the surface of the soup.

Spicy Butter Swirls

2 tablespoons butter	¼ teaspoon ground allspice
½ tablespoon Tabasco	2 tablespoons molasses
2 tablespoons heavy cream	¼ teaspoon ground cloves

Put all of the ingredients in a small saucepan and bring the mixture to a simmer, stirring frequently. Remove from the heat, and allow the mixture to cool to room temperature.

Bay Fortune Seasoning

To make Bay Fortune Seasoning, simply combine equal parts, by weight, of whole dried bay laurel leaf, coriander seed, and fennel seed. Grind together in a spice grinder and store powder in an airtight opaque container (light will damage the flavor of this seasoning).

evening can reserve a spot in a glassed-in section of the kitchen, where they can witness the chef preparing a seven-course meal just for them. The inn is open from Victoria Day weekend in May until Canadian Thanksgiving weekend (U.S. Columbus Day) in October. For details or reservations, call (902) 687–3745 in the summer or (860) 563–6090 in the winter, or write to The Inn at Bay Fortune, Souris, PE C0A 2B0, or visit www.innatbayfortune.com. Rates are deluxe.

Apart from the gourmet delights, the inn is a cozy place with an interesting history. It was the former summer home of playwright Elmer Harris, who wrote the 1940s play *Johnny Belinda*. After this was a huge success on Broadway, it was made into a movie. The playwright's summer home was a writers' colony where many of his friends summered and wrote. Eventually it became the home of actress Colleen Dewhurst, well known in her many film roles and also as Marilla in the television series *Anne of Green Gables*. She was the wife of George C. Scott, whose son was married here.

When the beloved actress died of cancer in 1991, her summer home was made over into an inn. The place has a lovely view of the bay.

Hills and Harbors

After enjoying Bay Fortune, continue south along Route 2 until you reach Dingwells Mills, where you'll turn left onto Route 4 and continue to Pooles Corner. Then turn left onto Route 3 and continue until you reach **Brudenell River Provincial Park.**

This park has quite a lot to offer in the way of pleasant diversions: trail rides, canoe and kayaking adventures, a championship-level golf course, a riverside beach, and a marina for water sports. If camping is not your style, there is a collection of chalets along the river, although they seem quite small and boxy and lacking in privacy. Organized activities emphasize the natural setting, with walking trails lined with wildflowers or through marshland. Bike paths lead to Georgetown and Cardigan, at 5 and 7 miles (7 and 11 km) respectively, with the Cardigan path traversing the Confederation Trail. To make campsite or cabin reservations, call (902) 652–8966.

The golf course at *Brudenell* has been host to numerous national and Canadian Professional Golf Association tournaments. Its pristine riverside setting, immaculate greens, and tree-lined fairways offer a challenge to golfers of all levels.

At Brudenell you can rent horses and go on a romantic, not to mention scenic, trail ride along the beach at sunset and other times, accompanied by an experienced guide. These are available only by reservation. For information call *Brudenell Trail Rides* at (902) 652–2396. There are several other exciting diversions in this area, including an opportunity to go sea kayaking along secluded offshore islands and sandy coves.

The marina comes in handy if you are interested in taking a look at a harbor seal colony. *Cruise Manada,* run by Captain Dan Bears, departs from the

Collector's Side Trip!

During the second-to-last weekend in September, antiques and collectible fans will have a field day at this end of the province. A loop of road that follows the coast from Cape Bear to Orwell Corner (more or less), is home to the *70-Mile Coastal Yard Sale,* which features over a hundred yard-sale sites along the route. Many of these are multifamily sites with lots of treasures culled from old farmsteads and Grandma's trunk. No need to pack a lunch; lots of food is available en route, everything from home-baked goodies to barbecue, chili, chowder, and sandwiches. Hot coffee and soft drinks are also in abundance.

Many gift and craft shops hold special sales along the route, and there is an art show and sale at the Little Sands United Church. Entry points to the sale will have maps of the route.

This sale happens rain or shine.

When you get tired of collecting, you just have to stop along the shore to visit some of the beautiful lighthouses in the area. Besides Point Prim's lovely redbrick lighthouse, you can visit Cape Bear's lighthouse and the nearby Marconi Station, where the *Titanic*'s distress signal was first received.

Montague Marina at various times throughout the day. Along with the cruise, Bears takes his passengers to a mussel farm where The Island's famous Atlantic blue mussels are grown. The whole trip takes two hours. If you are lucky, you may see a whale, harbor porpoise, or osprey in addition to the many seabirds in the area. The cruise is $22 for adults, with discounts for seniors and children. For information call (902) 838–3444.

Stay at nearby Montague or try camping at Panmure Island. To get to ***Panmure Island Provincial Park,*** drive east along Route 17 from Montague. Panmure Island offers two kinds of beaches: one fronting St. Mary's Bay and one open to the gulf. Set in a lovely pastoral area, the view of the ocean and the spaciousness of the hundred-acre campground are a bargain, with camping fees starting at $21 daily. For information on this or other camping areas in the eastern end of The Island, write to P.O. Box 370, Montague, PE C0A 1R0, or call (902) 838–0668.

Where do the buffalo roam these days? This wouldn't seem to be a likely question if you're on Prince Edward Island, but you will find a herd of buffalo at ***Buffaloland Provincial Park,*** just 3.8 miles (6 km) south of Montague on Highway 4.

In May 1970 fifteen young buffalo arrived on The Island as a gift from Saskatchewan to the government of P.E.I. Culling the herd keeps their number down to about 25.

The park is bisected by a long fenced-in column that people can walk down to get a feeling of being surrounded by a herd of wild buffalo. A raised platform with steps makes it possible to look out over the herd.

Calves are born in May or June. In the past the herd has reached 60 or 70 head before culling. To thin the herd the animals designated for slaughter are put out to pasture. The day I visited, several carloads of Mi'Kmaqs from Nova Scotia were there to take a look. They had just been to the big annual Abegweit Powwow at Panmure Island.

A herd of buffalo is something to see in the spring, when the animals are in heat. The elder bull buffalo make a circle around the females to protect them at the first sign of humans dropping by to take a look. If you get too close, they'll charge right at you and ram into the fence, which doesn't look like a very sturdy defense.

Interpretive signs explain details of the life of the buffalo. On sunny days it takes a lot to coax them out from under the trees at the back of the park, so if you have time and want to see the buffalo at their best, pick an overcast morning or early evening that's not too hot. Admission to Buffaloland is free.

Buffalo are not the only unusual animals to be herded in this end of the Island. Several farmers have begun their own herds of alpaca. These animals provide a fleece that is as soft as silk and is lanolin-free, making it an ideal hypoallergenic fiber with superior draping qualities. Farmers have been so successful in producing alpaca wool here that some is exported as far away as Pakistan. You can buy some locally produced alpaca knitwear at a shop in Murray River called *Spit'n Image,* at 649 Dover Road. They are open year-round, and specialize in 100 percent certified organic alpaca yarn of superfine quality and use no dyes or chemicals. All items made by Spit'n Image are individually handcrafted using 100 percent certified organic yarns. They also sell organic yarns for your own knitting projects.

Next drive southeast to *Murray Harbour,* a nice out-of-the-way fishing community. When you reach Murray River, cross the bridge and exit left onto Route 18 in the direction of Murray Harbour.

From Murray Harbour you can drive in either direction on Route 18, but if you take the inland route you will soon reach a fork in the road to Route 4. Turn southwest toward Little Sands. Here you will find the charming little *Rossignol Estate Winery.* In addition to its seven acres (three hectares) of hardy Franco-American hybrid wine grapes, the winery has recently experimented with greenhouses to grow the more tender varieties of wine grape, such as Chardonnay, Cabernet Franc, and Pinot Noir. The result is that the postcard-pretty winery has garnered several All-Canadian Wine Championship awards. At the winery's retail outlet and art gallery you can sip some of these or select from a variety of fruit-based wines.

While imbibing, take time to enjoy the spectacular view of Northumberland Strait and the shoreline of Nova Scotia. The winery is open May to October, Monday to Saturday from 10:00 A.M. to 5:00 P.M., Sunday from 1:00 to 5:00 P.M.

A quaint bed-and-breakfast establishment is *Bayberry Cliff Inn,* only 0.6 mile (1 km) west of the winery on Route 4, Little Sands, a few minutes' drive from the Wood Islands ferry terminal. This place overlooks a cliff, offering a spectacular view of the ocean, with five different levels and a number of sitting areas and balconies.

Room rates are moderate, with weekly rates available. For more information call (902) 962–3395.

At this point you are within minutes of a ferry to Nova Scotia, but if you want to linger another day on The Island, continue for a half hour on TCH Route 1, the same stretch of the TCH that passes in front of the ferry terminal.

You will come to a sign indicating the *Orwell Corner Historic Village,* reached by taking a right turn after the junction of Routes 1 and 23, up a small hill and at the start of a clay road. This site re-creates the life and times of a small crossroads agricultural village from the last century. The village includes a farmhouse from 1864, a smithy, and a shingle mill, which I haven't seen anywhere else in the Maritimes. Timing is a factor here: If you come on a Wednesday, you'll be able to take part in a really good ceilidh, one of the best of these traditional Gaelic parties on The Island. Events during the harvest and Christmas seasons make the village particularly picturesque. Other events at the historic village are scheduled throughout the year. To check the schedule, call (902) 651–8510.

The village operates cooperatively with the nearby restored homestead of one of Prince Edward Island's most noteworthy citizens. Sir Andrew Macphail was a physician and professor at McGill University in Montreal. He was also an author intensely interested in sustainable agricultural and forestry development. At age fifty he volunteered to work with a field ambulance corps in World War I. He was knighted by the King of England on New Year's Day 1918.

His birthplace is now called the *Sir Andrew Macphail Homestead,* a 140-acre (56-hectare) site with a reforestation project, including a tree nursery and wildlife gardens. A nature trail meanders along the side of a stream. Visitors can dine or have tea in the facilities provided in the restored home, which also boasts a large conference room in the former dining room. Dinner is quite reasonably priced, and the restaurant is licensed to serve alcohol. For details of upcoming events at the homestead, call (902) 651–2789 in season, or visit www.islandregister.com/macphailfoundation.html.

From Orwell Corner you can backtrack in the direction of the Wood Islands ferry. There is just one more thing that you ought to do to make your Prince Edward Island sojourn complete: Turn left off TCH Route 1 onto Route 209 and visit *Point Prim Lighthouse.*

Point Prim is a charming peninsula that seems like a little world unto itself. You can visit the lighthouse here and, just to the west of it, the *Point Prim Chowder House.*

Point Prim Chowder House Irish Moss Pudding

⅓ cup Irish moss (packed)

4 cups milk

¼ teaspoon salt

1½ teaspoon vanilla

1. Soak moss for 15 minutes in enough water to cover; drain.
2. Pick over the Irish moss, removing the undesirable pieces.
3. Add moss to milk and cook in double boiler for 30 minutes.
4. Add salt and vanilla. Pour through a sieve.
5. Fill molds and chill. Serve with a fruit topping.

Of all the old lighthouses on The Island, the Point Prim dates back the farthest, to 1845. The 60-foot tower is the only round brick lighthouse in the entire country. You can climb inside to the polygonal lantern house and catch a spectacular bird's-eye view of Northumberland Strait while you check your pulse.

Once you've worked up an appetite, drop by the Point Prim Chowder House (902–659–2023, in season) and try the Irish moss pudding. When recipes are made with this ingredient in other parts of P.E.I., they call it seaweed. But the owner of the Chowder House hates that terminology, because it's not really seaweed. (You can also buy some dried Irish moss to take home for your own culinary experiments.)

Places to Stay on Prince Edward Island

BAY FORTUNE

The Inn at Bay Fortune
off Route 310
(902) 687–3745
A lovely private setting.
Deluxe.

BRACKLEY BEACH

Shaw's Hotel
Route 15
(902) 672–2644
Canada's oldest continously
operating inn is a step
back in time. Charming.
Moderate.

CHARLOTTETOWN

The Great George
58 Great George Street
(800) 361–1118
(902) 892–0606
fax (902) 628–2079
www.thegreatgeorge.com
Comprising a cluster of

restored Heritage buildings,
the inns are fitted with
antiques, claw-foot tubs
or Jacuzzis, and an
exercise room.
Deluxe.

The Shipwright Inn
51 Fitzroy Street
(888) 306–9966
(902) 368–1905
fax (902) 628–1905
A Heritage property.
Deluxe.

GRAND TRACADIE

Dalvay by-the-Sea Inn
off Route 6
(902) 672–2048
The perfect romantic
getaway.
Deluxe.

GREENWICH

Greenwich Gate Lodge
off Route 2, overlooking St.
Peters Bay
(877) 961–3496
www.greenwichgate.com
Walking distance to St.
Peters Bay Landing Park and
Confederation Trail.
Standard to moderate.

LITTLE SANDS

Bayberry Cliff Inn
Route 4
(5 miles/8 km east from the
Wood Islands ferry dock)
(902) 962–3395
Eclectic inn near Wood
Islands ferry. Great views.
Adults/older children
preferred.
Moderate.

SOURIS

Matthew House Inn
15 Breakwater Street
(902) 687–3461
Victorian Heritage estate.
Deluxe.

Rollo Bay Inn
two and a half miles (4 km)
west of Souris at the juncture
of Route 330 and Route 2
(877) 687–3550
www.peisland.com/
rollobayinn
Queen Anne decor, elegant
dining room.
Standard to moderate.

STANLEY BRIDGE

**Stanley Bridge
Country Resort**
junction of Routes 6,
224, and 254
(800) 361–2882
(902) 886–2882
fax (902) 886–2940
Great location for prime
beach area, good facilities
for families.
Standard to deluxe.

TIGNISH

Tignish Heritage Inn
Maple Street
(877) 882–2491
(902) 882–2491
Converted convent at
beginning of the
Confederation Trail.
Moderate.

TYNE VALLEY

The Doctor's Inn
Route 167
(902) 831–3057
Beautifully landscaped
village home. Good food.
Standard.

VICTORIA BY-THE-SEA

Orient Hotel
Main Street
(800) 565–6743
(902) 658–2503
Historic.
Moderate.

WEST POINT

West Point Lighthouse
Route 14
(800) 764–6854
(902) 859–3605
Canada's first inn housed
in an active lighthouse.
Moderate.

Places to Eat on Prince Edward Island

BAY FORTUNE

The Inn at Bay Fortune
off Route 310
(902) 687–3745
Outrageously scrumptious
food. Reserve ahead to
avoid disappointment.

GRAND TRACADIE

Dalvay by-the-Sea
off Route 6
(902) 672–2048
Excellent food and setting.

HOPE RIVER

**St. Anne's Church
Lobster Suppers**
Route 224 (off Route 6)
(902) 621–0635
Over thirty years of
operation, St. Anne's Church
has set the standard for The
Island's church-based
lobster suppers. Open
Monday through Saturday
from 4:00 to 9:00 P.M.
Closed Sunday.

MIMINEGASH

Seaweed Pie Cafe
Irish Moss Interpretive Centre
Route 14
(902) 882–4313
Also featuring mussels, crab
cakes, and seafood
chowder.

MONT-CARMEL

Étoile de Mer
Acadian Pioneer Village
Route 11
(902) 854–2227
Acadian and seafood
specialties.

NEW GLASGOW

**New Glasgow
Lobster Suppers**
Route 258
(902) 964–2870
Lobster straight from their
own saltwater pond. It
doesn't get any fresher than
this. A big place, reservations
not needed. In operation for
more than forty years.

NEW LONDON

**New London Seafood
Restaurant**
(902) 886–3000
On the wharf.

NORTH CAPE

**North Cape Lighthouse
Wind and Reef Restaurant**
Route 14
(902) 882–3535
Fresh seafood.

ORWELL CORNER

Point Prim Chowder House
Route 209
(902) 651–2789
Great setting and seafood
selection. Contact through
artists' co-op.

ORWELL CORNER HISTORIC VILLAGE

Sir Andrew Macphail Homestead
Route 1
(902) 651–2789
Lunch and afternoon tea, plus hearty suppers during summer on Thursday, Friday, and Saturday.

OYSTER BED BRIDGE

Cafe St.–Jean
Route 6
(902) 963–3133
Listen to live east coast music and eat scrumptious food in this relaxed rustic setting overlooking a river. Fifteen minutes from Charlottetown, twelve minutes from Cavendish.

SUMMERSIDE

Flex Mussels
175 Harbour Drive
Spinnakers' Landing
(902) 954–0022
Closes mid-September.

TYNE VALLEY

The Doctor's Inn
Route 167
(902) 831–3057
Organic yet classic dining.

Nova Scotia's Sunrise Trail and Atlantic Coastline

If you have followed the routing outlined in this book to explore the Maritimes, you will have entered Prince Edward Island from New Brunswick and exited P.E.I. via Nova Scotia.

You will no sooner arrive in Nova Scotia than you will be pointed toward Cape Breton, a route commonly followed by travelers to the area. This often leads to an unfortunate bypass of much of the Northumberland Strait coast. The Tatamagouche Bay area has one of the most benign microclimates in the Maritimes, and is home to a vineyard in the area of Malagash. The waters of the Northumberland Strait are warm and small beaches dot the sheltered coastline.

Sunrise Trail

Although this book is planned so that visitors can travel in one unbroken clockwise route, the two highlights of this area warrant a side trip if you are coming in from Prince Edward Island. If you are entering Nova Scotia's Sunrise Trial from the Glooscap Trail, the area is equally accessible. To avoid confusion, I will outline the routing as if you were driving west from Pictou. On Highway 6—the Sunrise Trail—34.5 miles (54 km) west of Pictou, you will come to ***Tatamagouche,*** a cozy village

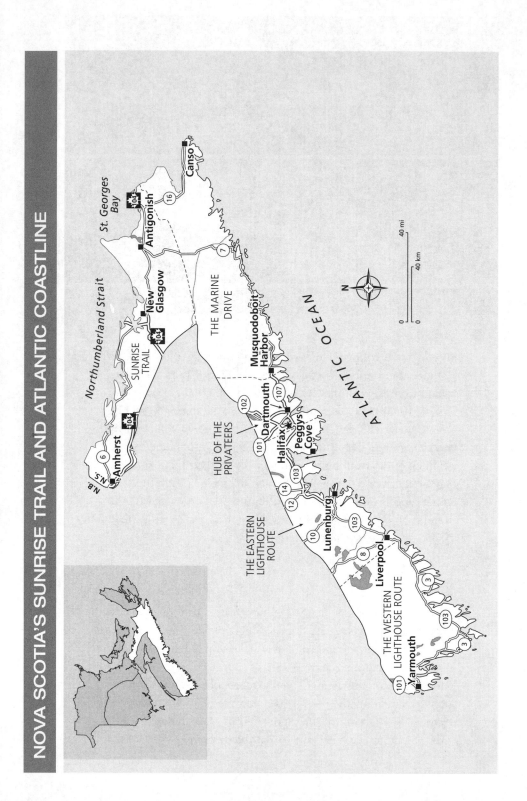

overlooking sheltered ***Tatamagouche Bay.*** The town has a number of children's summer camps. It's also the location of one of the few inns in North America that feature a train station and railcars for accommodations.

The terminus that now houses the ***Train Station Inn*** was rendered obsolete in 1973 and eventually came into the hands of railway buff Jimmy LeFresne. As a child LeFresne lived next to the station, and the old stationmaster even taught him how to use the telegraph. "Other kids had toy trains to play with!" LeFresne told me.

To keep the defunct station from being torn down, LeFresne leased the building for $50 a month from the time he was eighteen until eventually he was able to buy it outright in 1989, when trains stopped passing through.

trivia

In the late nineteenth century, a giantess from Tatamagouche by the name of Anna Swan (1846–1888) married a giant named Martin Van Burin Bates, making them the world's tallest married couple. She was 7 feet 5.5 inches (227 cm). Her husband was 7 feet 2.5 inches (220 cm).

Over time, he obtained seven cabooses and a boxcar. The upstairs of the station has three bedrooms. It used to be the stationmaster's quarters.

The cabooses have been converted into bedroom suites full of railway icons: old train posters, toy trains, pillowcases with steam-locomotive motifs, and books on old railways. To reserve your very own caboose, call (888) 724–5233 or (902) 657–3222. Rooms in the station and cabooses are moderate. Breakfast at the ***Jitney Cafe*** downstairs in the station house, or eat in their dining car, which features lobster suppers.

TRUDY'S FAVORITES

Sherbrooke Village

Maritime Museum of the Atlantic,
Halifax

Halifax Public Gardens,
Halifax

Tancook Islands

The Chester Playhouse,
Chester

Oak Island

Kejimkujik Seaside Adjunct,
Kejimkujik National Park

Ross-Thomson House,
Shelburne

Barrington Woolen Mill,
Barrington

Firefighter's Museum,
Yarmouth

boxcarjimmy

"There's more to buying a railcar than one might expect," says railway buff and Train Station Inn owner Jimmy LeFresne. First LeFresne tracks down a caboose that's about to be sold by its railway. With fewer trains in operation, that's no easy task. Sometimes LeFresne even buys a caboose before its retirement date and rents it to the railway for its remaining working years.

Next there's the expense. The cost of hiring a flatbed, a truck, a crane, and an operator to lift the caboose onto LeFresne's stretch of rails often exceeds the cost of the caboose itself—and that's without considering the money needed to transform it into a cozy hotel room!

And complications can arise. LeFresne tells about the time he lost a caboose. "It went missing shortly after I bought it," he says. "It seems some brakeman, tired of hanging out of the back of a boxcar, thought it was an extra caboose and put it on the train." That "loose caboose" was later spotted traveling through Burlington, Kingston, and other points in Southern Ontario.

After a short detour inland along Trunk 311 from Tatamagouche, you will come to the **Balmoral Grist Mill Museum,** in the village of Balmoral Mills. This little museum is open from June to mid-October, Monday to Saturday from 9:30 A.M. to 5:30 P.M. and Sunday afternoon from 2:00 to 4:00 P.M. Even when it isn't open, I love just stopping here to eat my picnic lunch next to the charming mill and its stream. This mill has been in operation since 1874. The site features a 0.6-mile (1-km) nature trail through glorious scenery, including a gorge, and the mill itself is pretty enough to paint. There are two daily two-hour-long demonstrations of the mill in operation, at 10:00 A.M. and 2:00 P.M. The result is a surprisingly nutty-tasting whole-wheat flour of oats, barley, rye, and buckwheat. The museum gift shop sells the freshly ground grain. A small admission is charged.

Continuing along that same coastal Highway 6, you will come to a village known as **Malagash.** A series of grape-cluster signs will indicate the **Jost Winery,** just outside of town. Pronounced "Yost," this is a vineyard and winery started in the early 1970s. Because the vineyard is located downwind of the sheltered Northumberland Strait, the area is particularly warm and beneficial to wine grapes. The result is that Jost wines have garnered a number of international awards over the years, including several gold medals.

The Jost vineyard stretches over forty-five acres (eighteen hectares), and has a shop and visitor center where you can take a wine tour from mid-June to mid-September daily at noon or 3:00 P.M. Afterward, you can picnic under the Jost arbor, with a bounty of the shop's wine and cured meats and gourmet cheeses made by other local producers.

The afternoon I visited, the temperature was ideal for a picnic. Lunch consisted of a bottle of Marechal Foch, cardamom-spiced Gouda cheese from Buttercup Farms in Bridgewater, and salami from a nearby smokehouse. Jost also makes barbecue grilling facilities available to visitors on its licensed deck.

The vineyard also has added a selection of festivals to its summer visitors schedule. These include a wine fest near the end of June and a "grape stomp festival" toward the end of September. At this festival competing teams squish grapes for charity, while spectators cheer them on. Exact dates for these festivals change from year to year, but if you can gather a team that has a yen to stomp on the fruit of the vine, check out www.jostwine.com for specific dates. Call (800) 565–4567 or (902) 257–2636, or fax (902) 257–2248.

After Malagash, return to Highway 6 and retrace your steps to Pictou. *Pictou Lodge* was originally built by the Bungalow Camps Company in 1922. The original dining room is in a huge log house that still retains all of its rustic appeal. It features luxurious dining in a room made cozy by a huge stone fireplace. Guest accommodations consist of large three-bedroom log cabins decorated with many of the original furnishings. They also feature big old-fashioned claw-foot tubs like the one Grandma luxuriated in. Prices for Pictou Lodge run from moderate to deluxe. For advance reservations, call (888) 662–7484 or (902) 485–4322.

A small beach running along one side of the lodge is good for beachcombing and walking. You may prefer to swim in the heated pool that is near the cabins. A small man-made lake is used for water sports. You can also hike on nearby *Munro's Island.* This small wilderness is unspoiled by motorized vehicles.

trivia

More than 600 men have died in mine disasters in Pictou County's underground coal seam. Many deaths were due to methane gas explosions.

You will be able to see deer, ducks, osprey, eagles, geese, and possibly even a fox on this island, now owned by the Nature Conservancy of Canada.

The town of *Pictou* is just 3 miles (4.8 km) west of Pictou Lodge. Braeshore Road will take you right into town. Visiting Pictou is a good way to connect with the origins of Nova Scotia, since this was the point of entry of many of the province's original Scottish settlers. Of course, this was the reason for renaming Acadia "Nova Scotia" in the first place, to encourage would-be Scottish settlers to think of it as their new homeland. (Nova Scotia means "New Scotland" in Latin.)

The settlers first arrived in 1773 on the ship *Hector,* which carried more than 200 passengers, including thirty-three families and twenty-five single men.

The province's first Highland Scots came too late in the season to plant crops, having been blown off course by a fierce gale near Newfoundland. People onboard the ship also suffered from smallpox and dysentery outbreaks that claimed the lives of eighteen children before the ship reached land. Immigration to New Scotland reached a peak in the early 1800s. Between 1802 and 1807, historians recorded the arrival of more than 25,000 Scots in Cape Breton alone.

The original *Hector,* which brought the first Scottish families, was a fully rigged Dutch ship known as a flute, characterized by its flat bottom with full pear-shaped ends. Captained by John Speirs, the ship was reputed to have a smuggling past. Provisions were rationed: a daily pint of water and three pounds of salt beef, four pounds of bread, and four pounds of oatmeal a week. Because the storm delayed their arrival by two weeks, provisions started running out at the end of the voyage. Vinegar was added to green, scummy water to make it drinkable. Moldy oatcakes that had earlier been discarded were retrieved and shared to stave off starvation.

You can explore all this history at the **Hector Heritage Quay** and visit a full-size replica of the *Hector,* which was built right here on a dry dock outside the interpretive center. In the center are a number of wax models and displays depicting the passengers aboard ship. A small admission is charged.

You can watch a blacksmith turn out iron tools and candlesticks, which are for sale. Gift shops on the quay feature excellent local crafts, pewter, and music CDs by noted east coast artists.

If you are in the mood for some pub crawling, be sure to check out **The Old Stone Pub,** 300 feet (90 m) or so past the quay on Depot Street. This favorite local hot spot occupies the bottom floor of a brick-and-sandstone building that dates back to 1870. This former customs house (until the 1950s) offers visitors a chance to enjoy live music Wednesday and weekend nights.

Upstairs, but through a separate entrance on the opposite side of the building, you will find the **Customs House Inn,** run by twin brothers Dave and Doug DesBarres. I should add that due to the solid construction of the building, sound from the downstairs pub does not carry, so you can sleep soundly in their king-size beds.

The building is a registered Heritage property and is charmingly furnished and decorated to reflect its history. It also has first-class modern fixtures, like high-speed wireless Internet and cable television. Breakfast is included in the price. Prices are moderate. For reservations, call (902) 485–4546.

Another delightful place to stay, and quite possibly the best bargain in town, is the 1865 **Auberge Walker Inn.** The inn is in a pre-Confederation building that has been decorated with many period pieces. A large-screen television draws guests to the living room, where they can socialize with other

TOP ANNUAL EVENTS

The Greek Festival,
Halifax (first weekend in June);
(902) 479–1271
Sponsored by the local Greek church, this event has mushroomed into one of the city's favorite parties.

The Multicultural Festival,
Dartmouth waterfront
(third weekend in June);
(902) 455–1619
Lots of exotic food, dance, and crafts. A great chance to graze rather than eat a sit-down meal.

The Antigonish Highland Games,
Antigonish (early July);
(902) 863–3330
Lots of burly guys in kilts throwing objects the size of trees. Ale, a parade, and highland dancers galore.

Maritime Old-Time Fiddling Contest,
Dartmouth (second Wednesday in July through Sunday);
(800) 565–0000
Excellent acoustics, the region's top fiddlers, and intense competition make this a mecca for any fiddle fan.

The Wooden Boat Festival,
Mahone Bay (first week of August);
(902) 624–8443
The bay's biggest party of the year. Explore the boatbuilding heritage of an area noted for its rumrunners and privateers.

Lunenburg Folk Harbour Festival,
Lunenburg (second Wednesday in August through Sunday);
(902) 634–3180
The picturesque waterfront and assorted venues are filled with the best folk musicians and fans from across the region. The daytime concerts are free.

Halifax International Busker Festival,
Halifax (mid-August);
(902) 429–3910
A good event if you like crowds. Sample an act or two, then visit Halifax's charming waterfront and downtown areas.

The International Woodsman's Competition,
Greenfield (second weekend in August);
(800) 565–0000
Unusual and fun. Local lumberjacks try their luck at logrolling, tree climbing, and many other lumberjack job skills.

Atlantic Fringe Festival,
Halifax (early September);
(800) 565–0000
"Out there" theatrical events and related activities for the artsy crowd.

visitors. The continental breakfast (included in the price) is served in a sunny, elegant dining room. Rates are standard to moderate.

The friendly owners, Laurent and Jacqueline LaFlèche, have unearthed old photographs and the original architectural plans of this historic home. To reserve a room, call (800) 370–5553 or locally at (902) 485–1433. The inn is on Coleraine Street, 1 block from the Hector Quay.

As you leave Pictou, you will reach a fork in the road and signs indicating the turnoff for Highway 104, which leads to Stellarton and New Glasgow (8 miles, or 13 km). Take this road, also known as the Old Haliburton Road, until you find the **Hector Exhibit and Research Centre** and **McCulloch House Museum.** The home of the founder of Pictou Academy, McCulloch House dates back to 1806 and overlooks a charming beaver pond.

Thomas McCulloch was an avid naturalist, and his collection was studied in 1833 by the visiting John Audubon, who personally presented him with his prints of wildlife. On the same property is the Hector Exhibit and Research Centre, which houses the records of the Pictou County Genealogy and Heritage Society. This is an excellent resource for people of Scottish descent who wish to trace their roots. The center also has a rotation of exhibits put on by local societies and craft guilds, and items are sometimes for sale. For information call (902) 485–4563.

New Glasgow and Stellarton are two closely linked communities; you can easily travel from one to the other without using the main highway. Your first stop in the area should include a visit to the **Nova Scotia Museum of Industry** in **Stellarton,** just off Highway 104 at exit 24, which brings you to the museum's doorstep.

This is a great museum to visit with children, who seem to be endlessly fascinated with old machinery and interactive displays. Visitors will be handed a time card and asked to punch a time clock, as if they were showing up for work. Kids will continue to get their card punched as they proceed through the exhibit, which advances in time, keeping apace with the improvements in technology.

The museum is the size of seven hockey rinks, making it the province's largest museum. It has to be big, because of the heavy machinery, steam locomotives, and cars that it houses. One of the most noteworthy items is the Samson steam locomotive, the oldest surviving steam locomotive in Canada. (The steam chamber is encased in wood, making it resemble an oblong whisky barrel.) The Samson arrived in 1839, twelve years after the General Mining Company obtained a lease to mine coal in the province. This marked the beginning of industrialization in Nova Scotia.

Early automobiles are also featured in the museum—from the Victorian horseless carriage, a one-of-a-kind two-horsepower vehicle made in Hopewell in 1899, to the 1912 McKay Touring Car. The McKay was the product of a local enterprise that was in operation only from 1912 to 1914, during which time only 175 were produced. These posh automobiles sold for $2,300, a lot of money at the time. Admission is charged.

When you exit the museum, follow Route 374, also known as the Stellarton Road, to **New Glasgow.** Just as you cross the small bridge that traverses the East River, you will come to the most historic section of town and New Glasgow's oldest building, which houses one of the town's liveliest pubs. Built in 1841, the Squire Frasier Building was made from stone ballast used in the ships that brought the town's British settlers. You will find it just a block from the waterfront.

Abandoned for three years, the ground floor of the building has been turned into a pub by an Irish couple, the Margesons. Now called **The Dock, Food, Spirits and Ales,** it stands as one of the biggest drawing cards to date in the town's revitalized riverside and features an outdoor patio.

"It's certainly given people an opportunity to come into the oldest building and to see it as it used to be," said owner Carmel Margeson, a native of Cork, Ireland, whose family owns a pub in Ireland. Since a river runs through New Glasglow, customers sometimes arrive by boat, docking at the nearby marina. The Dock has a variety of imported ales on tap, and Irish, Nova Scotian, and Canadian flags decorate the front of the pub, just so you know where their hearts are.

At the beginning of the railway era, some locomotives ran on all-wooden tracks and covered only short distances, because they were used for hauling goods from a mine or factory to a pier. Later technological improvements involved substituting iron and steel in the construction of railroad tracks. In downtown New Glasgow you'll find the **Sampson Trail,** a pleasant promenade approximately a half mile long between downtown New Glasgow and downtown Stellarton. This trail is on the railroad bed of the first iron-and-steel railway in Canada and is named for the first locomotive to run on it, the Sampson, which was used to haul coal from the mine to the dock.

The **Thorburn Rail Spur** yields another trail and access to a marshland area with bald eagles and rare species of flora and fauna.

Before you leave New Glasgow be sure to visit the **Carmichael Stewart House Museum,** on Temperance Street. This is designated in downtown New Glasgow by a series of signs and arrows indicating, simply, MUSEUM. A sign outside the building is labeled PICTOU COUNTY HISTORICAL MUSEUM. Despite the multiple designations, it's all the same place.

The Carmichaels were wealthy shipbuilders who produced a missionary sailing ship that went to the South Seas in search of Christian converts. The ship itself was paid for with donations from schoolchildren in Canada, Scotland, and England. Apart from shipbuilding artifacts, what I found most noteworthy about this museum collection was the variety of antique clothing, including a century-old wedding dress and several handmade christening gowns.

Because there are a limited number of mannequins, the museum guide tries to change the costumes often, so repeat visits will still yield fresh surprises.

The museum is open June to August, Monday to Saturday from 9:30 A.M. to 4:30 P.M., Sunday from 1:00 to 4:30 P.M. Admission is free, but donations are welcome.

Just outside New Glasgow is one of the area's best-kept secrets. **Melmerby Beach** has my vote for the warmest saltwater beach in Nova Scotia. To get there, take Route 289 north on Little Harbour Road in downtown New Glasgow until you reach the junction with Route 348. Take a right turn from here to get to Melmerby Beach Provincial Park. The beach came by its name because a French ship, the Melmerby, ran aground here. It's not surprising, since the water is shallow for a considerable distance. Lifeguards are on duty all summer long, and there are changing facilities.

Backtrack on Route 289 to New Glasgow to reconnect with Highway 104. Continue east until you reach the community of **Barneys River Station.** Turn right off the main highway and follow Barneys River Station Road a few hundred feet until you see a sign indicating the **School House Museum.** This tiny one-room schoolhouse, built in 1865, accommodated forty-two pupils at its peak. It closed in 1971.

A number of artifacts related to the old school were resurrected in the community, and the effect is a convincing step back in time. Having been a Nova Scotian schoolgirl in the early 1960s, I can attest to the authenticity of the classroom setting, right back to the double desks and inkwells, the mint-condition schoolbooks, and even the strap used to administer punishment for naughty behavior. The old schoolhouse is open July and August, Tuesday to Saturday from 11:00 A.M.to 5:00 P.M., Sunday from noon to 5:00 P.M. Admission is free, but donations are welcome.

From Barneys River Station you can continue on Highway 104 to **Antigonish.** While in Antigonish, be sure to stop into the **Lyghtesome Gallery,** on Main Street, one block north of Church Street, which is directly off Highway 104. A number of excellent artists work in the Antigonish area, and many of them are represented by the Lyghtesome. One of the region's most noteworthy painters, Anna Syperek, has works shown here. It's not a terribly big gallery, but the range of work is worth a visit. They also carry a variety of Celtic pewter ornaments, some very fine weaving, jewelry, and books of local and historical interest. They are open year-round, Monday to Saturday from 10:00 A.M. to 5:00 P.M. In the winter they close at 3:00 P.M. on Saturday. They publish an exhibition schedule, as well as profiles of their artists, online at www.lyghtesome.ns.ca.

If you happen to be in the vicinity of Antigonish at the end of the first week in July, you can enjoy the **Antigonish Highland Games.** Plan to stay for a few days, but expect to find hotel rooms in short supply. This may mean

The Gloomy Bard of Barneys River Station

In the early days of Barneys River, many Highland Scots came to live in the neighborhood. Among them was a poet, or bard, who was highly esteemed in his native Scotland. *John McLean,* the "Bard of Coll," settled here and became disillusioned with the hard life of a settler. Many of his finest works were composed here, but the one that really left his mark has a title that translates from Gaelic as "The Gloomy Forest."

Following his presentation of this homesick lament in Iona, Cape Breton, 500 of his fellow countrymen decided to abandon their hope of making a life in "New Scotland" and left for the presumed greener pastures of New Zealand.

The bard John McLean didn't leave Nova Scotia, but he did move to James River, in Antigonish, where he and his poison pen remained until his death.

staying outside of town so that you can take part in the biggest and longest running highland games outside of Scotland.

The core of the games are musical performances from pipe-and-drum bands, highland dancing, and, of course, the ancient heavyweight events such as the caber toss. A caber looks like a spruce telephone pole and is tossed in a two-handed motion by hunky men in kilts. Competitors come from Scotland, Australia, and the United States.

Celtic music is featured under the big top at Columbus Field. Expect to hear some of the finest fiddling in eastern Canada. Along with the highland games, Antigonish has other delights you can sample. The long-standing summer theater, called Festival Antigonish, has professional actors presenting plays written by local authors. It's possible to check out the program of events by visiting www.festivalantigonish.com.

Upon leaving Antigonish, you're faced with the choice of continuing along Highway 104 until the Canso Causeway and Cape Breton, or turning eastward at exit 32 and joining Highway 7, also known as the Marine Drive, which skirts the Atlantic Coastline and will eventually bring you to Nova Scotia's capital, Halifax.

The Marine Drive

One Guysborough county highlight must be a visit to the town of *Sherbrooke Village,* which, starting in the 1860s, was the site of a massive gold rush that went on for twenty years until it suddenly collapsed. The remains of those days are a collection of thirty perfectly preserved buildings fronting the beautiful St.

Marys River. These include a school, drugstore, courthouse, blacksmith shop, and barn (complete with horses). House after house is filled with artifacts from the town's golden era.

Costumed guides explain the history of Nova Scotia's gold rush. The economic activity of Nova Scotia gold rushes of the last century produced an income higher than that of the Klondike gold rush. Several old mines are still around in the province, and a few are reopening thanks to modern technology.

Sherbrooke Village has its own costume department, where staff members create authentic outfits from the village's heyday. I recommend that you visit their workshop to get a sneak peek at the behind-the-scenes work of historic re-creation. It's worth mentioning that needlework is very high quality in this area, and if you're in the mood to buy a quilt to take home, you'll find many good examples in craft stores in the area. The Sherbrooke Village museum staff organizes a variety of special events throughout the year, including a Courthouse Concert Series and parties revolving around themes such as harvesttime or cider-making. See http://museum.gov.ns.ca/sv/ for details. Sherbrooke Vil-

Chair-Making at Sherbrooke Village

At the *Woodturner and Chairmaker's Shop* in Sherbrooke Village, you can get an excellent feel for the art of making reproductions of 1860s-style furniture. On the day we visited, the carpenter demonstrated the use of a long wooden trough attached to a kettle. Strips of white ash, "the poor man's oak," were heated in the trough, which became a steam chamber when the water in the kettle boiled. The strips were heated for an hour for every inch of thickness, then removed and bent into shapes dictated by wooden forms.

Chair seats are carved out of wood with hand tools. For finishing, the carpenter uses modern sandpaper, a compromise solution. Dennis told us that in olden days, sandpaper was made by locals from animal-hide glue and various grades of sand. The finest grade of sandpaper was made from fish skin. "Sandpaper didn't come in all the grades we have today," Dennis said. "A carpenter just had to go by the feel of it and be his own judge."

No two chairs made in this traditional way are ever exactly alike. In fact, not even the spindles are absolutely consistent. It's the slight irregularities that distinguish a handmade reproduction from modern machine-made chairs. Chairs made throughout the summer in this small shop are sold for $100 to $300.

Sherbrooke Village is open daily from June 1 until mid-October. Some of the village's houses are still privately owned and occupied by families year-round, so it is never totally deserted, but you will not be able to go inside the buildings in the winter.

lage is open daily from June 1 to October 15, from 9:30 A.M. to 5:30 P.M. Admission is charged. For details, call (888) 743–7845 or (902) 522–2400.

If you are eager to spend more time in this area, you can find cabins, some overlooking the rapids of St. Marys River, at **Liscombe Lodge.** You can enjoy a closeness with nature on a par with wilderness camping, while still benefitting from the luxuries of a cozy lodge. In the dining room I had a feast of plank salmon and was able to watch an assortment of colorful songbirds at a feeder just a few feet away. There was also a very people-friendly groundhog on the premises, who seemed to be as interested in the guests as we were in him. The lodge offers an indoor pool and a fitness center, as well as access to a wide range of outdoor sporting equipment and guides. For reservations, call (800) 665–6343. Rates are moderate to deluxe.

If you're just passing through, you might want to drop by the restaurant to enjoy a bite or to check out the dozens of locally handmade quilts and other crafts that adorn the post-and-beam ceiling of the main lodge's second floor. These items are for sale.

There are several good excursions that you can take at Liscombe Lodge. Guests can take a harbor cruise on the lodge's flat-bottom boat to visit an island, where you have a good chance of seeing eagles.

There are also good walking trails, including one that leads to a salmon ladder, a man-made series of rapids that were constructed to aid the fish in their annual migration. After the salmon ladder was constructed, the river's course was partially rerouted so that half of it would flow through the ladder.

You can take a footbridge that traverses the river just down from this ladder. Maps of this 5-mile (8-km) trail are available at the lodge desk. If you are driving a vehicle with a high undercarriage and good shock absorbers, you can travel the rough road right up to the footbridge or salmon ladder. Otherwise, it's a four-hour hike, round-trip.

After Liscombe, continue west along Highway 7. You will see a Nova Scotia Provincial Government campground marker indicating **Taylor Head Beach,** one of the unspoiled wonders of the province. Turn left and drive a short way to the shore along a small peninsula. Taylor Head Beach has a wonderful white-sand beach that looks striking against a backdrop of dense fir trees. The area includes a 3.6-mile (6-km) hiking trail. Along this coastline you stand a good chance of seeing not only eagles, but also great blue herons in flight, with their exceedingly long legs dangling behind them. The best thing about Taylor Head is that it is truly undiscovered, so don't tell anyone.

After you exit Taylor Head, you will come almost immediately to the community of Tangier. This stop involves some advance planning. So, assuming that you've been reading ahead a little bit, here goes. Tangier is the headquarters of

Woodstock Grows Up

The wonderful three-day *Stan Rogers Folk Festival* is held in Canso, usually in late June. It has grown to include more than 50 musical acts from around the world, performing on six stages. Stan Rogers was a local folksinger/songwriter who penned many popular ballads that can best be described as "working man's anthems." After he died tragically in a plane crash, his hometown became host to this festival, which runs at the beginning of the summer. You can check festival times and book your tickets in advance by calling (888) 554–7826. The Stan Rogers Folk Festival is clean, well organized, and family friendly, with a wide range of people in attendance. It has a hint of the Woodstock-generation aspect—now that they've grown up and found jobs—that is reflected in the event's congenial yet wholesome atmosphere.

To get to Canso from Antigonish, continue on Highway 104 toward Cape Breton until you reach the Route 16 exit at Junction 37. Take Route 16 east to Canso. After the festival you can rejoin the Marine Drive by taking Route 316 south, all along the Atlantic coast.

Dr. Scott Cunningham, biologist, writer, and, most important for our purposes, sea kayaking expert. He takes groups on a number of sea kayaking expeditions along these shores through his company *Coastal Adventures,* the longest-running sea kayaking operation in Atlantic Canada.

Cunningham has published a book, *Sea Kayaking in Nova Scotia,* and, in addition to circumnavigating the province in 1980, he has extensively explored other regional wilderness areas. His tours take from three to eight days and cover the biology, geology, and history of the shorelines explored. All gear is supplied, apart from tents, sleeping bags, and personal items. Coastal Adventures also offers daylong trips for $100. For details, you can visit www.coastal adventures.com, e-mail coastal@dunmac.com, call (877) 404–2774, or fax (902) 772–2774.

The first thing that comes to mind when you mention Tangier to gourmets throughout the region is *Willy Krauch and Sons Ltd.,* home of the ultimate wood-smoked Atlantic salmon, which is also endorsed by Her Majesty the Queen. It is truly incredible melt-in-your-mouth salmon. You can visit and shop at the Krauch smokehouse, located right on Highway 7. While there, be sure to try the hot smoked lemon-pepper salmon. Chances are you'll find you've devoured your entire souvenir before you even get home. Thankfully, they'll ship salmon anywhere. For details call (800) 758–4412 or (902) 772–2188.

Continue south along the Marine Drive until you reach the little communities of Jeddore and Oyster Pond. All along this highway you will pass through centuries-old fishing communities. Some of these date back to the era of the Acadians.

You can get a glimpse into the lives of these hardworking fishing folk at the ***Fisherman's Life Museum,*** in Jeddore. This was the homestead of Ervin and Ethelda Myers, parents of thirteen daughters. Ervin was an inshore fisherman who also worked in the woods each winter.

Costumed guides use the home's woodstove to do their morning baking, and on the day I visited, they offered me tea and traditional ginger snaps right out of the oven. The ladies were also busy making hooked rugs from scraps. The residents of this home enriched the poor coastal soil with seaweed mulch, manure, and compost. Sheep still graze in the yard of the one-and-a-half-story house. To make their own yeast and cold medicines, the Myers grew hops near the orchard. Century-old dishes still grace the kitchen cupboards. A lady's coquettishly embroidered bloomers lay on the master bed, as if waiting for their owner. "Wouldn't Ethelda be mortified if she saw her bloomers on display?" chuckled one of the guides.

The museum is open from June until mid October Monday to Saturday from 9:30 A.M. until 5:30 P.M., Sundays 1:00 to 5:30 P.M. A small admission is charged.

If you are looking for some countryside peace and quiet that's only three-quarters of an hour from Halifax or the airport, try the ***Salmon River House Country Inn*** in Head Jeddore, just a mile from the museum. A Heritage inn located along the Salmon River, it includes several cottages as well (two are off-site and oceanside). The owners also operate the Lobster Shack. They offer outdoor activity and weekend packages, including a lobster supper package. The three-and-a-half-star inn won the provincial tourism association's top food and beverage award for 2001. Prices are standard to moderate. For reservations, call (800) 565–3353 or locally at (902) 889–3353. You can also take a peek at www.salmonriverhouse.com.

Hub of the Privateers

They don't teach this in local history lessons, but the truth is, piracy was big business in Nova Scotia once the British got hold of the territory. After hostilities broke out with the renegade colonies to the south, Britain took full advantage of the colony's strategic position and commissioned all sorts of ships for "privateering," which was piracy by all intents and purposes. Young men signed on with privateers as a way of avoiding being "press-ganged" into service with the notoriously brutal Royal Navy. Add to this the fact that Britain was almost constantly at war with somebody or other, and you can see that the high seas represented a tremendous career opportunity for the adventurous sort with a strong stomach. Captured booty was taken to Halifax, where it was "libelled off" in public auctions and the proceeds split between the shipowners, the court, and government officials.

It was this piracy and war that really gave Halifax a leg up. Even the cobblestones of the city's first streets were quarried from the shattered ruins of Fortress Louisbourg, which fell to the British shortly before Halifax's founding. Some areas of downtown *Halifax* still contain these stones, such as the Granville Street entrance to the art college. But after the War of 1812 drew to a close, piracy was no longer government endorsed.

trivia

The population of the Halifax Regional Municipality in 2004 was 39.5 percent of Nova Scotia's total population. That's 370,000 inhabitants.

Halifax's waterfront is still a fun place to hang out, pirates or no, because the city boasts a lively music scene, excellent shopping for local arts and crafts, and gourmet seafood.

Driven by the demands of six universities full of students, the nightlife can be relaxed, fun, and easy on the wallet. For both visitors and locals, the focus of interest stretches from Argyle Street, a few blocks from the harbor, to Historic Properties, with its restored waterfront buildings from the nineteenth century. Early each August the *Halifax International Busker Festival* draws street entertainers from around the world.

Overlooking the city, the fortress to which the city owes its birth, *The Citadel,* provides a stunning lookout. *Point Pleasant Park* is an extensive rustic park at the tip of Halifax's posh south end. The city also boasts large traditional English-style gardens.

Opinions about Halifax are as varied as the people who live here. The city is an eclectic mix that somehow manages to be avant-garde. The downtown is full of funky little cafes decorated with original paintings and folk art. The cafe culture is no doubt a by-product of the Nova Scotia College of Art and Design. Called NSCAD by locals, the school was founded by the one-time governess of the King of Siam's children, Anna Leonowens, whose day job was immortalized in the movie *The King and I*. For many years NSCAD was the only degree-granting art college in Canada.

NSCAD has left an indelible stamp on the funky downtown core of Halifax, as has the city's seafaring past. The Privateer's Wharf and the shops down by the waterfront are converted old-time warehouses from the Age of Sail. You are as likely to hear an avant-garde band perform original music that has won fans from all over Canada as you are to watch a crowd of Maritimers pouring onto the dance floor to the tune of "What Shall We Do with the Drunken Sailor?" —a traditional Halifax jig if ever there was one.

Where to go when in Halifax? A lot of visitors stop at three of the city's cemeteries, their interest piqued by the city's considerable connection to the *Titanic* disaster. Halifax was the port where the bodies of the victims were brought for identification and, sometimes, burial. The bodies were scooped from the freezing North Atlantic by a steamship, the *Mackay-Bennett,* which normally laid and repaired telegraph cables on the ocean floor.

trivia

The official name of Halifax's harbor is Chebucto Harbour, which in Mi'Kmaq means a "great long harbor." The Mi'Kmaq weren't exaggerating. It is the world's second-largest natural harbor.

The steamship, which was crewed with Nova Scotians from across the province, retrieved 306 bodies. When its supply of ice and embalming fluid was exhausted, it was joined by another local ship, the *Minia*. In all, 328 bodies were recovered from the water. Burial at sea followed for 119 victims, whose bodies were too damaged to preserve. Each victim was identified by a small canvas tag, numbered to indicate the order in which he or she was taken out of the water. These numbers are to be found on the victims' headstones. In many cases they are the only identification marks given, apart from the date of death shared by all the headstones: April 15, 1912.

A total of 150 casualties of the *Titanic* disaster are buried in three of Halifax's graveyards. At the ***Fairview Cemetery,*** 121 are buried in a curved arrangement resembling a ship's hull. You will find the gravesites near the intersection of Windsor Street and Kempt Road, overlooking Bedford Basin. This is where James Dawson's remains lie buried. Dawson (victim number 227) was a third-class seaman, an Irish coal trimmer—not an artist as the *Titanic* movie portrays him.

Most Halifax residents know that the James Dawson frenzy was a case of mistaken identity and the charms of a Hollywood idol. What is generally not known is the story of another case of mistaken identity involving a victim buried at the ***Baron de Hirsch Jewish Cemetery,*** final resting place of ten *Titanic* victims. This graveyard is just south of the adjacent Fairview Cemetery but is not generally open to the public.

Here is buried the fugitive Michel Navratil, a man who assumed a false identity and name, Louis M. Hoffman, in order to make off with his two children, whom he had kidnapped from his estranged wife in France. When the great oceanliner was sinking, Navratil handed his two sons over to the lifeboat crew, never revealing that the two boys were also traveling under false identities. The children survived the sinking, and were called the "Orphans of the *Titanic*" by newspaper headlines around the world until their mother recognized their pictures and traveled to America to reclaim them. Although by this time Navratil's true identity was known, his body was not exhumed; it remains buried in the Jewish cemetery, under marker number 15.

The third *Titanic* graveyard, **Mount Olivet Cemetery,** is on Mumford Road, near Dutch Village Road. Many of its nineteen victims are unidentified. It does hold the grave of a *Titanic* band member, John Clarke, a native of Liverpool, England. He and his other band members are reported to have continued to play on deck until the last of the lifeboats were filled and the waves began to claim their first victims.

Halifax is no stranger to marine disasters. Decades before the sinking of the *Titanic* came the disaster of the SS *Atlantic* (also launched by the White Star Line). The *Atlantic* ran aground in Terence Bay, just outside Halifax Harbour. Less than half the ship's approximately 1,000 passengers escaped with their lives. Divers like to explore the wreck of the *Atlantic* where it lies offshore in only 80 feet (24 m) of water.

The most famous of the city's disaster connections is the Halifax Explosion, depicted along with the story of the *Titanic* and the SS *Atlantic* at the **Maritime Museum of the Atlantic,** located on Halifax's waterfront.

The 1917 Halifax Explosion was the largest nonnuclear man-made explosion in history. Caused by the collision of two ships, the munitions ship *Mont Blanc* and the *Imo,* formerly a White Star ship, the explosion killed 1,635 people.

The museum also displays Canada's first hydrographic vessel, the CSS *Acadia,* which makes for a fascinating afternoon of ship exploration. Hydrographic vessels are used to map the ocean floor. Included in this complex is a restored ship's chandlery (supply store), William Robertson and Son, with lots of authentic marine curios. The museum is open year-round. Admission is charged. Summer hours extend from May 1 to October 30, Monday to Saturday from 9:30 A.M.

to 5:30 P.M., Tuesday until 8:00 P.M., and Sunday from 1:00 to 5:30 P.M. After October 30, the museum is closed on Monday, and doors are locked at 5:00 P.M. every day but Tuesday, when they close at 8:00 P.M. The CSS *Acadia* is not open off-season. For details, call (902) 424–7490.

One positive offshoot of the Halifax Explosion was the subsequent recon-struction of the north end of the peninsula, the area most devastated by the blast. Known as **The Hydrostones,** the now-quaint neighborhood of Tudor-revival houses boasts European-style markets, several cozy dining establish-ments, and upscale shops along Young Street. Bubbling over with the atmosphere of an English garden suburb, the area takes its name from the building material used to create the 86 buildings of Canada's first public hous-ing project. (Hydrostone is a mixture of crushed stone, sand, gravel, and port-land cement molded under intense pressure.)

If disasters and ships are not your thing, gravitate toward the beautiful **Halifax Public Gardens,** and from there meander along Spring Garden Road toward the harbor.

Between these two points, you will find countless coffee shops; all manner of restaurants, pubs, and fish-and-chips wag-ons; bohemian types, college students, and out-of-towners.

The seventeen-acre (seven-hectare) Public Gardens were originally created as a private garden in 1753, only four years after the founding of Halifax. In 1836 they were taken over by the Nova Scotia Horticultural Society. Since 1889 the park has been enclosed by a wrought-iron fence, punctu-ated by an ornate pair of ornamental gates imported from Glasgow, Scotland.

giftofthanks

As a thank-you for the food, shelter, and clothing Bostonians gave to the people of Halifax in the aftermath of the explosion, Nova Scotia gives the city of Boston an annual Christmas gift. It is a large evergreen tree, illuminated with great ceremony in that city's downtown.

The gardens are now recognized as the finest original formal Victorian gardens in North America. They have rhododendrons so massive that you can walk under a huge canopy of leaves, hidden from the passersby on the other side. The duck pond in the middle of the garden leads into a stream, lined with irises and day lilies, that passes under a small arching stone bridge. Swans share the pond with the ducks, and if you arrive at a propitious time of year, you may catch glimpses of baby swans and little ducklings dutifully swimming after their mothers. Along with the carefully tended roses, there are floating flower beds in French Formal and English Romantic styles. The Vic-torian bandstand in the center of the park is the site of free concerts on Sun-day afternoons.

No admission is charged for the gardens, which are open dawn to dusk daily but closed during the winter months.

Across Sackville Street, which borders the gardens on the north side, you will see greenhouses. Next to them a charming stone house, Public Gardens Cottage, dates back to the life and times of Richard Power, one-time gardener to the duke of Devonshire in Ireland. His descendants tended the gardens until the 1960s.

It is possible to find a low-key, elegant, secluded-feeling place to stay, right in the city. My choice for a relaxing stay is the ***Halliburton House Inn,*** located at 5184 Morris Street, a few blocks south of the corner of Barrington Street and Spring Garden Road, which informally marks the end point of most of downtown's clubs (just far enough that the noise of the clubs won't keep you up at night, but close enough that it's a five-minute walk to hopping nightlife).

trivia

Canada's first newspaper was the *Halifax Gazette*, published in 1752.

The Halliburton House Inn comprises its original Heritage house and two adjacent buildings. At the back of the inn is a series of garden courtyards, some ultraprivate and attached directly to the suites. It has an excellent restaurant with a menu showcasing seafood and wild game, and several dining rooms from which to choose, including a private dining room suitable to small meetings or intimate tête-à-têtes. Among the twenty-nine guest rooms, several have their own working fireplace. My favorite, complete with Jacuzzi and king-size bed, has its own verandah.

The main building, dating from 1809, is the former home of Sir Brenton Halliburton, chief justice of the Nova Scotia Supreme Court. The home briefly served as the Dalhousie Law School from 1885 to 1887. To reserve a room at the antiques-filled inn, call (902) 420–0658, or check out the Web site at www.halliburton.ns.ca. Rates are moderate to deluxe.

For a small city, ethnic food abounds, with lots of Lebanese, Italian, Greek, Vietnamese, Thai, East Indian, and vegetarian places awaiting your discovery. Later in the evening embark on a pub crawl, a sport heavily favored by the city's many university students.

The Eastern Lighthouse Route

Take a Canadian 10-cent piece in your hand and examine the sailing ship that enjoys equal billing with Her Majesty the Queen. That is the famous Nova Scotia sailing ship the **Bluenose,** as photographed by W. R. MacAskill. For two

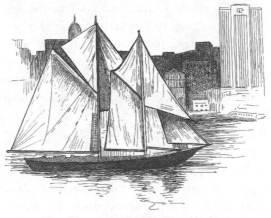

The *Bluenose II* in Halifax Harbour

decades during the early part of the nineteenth century, this schooner won one international race after another. Eventually, it came to symbolize the pride of Canada's seagoing easterners. A replica of the *Bluenose* (the *Bluenose II*) graces Halifax Harbour today.

MacAskill, whose famous photograph found its way onto the Canadian dime, also made famous another Nova Scotian landmark: **Peggys Cove.** This once-isolated fishing cove has become so synonymous with "quaint fishing villages" that it has become anything *but* off the beaten path. Now busloads of tourists come to soak up the "unspoiled beauty" of this village.

Those who consider a pilgrimage to Peggys Cove mandatory do themselves a disservice if they do not continue farther down the **South Shore** to the historic villages and other unspoiled and largely untouched coastal communities along Highway 3, which is provincially designated the Lighthouse Route.

During the Colonial era the British Crown supplied Nova Scotian privateers with letters of marque, entitling them to loot and plunder enemy ships. This freewheeling approach to the seafaring tradition was revived during the era of Prohibition, when rumrunners smuggled contraband booze into the United States from the tiny fishing communities that dot the South Shore. From the south end of Halifax to the southernmost tip of the province, some of the grandest old homes had their beginnings as the houses of sea captains who owed their wealth to their success on the high seas and in hidden coves.

To reach the South Shore from Halifax, follow the "shore road," also known as Route 333, which will give you a glimpse of the many unspoiled coastal communities, such as Seabright, French Village, and Indian Harbour, that line **St. Margarets Bay.** You can also drop by Peggys Cove if you really have to take a look. If you want to bypass this area and get into the South Shore more directly, take Provincial Highway 103, which you can also access from Route 333 at exit 5. At this point you will have reached the head of St. Margarets Bay.

City dwellers looking for a good beach often head to this bay because it is shallow and runs sufficiently far back that the water is reasonably warm in late summer. Several beaches that offer excellent swimming are in Hubbards and Queensland.

There is a charming little Heritage inn and restaurant located in Hubbards, which makes the local beach communities even more enticing during a short jaunt from the city. The **Dauphinee Inn,** at 167 Shore Club Road, is the second-oldest inn in the province, having operated since 1920. It overlooks a small inlet, just off the main road, so you can spot it easily. The little restaurant is also very cozy, with a panoramic view of the shore, and it features assorted packages, in which all the details are worked out for rooms, a candlelight lobster dinner with wine, for example, and the use of a canoe or bicycle. Rates are moderate. For information, call (800) 567–1790 or (902) 857–1790, or visit www .dauphineeinn.com. The inn is open only during the summer.

If you follow along Route 329, you'll reach the point of the peninsula that separates St. Margarets Bay from **Mahone Bay.** Here you will also find a provincial picnic park and Bayswater Beach, with its broad stretch of white sand. From time to time seals can be seen sunning themselves nearby.

The name Mahone actually is derived from the French word *mahonne*, which was the kind of vessel favored by French pirates. Foremost among the bay's islands are **Big** and **Little Tancook Islands.** The islands can be reached by a small pedestrian-only ferry that runs two to six times daily, depending on the day of the week. For details on the ferry, call Tancook Island Transportation at (902) 228–2340. Avoid taking the last ferry of the day to Tancook if you want to return the same day, because it docks on the island for the night.

In earlier days the combined population of the two Tancook Islands exceeded 1,100. Isolation, a downturn in the fishing industry, and the need to move off the islands for junior and senior high schooling all contributed to the population shrinkage. Locals get around mostly with all-terrain vehicles or dirt bikes, but some other vehicles have been brought to the island, although the ferry carries only passengers.

The shallow, pebbly swimming beach at Southeast Cove on Big Tancook Island is quite warm and accessed by a pleasant hike through the island.

The first Europeans on the islands were German farmers who settled here because they could let their cattle range freely. They soon discovered that the soil was perfect for growing oversize cabbages; even today Tancook is noted for its superb sauerkraut. You can't miss it in local grocery stores. It is imaginatively labeled "Tancook Sauerkraut" and comes packaged in something resembling a red-and-white-striped milk carton.

The permanent residents are now most commonly involved in the fishing industry; historically, they engaged in schooner-building. In addition to the company of seagulls, the thrill of isolation in a completely out-of-the-way seaside setting, and nature trails, Big Tancook Island offers a bed-and-breakfast, a canteen, a grocery store, and a gift shop.

Two colorful villages overlook Mahone Bay. On three fingers of one peninsula you will find **Chester.** Its first residents were transplanted Bostonians, in 1759. These were followed by United Empire Loyalists, along with the French, German, and Swiss.

Its early links to New England did not spare Chester from being the focus of raids by American privateers. In 1782, while the village's men were off gathering firewood, three such ships threatened to sack the defenseless village. The broomstick-carrying women of the village marched back and forth along the hill above the community, the red linings of their cloaks worn outward. The privateers, thinking that the village was guarded by British redcoats, decided to sail farther south and sack neighboring Lunenburg instead.

Check out one of the colorful platters or bowls made by folk artist Jim Smith, who operates **Nova Scotia Folk Pottery** on Front Harbour during the summer months. The **Warp and Woof** on Water Street carries local crafts as well as imported items needed to make your seaside holiday more comfortable, like cottage rugs that will hold up to hard wear, and fashionable sun hats, as well as rain slickers. There is also a selection of local hooked rugs (generally nautical in theme), as well as CDs by Nova Scotia musicians. Staff claim that theirs is the oldest tourist shop in the province.

For the past hundred years or so, Chester has been the summer retreat of sailing enthusiasts, from the descendants of U.S. president Grover Cleveland to the presidents of universities, along with a smattering of cabinet ministers, former prime ministers, and famous authors. The affluent summer crowd swells the village's permanent population by as much as 30 percent, giving it both a touch of cultural vibrancy and the lotus-eater quality of exotic haunts. There are gleaming yachts, Jaguars and Mercedes, seaside eateries with trendy menus, and Cape Cod architecture without the New York crowd. Yet few people in neighboring Halifax give Chester a second thought except in mid-August during **Race Week,** which since 1904 has been the culmination of the social season.

The race draws sailors from Boston and beyond, filling the bay with sleek yachts. Parties spring up everywhere, and people flock to the **Chester Playhouse.** This venue was purchased and then donated to the village by financier and author Christopher Ondaatje. The Chester Playhouse playbill for the summer can be viewed at www.chesterplayhouse.ns.ca. Every summer something new and fresh keeps the regulars coming back.

Chester can be explored in an hour, but savored in a month or two. Do not miss a visit to *Julien's Bakery,* three streets back from the harbor, at 43 Queen Street. The cafe is named for Didier Julien, a Master Baker, *Patissier,* and *Chocolatier,* who began training as an apprentice in France at age fourteen. The cafe now has a shop in Lunenburg and a cafe in the Hydrostone neighborhood in Halifax. They also have great sandwiches to take away for the road, and a front patio where you can enjoy your scrumptious baked goods along with beer or wine. The coffees are Paris-worthy and the "calorific" almond croissants are worth gaining a few inches around the waist. (Be forewarned: These are dipped in rum syrup, filled with almond cream, topped with almond cream, and baked again). They also have totally decadent triple-chocolate cakes. The baking for all three shops comes from this location's wood-fired oven (for that authentic French bread crust) and is delivered daily to the Lunenburg and Halifax sites. You'll think you died and went to Paris.

The influx of well-heeled summer visitors with discerning palates and a taste for seafood has kept restaurants hopping. A favorite watering hole, *The Fo'c'sle,* is the oldest of these, and is located just across the street from Julien's.

One street downhill from Julien's is *Chez Glass Lass,* an amazing glasswork shop in the town's core at 65 Duke Street. This is the retail outlet and smaller workshop of a larger glassworks called *Kiln Art* at the edge of town. The Duke Street shop does have a smaller kiln on-site and some of their incredible fused glass is made there. The shop manager showed me how the one-of-a-kind pieces are made using finely powdered glass, which comes from surplus glass left over from stained-glass rough edges. This is dripped and drizzled into patterns to make amazing world-class plates, place settings, lamp shades, windows, and other whimsical objets d'arts. My personal favorite is a place setting inspired by Chagall. Many of Halifax's posh hotels use pieces from this glassworks for their fanciest presentations. You can check out some of their work on their Web site at www.kilnart.ca.

This community's naming follows a very royalist pattern. Right after Water Street, which fronts the harbor, comes Duke Street, then Queen, then, one block further up the hill, King Street. Where King Street intersects Pleasant Street, and just one block away from the waterfront, you can view the artistry of renowned painter Jose Antonio Valverde-Alcalde, who has a summer home here, at the *Valverde Studio Gallery.* The artist's work is held in Spanish Embassies in Ottawa and Copenhagen, as well as by major corporations and by the King and Queen of Spain. The gallery is open from May through September Monday through Saturday 11:00 A.M. to 5:00 P.M. and Sunday noon to

5:00 P.M. Reach the artist by phone at (902) 275–5341, or visit his Web site at www .valverdestudiogallery.com.

Farther along Provincial Highway 103 or closer to the shoreline on High-way 3, you will pass **Oak Island,** reputed to be the site where Captain William Kidd hid his treasure. For two centuries people have risked their lives (and sometimes lost them) trying to get at the treasure supposedly hidden under an elaborate network of underground tunnels.

Continuing along Highway 103, you'll come to Mahone Bay, which has several star attractions tucked in among this sailor's paradise and its bay with 360-odd islands.

The pretty shoreline, dotted with churches, is a postcard waiting to happen. Pull into the **Innlet Cafe,** situated at the perfect bend in the road for photographing Mahone Bay. Set up your tripod or prop your camera on the stone retaining wall at the front of the cafe, and you will get a picture of one of the most photogenic spots in the province.

This village gives the impression of being a bit busier than Chester, since a number of craftspeople have set up shop here.

It seems that few can resist buying a quilt when visiting this part of Nova Scotia. Foremost among the shops offering stunning patchwork apparel and quilts is **Suttles & Seawinds,** on Mahone Bay's Main Street. Nearby is **Birdsall-Worthington Pottery Ltd.** They specialize in commemorative dishes, such as birth, wedding, graduation, and anniversary plates, as well as handmade ear-rings. Across the street you will find **Amos Pewter,** which is part of a net-work of econo-museums. The workshop combines the elements of an artisan shop and demonstrations of the skill used to produce their product. The shop features a wide range of useful household goods and decorative objects. At the back of the shop is the studio, which overlooks the harbor and garden. From this vantage point you can watch the final finishing on some pewter, or take part in some crafty business: For a small fee, you can make a pewter object of your own to take home. Another shop worth a visit is the upscale **Teazer,** on Edgewater Drive, which is noted for fine local crafts and quality clothing.

Privateers figured prominently in the community's history. During the War of 1812, an American ship, *The Young Teazer,* was chased into Mahone Bay by a British warship. One of the crewmen aboard the privateer was a British deserter who set fire to the ship's powder magazine rather than be captured by the British. The resulting explosion killed twenty-eight on board.

The flourishing shipbuilding trade of old-time Mahone Bay brought with it considerable wealth, as shown by the many stately old Victorian, Georgian, and Cape Cod homes here. Many Main Street businesses occupy buildings formerly ʳ shipbuilders. A walking tour brochure gives a closer look at the local ture. It's available at the **Mahone Bay Settler's Museum,** at 578 Main ᴖᴛᴇᴇᴛ. The village hosts a wooden-boat festival at the beginning of August. It includes workshops, demonstrations of maritime skills for all ages, schooner races, and boatyard tours. Admission is free. For details, call (902) 624–6263.

After Mahone Bay continue along Trunk Highway 3 until you reach **Lunenburg,** the birthplace of many famous ships. It was here that the *Bluenose* and its replica were built, as well as the full-scale replica of the HMS *Bounty* used in the Marlon Brando version of *Mutiny on the Bounty.*

As far as picturesque fishing villages go, they don't get any prettier than Lunenburg and its harbor, proof of which you will find on the back of a Canadian $100 bill.

The most noteworthy of the buildings forming the UNESCO World Heritage Village's shoreline is the **Fisheries Museum of the Atlantic.** The large red building itself has several stories of presentations on the tough life of a fisherman, an aquarium, and an eatery, along with several fishing vessels, including the schooner *Teresa E. Connor.* Built in the 1930s, this boat served in the fisheries for twenty-five years. Inside the building, you'll find the aquarium showing the variety of fish harvested for food. My personal favorite is the Lump Fish, which has a cartoonlike appearance as it leaves its mouth stuck to the glass whilst maintaining a deadpan expression (well, as deadpan as a fish can be expected to manage).

On the second floor of the Fisheries Museum is a monument to the many sailors who lost their lives during fierce storms. A map shows the hundreds of ships that wrecked on Sable Island, and a detailed display tells the story of the half dozen schooners that succumbed to the North Atlantic in 1926 and 1927, during what are called the August Gales. A small chapel adjoins the display and family members of the many lost Lunenburg sailors are invited to sign a book of remembrance. The chapel also features the mariner's version of the Bible's twenty-third psalm, which begins, "The lord is my pilot, I shall not drift . . ."

The museum also features models and relics of many of the famous sailing ships that originated from Lunenburg, most notably the wheel of the original *Bluenose,* in its day the fastest sailing ship in the world. Admission is charged. The museum is open daily from 9:30 A.M. to 5:30 P.M.

One of the big outcroppings of this is a strong tradition of folk music and art, as evidenced by the **Lunenburg Folk Harbour Festival,** held the second weekend of August every year from Thursday through Sunday. This is a really great party well worth attending, so keep it in mind when you time your visit.

There is also an annual crafts festival, in which many local artisans display their wares. It is timed to take place the second weekend in July. Since the town is so pleasant and picturesque, many craftspeople and artists live in the vicinity. Lunenburg has nineteen art galleries, mostly clustered in a five-block area, making it the perfect place to buy paintings and other art for home decor. It is not unusual to have art dealers from out of the country arrive with a van and fill it with paintings created in this noteworthy artist enclave. Visit *Mauril Art Studio,* where one artist of note, Mauril Desbiens, has works in a variety of medium, which he sells all over Europe and North America. Loaded with vivid color, and depicting the rugged coastal life of the South Shore, his works are also available as prints.

In Lunenburg you can stay at the historic *Boscawen Inn,* built in 1888. It is located at 150 Cumberland Street, overlooking the harbor. Its twenty guest rooms are furnished with antiques. Rates are standard to moderate. The restaurant is also highly rated and participates in the "Taste of Nova Scotia" program. For reservations, call (800) 354–5009 or (902) 634–3325.

What really gave Lunenburg its color was the influx of large numbers of German Protestants by boat from Halifax at its founding in 1753. *Deutsch* (German) soon became "Dutch" in everyone's parlance, so everyone began calling them the Lunenburg Dutch. Their descendants have put an indelible stamp on the local lingo. The accent is strong and verbs sometimes find their way to the end of the sentence.

The German connection continues today. Many German nationals have recently purchased homes along this coast for use as summer homes, which they fly to annually, thanks to cheap and convenient air connections and a strong Euro currency.

When you are in Lunenburg, do not miss up a chance to eat at *Magnolia's Grill,* at 128 Montague Street, one block up from the harbor. It's a small place, yet word of its great food is an open secret, so plan to either make a reservation at (902) 634–3287 or go early and ask for a spot on their waiting list. (Plan on perhaps an hour-long wait.) The food is wonderful, especially their Creole Peanut Soup, their seafood, and their tangy calamari. Desserts are sublime. The atmosphere is convivial and quirky, with a collection of foreign currency on the wall, ceramic knickknacks, and photos of everybody from Princess Diana to the late Prime Minister Pierre Trudeau, as well as the usual smattering of movie stars, who've graced Lunenburg with their presence in the past. (That's not so unusual. Recently, Alicia Silverstone was here filming in Chester.) With only six booths and two tables, Magnolia's is tiny, quaint, and open for the summer only. In the winter, you will have to resign yourself to their take-out soup business.

Before leaving the town, plan to stroll around and look at some of its lovely architecture. Of all the buildings, by far the most imposing structure is

Lunenburg Academy, built in 1894 high atop Gallows Hill, where it can be seen for many miles around. This is the province's only surviving academy building dating from the nineteenth century. It is full of all sorts of Victorian bits of fancy: oval-shaped portholes, towers, decorative shingles, and intricate bracketry. And when you reach the hill where this municipal, provincial, and federal Heritage building stands, you are presented with a panoramic view of the town's many beautiful old homes.

Traveling south from Lunenburg, take a fifteen-minute detour off Highway 3 and travel on Route 332 in the direction of East LaHave. Just before you reach this point you will come to the head of Rose Bay and a small sign indicating the exit to *The Ovens.* This is a sight you must not miss, for here was the scene of a major gold strike in 1861.

It still holds some gold deposits to this day. For a small admission fee, you can enter the park and pan for gold along the beach. It's easy to get on-the-spot prospecting lessons, because the beach is the regular haunt of helpful amateur prospectors. The management also gives periodic demonstrations of proper technique.

After an afternoon of panning I must confess that my family came away with six grains of gold. Not much, but the experience was greatly enhanced by the kids' "get-rich-quick" fantasies and by the occasion to hang out with some real gold diggers.

At The Ovens you can descend a series of concrete steps set into the side of sea caves. These are so massive that they are legendary to the Mi'Kmaq, who believe that a brave once traveled from one of these caves to a similar one on the Bay of Fundy, on the other side of Nova Scotia. Once you get to the bottom of the steps of some of the bigger caves, you will be treated to the earthshaking boom of the waves as they crash against the rocks. You can also take a boat with a guide, who will lead you right into the biggest caves.

The Ovens has campsites and some log cabins for rent, a pool, and a restaurant with a surprisingly good menu, considering its secluded location. Rates are standard to moderate. For reservations call (902) 766–4621.

After visiting The Ovens, take Highway 332 back to Route 3 outside Lunenburg and then turn south at exit 12, onto Provincial Highway 103. After a half hour's drive, you will come to *Liverpool,* once favored by the privateers.

From 1750 until the War of 1812 ended, Nova Scotia's and, in particular, Liverpool's ships were commissioned to roam the high seas in search of vessels to plunder. Liverpudlian Enos Collins, owner of a privateer ship called *The Packet,* was rumored to be Canada's richest man; he died with a fortune of $10 million.

The wealth brought in is evidenced by the historic buildings and museums here, recalling the wild days of the town's youth. Liverpool is the site of the oldest house in the entire collection of Nova Scotia museums. To find it, exit Provincial Highway 103 on Main Street and proceed in the direction of Moose Harbour. Just after Bristol Avenue you'll see the museum at 105 Main Street, set far back on a lawn that it shares with the county museum.

Called the ***Perkins House,*** after its original owner, this one-and-a-half-story building was the home of a twenty-seven-year-old Connecticut widower who came to Nova Scotia in 1762. Here he successfully established himself as, among other things, a justice of the court of common pleas, a judge of probate, and a member of the legislative assembly.

In this simple home, Simeon Perkins entertained privateer captains, governors, and traveling men of the cloth. He wrote about his life in a diary that he kept faithfully from 1766 until his death in 1812. It now serves as a valuable historical record on the early life of this province's settlers. The excerpts of Simeon Perkins's diary make for fascinating reading, and are well worth buying for only $4.00. Entitled *The Boston Tea Party and the American Revolution,* the book gives a fascinating account of the coming revolution, told through the eyes of this transplanted New Englander who still corresponded with relatives back home. Here's an excerpt from early 1774: "There is a tumult at Boston, occasioned by the East Indies Company sending quantities of tea to Boston, and other places in America. 342 chests of tea December last were destroyed by a number of people dressed as savages. Benjamin Arnold says that Capt. Snow has two letters for me, sealed in black, which I am fearful foretells of death in the family . . ." A small admission is charged. It is open June 1 to October 15 Monday to Saturday from 9:30 A.M. until 5:30 P.M. and Sunday from 1:00 to 5:30 P.M.

Perkins raised six daughters and two sons here, but Liverpool wasn't the most tranquil place. In 1783 Americans landed at nearby Fort Point and overran the town. Through the efforts of Perkins, they were repulsed.

Perkins House, Liverpool

All parts of the diary that were written in Nova Scotia have been published by the Champlain Society. The original is on display at the **Queens County Museum,** which is adjacent to Perkins House. This museum represents the warehouse of Perkins's business.

If you have any ancestral roots from this end of Nova Scotia, this is a good place to trace them. The building, which is operated by the historical society, houses the Thomas Raddall Research Room, which features a library and genealogical records for Queens County. Thomas Raddall, one of the province's most noteworthy writers, published many novels set in Nova Scotia. It has the same hours as Perkins House next door. A small admission is charged.

Explore your artistic side at the **Gallery of Roger Savage,** at 611 Mersey Point Road in a bedroom community called **Mersey Point.** To get there take the next right turn after Perkins House and drive down School Street toward the Western Head Lighthouse. The drive takes about fifteen minutes.

Savage is one of the region's most highly esteemed artists. He not only does paintings of coastal landscapes, but also creates watercolors, portraits, and lithographs. For information or to register for a workshop, call (902) 354–5431. Roger is a plein air painter, executing his works on the spot. During my latest visit he showed me the results of a week-long painting expedition on Sable Island. His wife, Isolde, rents out two rooms in their home, each with its own private entrance and patio overlooking the sea. Every morning guests discover a trolley outside their bedroom with a prearranged selection of breakfast items, complete with your own toaster, so you can enjoy your morning meal at your leisure. The Savages also provide guests with quirky tip sheets and an informal sketch/map of the local area so they can explore on their own. To reserve one of the two bedrooms in his home or for details, visit www.bbcanada.com/galleryguesthouse.

Downtown Liverpool is worth time meandering. Have coffee and home-baked treats at the Woodpile on Main Street, then drop in next door at **ADJA Studio and Gallery,** at 177 Main. When I visited, the shop carried works by close to a dozen locally based artists and crafts people, many of whom show in other regions during the winter months. They also feature wonderfully eclectic jewelry, 80 percent of which is made in the shop itself.

On the same side, and another block further down at 219 Main Street, is the **Sherman Hines Museum of Photography,** which is affiliated with the Rossignol Cultural Centre just around the corner. If you are a photography buff, this is the must-see collection that will make your holiday complete. Sherman Hines is one of the region's most renowned photographers. Since 1996 his collection of photographic artifacts and vintage photography has been housed in this building, Liverpool's old town hall, which dates from

1902. Flanking the stairs leading to the second-floor display are movie projectors from the hundred-year-old Astor Theatre, containing some parts that date back to 1917.

The museum has the largest box camera (complete with baffles) that you or I will see in our lifetimes. It is as big around as a dining room table, and had to be carried on the back of a wagon. The museum has wonderful old daguerreotypes (glass-imprinted photographic positives), some in the form of lampshades, and one by famous photographer Wallace MacAskill, which has been used in a firescreen. The collection has one room containing all the attributes of a well-equipped Victorian photography studio. Stereoscopic viewers, magic lanterns, and an extensive collection of cameras serve as a complete history of the art of picture taking.

Around the corner, at 205 Church Street, the *Rossignol Cultural Centre* aims at giving a comprehensive experience, featuring under one roof a variety of museums, art galleries, libraries, and wildlife (mounted and stuffed for your viewing pleasure). The museum shares it name with a large lake in the Kejimkujik area, hence its authentic 1930s trapper's cabin and displays on hunting, fishing, and the Mi'Kmaq culture. Displays cover the gamut from the serious to the tongue-in-cheek, ranging from a museum containing apothecary items from a Halifax drug store that survived the Halifax Explosion, to a Folk Art Museum, and even an Outhouse Museum, dedicated to the little shack out back. The Hines Museum and the cultural center are open mid-May to mid-October Monday to Saturday from 10:00 A.M. to 5:30 P.M. In July and August, they also open on Sundays noon to 5:30 P.M. A small admission is charged and covers both facilities. Contact them at (902) 354–3067 or www.rossignolcultural centre.com.

Flowing down from Lake Rossignol deep in the interior, the Mersey River wends its way to the sea right through the center of Liverpool, the two sides of which are connected by a small bridge. Just after leaving this earlier cluster of shops and museums on Main and Church Streets, turn onto Route 3 and cross the bridge. Just before the signposts directing people to exit 19 on the main highway is a small railway station, set back from the road. This is the site of the *Hank Snow Country Music Centre,* which shares space with a small railway museum and the *Nova Scotia Country Music Hall of Fame.* People of a certain age will remember Hank Snow, if for nothing else than his timeless mega-hit "I'm Movin' On," which included in its recording a lonely train whistle. The museum attendant will gladly play you the famous song, and train whistles are among the items for sale in the center, which hosts an annual Hank Snow Tribute and was featured on the Nashville Network. Hank Snow was born and raised just 2 miles (3 km) from this station. Abused by his stepfather, he frequently slept at this very train station. Eventually, he shipped out as a cabin boy at age twelve. Soon afterward he began listening to country music greats. Inspired by them, and starting with a Halifax radio show in 1935, he went on to a successful international career, as evidenced by the many album covers that grace the walls. The museum contains a guitar made from a piece of the floor of the Grand Ole Opry, stage outfits from his storied career, and, most notably, two of his convertibles from his glory days as an international star. (Check out the 1947 Cadillac in mint condition.)

Snow was not the only star from this area. He was preceded by Wilf Carter and followed by Carol Baker. Some of their memorabilia are also displayed at the center. After you visit the museum, and see just how far his wanderlust took him, you'll understand what inspired such songs as "I've Been Everywhere." The center is open year-round. From mid-May to mid-October, hours are Monday to Saturday from 9:00 A.M. to 5:00 P.M., Sunday open at noon. In the winter months, the center opens Monday to Friday from 9:00 A.M. to 4:00 P.M. A small admission is charged. Contact the center at (902) 354–4675; www.hanksnow.com.

There are a number of cozy places to stay in the area, two of which are located near wonderfully unspoiled beaches. One, **White Point Beach Resort,** is rated three and one-half stars and is quite popular. It occupies the shoreline of White Point Beach. Sometime during your travels though the region you'll find yourself tempted to consider getting a summer cottage. Then again, you might decide that you'd rather leave the laundry, the cooking, and the organizing to someone else, so that you can just play. Besides, who wants to run the risk of being a freeloading relative's new best friend, which is always a danger when you seek out the Robinson Crusoe experience. White Point is organized to meet these two seemingly conflicting needs. You can have the feeling of a cottage of your own, yet you can enjoy room service when you want it. You can enjoy your space your way, but you can have maid service instead of having to be an indentured servant to your kids during your holiday. White Point offers a wide range of accommodation options, including cottages with fully equipped kitchens. But when you're all played out, you could simply putter down to the main lodge and partake in one of their expertly prepared meals.

The formula seems to work very well. Nightly bonfires, game rooms, lots of kid-friendly activities, a CPGA-rated golf course, indoor and outdoor pools, and a stretch of beach that seems like the end of a very private world all combine to create a great personal getaway. Rather than having to own all the toys necessary to recreate at the beach, you can just rent everything from sea kayaks to boogie boards to wetsuits by the hour. White Point Beach Resort has combined the best elements of a "boutique hotel" and cottage country. It now involves various permutations, such as membership in their golf course, and the potential to purchase a holiday home in the community, or simply rent by the week or the night. Then, if a sudden unexpected in-law arrives, you can send him to the main lodge to indulge in the substantial and scrumptious buffet or take his pick from the à la carte menu. The pork ribs fall from the bone, the fish is done to perfection (tender, not dry), and their desserts need to be worked off doing twenty laps in the pool.

People who want to be closer to the action can get a room in the main lodge. Since there is an indoor pool, facing the ocean, even in the coldest months you can swim in warm water while watching the North Atlantic surf outside. The resort has perfected its vacation packages (some are geared towards women on the run from the kids and the house, others are designed for golfers). Buses can collect people from Halifax, for example, and bring them for a holiday. If you drive, there are two exits off Highway 103, exit 20a or 21. It would seem confusing, but the whole complex is on a point of land jutting out to the sea and all roads seem to lead to White Point, with multiple signs helping you find your way. You can also reach it by driving south from Liverpool on Route 3, the smaller coastal road. As you pull into the complex, signs warn you to slow down for children and bunnies. They aren't joking. The place is overrun with very tame bunnies, who invariably are being hotly pursued by children looking to pet them. Rates and options vary widely, so it's best to read through the various options on their Web site at www.white point.com. You can reach the lodge by calling (800) 565–5068. Rates are moderate to deluxe.

A much smaller-scale set of beachside villas can be found at neighboring Summerville Beach, at a place called ***The Quarterdeck Beachside Villas and Grill.*** It provides intimate two-story condo-style accommodations overlooking the tranquil, spotless white sands of Summerville Beach, on a site that was occupied by much older rustic cottages for fifty years. The new villas are so close to the shoreline that you are lulled to sleep by the steady lapping of the waves.

If you are in the mood for an early-morning hike, walk to the far southern end of the beach and then cross over a small arm of water via a one-time rail crossing. This leads to another tranquil little cove, where you can watch shorebirds do their thing. The beach is home to piping plovers and sandpipers.

Each villa has lots of pleasant little extras: propane-powered fireplace; two bathrooms, one featuring a Jacuzzi complete with rubber ducky; well-equipped kitchen facilities; a patio overlooking the ocean; and a second-floor deck, also facing the sea. The walls are decorated with original artwork, all for sale.

The restaurant here overlooks the ocean and serves plank salmon, among other delicious fare. The Quarterdeck is off Highway 103; turn at exit 20 and head for Summerville Beach. For information and reservations, call (800) 565–1119 or (902) 683–2998. For details, visit www.quarterdeck.ns.ca or e-mail quarterdeck@eastlink.ca. Rates are moderate to deluxe.

From Liverpool you have the option of turning inland onto Route 8 to experience the wilderness of **Kejimkujik National Park** (or Keji, as it is generally called by locals), or you can continue heading south on either Route 3 or Highway 103 (which briefly overlaps Route 3) around the tip of Nova Scotia, and reserve Kejimkujik for later. In the next section we will continue to follow the route southward, toward Yarmouth, the southern gateway to the province.

Even if you want to head straight to Yarmouth on Highway 103, if you don't mind a brief detour you can visit a very quirky collector, antiques dealer, and artist. If you're up for the magical mystery tour, when leaving Liverpool take exit 19 on the 103 and turn inland for 12 miles (just under 20 km). Just after the turn-off to Middlefield (easily noted by the presence of a senior citizens' complex on your right), you will arrive at Twelve Mile House, which starting in the mid-1800s was a stagecoach hotel. This is marked by a faded sign that is hard to see and easily overshot before you realize where you are. But you will also notice that the front door is marked by a race car–style checkered flag hanging from a broomstick.

Dennis Teakle of **Teakle and Butler Antiques** is an artist who grew up about 6 miles (10 km) from Algonquin Park in Ontario (stomping ground of world-famous artist Tom Thompson, not to mention a number of the Group of Seven painters who were to follow him into the wilderness). Their influence shows in his work, which is vibrant and bold. He also deals in some antiques. On the afternoon I visited, Dennis was cutting wood to make frames for a number of his paintings, which were slated to be shown in a gallery in Ontario. The sound of a band saw made it impossible for him to hear my knock, but the barking and snarling of several dogs (large, with big snapping teeth, I presume) could be heard over the gratefully high solid-wood fence. Luckily, these alerted him to my presence, since his screen door was barricaded. Eventually the band saw stopped and a smiling Dennis emerged, covered in sawdust. After a brief introduction, he led me through the eclectic house (which does not appear to have undergone any radical renovation since its days as a stagecoach hotel). His studio was packed with expressive oil paintings on board, allowing for easy storage and transport. His entire house is full of an impressive collection of Oriental art that he was happy to show, but much of it is not for sale. Many of these pieces are hundreds of years old and have been selected with an expert eye for their authenticity and value. With such a long history of seafaring traders who covered the globe in the golden age of sail, Nova Scotia appears to hold exotic, unexpected treasures that belie its small population and size. You might want to call ahead to make sure he's receiving visitors, at (902) 685–2779.

The Western Lighthouse Route

Just past the town of Liverpool, on Highway 103, is a wonderful but little-known wilderness area. It is the nesting ground of endangered species, an unspoiled stretch of shoreline completely lacking in "development." During the piping plovers' mating season, parts of this area are closed to the public.

In 1985 the province handed over 5,400 acres (2,160 hectares) of this land to the National Park Service, which now administers it as part of Kejimkujik National Park. Called the *Seaside Adjunct,* it offers two pristine beaches, both 2 miles (3 km) long, completely unspoiled wilderness, and rocky headlands. (There are no facilities for human visitors, so plan accordingly.) It is very easy to miss the road for the Seaside Adjunct, so as you drive south down the one and only stretch of highway (Route 3/Highway 103), be on the lookout for the Port Joli Community Centre. Take a left here and follow a gravel road to the Seaside Adjunct. It is well signed.

Along with birds, you may get a look at some coastal seals as they frolic in the waves off this blissfully solitary shore.

Just south of the Seaside Adjunct, off Highway 103 and about 25 miles (40 km) from Liverpool, you will come to the *Port l'Hebert Pocket Wilderness.* Look for a sign on the road 6 miles (10 km) after Port Joli and just before you reach the Shelburne County line.

At Port l'Hebert you will find about 2 miles (3 km) of graveled walking trails that cut through 150 acres (60 hectares) of woodlands and salt marshes.

The Endangered Piping Plover

The *Seaside Adjunct* is a nesting ground of the ill-fated piping plover, which has become increasingly rare due to its unfortunate habit of laying eggs in piles of rock near the shoreline. The spotted eggs look decidedly like rocks, which would be a nice form of camouflage if only they didn't get stepped on by human passersby.

Bear this in mind if you decide to walk along the pristine beaches of this coast: What may look like a rock may actually be the egg of an endangered baby bird. So crucial is this area to the survival of piping plovers that parts of the annex are closed from late April to late July so that the birds can hatch safely.

These paths stretch from the small parking lot on the side of the highway where you turned off to the shores of a tiny bay called Port L'Hebert Harbour, which draws its name from an apothecary who sailed with Samuel de Champlain in 1604. Louis l'Hebert's name lives on at Louis Head as well.

These lands are the wintering grounds of a flock of Canada geese. They need eel grass, open water, and as little disturbance as possible to get through the winter; few places suit them as well as this site. Due to its importance, the Canadian Wildlife Service has designated the marshy shoreline a waterfowl sanctuary.

The trail is quite an easy walk, with some boardwalk aiding your travel, but if you stray from the path you may discover your feet sinking into the bog. The water looks quite uninviting here, stained as it is a murky tea-brown. In fact, however, it is nutrient-rich, and the salt marshes that border this bay are nurseries for all manner of sea life. Before white settlers arrived, inland Mi'Kmaq families came here to gather shellfish and to fish.

trivia

The Nova Scotia Loyalists had a banner on which was inscribed the Latin word: *resurgam*. It means: "I shall rise again."

Once you have finished stretching your legs, return to your vehicle at the end of the trail loop and head, camera-ready, 12 miles (20 km) south on Route 3 to the scenic village of **Lockeport.** This is the site of the province's first officially designated Heritage streetscape, which slates it for historic preservation. **Crescent Beach,** which runs along the entrance to the town, was once on the back of the Canadian $50 bill.

A visitor information bureau overlooks the beach. Here you can change into a bathing suit or arrange for the rental of a nearby cottage. Be sure to check out the tile mural by local artist Rebecca Tudor, whose studio is in Sable River. (Her work also appears on the floor of the Shelburne Visitor Center.) Natural elements such as tulips, wildflowers, and fish blend in her pieces to create a harmony reminiscent of Tiffany's elegant stained-glass windows.

The road to Lockeport runs the length of the beach, giving the impression that you are driving along a sandbar to an island. Its location off the main highway adds to the impression that you are visiting a separate island.

Apart from strolling around the tiny village taking pictures, there is not a lot to do here. When your interest is sated, get back in your car and head farther south on Route 3 to a string of villages peopled by the descendants of Loyalists from Nantucket and Cape Cod who came to this area after 1760.

From Lockeport it is only a half-hour's drive to **Shelburne** along Provincial Trunk Highway 3 until you reach exit 25. Following the road will lead you into the town's historic waterfront **Dock Street.**

Try to park near the visitor center, which is built right at the water's edge. From here all of the historic area is to your left as you face the water.

In Shelburne you can visit the **Ross-Thomson House,** a remnant from the era of the United Empire Loyalists. It is located on Charlotte Lane, which intersects Dock Street, quite near the harbor. As you walk inside, the most striking thing is the rich patina of the building. Goods from the era of the former store are laid out as if the company were still in business, right down to birch brooms and wooden toys.

In early 1783 the shores around here were the landing site of some 5,000 settlers from New York and the Middle Colonies of America. Acting on the promise of free land, tools, and provisions, many had chosen to leave the new republic and head north to live under British rule. This first wave of settlers was followed by another wave in the fall, many of them entrepreneurs.

By the following year the population of Shelburne was double that of Halifax, and larger than Montreal or Quebec at the time. In fact, at its peak it was the third-largest town in North America. Because of the huge influx of colonists, it has become one of the continent's genealogical treasures.

The Ross-Thomson House is the last original store building from that era. It was the site of intense trading. The owners, a pair of brothers originally from Scotland, sold local wood; fish and salt from Turk's Island; tobacco, rum, sugar, and molasses from the West Indies; fine goods from Britain; Portuguese wine; and many other local and imported items.

Little by little, however, the town's population began to dwindle. The lack of arable land meant that when the government withdrew from distributing food, living here became increasingly difficult. By the 1820s the town had shrunk to a mere 300 souls.

The building is typical of the type favored by the Loyalists. The house shows a

trivia

The first solo circumnavigation of the world was made by Nova Scotian–born sailor Joshua Slocum, aboard the *Spray.* He started his journey in April 1895 and finished over three years later in July 1898.

strong New England influence, with its gambrel roof and gables. Finished with heavy plank doors, the house had the added security of studs, bars, and a double lock. For a time the house served as the town post office; the shutter on the north window has a slot into which late mail could be slipped.

The house also features a "Loyalist Garden" out back, which demonstrates how day-to-day provisions were grown by people like the Ross brothers and the Thomson family 200 years ago.

Upstairs in the house, you will find an exhibit on the Shelburne Militia. The Ross-Thomson House is open daily June to mid-October from 9:30 A.M. to 5:30 P.M. A small admission is charged. For details on the museum, call (902) 875–3141.

Much of Shelburne's Loyalist past is still in evidence in the town, as shown by the number of buildings still standing that date from the time of the American War of Independence. Among these, one has been turned into a small inn, overlooking the harbor. Called *Cooper's Inn,* it dates from 1785 and has been sufficiently preserved and restored that it has received an award from Heritage Trust Nova Scotia. Like all the other buildings on Dock Street, it is finished in deepbrown shingles. Located near Ross-Thomson House, this building was constructed under the direction of a blind Loyalist merchant named George Gracie.

Through the centuries it has housed mariners, shipbuilders, gentlemen esquires, merchants, and coopers. It is open from April through October. For reservations call (800) 688–2011 or (902) 875–4656. Rates are standard to moderate, with breakfast included.

Cooper's Inn, along with several other places on Dock Street, was part of extensive restorations undertaken prior to a visit by the newly married Prince and Princess of Wales in 1983.

Because of the facelift, the harbor area is quite a pleasant place to roam aimlessly and soak up atmosphere. Think of it as time travel. It is sufficiently authentic that it was used as the location for the 1995 movie *The Scarlet Letter.*

More information on the Loyalist era can be found at another Dock Street locale, the *Shelburne County Museum.* For those of you who have families dating back to Revolutionary days and a link to Loyalists who settled in Nova Scotia, this is the place to track down some family history. The museum has extensive genealogical records. There are even eighteenth- to twentieth-century newspapers on microfilm so that you can peruse the old news at your leisure. The museum is open year-round, with summer hours daily from 9:30 A.M. to 5:30 P.M. For information call (902) 875–3219. A small admission charge entitles you to entry at all four of the village's museums.

moviemaking magic

You will no doubt wonder how the asphalt was hidden from the camera during the filming of *The Scarlet Letter*. The solution was to truck in loads of dirt and cover the paving. No detail was too small to ignore during the making of the movie. To ensure that the white houses of a distant point were not in the background, for example, the set designers had bushes strategically planted to obscure the distant shore.

Another source for genealogical information is next door to the museum, at the *Shelburne County Genealogical Research Centre.* A certified genealogist on staff assists people in tracing their Nova Scotian roots. Members of the Shelburne County Genealogical Society can search records for free, but a small fee gives you access to considerable research.

The center has indexed church records and vital statistics, an in-depth census, and the international genealogical index, as well as records for the whole county. It also keeps newspaper statistics on various people and information on Heritage homes in the area. Not all the families in this area were Loyalists: A number of Welsh, Icelandic, and Scottish people settled here. Blacks from the United States also settled in nearby Birchtown at the time of the Revolution.

Of particular interest is the history of **Birchtown,** named for General John Birch, the New York commander who gave protection to Loyalist blacks, whose direct descendants still live here. At the time of the Revolution, many black American slaves chose to take sides with the British, who promised them their freedom. Expecting equal treatment with other Loyalists, they came to live under British rule. But few of them received the land that the white Loyalists received as a matter of course, and those who did get land received substandard lots.

In 1783, when the village was settled by 1,500 freed slaves, it was the largest free black settlement in North America. But by 1792 the settlers in Birchtown were fed up, and they joined other black Loyalists in the province who had decided that a return to Africa was in order. That year 1,200 of them left the colony and founded Freetown in Sierra Leone.

Recent archaeological digs in the neighborhood of Birchtown have revealed remnants of the early days of these settlers.

The Shelburne County museum and its Genealogical Research Centre are open year-round Monday to Saturday, from 9:00 A.M. to 5:00 P.M. There are reduced hours in winter. For information, call (902) 875–4299.

One other Dock Street site is worth a special mention: **The Dory Shop.** You may have visited a dory shop along the Lighthouse Route (Route 3), but if you haven't, this one is operated by the Nova Scotia museum system and comprises three stories of dory-making memorabilia. A factory from 1880 to 1970, it is all that is left in the town of seven dory shops. It opened as a museum in 1983 and featured as its star attraction master builder Sidney Mahaney, who made dories according to the traditional methods he learned in his youth. Mahaney began building dories at age seventeen and continued until his death at age ninety-six in 1993. One of his miniature dories was given to Prince William as a present.

A large photograph of Mahaney, decked out in a Nova Scotia tartan shirt, acts as a backdrop for his last hand-built dory, displayed here. In the early days, this particular shop produced two dories a day, and sold them for $18.00 apiece. When Mahaney started in 1914, his wages were 45 cents a day. (They reached their peak back then at $2.00 a day, after a man had received a raise every three years.)

On the premises you will find an information booth that can fill you in on local events. The shop is open daily mid-June to mid-September from 9:30 A.M. to 5:30 P.M. Call (902) 875–3219.

After Shelburne, resume your drive down the Lighthouse Route (Highway 3) or Highway 103 until, twenty minutes later, the roads converge at the head of Barrington Bay in a village called Barrington Passage.

If you ever had the urge to get onto a Cape Islander boat, here is your chance. The Barrington Passage Tourist Bureau has one you can visit. (It's also on Highway 3.) *The Seal Island Light Museum* is open to the public, and you can climb the five stories to the top, which offers a panoramic view of the bay.

trivia

The world's second most abundant seal species is the harp seal, seen every winter off the Atlantic coast.

Continue along Highway 3 in Barrington until you cross the Barrington River, indicated by a road sign. Here you'll find the *Barrington Woolen Mill,* where you can get a good look at an old-time water turbine–powered woolen mill. This had its beginnings in 1882 as a community enterprise, to provide fishermen with wool clothing. Inside the mill is a magnificent wall hanging woven by Bessie Murray. In addition to its depiction of Nova Scotia's history, the wall hanging features a piper wearing the Nova Scotia tartan, which was designed by Murray. This was the origin of the tartan, and the wall hanging you see here was its unveiling, as it were. Outside is a pleasant picture: The mill overlooks a rushing stream and is quite lovely.

For several decades the mill was an important supplier of specialized woolen goods for the people of this region. It is now part of the Nova Scotia Museum System and features jennies, looms, a dye house, and equipment for scouring wool. It is open June 1 to September 30 Monday to Saturday from 9:30 A.M. to 5:30 P.M., Sunday from 1:00 to 5:30 P.M. For information call (902) 637–2185. A small admission is charged.

A change of pace from the dory shops and elegant old homes is the *Old Meeting House in Barrington,* located at the head of Barrington Bay. The barnlike meetinghouse was built in 1765 by pilgrims who used it as a place of worship and for public meetings. It is the oldest New England–style meetinghouse in the province. Barrington Township itself was founded in 1761 by fifty families of Cape Cod planters, who brought their religion, customs, and building style north with them.

Be sure to stroll through the graveyard adjacent to the building, where you will see the markers of many of the area's early settlers. One fine day, in the middle of a funeral on the morning of May 4, 1783, the mourners noticed a great cloud of white sails crowding the harbor mouth. There they saw the singular event that was to transform Shelburne into one of the most important towns on the continent. That morning a convoy of transports carried into the harbor thousands of United Empire Loyalists, newly exiled from their New England homes.

The meetinghouse is open June 1 to September 30 Monday to Saturday from 9:30 A.M. to 5:30 P.M., Sunday from 1:00 to 5:30 P.M. For details call (902) 637–2185.

You can live in Nova Scotia for decades and never visit the remote fishing villages of the southernmost tip of the province unless you are headed for one of the ferries to Portland or Bar Harbor, Maine. This is decidedly off-trail and well worth some lazy puttering.

As for archetypical fishing villages, they don't get more authentic than **Clark's Harbour,** Cape Sable Island, the southernmost part of Nova Scotia. Once the British won their final battle with the French, this whole area opened up for settlement, in large part encouraged by the expulsion of the Acadians and supplemented by the American Revolution, which followed a few years later.

One of the first places to be settled by exiles from the other colonies was **Cape Sable Island.** In 1761 the island was settled by forty families from outer Cape Cod. The following year a number of whalers and their families from Nantucket moved into neighboring areas. Even Halifax Harbour's eastern waterfront was a site of a Cape Cod whaler settlement, as evidenced by some of the houses near the Old Dartmouth waterfront.

On Cape Sable Island especially, traces of the Cape Cod housing style and even the accents linger. Fishing and related industries have always been its mainstay. It was here in 1907 that the Cape Island boat was first built for fishing off the coast. To this day it is the standard for small fishing boats to withstand the cruel seas of the North Atlantic.

They are not as elegant as the schooners of yore, but the Cape Islander, like the dory, is outstandingly seaworthy, sitting high in the water. The standard Cape Islander is 38 feet (11 m) long, with a 12-foot (3.6-m) beam. The old ones had a pulpit on the bow for harpooning.

Stay on Highway 3 as you proceed around the southern tip of the province and you will see a string of small fishing and farming communities peopled by the descendants of Loyalist planters and returned Acadians, among others: Ste.-Anne du Ruisseau and **West, Middle West,** and **Lower West Pubnico** are a few of these villages, partially peopled by

trivia

The first shipwreck in Canada was the *Delight,* which ran aground on Nova Scotia's Sable Island in 1583. Since then, more than 500 ships have met their end on this island, known as the "Graveyard of the Atlantic."

the descendants of the Acadians who originally settled here in 1653. If you look carefully, you will see traces of these early days, from an old stone bridge to the ***Musée Acadien,*** or Acadian Museum, in West Pubnico.

This Acadian Museum is a homestead dating back to 1864. Today it contains artifacts from Acadian pioneer days along with land grant documents from the 1700s. To visit turn off Highway 3 onto Highway 335 and drive east for 3 miles (5 km) until you reach West Pubnico. A small admission is charged. It is open from early June to September 15, Monday to Saturday from 9:00 A.M. to 5:00 P.M., Sunday from 12:30 to 4:30 P.M. For details call (902) 762–3380.

The name Pubnico is derived from the Mi'Kmaq word for "cleared land." The actual village of Pubnico (not Middle West, West, or Lower West) was settled by transplanted New Englanders who came in 1761, filling the void created by the expulsion of Acadians from the region.

Just before you reach Yarmouth proper, turn off Highway 3 at Arcadia and follow the sign for Kelly Cove and ***Chebogue Point.*** Soon after joining the lupine-edged shore road, you will come to the tiny ***Town Point Cemetery.***

Apart from the many old settlers who found their final resting place here, a sad and beautiful love story is linked to the place. Among the weathered headstones you will find a life-size carving of a woman reclining, as if asleep, on sheaves of wheat, sickle in hand. This is the grave of one Margaret Webster, who died in 1861. Several years before her death, her Yarmouth-born husband was a young medical student in Scotland.

One day he was walking through the fields when he came upon just such a sleeping figure. He paused for a long time to watch the beautiful woman, exhausted by her work, catching forty winks. When the woman awoke, he introduced himself, and soon a relationship developed. The two were married, and that would have been the end of the story had his new wife, Margaret Webster, not died suddenly.

The bereaved young man returned to Yarmouth, where he searched until he found a talented artist to make a marble effigy of his young wife, who reclines to this day, seemingly asleep, on the sheaves of wheat where her husband first fell in love with her.

It's just a statue and a sentimental side trip, but the detour is worthwhile. The roadside is strewn with lupines, and if you look out over the water, you will get a sweeping view of the Tusket Islands.

Westbound from Yarmouth, the Lighthouse Route takes on a new name, the Evangeline Trail, in honor of Longfellow's epic poem about the banished Acadians. Therefore, you will enter ***Yarmouth*** on the very last leg of the Lighthouse Route and meet the beginning of the Evangeline Trail where Highway 1 meets Highway 3.

The junction is also the corner of Starr's Road and Main Street, down by the waterfront in beautiful downtown Yarmouth, with a population of almost 8,000. From this corner take a left, continue half a block, and keep your eyes open for the *Firefighter's Museum* on your left at 451 Main Street.

If you are arriving from Maine on a ferry, you'll be departing the boat just slightly farther down that same waterfront road. In this case, as you drive off the Marine Atlantic Ferry, turn left onto Main Street. Continue past the Parade Street intersection to 451 Main Street on your right. The Firefighter's Museum is the only provincial firefighter's museum in Canada. It has every type of fire engine ever in use in Nova Scotia, as well as all kinds of other vintage firefighting gear.

There is an 1880 Silsby Steamer that looks like a madman's boiler on wheels. A bright-red hand pumper dates back to 1819; it is so dinky that one expects to see a monkey and organ grinder next to it and a hot roasted-chestnut concession operating out of it. The shiny metal doodad-covered Holloway Chemical Engine from 1892 is so ornate that it could donate parts for Cinderella's carriage. Apart from the three horse-drawn steamers, the museum has some antique toy fire engines and other nostalgia for anybody who ever wanted to grow up to be a firefighter.

Firemen swear this is the best collection they've ever seen anywhere. In addition to possessing a fleet of mint-condition firetrucks, the Firefighter's Museum takes the bait for unusual stories. Check out the photo display on the Circus Ship Fire of 1963, where the local firefighters were called upon to save the lives of cheetahs, a Brahma bull, a zebra, and a llama. It may not have been the most dangerous fire they ever tackled, but it presented its own set of hazards. All were saved but the zebra.

The *National Exhibit Centre,* in the same complex, features traveling exhibits. For more information write to 451 Main Street, Yarmouth, NS B5A 1G9, or call (902) 742–5525. A small admission is charged. Hours for the complex are Monday to Saturday 9:00 A.M. to 9:00 P.M. in July and August. The rest of the year the complex is open Monday to Friday from 9:00 A.M. to 4:00 P.M. but closes daily from noon until 2:00 P.M.

Yarmouth's shoreline is a working waterfront, including a ferry dock, fish processing plants, and a fishing fleet. In addition, it is a major point of tourist entry for Nova Scotia. For easy exploring, the 3-mile (5-km) stretch of shoreline includes walkways, marina berths for pleasure craft, and a refurbished railway station dating back to the 1800s. The restored *Parker Eakins Building* houses a microbrewery and bakery with an informal dining room on the second floor.

Before leaving Yarmouth, you may want to explore local history at the *Yarmouth County Museum,* 22 Collins Street. The museum is a great place for would-be sailors. The collection of Age of Sail artifacts, including ship portraits and models, is drawn from a seafaring past that saw Yarmouth as the home of the third-largest merchant navy in the world. When sailing ships ruled the day, this little town boasted the world's highest per capita ship tonnage. The remnants of this legacy are found at this museum, including one of the largest collections of marine paintings in the country as well as a lighthouse lens, a stagecoach, historic costumes, furniture, tools, and glass. For more information, call (902) 742–5539.

To get to the Yarmouth County Museum from the Firefighter's Museum, turn left when you exit the building and go south down Main Street toward the ferry terminal, until you get to the Collins Street intersection. Turn left again and you will be at the door of the museum. A small admission is charged. The museum is open June 1 to October 15 Monday to Saturday from 9:00 A.M. to 5:00 P.M. and Sunday from 2:00 to 5:00 P.M., and October 16 to May 31 Tuesday to Saturday from 2:00 to 5:00 P.M.

After leaving the museum, get back onto Main Street and continue past Starrs Road. Turn left on Vancouver Street, then take a left again onto Route 304. Follow this route to Overton and *Cape Fourchu.* In a matter of minutes after leaving the town of Yarmouth, you'll be deep in the heart of photographer's heaven: Cape Fourchu is one of the most photogenic lighthouses in the province, set at the tip of a rugged granite coastline. (At one point a high wall en route to Cape Fourchu protects cars from the waves on rough days, and the road seems precariously close to the water.) The original lighthouse, built in 1840, was replaced by a more up-to-date facility in the 1960s.

Just past the lighthouse is the *Leif Eriksson Picnic Park,* allegedly the landing site of the famous Viking explorer. Apart from its historical significance, the park overlooks spectacular coastline and offers visitors a good spot to picnic, tables and all.

After this stop head back to town until you reach the end of the little peninsula.

This is the end of the Lighthouse Route and the Atlantic coastline. From here the communities change from descendants of the Germans and Loyalists, whalers and privateers, to communities with a strong Acadian heritage. To explore this next region turn right onto Route 1.

Places to Stay on Nova Scotia's Sunrise Trail and Atlantic Coastline

HALIFAX

Halliburton House Inn
5184 Morris Street
(902) 420–0658
Converted Heritage brick
homes. Four-star dining.
Moderate to deluxe.

Lord Nelson Hotel
1515 South Park Street
(800) 565–2020
(902) 423 6331
Luxuriously refurbished
landmark hotel. Overlooks
Halifax Public Gardens.
Moderate.

HEAD JEDDORE

**Salmon River House
Country Inn**
Route 7
(800) 565–3353
(902) 889–3353
The right balance between
the great outdoors and
proximity to the city, with
excellent on-site food.
Standard to moderate.

HUBBARDS

Dauphinee Inn
167 Shore Club Road
(800) 567–1790
(902) 857–1790
Heritage inn full of charm
in a seaside setting,
featuring lobster and the
great outdoors.
Moderate.

LISCOMB MILLS

Liscombe Lodge
Marine Drive (Route 7)
(800) 665–6343
(902) 779–2307
Beautiful rustic setting.
Moderate to deluxe.

LIVERPOOL

White Point Beach Resort
Highway 103 exit 20A
or 21 to Route 3
(800) 565–5068
(902) 354–2711
Large resort overlooking
White Point Beach. Try the
plank salmon and other
seafood specialties. Offers
children's programs.
Moderate to deluxe.

LUNENBURG

Boscawen Inn
150 Cumberland Street
(800) 354–5009
(902) 634–3325
Romantic Victorian elegance
with lots of nice touches.
Standard to moderate.

**The Ovens Oceanview
Cottages**
Route 332
(902) 766–4621
Cabins set high above
the coastal cliffs. Sea-cave
boat tours available.
Standard to moderate.

PICTOU

Auberge Walker Inn
34 Coleraine Street
(800) 370–5553
(902) 485–1433
Restored Heritage inn.
Standard to moderate.
Includes breakfast.

Customs House Inn
38 Depot Street
(902) 485–4546
Historic building with first-
class modern fixtures.
Moderate. Includes
breakfast.

Pictou Lodge
Braeshore Road
(east of Pictou)
(888) 662–7484
(902) 485–4322
A rustic hideaway.
Moderate to deluxe.

SHELBURNE

Coopers Inn
Dock Street
(800) 688–2011
(902) 875–4656
Lovely garden,
complimentary wine and
chocolates, and great
breakfasts come with cozy
rooms in historic house.
Standard to moderate.

SUMMERVILLE BEACH

**Quarterdeck Beachside
Villas and Grill**
Highway 103 exit 20 to
Route 3
(800) 565–1119
(902) 683–2998
Fall asleep to the gentle
lapping of the waves just
outside your window at this
well-appointed home away
from home.
Moderate to deluxe.

TATAMAGOUCHE

Train Station Inn
21 Station Road
(888) 724–5233
(902) 657–3222
A must for railway buffs.
Choose from rooms in the
station or rent your very
own caboose.
Moderate.

Places to Eat on Nova Scotia's Sunrise Trail and Atlantic Coastline

ANTIGONISH

Lobster Treat
Post Road, off Highway 104
(902) 863–5465
Family restaurant housed in
former schoolhouse.
Competitive prices, surf 'n'
turf options.

HEAD JEDDORE

**Lobster Shack at Salmon
River House Country Inn**
Route 7
(800) 565–3353
(902) 889–3353
Feast on lobster in cozy
restaurant overlooking
Salmon River Estuary and
the Atlantic.

LISCOMB MILLS

Liscombe Lodge
Marine Drive (Route 7)
(800) 665–6343
(902) 779–2307
Great natural setting.

LOURNEVILLE

Amherst Shore Country Inn
Route 366
(between Amherst and
Pugwash)
(902) 661–4800
By reservation only.

PICTOU

Braeside Inn
126 Front Street
(902) 485–5046
Overlooking harbor.

Pictou Lodge
Braeshore Road
(east of Pictou, and 2.5
miles/4 km from P.E.I. ferry)
(888) 662–7484
(902) 485–4322
Extensive midday buffet.

STELLARTON

The Heather Hotel
TCH 104, off exit 24
(902) 752–8401
Intimate dining room,
excellent service.

TANGIER

Willy Krauch and Sons Ltd.
Route 7
(800) 758–4412
(902) 772–2188
Provides smoked salmon
to the Queen.

TATAMAGOUCHE

**Balmoral Motel and
Dining Room**
Main Street
(902) 657–2000
German and Canadian
cuisine.

**Jitney Cafe at the Train
Station Inn**
21 Station Road
(888) 724–5233
(902) 657–3222
Wholesome breakfasts;
dinner options include
chowder and lobster. Open
year-round.

Western Nova Scotia

Along the Nova Scotian shoreline of the Bay of Fundy is a culture that has withstood massive deportation and centuries of isolation. As visitors ramble along Route 1, the little communities of this Acadian heartland stretch one into the other, giving the impression of a massive church-dotted "Main Street" that extends right through the villages where the French first set up shop on their Canadian adventure.

This region boasts the first-ever European settlement on Canadian soil. It was from here that the governments of France and, later, England ruled the whole region of Acadia, which included Nova Scotia and New Brunswick.

Possession of the area fluctuated between the English and French armies. In the end, when France lost control for good, the settlers' neutrality came into question. Finally the new military commanders made a decision that was to echo as far south as Louisiana.

The Land of Evangeline

It was from the shores of Northwestern Nova Scotia that thousands of Acadians were forced to board ships that would disperse them along the eastern seaboard and as far south as

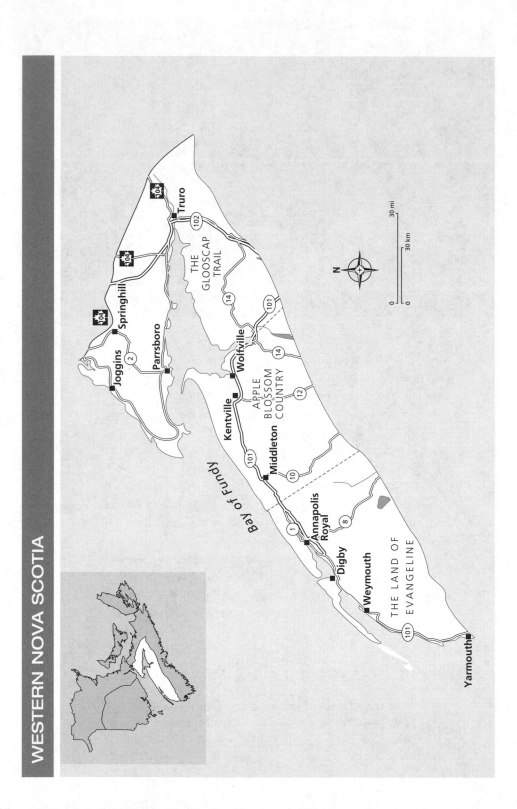

WESTERN NOVA SCOTIA

Louisiana, where they eventually became known as Cajuns. Legend has it that a young Acadian couple, Gabriel and Evangeline, was separated on their wedding day. This story was told in many guises, and eventually became the inspiration for the famous poem "Evangeline," by Henry Wadsworth Longfellow. The region is now named after Longfellow's heroine.

The Acadians, once exiled from Nova Scotia and now returned, can boast of a thriving francophone culture and lively community life.

The Evangeline Trail, which is actually Route 1, begins in Yarmouth (end point of the Lighthouse Route), at the intersection of Main and Vancouver Streets.

Traveling east along this historic route, you will shortly come to *Sandford,* a scenic harbor and home of what is claimed to be the *world's smallest wooden lift bridge.* To see this bridge, turn left at the Sandford breakwater and drive right down to the wharf. The wharf is strewn with mountains of seashells, which in photographs look like abstract art. From here you will see what initially appears to be an upside down V. This is the bridge. A winch operates it, with the help of whoever is standing by, but the bridge is never flat, allowing small boats to pass under easily. Crossing it is like walking up and down a steep ramp.

Along Highway 1 you'll drift through Beaver River, Salmon River, and then the gorgeous *Mavilette Beach,* which winds for about 1 mile (1.6 km) along the shoreline to Cape St. Marys.

This is undoubtedly one of the prettiest beaches in this end of the country, although the water temperature is low enough to chill champagne. There are a provincial picnic park and walking trails along the grassy dunes. Boardwalks protect the sea grasses, which are all that holds the sand back from the relentless forces of Mother Nature.

TRUDY'S FAVORITES

World's smallest wooden lift bridge,
Sandford

Oaklawn Farm Zoo,
Aylesford

Brier Island,
Digby Neck

Apple Blossom Festival,
Annapolis Valley

Balancing Rock,
Digby Neck

rafting on the tidal wave,
Maitland

Annapolis Royal Historic Gardens,
Annapolis Royal

Fundy Geological Museum,
Parrsboro

Habitation at Port Royal

World's Smallest Wooden Lift Bridge

Beachcombing on the fine white sand can yield a wide choice of shells and driftwood. Be aware that the extensive sand flats of low tide are a temporary thing; here you will be reminded that the Bay of Fundy has the highest tides in the world. What people often don't realize is how fast the water level can change. But as the water rises, the sand heats it up to a less brutal temperature for swimming.

There is excellent seafood at the **Cape View Diner,** in particular whole fresh lobster and Acadian specialties. Alongside are the Cape View Motel and Cottages. For reservations, call (902) 645–2258, or write to P.O. Box 9, Salmon River, Digby County, NS B0W 2Y0. Rates are standard.

Farther along on the route is **Smuggler's Cove,** a rocky stretch of shoreline with massive sea caves that are well known in the area because of the area's historic link to smuggling and rumrunning. The contraband was hidden in the "caves" that the waves carved out of the rock and that are hidden during high tide.

I visited this place years ago and had to climb down the cliffs with ropes. Now you can go down a set of steps, and the headland above the cove has been made into a provincial picnic park.

These days smugglers have been replaced by people in sea kayaks entering the caves. Indian legend says that a brave once traveled between the largest of these sea caves and one at The Ovens in Lunenburg County; most kayakers don't go in much farther than the rumrunners did.

In **Church Point** (by its French name, Pointe de l'Église), a short way up the road, is **Université Ste.-Anne,** which is the province's French-language university. Especially because of the university's existence, this is a culturally rich area. The school acts as a magnet for Acadian artisans in Nova Scotia. The university archives also offer visitors with Acadian French ancestors a chance to trace their roots.

The campus lines the shore and is stretched out alongside the road. Just beyond it is *Église Ste.-Marie* (Church of St. Mary), the tallest wooden church in North America, which you can see from far off. This church was actually designed in France. The 185-foot (56-m) steeple had to be secured against hurricane-force winds with 40 tons (36 metric tons) of stone ballast. To make "stone" pillars to support the roof, the builders used tree trunks covered with plaster. The "marble" arches are wooden also. Small booklets covering the history of the village and its church are sold here, and a bilingual guide is available for tours. The door of the church is always open in the daytime.

In Search of the True Story of Evangeline

It is said that Longfellow heard the story of Evangeline and Gabriel from a minister at a dinner party with Longfellow's friend Nathaniel Hawthorne. (By that time, nine decades had passed since the expulsion.) This inspired the famous epic poem of the same name. Historians now feel that there may have been a woman such as Evangeline, but accounts of her life vary. History buffs have tried to pin down the real story for decades, but have come up with more fiction than fact.

Longfellow's story of Evangeline holds that she was separated from her lover on her wedding day. Eventually, after wandering the countryside futilely in search of him, she became a nun in Philadelphia. At the end of her days, the poem has her encountering her former fiancé, ill during an epidemic. He dies in her arms. Other versions of the story include several family sagas that run on parallel tracks. Perhaps the closest to historical accuracy comes from a 1907 novella called *Acadian Reminiscences: The True Story of Evangeline,* by Felix Voorhies, a member of the Louisiana House of Representatives. In his story, the heroine and her lover were named Emmeline and Louis. They tried to flee the village of St. Gabriel in old Acadie before the deportation, but they were caught by the British and were separated. Emmeline was sent to Maryland and came to Louisiana via the Tennessee and Mississippi Rivers. According to this author, Emmeline met Louis again in Louisiana. But by that time, he was married to another. In his story, she subsequently lost her sanity, withered away, and died.

Regardless of the lack of historically verifiable facts of the case, roughly ten thousand Acadians were packed off with no regard for family ties, so many tragic Acadian family sagas existed, including the long separation of lovers. But few were as melodramatic as the literary creations of the authors who dramatized the tragic tale of Evangeline.

The Great Expulsion

The Acadians of Southwestern Nova Scotia are descendants of French deportees from the Great Expulsion of 1755.

When Nova Scotia's governor lifted the ban against Acadians in 1765, almost 800 of the deportees gathered in Boston and, over the next four months, walked more than 1,000 miles (1,600 km) back to Nova Scotia. Some ran out of steam by the time they got to the Saint John River Valley and decided to settle there. Fifty remaining families continued on until they reached their old homesteads—only to discover that their homesteads had been given to new British settlers. These displaced Acadians wandered the Annapolis Valley until 1767, when the district of Clare was established for them. Joseph Dugas Sr. and his family were the first to settle there, followed the next year by thirteen more families.

The last survivor of the Acadian deportees who returned to Nova Scotia, Marie Babin Surette, died in 1862 at age 110. She is buried on Surette's Island, near Tusket.

If you continue along Highway 1 after Church Point, you will come to *Grosses Coques.* Keep on your toes, though, because in a flash it turns into *Belliveau Cove.* Belliveau Cove Wharf is one of the prettiest little wharves in this part of the province, with its boats stranded at low tide and a tiny lighthouse to the left.

This place is a good spot to explore shore ecology, particularly periwinkles. There are several different species of periwinkles (the gastropod, not the ground cover), and they are abundant in the Bay of Fundy area because of the tides. If you go down to the shore to look for them, be sure you know when the tide is due to come in, because the beach—and your route out—might end up underwater in an astoundingly short period of time.

The water can rise more than 50 feet (15 m) in some areas of the Bay of Fundy, to the highest levels anywhere in the world. This once caused Joe Howe, Nova Scotian patriot, journalist, and eventually provincial politician, to exclaim in response to a parliamentary put-down, "How high do *your* tides rise?"

His nineteenth-century rebuke still gets a chuckle in some places these days, perhaps making it a record for old jokes. Just keep it in mind if you decide to leave your shoes on a rock somewhere and go strolling out on a large expanse of shoreline.

Just before Grosses Coques ends and Belliveau Cove begins, the road crosses a small river. Immediately after this point a small sign will direct you to the old *Acadian Cemetery.* You'll drive down a road that stretches to the shore, where boardwalks offer the possibility of a walk along windswept *Major Point Beach.*

Nature lovers will appreciate the rugged scenery at this end of the province and the opportunity to watch migratory birds, see wildflowers, and spy whales and dolphins offshore. Artists find the area inspiring, too; you'll find a number of them here.

A tiny almost closetlike chapel has been erected at the site of the Acadian Cemetery. At the time of the Expulsion of the Acadians, many of them hid in the woods, aided and abetted by their Mi'Kmaq allies. Some made their way to Cape Breton, which was then still in French hands. But others quietly resumed life here after a time, and their earthly remains eventually came to join those of their ancestors, the first white settlers in Canada, in the Grosses Coques Cemetery. The original rough wooden crosses have been replaced by new ones, which are arranged in exactly the same way as the former markers. The handful of souls put to rest here were buried as far back as the 1770s.

Following Route 1 in the direction of Halifax, you'll come next to the tiny village of St. Bernard. From far off you will see arising out of the countryside *L'Église St.-Bernard* (Church of St. Bernard), a massive granite Gothic church, built entirely by the congregation. Construction, which began in 1910, was not completed for thirty-two years. The church is enormous; it can easily accommodate a thousand people, a congregation comprised of several villages. Building materials were supplied by the local population, making the creation of the church a small industry in itself. The stone was quarried in Shelburne and then hauled by train for 120 miles (193.5 km).

Note that L'Église St.-Bernard is at a crossroads in the highway called Junction 28, after which Route 1 is essentially swallowed up by TCH Route 101.

Following the coastal route, you'll come to **Gilbert Cove,** which has a pretty little lighthouse that has been restored. The lighthouse and grounds are worth visiting, and there is a spot for picnicking here.

About 10 miles (16 km) past Gilbert Cove on Highway 101, you will reach Digby. From Digby follow Route 217 down a long narrow peninsula ending in a ferry ride to **Long Island,** followed by another short ferry ride to **Brier**

TOP ANNUAL EVENT

The Apple Blossom Festival,
Windsor to Digby (last weekend in May);
(800) 565–0000
Just a drive through the valley at this time
is worthwhile for the scenic beauty.

Island. The whole narrow strip of land is referred to as ***Digby Neck***—part of the Bay of Fundy's "trail of lava" that runs along the coastline. Boats run hourly twenty-four hours a day, leaving the mainland on the half hour.

Along with Digby Neck's offer of dolphins and five species of whales, the site is crisscrossed in the spring and fall by three flyways of migratory birds from the Arctic, Europe, and Canada. Bird-watchers have a chance to spot specimens from 130 species, including grebes, kittiwakes, and razorbills. The island is also home to fifteen different varieties of wild orchid and is dotted with the yellow-and-white blossoms of the mountain avens, a flower found only in northern Canada, the White Mountains of New Hampshire, and Eurasia.

On top of all this, Digby Neck is one of the best places to get a look at the bizarre igneous (lava-based) rock formations that you will no doubt see photographs of in many local tourist publications. The best place to see the rocky cliffs is a spot on Long Island marked quite inconspicuously by a hand-painted sign announcing ***Balancing Rock.*** It's easy to zoom past this small sign just beyond Tiverton as you race to meet the ferry to Brier Island. The ferry departures are timed so that there is no waiting if you drive immediately from one boat to the next.

Despite the lack of fanfare, this is a fascinating side trip. Follow along the wooded path's well-marked trail past ferns and mature trees. After twenty minutes, you will reach a boardwalk that rapidly turns into a series of wooden steps that wind their way down the steep rock cliff. At this point you will see

Where the Whales Are

There are a number of companies that take people to see whales. I went out with ***Brier Island Whale and Seabird Cruises*** (902–839–2995, fax 902–839–2075). They have a large ex-fishing boat, and the captain maintains constant radio contact with other ships in the area to track down the whales. It took about an hour to locate one.

Once we did, the captain repeatedly circled around, bronco-fashion. We circled ever closer and closer to the whale. It would breach (that is, leap into the air) at regular intervals, then shoot forward and lunge neatly back into the sea, with its tail fins skyward. Getting anything other than a snapshot of tail fins is a challenge, demanding foresight, an eye on the whale's trajectory, and quick reflexes. Seasickness tablets came in very handy.

Over the course of the year, five different species of whales come here in search of food. They are finback, minke, humpback, sperm, and North Atlantic right whales. We saw a group of minke whales, one of the smaller species. I got lots of pictures of a whale's tail as he or she went back under.

the most dramatic example of ancient volcanic fury. At the bottom, huge basalt boulders form a coastline that looks like the Viking god Thor had thrown handfuls of lightning bolts at the shore.

The biggest bolt is at the last step: Jutting out improbably from the cliff, it exceeds the height of three grown men. It seems as precariously balanced as a bowling pin in a juggling act, as if the slightest breeze could send it crashing to the jagged volcanic rocks below. At this point, it is easy to imagine oneself at the end of the world, in a land before time.

There are only a few choices for accommodation if you want to enjoy some nature walks and explore Long Island further. In *Sandy Cove,* a pretty community flanked on both sides by beaches, you can stay at the *Olde Village Inn* on Route 217 west. This inn is in a structure that dates back to the nineteenth century. Sandy Cove is a promising spot for rockhounding. For reservations call (800) 834–2206. Rates are moderate.

On Brier Island you can stay at the *Brier Island Lodge,* which also has a good restaurant. You can't miss the lodge; you can actually see it from Long Island as you approach Brier Island by boat. Its main building is a huge log structure built on a headland to the far right end of the island. The hoteliers can book whale-watching tours for you and provide maps of the island. Rooms are standard to moderate. For further information call (800) 662–8355 or (902) 839–2300. They have a three-star Canada Select rating. For more details on the lodge, visit www.brierisland.com.

Due to the depth of its tides, the waters of the Bay of Fundy have a high salt content. Consequently, they are teeming with zooplankton, which in turn attract herring and mackerel, the favorite snacking foods of whales. The result is that the tiny 3-mile-long (5-km) Brier Island is renowned for whale- and dolphin-watching. Sightings are guaranteed on the daily *whale-watching cruises,* with different species making their appearance at varying times of the year.

A number of naturalists have assured me over the years that the best time to witness the coy display of whales in love and its attendant splashing is in the early weeks of August. Since many people seem to be in the know about this, rooms at local inns are more likely to fill up early at that time, so plan to book ahead.

Along with enjoying the wildflowers and the animals, you can take a long walk along the shore to see the massive, spectacular basalt rocks. Many of the best hikes are detailed on the map supplied by the Brier Island Lodge. One trail starts virtually at the backdoor of the lodge. The innkeeper, Virginia Tudor, lends out her dogs as four-legged trail guides who will take you for an hour across the width of the island until you reach *Seal Cove,* a favored locale for watching seals frolicking on the shore, before leading you back.

At the southwest tip of the island, a narrow footpath at Green Head cuts across a grassy bog, moss-covered rocks, and eventually into an area of basalt cliffs. Across the water, you will see the towering cliffs of Peters Island, a bird sanctuary that plays host to thousands of arctic terns. They stop here briefly on the way to Antarctica, following the longest migratory path in the world.

Late in the day, as the sun turns red, you can still distinguish Peters Island's rocks, like a jagged basalt layer cake, which the sun tints to a sparkling salmon-pink hue.

Virginia Tudor told me that most of their visitors over the years have been naturalists, who come to study the wildlife. She pointed out that two-thirds of the island are held by the Nature Conservancy. Another interesting fact about Brier Island is that most of the residents have relatives on Grand Manan Island. Years ago, Tudor explained, before roads came in, the people in this area got around only by boat, so the closest communities included Grand Manan, which even by today's standards would seem to be quite a drive.

Although small, Brier Island has three lighthouses. More than sixty shipwrecks have occurred around the island. The salvage has formed part of its enduring legacy. The **Oddfellows Hall,** for example, is a fraternal lodge built completely of salvage from the 1908 shipwreck of the *Aurora*. You'll see bits and pieces of old boats all over Brier Island.

When you want to leave Digby Neck, you will be returning by the same two ferries, the *Spray* and the *Joshua Slocum,* this time for free, since you have to pay only to get on the islands, not off them. (Note that both ferries are named in honor of famous Digby-area sailor Joshua Slocum, who was the first to sail single-handedly around the world in his ship, the *Spray.*)

Once off the islands, drive right off the boat onto Route 217 and continue until you get to the point where this long peninsula was connected to Nova Scotia in the first place. Take Junction 26 and turn onto Route 303, which will take you into **Digby.**

This is the docking site of the ferry from New Brunswick. The wharf in Digby also is home to the world's largest scallop fleet, hence the presence throughout the province's menus of Digby scallops.

The area offers excellent photographic opportunities, as well as golfing. One spot favored by golfers is the **Pines Resort Hotel,** which includes a Norman-style mansion and cottages scattered upon landscaped lawns. For reservations call (800) 667–4637 or (902) 245–2511. Rates are deluxe.

A cozy, conveniently located place to stay, with a two-and-a-half-star rating, is the **Mountain Gap Resort.** It is just a short drive farther north of Digby, in **Smiths Cove,** making it a good staging point for either a trip to Digby Neck or day trips to Annapolis and neighboring areas. To get to Smiths Cove, take either exit 24 or 25 off Highway 101.

Mountain Gap Resort has all the amenities, including a pool and tennis court, and a calming atmosphere, with its many perennial flower gardens trimming the cabins and pathways. Nightly bonfires here are a good excuse to hang out on warm summer nights. The inn is built on a grassy headland overlooking a tidal beach, accessible by wooden steps.

If the salty sea air is making you too tired to want to roam the nearby town in search of nightlife, the nice thing about the inn is that you can find nightlife of a kind right on the spot. Slocum's Pub is a friendly little bar, with outdoor seating as well in the middle of the complex. It has live entertainment most evenings, but not of the overwhelmingly noisy variety that would spoil the tranquility of the place.

There is also a lovely knotty-pine restaurant, featuring everything from prime rib of western beef to the local specialty, râpure pie. Seafood options are also in abundance.

Mountain Gap Resort arranges a number of different holiday packages, in particular those built around golf and whale-watching. To reserve a room or package, call (800) 565-5020. Rates are moderate.

Continuing along Route 1 for a very short time you will reach exit 23, where you will have an important choice to make: Turn inland for a side trip to *Bear River,* or continue along the coastline to *Upper Clements* and then *Annapolis Royal,* leaving Bear River as part of your inland detour en route to Kejimkujik National Park. In either case, the drive is an outrageously picturesque one. Bear River is nestled in a deep valley, cleft in two by a river that flows from Smiths Cove on the shore of the Bay of Fundy. Owing to the bay's high tides, this river swelled sufficiently that it allowed large ships to frequent the docks of Bear River. Years ago, this meant that the flow of ships provided a vital lifeline, and the tiny village-run *Bear River Heritage Museum* attests to this village's shipbuilding and trading history with a display of old-fashioned shipbuilding tools in its front parlor. A total of five rooms gives a fairly accurate picture of Bear River, from about the time of the Great War, when some of its young men left for Europe to fight. The room at the back of the museum is kitted out in all the equipment necessary to run a school from that era, and a set of costumes that children are invited to play with as a reward if they manage to be patient enough to get through the displays.

The little community straddles both sides of the river, crossed by a small bridge, with many of the buildings flanking the river supported by stilts. It is a haven for the artistic type, and the neighboring area is home to a band of Mi'Kmaq who take active part in activities at Keji. A number of artist and craft studios are there, but much of the artisans' work can be seen at a shop called *Flight of Fancy,* which has a fairly representative selection. This is on the north side of the bridge and is chock-a-block with high-quality work by artisans not just from Bear River but all over the province. It's open daily from 9:00 A.M. until 7:00 P.M. from May to November.

Curiously enough, Bear River is like an open secret, a tiny, unspoiled hideaway and so quaint it comes as a shock that it has not really been discovered except by a small eclectic mix of artistic types. There are some places to stay here, and a few places to grab lunch, which would make it a great side trip from either the area of Annapolis Royal or South Milford. For a longer stay, check out the *By the Brook* bed-and-breakfast, housed in an 1870s captain's home. It is affiliated with a set of housekeeping suites, complete with private patio, at *The Carriage House.* Call (902) 467–3612 to reserve. Rates are standard.

After Bear River, either backtrack to Route 1, and exit 23, so that you can enjoy Upper Clements Park, or drive in a loop to South Milford and take in Annapolis Royal and Upper Clements after visiting the interior. *Upper Clements Park* is the largest amusement park in Atlantic Canada. Admission fees to the park come in two varieties: the park only, or an all-day or half-day ride pass. The park has, among other things, a rattly wooden roller coaster that covers a large hilly section of what was once an apple orchard. If the roller coaster is your reason for visiting the park, be sure to ask if it is in operation on that particular day before you plunk down your cash for a ride pass.

As you exit this park, you'll notice the sign for the *Upper Clements Wildlife Park* about a mile and a half (2 km) along on the same road. If you didn't stop by here before visiting the amusement park, you may want to now. Admission is included in your fee to get into Upper Clements Park. You can stretch your legs while you take a look at some native Nova Scotian species such as cougar, porcupines, fox, groundhogs, deer, and moose. You may also see the queen's royal red deer as you stroll along the walking trails.

Past Upper Clements you'll have the opportunity to visit the village of Annapolis Royal, which recalls the times of eastern Canada's first European settlements.

The community, which boasts the oldest thoroughfare in the country, is one of the prettiest little villages in this end of the province. It is small, but its historical significance ensures that a considerable number of people visit in the summer. The village has retained its well-mannered charm and historical character, however. There are lots of beautiful, big old homes, many of which have been turned into bed-and-breakfast establishments or inns.

If you want to spend your stay in Annapolis Royal soaking in romantic ambience and royal memorabilia, consider the *Queen Anne Inn,* the striking facade of which is hard to miss. This is a substantial three-and-a-half-story Victorian building practically facing the town's lovely gardens. Downstairs is a tastefully appointed dining room and sitting room, while the upstairs contains ten bedrooms, each with wonderful canopy or four-poster feather beds with all the Victorian frills. (You will sink into these and imagine you've gone to heaven.) Throughout the historic inn you will find books about the area's history, gardens, and (emphasizing its historical ties to royalty) lots of pictures of former kings, queens, and the occasional glamorous princess. The inn also has two other guest cottages in a lovely garden setting. The downstairs of the main building has a striking hardwood floor made of alternating mahogany and ash to create a striped effect. Throughout the building, which dates from 1865, are period furnishings and antiques.

Innkeeper Greg Pyle is an amusing guy who originates from the prairies, but always had a dream to learn how to sail, which eventually brought him here. He's a great source of information about the town's interesting goings-on. In particular, he pointed to the Annapolis Region Community Arts Council's annual ***Paint the Town*** event. This takes place the third weekend in August, when artists set up their canvases all over town to paint. Visitors can watch the works in progress, and at the end of each day it's all sold off in a silent auction at the local Legion hall. In 2006 eighty artists and craftspeople participated.

The Queen Anne boosts other local events, like the town's ghost walk, and has hosted encampments from historical reenactors such as the "Orange Rangers" that gave the inn's front lawn a bit of an authentic time-travel effect.

Queen Anne Inn

(Not to worry, they have five acres of manicured lawns to accommodate just such an event.) Pyle has arranged to have a weekly visit from the town crier, who arrives every Saturday morning to tell guests eating breakfast in the dining room about the farmers' and traders' market to be held further downtown. When we visited, the town crier was a huge hit, a font of information about his dashing British military garb dating from the late 1700s.

"We try to give you more than you expect," says Pyle, who arranges everything from massage therapy with a qualified local therapist to whale-watching tours with several boats. He also can put together an individualized holiday request in the manner of a European concierge. During tourism's shoulder season, he points out, guests could opt to rent out the entire building and turn it into their own manor for a family reunion. He also is promoting mother-and-daughter weekends. Rooms include satellite television, CD players, DVD players on request, and some rooms have Jacuzzi tubs. Air-conditioning is effective, but inconspicuous. Open from the first of May until the end of November, the inn serves a complimentary three-course breakfast to guests. Sumptuous dinners are available for guests and nonguests. On warm summer nights, they can be served on the back patio, overlooking beautiful gardens. To reserve, call (877) 536–0403 or (902) 532–7850. Rates are standard to deluxe.

A walking tour, mapped out in a brochure called "Footprints and Footnotes," is available at most village businesses. Following the tour at a leisurely pace should take you about an hour.

The "Footprints and Footnotes" walk begins with a monument erected on the site of a Mohawk fort built in 1712. You can see this cairn down on the waterfront, on Lower Saint George Street. At a time when the British and French were constantly wrangling for supremacy on mainland Nova Scotia, the Mi'Kmaq sided with the French, with whom they had been trading for many years. As a countermeasure, the English brought in one hundred Mohawk braves from New York State in 1712.

Farther along Lower Saint George Street is a one-time inn and tavern, now the *O'Dell Museum.* The founder of this establishment was once a dispatch rider for a pony express that in 1849 became the Associated Press in New York. Today in this restored inn, you'll find a collection of Victorian costumes, furnishings, and shipbuilding artifacts. Back in the days when it catered to cosmopolitan travelers, the best rooms in the house could be had for $1.50 a night. For information, call (902) 532–7754. The museum is open daily June 1 to September 30 from 9:30 A.M. to 5:00 P.M., Sunday from 1:00 to 5:00 P.M.

The O'Dell Museum's front desk has a display of antique silver plate, along with a sobering demonstration of the damage wrought by over-polishing. By far, the museum's biggest draw is its shared function as *The Genealogy Centre of the Annapolis Heritage Society,* which focuses primarily on Annapolis Royal and its neighboring townships. In one corner of the museum's entrance there is a selection of books for sale covering local genealogy, tracing the family lines of many of the early settlers. The center also covers the early Acadian settlements prior to 1755. The center's collection includes genealogies, local histories, cemetery and probate records, old scrapbooks, microfilms of vital statistics for Annapolis and Digby Counties, church records, and deeds. If you had ancestors in the area, this is a great place to start exploring your family tree.

The local historical society co-manages this and another small building, the *North Hills Museum,* in Granville Ferry. This place is right on Granville Road, en route to the Habitation at Port Royal, so it's worth a peek while you are in the neighborhood. This 1764 farmhouse was the private home for many years of an antiques collector who concentrated on the Georgian era. Now housing his donated collection, the building contains eighteenth- and nineteenth-century English furniture, porcelain, and eighteenth-century glass and paintings by four renowned Royal Society of London painters. The barn has an original Acadian *aboiteaux,* a wooden contraption used to drain salt water from marshes and retain fresh water. The museum is open from June to mid-October Monday to Saturday 9:30 A.M. to 5:30 P.M. and Sunday 1:00 to 5:30 P.M. and donations are welcome.

This end of Saint George Street can get very lively during the *farmers' market,* which is held weekly on Saturday morning all year long and Wednesday afternoon during July and August. A lot of crafts from near and far show up here, along with the vegetables and the potato pancakes. Just around the corner, at 170 Saint George Street, you can also visit a potter's shop and studio at *Catfish Moon,* where the specialty seems to be dishware, cute pet feeding bowls, and assorted fun knickknacks with a humorous cat, dog, or fish theme. They also ship items, and samples of their work can be viewed at www.cat fishmoon.com.

A short way farther into town on this same thoroughfare is the *Bailey House,* built in 1780 by an artificer at Fort Anne. It was once the home of wealthy United Empire Loyalists whose social standing was so lofty that they could host a grand ball for the Duke of Kent.

A few blocks farther down the street is the *King's Theatre,* built in 1922. This was the home of Henry Goldsmith, a lawyer and great-grandnephew of playwright Oliver Goldsmith, who wrote *She Stoops to Conquer.* The building is now used as the venue for the Annapolis Royal Arts Festival, held every September, and plays and films are shown here year-round.

Just across the street from the theater is the *Old Post Office,* the site of which was home to Colonel Samual Vetch, the captor of Port Royal in 1710.

Following Confederation, the newly formed government built a château-style post office and customs warehouse on the site.

Two other houses are worthy of mention: the **Adams-Ritchie House,** dating from 1712, and the **Sinclair Inn,** dating from around 1710 and including elements from three early buildings that served as a hostelry.

The Sinclair Inn Museum is one of the most fascinating houses you will see in town, since they have literally picked it apart, down to the bare bones. When you walk inside the doors, you will see exactly what I mean: Only the timber frame seems to be keeping it together. You can examine the walls to learn how they were constructed in early colonial times using wattle and daub, known as *torchis* to Acadians. This was a mixture of clay and marsh grasses supported by horizontal staves, which were spaced about five inches apart and strung between rough-hewn timbers that were notched to hold the staves. Parts of the floor of the Sinclair Inn are now completely open to view, covered only by thick plates of glass, so that you can view the foundations.

Since the building is really comprised of three homes that were amalgamated, you can also see examples of mid-1700s plaster and lath walls, which by then were considered the most effective way of sealing the house from cold air. One of the three houses incorporated into the Sinclair Inn dates back to 1710, and was built by silversmith Jean-Baptiste Soulard, who kept his shop here and also served as the French King's gunsmith just before the British take-over, making this the oldest still-standing Acadian building in Canada. By 1714, Soulard sold the home to John Adams and moved to Quebec with his wife. There's an unusual strategy to take you though the history of the home: You can visit the ghosts in the basement who will recount stories from their lives, including that of Louise Comeau, Soulard's wife. The Sinclair Inn is open in summer daily 9:00 A.M. to 5:00 P.M. and in winter Monday through Friday 9:00 A.M. to 5:00 P.M. and Saturday 1:00 to 4:00 P.M. A small admission is charged.

The Adams-Ritchie House used to be the site of government meetings when Annapolis Royal was the provincial capital (before Halifax was founded). One of the fathers of confederation, Sir Thomas Ritchie, was born here. It now houses **Leo's Café,** which has lunch and casual afternoon dining, but closes early. If your appetite hits later in the evening, eating out can be a stretch. For good supper fare, competently made, try the **Garrison House Inn,** at 350 Saint George Street, or the Queen Anne Inn. Chefs in both places can be relied upon to use only the freshest ingredients and to not cut any corners in your dinner's preparation. If the appetite strikes after 9:00 P.M., however, your only choice is the pub. Reportedly, palatable food is also available at odd hours at the local golf course.

After lunch at Leo's, resume your walk by continuing along the same thoroughfare until you reach **Fort Anne.** This national historic site represents the fourth and last French fortress built at this site. Only three buildings remain out of sixty that once stood on this spot.

Fort Anne comprises pieces of several different forts, dating from different eras and ruled by different countries. From the fort's hilly defenses you will get a nice view of the harbor and a stretch of lowland originally reclaimed by a dike constructed by the Acadians.

The original fort was constructed by the French here in 1643. The powder magazine, which dates from 1708, is the last remnant of the French fortifications. The earthworks, which look like empty moats, have been left in the state in which they were found. They are among the oldest historic features in the entire National Historic Parks System.

If you visit the museum housed in the field officers' quarters, which the Duke of Kent had constructed in 1797, you can get the whole story of the English-French conflict that raged for many years in this region. One room is dedicated to the story of the Acadian settlers. Other rooms feature collections of old military badges and buttons and lots of antique weaponry.

You will be strolling through Fort Anne's star-shaped fortifications, its beautifully tended lawns, and its earthworks dating from 1702. They offer a magnificent view of the basin.

After visiting the fort complex, return to Upper Saint George Street (Lower Saint George Street becomes Upper about halfway through the village) and continue walking past the Military Cemetery and onward past Prince Albert Road until you come to the **Annapolis Royal Historic Gardens** on your right.

Acadian Cottage at Annapolis Royal Historic Gardens

The ten-acre (four-hectare) gardens are abutted by reclaimed marshland and a wildfowl sanctuary. The gardens contain more than 200 varieties of roses, with a total of 2,000 bushes. Some varieties of these roses were grown by the early Acadian settlers. At their peak, in midsummer, some roses cascade over a huge rough-hewn log pergola. There is a small replica of an Acadian cottage, complete with a kitchen garden, or *potager,* containing the ingredients for traditional Acadian soups, or *potages.*

Traditional English gardening is represented in the form of the Governor's Garden, carefully tended in eighteenth-century style. There is also a Victorian garden, accented by a 300-year-old elm tree. If you compare this garden with Halifax Public Gardens, the most striking difference is that much of this garden is built along an incline, which gradually descends to a marshy area bordering the shore. Make sure you descend to this point in the gardens, the site of the early Acadian dikes. In early September the reclaimed marshes are full of Norfolk grass, which is taller than most men. This bushy, reedy grass was used for centuries as thatch on cottage rooftops in Europe and in Acadia's early settlements.

This is the end point of the Annapolis Royal walking tour's route. Once you return to your car, if you cross a small bridge to the village of **Granville Ferry,** you will be entering yet another narrow peninsula similar to Digby Neck. Pause for a moment after crossing the bridge and look back across the water at Annapolis Royal. On a clear day this has to be one of the prettiest vistas the province has to offer.

Drive southwest on Route 1 for about 6 miles (10 km) and you will come across an old wooden fortress.

This is the **Habitation at Port Royal,** a re-creation of the oldest European settlement on the continent north of Florida. This reconstruction, built in the 1930s, was based on the records of the inhabitants of a fur-trading post here that dated back to 1605. Historians have never been able to ascertain the exact site of the original Port Royal, but this is definitely in the ballpark if not right at home plate. It was here that the Order of Good Cheer was formed to boost morale during the long winter nights.

Several of the post's inhabitants had literary inclinations, in particular a lawyer named Marc Lescarbot, who wrote copious notes about his year at the site. To amuse the bored pioneers, he created theatrical pieces that were performed for the inhabitants in what he named the Theatre of Neptune. This eventually was honored in the selection of a name for Canada's first professional repertory theater, Neptune Theatre, located in Halifax.

It is because of Lescarbot's notes, and those of Samuel de Champlain and Père Pierre Biard, a Jesuit priest, that historians were able to learn so much about the early days of the Acadians in Nova Scotia. One of the things that

Habitation at Port Royal

strikes the visitor most at this carefully re-created fortress is the size of the beds. The original inhabitants of Port Royal were a stocky lot, with beds that could hardly accommodate Snow White's pals, by modern standards. They were also quite elevated and canopied to retain warmth.

The little charcoal-colored rectangular fortress, with its stone-covered central courtyard and rugged furnishings recalling farm settlements from seventeenth-century Normandy, is so startling in its authenticity that it feels like you have time-traveled. It is hardly a stretch of the imagination to picture the original traders going about their business in the 1600s. This illusion is helped along by the many costumed interpreters, French-accented Acadians from the local area. Wearing *sabots*—wooden shoes—the interpreters do everything from cutting wood into shingles to maintaining a lookout for enemy attacks. Their clothing is made from handwoven material carefully sewn in the manner of the original inhabitants.

Be sure to see the fur-trading room, where the wealth of hides and commercial paraphernalia really re-creates the feeling of this old fur-trading post.

Leaving Port Royal, backtrack roughly a mile (1.6 km) in the direction of Granville Ferry and then turn left along the Hollow Mountain Road, an unpaved byway that is nevertheless quite passable in dry weather. When you reach the end of this secondary road, you'll be facing the Bay of Fundy. If you turn left again, you will soon be in **Delaps Cove,** which has some of the most noteworthy hikes in the province.

It is along this stretch of Fundy coast that the province's unusual prehistoric past is most evident. Basaltic lava flows have hardened into crystals, which have been worn and shaped by the relentless forces of the tide. Anyone who has visited the coast of a volcanic island—for example, the Canary Islands— will instantly recognize the rock formations as the result of hardened lava flows. The only thing that has shaped the lava somewhat differently here is the relentless crashing of the world's highest tides.

Whereas on Digby Neck you will see basalt cliffs leaning precariously like primeval towers of Pisa, here the rocks are sometimes softened into hard round beach boulders or natural basalt pools that fill up at high tide, allowing the brave and hardy to take a chilly dip in the tidal waters.

Delaps Cove is the one-time settlement of freed black slaves from the United States, who lived here on land granted to them by the Crown. Their old farms have now returned to the wilderness, cleft in two by old logging roads.

If you wish to go on a wilderness trek here, plan on at least two hours for the journey. Finding the area's two trails is easy: Simply follow the signs marked DELAPS COVE WILDERNESS TRAIL. The trails are a little farther up the road than the wharf; if you actually descend to the cove itself, you've gone too far. You can leave your car at the parking lot at the designated trail entrance just before the descent to the cove.

You have a choice between the ***Bohaker Trail***, a 2-mile (3.2-km) oval that begins on an escarpment of rocks overlooking the bay, and ***Charlie's Trail***, a more challenging 2.5-mile (3.8-km) loop that starts a mile (1.6 km) or so farther down the rock-strewn logging road. Charlie's Trail requires better hiking boots that offer more stability, since the trail consists of harsh granite terrain. The payoff of taking the easier Bohaker Trail is a 43-foot (13 m) water-fall at its end. The Bohaker also allows you the delicate pleasure of salt sea mist mingled with the scent of black spruce.

An alternative walk is simply to follow the coast by walking along the huge basalt boulders that stretch past the government wharf. From here all up along the coast is a daisy chain of fishing wharves and tiny lighthouses that serve the small communities of Delaps Cove, Parkers Cove, Hampton, and Halls Harbour.

Boats along the coast are tied up flush alongside the wharves at high tide and are left immobilized 20 feet (6 m) or so below on the sea bottom when the tide goes out. Depending on when the tides are coming in, you may chance upon lobster boats being unloaded. The fishermen will gladly sell you lobsters from right off the boat if you are interested in boiling your own, Maritime style.

You can also follow this coast along the unnumbered shore road, turning inland at Hampton or Port Lorne to rejoin Highway 101. Or if you don't want to go that far on an old shore road, you can turn down at Parkers Cove, pro-ceed to Granville Ferry, and cross the small bridge that separates it from Annapolis Royal.

From here you can follow the Evangeline Trail into the Annapolis Valley's rich farmlands, or take a side trip into wilderness at a national park in the center of the province. To do this get onto Route 8 in Annapolis Royal and proceed inland toward *Kejimkujik National Park.*

If you do opt for the national park, plan to return to the Evangeline Trail, even though it means backtracking. Otherwise you will miss some of the prettiest countryside in this end of the country and some of the finest country inns and restaurants in the area.

There is a relaxing bit of wilderness just outside of Annapolis Royal at the *Milford House Wilderness Retreat* in South Milford, just 14 miles (21 km) inland on Route 8 from Annapolis Royal, as you are headed in the direction of Kejimkujik. This charming place predates the formation of the national park by many years. Milford House started out as a staging point for hunters and fishermen who were drawn to the wilds of Nova Scotia's interior as early as the mid-1800s. At that time, and for many years afterward, people visiting the provinces were only granted hunting licenses if they were traveling with a certified Mi'Kmaq guide, who would shepherd them through the woods safely. Only around 450 licenses a year were granted, and the experience of going into the interior, where one lake after another was connected by a river system that could take people from the region of Annapolis right down to Liverpool, was hugely appealing and exotic. Prospective adventurers would arrive in Yarmouth from New York or Boston via freighter, then take a stagecoach to points inland such as Milford House, where they were met by their native guides. A novel published in 1908, *The Tent Dwellers,* described the experience in detail, including the arrival at the main lodge of Milford House, which at that

Milford House

point seemed to be the last stop at the end of civilization. (Back then, the lodge kept drinks cold with ice harvested from the frozen lake in winter. So if nothing else, it was the last chance for a cold drink.)

The tiny community of South Milford's fortunes and lives have been so intertwined with the lodge and its many annual visitors that four generations of the same family have worked there. Many of the older guests have been coming since early infancy, making their connection to the place six decades long. It's now owned by a group comprised of long-time visitors who bought the place in the 1960s. When the main lodge burned down in 2000, locals came to the rescue of displaced guests, and local contractors worked over the winter until a new lodge (looking much the same as its predecessor) was erected by the following spring.

The original owners of the 600 acres of property allowed visitors to construct their own cottages on the land, with the proviso that guests would eat at the lodge and if they desired to give up the cottage they would allow the Thomas family (who originally owned the land) to buy the building. The result is that the complex includes twenty-seven secluded cabins, many dating back to the early 1900s, and often named for the original occupants. Each has wood-burning fireplaces (sometimes even in the bedrooms), verandahs, and a dock for a canoe. Even if you are a first-time guest, the rustic mementos left by previous holiday-makers and the collections of good vacation reading give you the impression that you are returning to your own very secluded and private family cabin in the wilds, with nothing much to do but de-stress.

The slow, steady march of civilization has meant that over the years the rustic cabins have acquired electricity, cooking facilities, and hot-water heaters, making the bathrooms modern enough that guests are not completely roughing it, but they are not spoiling themselves either. It's still like camping at Keji, but with just a touch of added comfort and civility. (Cold beer in the fridge, mosquito screens, and a good bed next to a crackling fire.) The whole point of Milford House is to escape the outside world, and get a Thoreau experience, with a hot bath thrown in.

The lodge itself has a wonderful licensed dining room, with hearty breakfasts and a respectable dinner menu and talented chef who can also pack picnic lunches for trips into the wild. Menus change twice weekly, but feature items like local roast duck, rainbow trout, or pork loin. Facing the lake is a screened-in porch where you can imbibe in a charming, bug-free idyll. Canoes are for rent, and the resort also features a tennis court, lawn croquet, and a well-stocked game room and children's play room. Trails are dotted with picnic areas and dogs are welcome. It's a very *On Golden Pond* atmosphere, which can come as a bit of a shock to first-time visitors. John Hentz, one of the shareholders, told me the story of a high-flying New York executive who loudly proclaimed on his first day, "You call this rustic! I call it downright primitive!" Two days later that same executive asked to extend his stay and was raving about how wonderfully close to nature he felt. Three of the cottages are fully winterized and available for wintertime rental, though the rest of the services wind down. For more information, call (877) 532–5751 or (902) 532–2617. Rates are moderate to deluxe.

Keji comprises 147 square miles (381 sq km) of land, in the center of which is a large lake fed by several rivers. Canoes can be rented by the day or week through **Wildcat River Outfitters,** at Jakes Landing inside the national park. Canoe rentals are $30 for twenty-four hours or $24 for a business day. Weekly rates are $100. The outfitter also rents bicycles, kayaks, and paddleboats and provides shuttle service to other points in the park, which is particularly useful for river trips. **Loon Lake Outfitters,** along Route 2 outside the park, can out-fit you with most of the equipment you'll need for wilderness camping and can even provide premade meals ready for cooking at your campsite.

If you need to stock up on food or other supplies before camping in Keji, or feel the need for one more quick meal made by someone else before forging off into the wild, you can stop at **M&W Restaurant and Variety Store.** This is actually two places in one, located literally just before the park's entrance, on your left as you drive from Annapolis Royal. It is spotless, friendly, well main-tained, and well stocked. Co-owner Marilyn Rowter makes great BLT sandwiches and home-style burgers and fries, among other necessities like pie. M&W has a lovely floral patio on one side of the restaurant, and the place has nice touches like Nova Scotia tartan tablecloths setting off its rustic pine decor. The restaurant is the first building you will see. Next to it is the variety store, containing the all-important bug spray and firewood, among other things. It includes a laundromat, making it a full-service civilization pit-stop. Some trailer parking is also available.

Rates for camping in the park are quite reasonable, but spots are in short supply. If you want to explore the park in the daytime but not camp, consider staying at the **Whitman Inn,** which has been operating nearby for eons. It is a pretty yellow country inn on the right-hand side of the road, just a five-minute drive farther down Route 8 past the park entrance. The Whitman Inn is a restored turn-of-the-twentieth-century homestead, still with its original furnish-ings, and boasting a library and parlor with books dating back to the 1800s. The Whitman Inn has its own restaurant, and people who are not guests of the inn stop by for their suppers as well, which is always a good sign. For details on this Heritage inn, call (800) 830–3855 or (902) 682–2226.

Take note that you have to pick your season well for a visit to Keji. At the tail end of August until the second week in September, it is lovely; but from late spring to early summer, you will be an all-you-can-eat buffet on two legs for the ticks and blackflies.

There is a standard campground at the beginning of the park, in an area called Jeremys Bay, where people rent sites by the night and prepare for or recover from their forays into the wilderness. For wilderness camping you will be expected to do some planning for your trip when you reserve your designated campsite in the park. Sites are spaced generously apart allowing for exceptional privacy. Due to the extremely small number of sites and their enormous popularity, park attendants recommend booking these spots up to sixty days in advance during the summer. In the early fall, my favorite time for Keji, these are far more available, but try to plan ahead anyway.

The park's wilderness campsites are clearly marked on their Web site, www.pc.gc.ca/pn-np/ns/kejimkujik/index_e.asp. The park's reception center also has detailed maps available with each wilderness site clearly marked; another, smaller map on the back shows the navigational buoys that you will need to find your way around if you are canoeing to your site. The park guides will also, if requested, show you a more detailed listing of all the wilderness sites, which describes their unique features. It is invaluable in choosing a site that suits your style. They also told me that the biggest problem campers face is getting disoriented while paddling in the lake and not being able to find their site. Frustrated campers sometimes give up and just put their tent anywhere, which is forbidden. Remember that you are allowed to spend only two days at each site, so plan your sites so that they follow a sequential pattern.

Be wary of leaving scraps of food lying around, and be sure to carefully dispose of any of the debris of human consumption. The numerous beaver and muskrat that you will see are not the only nonhuman inhabitants of the park. Bear, cougar, and lynx, not to mention other native Nova Scotian species, also inhabit this park. The last time I camped at Keji, I took the absolute worst book for my vacation reading: *The Cure for Death by Lightning,* which obsesses about bear attacks for at least the first hundred pages. While I admit that it compelled me to take scrupulous care of my pots and pans, it didn't prove to be good bedtime reading. There are bears in Keji, but sightings are rare. You're much more likely to have your site trashed by marauding raccoons.

Mi'Kmaq people camped in these lands many centuries before the white man. Petroglyphs that are visible when water washes over them are testimony to their early presence. The actual petroglyphs are protected now by fencing, so the only way to get up close is to join a tour by the park guides. These are held twice daily in the tourist season and must be reserved in advance, preferably the day before. Ask at the park's reception center, where you will be issued a free admission ticket after adding your name to their list. You might also want to view their twelve-minute film on the park and its wildlife and history, before venturing in.

Remember that Keji is a native heritage site, as well as a wilderness one, and Mi'Kmaq still maintain an active role in the park life. During my most recent visit, treasured hatchlings of endangered Blanding's Turtles were released into the wild following a colorful Mi'Kmaq naming ceremony on Merrymakedge Beach. Elders from the nearby Mi'Kmaq community chanted and drummed before the turtles were given their names. The Mi'Kmaq also are involved in other ways, from the petroglyph tours to traditional storytelling and encampments. Check at the main reception center for a detailed schedule of the activities.

Historians now know that people lived in Nova Scotia as early as 10,500 years ago, but they have not been able to ascertain whether these early inhabitants were the ancestors of the Mi'Kmaq who greeted and traded with the white men of the 1600s. The land may have witnessed the visits and passings of many peoples after the Ice Age slowly retreated and the trees and forests returned.

The pictographs that the ancient Mi'Kmaq left show elements from their nomadic life as hunters and gatherers. Moose are quite clearly depicted, as well as a snakelike creature, possibly Kipika'm, the Horned Serpent Person, a monstrous snake who lives in the Mi'Kmaq underworld. This character appears in all native legends in Canada, and even in Siberia. Anthropologists theorize that the serpent-creature elements of native oral history go back as far as 11,000 years, back to the original migration from Siberia across the Bering Strait land bridge.

An apt summary of Keji is that the park could easily serve as a destination in itself, for those interested in taking an extended canoe trip into the Nova Scotia of the ancient Mi'Kmaq.

I first visited Keji more than twenty years ago, and each time I return I am amazed at how the place has managed to retain not just its beauty, but also its magic. Every season has its own delights, from the rebirth of spring fauna and flora to the sensuous fullness of summer, the early morning mist rising off the lake, and the haunting call of the loon that echoes for miles. The key to Keji's continued brilliance lies in the tiny number of wilderness sites, giving a feeling of complete isolation. But don't let that fool you. We were still able to call Loon Lake Outfitters via cell phone from a site six hours' paddling away from Jakes Landing.

If you don't feel up to a wilderness camping experience in the cooler winter months, or just don't want to rough it all the way, you could extend the season by staying at the **Mersey River Chalets,** on Route 8, just 3 miles (5 km) before the park as you drive from Annapolis Royal. After you turn in from the main highway, expect to drive for a few minutes down their private road until you come to a clearing near the water. The setting is wonderful, with log-cabin construction lending a rustic close-to-nature feel, yet with all modern conveniences inside. A small reception cabin and gift shop will be on your left, and facing you will be their own licensed restaurant, **The Cascades.** One side of the restaurant features a patio overlooking a set of rushing rapids that run from one lake to the next. Inside, a striking multi-sided fireplace can be called into action on cooler days.

Mersey River Chalets features modern two-bedroom chalets with a full kitchen and a woodstove, and lots of hot water. On-site there are several com-plimentary sporting options, including tennis and canoes. If you want to be just a bit closer to nature, you can rent one of their Sioux-style tepees, which mer-cifully contain their own beds for soft-option camping.

Barrier-Free Nature

When it comes to mobility issues, my eyes were opened years ago following a ski accident that left me on crutches for months. Now aware of how seemingly minor things can affect a visitor's opportunity to enjoy a space, I always enjoy finding a setting that has managed to incorporate the principles of accessibility, or universal design, into its accommodations. Going even further is Mersey River Chalets, which has made a pristine corner of wilderness as available as possible to any guest that arrives at the door. Three of the resort's ten co-owners use wheelchairs, and as a result they understand accessibility issues better than any other nature retreat I've ever visited. They have applied their expertise and experience to create a place that can be used by groups or families with a wide range of physical abilities. Co-owner Tim Atkins pointed out that their chalets feature pocket doors that recede into the walls in the bathrooms, roll-in showers, doors with 3 feet (1 m) of clearance, and ramping. Beyond that, the grounds have an extensive set of boardwalks edged in low rustic railings, and a canoe dock rigged with an overhead lift so that people of differing physical abilities can get into a canoe.

This means a great deal to Mersey River's guests, some of whom come from as far away as Europe for a holiday where no one in the group is hampered in their enjoyment of nature. As I made my way down to the shoreline one day, I was greeted by an elderly German gentleman practically jumping out of his boots with excitement over the number of fish he and his son had caught together that day. Following closely behind, with the aid of two crutches, was his son. Watching this pair, I was reminded of co-owner Andrea Wegerer's comment that hotels often have ramps making rooms accessible, "But when you step out of the room, it's not accessible. Here you can access different activities and really explore nature."

Reach them at (877) 667–2583 or (902) 682–2443. They are open year-round. To explore their various accommodation options, check out their Web site, www.merseyriverchalets.com.

After Kejimkujik, backtrack to the Evangeline Trail, which you can rejoin at Junction 22, roughly 3 miles (5 km) before you return to Annapolis Royal. Alternately, you can continue to traverse the province via Route 8, and end up in Liverpool on Nova Scotia's south shore.

Apple Blossom Country

Provincial Highway 101 and its parallel trunk road, Route 1, from Annapolis Royal to Wolfville, run through some of the prettiest countryside you will ever see: rolling hills dotted with apple trees. These days even an occasional vine-yard can be seen, as grape growing becomes more and more popular.

Sheltered on both its western and eastern sides and lying along the fertile Annapolis River, the **Annapolis Valley** enjoys a miniclimate all its own. Spring comes earlier here than elsewhere in the province, summers seem warmer and sunnier, and fall holds out the tantalizing possibility of a profusion of gold, red, and fiery orange trees set amid the soft ochre glow of drying grass in the fields, all with warm Indian summer days thrown in. Winter along the coast is often unpredictable, with first a damp snowstorm followed by freezing rain and then a thaw. But here in the valley, the effect is often pure Currier and Ives, with snow-topped steeples, gorgeous winter scenery, and cross-country ski trails popping up here and there.

As you wind your way through this beautiful country, be sure to turn off at exit 16 in Aylesford to visit the **Oaklawn Farm Zoo.**

"We had no intentions of ever being a zoo," says Gail Rogerson. She and her husband, Ron, who own and run the Oaklawn Farm Zoo, had always just liked animals. They collected exotic pets on their Aylesford-area farm. For years Gail was a schoolteacher, and in 1975, her son's class visited the farm. The vis-its snowballed, and by the end of the 1970s, dozens of teachers were taking groups of students out to visit the farm.

It reached the point that people would drive up to the farm, insisting that it was a public place. Privacy became a thing of the past. "On a nice weekend our drive would be filled with strangers."

Forced to choose between moving away or opening their doors to the public, the Rogersons became the owners of the only zoo east of Montreal that features exotic animals such as lemurs, Japanese macaques, a gibbon (which you can hear from a long way off), camels, and a yak. You could spend hours watching the monkeys. Kids like the llamas. Several lions live here in spacious

About the Zoo's Zonkey

No, those aren't stockings on the donkey. A few years ago, Oaklawn Farm zoo owners Ron and Gail Rogerson had to deal with the problem of a lovesick zebra, for whom no suitable mate could be found. Eventually, a donkey was willing to make her a happy zebra, but the resulting offspring is a "terminal cross"—a sterile, mule-like progeny with no identifiable gender. This little "zonkey" looks just like a donkey except for the fetching pair of striped stockings that it appears to be wearing, and the war-paint stripes that run down its nose. Ron assures me that there is no reason for wildlife enthusiasts to be upset about the hybrid animal, since its mixed-up genetics will go no further than this particular zonkey.

quarters, among them, Rutherford, who once weighed in at a whopping 809 pounds. He is easily three times the weight of a lion in the wild, who would be kept trim by the struggle for survival, as Ron Rogerson explains. Rutherford greets visitors with the same self-satisfied nonchalance as Garfield, that other famous fat cat. Rutherford, however, has gone one better, with his name now entered in the *Guinness Book of Records*.

The zoo has a canteen where you can take a break from the hot midday sun, coin-operated vending machines that dispense snacks for feeding sheep and other small animals, and a gift shop in the two-story log-cabin reception building that features wild-animal sweatshirts and local crafts.

Be sure to check out the reception building's animal-head carvings on its second floor. Ten of the carvings are on the rounded ends of the joists. A cougar comes out of the end of two wall logs, while an owl stands out in bas-relief. Every carving represents an animal at the zoo, including resident and pet Badness the Pug.

The carvings are so subtly crafted that they trick the eye, so you have to search for them. Make a point of looking closely at the log ends and you will see a gibbon, an alligator, a llama, and a host of other critters. The carvings are the work of artist John Murray, who used a Haida Indian knife, traditionally used to make totem poles. Along with other artful pieces, the building has an almost-life-size papier-mâché zebra crafted by another local artist.

The Rogersons remind visitors that the principal concern of the farm is not to exhibit the animals but to provide a home for them where they can be at ease and breed. The zoo breeds registered dogs as well as exotic animals for sale to other zoos. Many of these animals are endangered in the wild, so their only hope of survival is through zoos and wildlife refuges. Oaklawn Farm Zoo is open April to November, with May and June weekdays the favorite times for school visits. Admission is charged. For information call (902) 847–9790.

All along this road between the valley and the Fundy coast you have been zigzagging the *North Mountain Range.* This was formed 200 million years ago at a time when the supercontinent began splitting into smaller continents. At that time rifts opened between the sandy plain around the Cobequid Hills of Truro, and basaltic lava was spewed out from the earth's belly, spilling out into the area. As it cooled, the North Mountain ridge was formed from the fractures and tilting, along with the rock formations of Digby Neck. The most spectacular result to come from this era of upheaval, apart from the Bay of Fundy itself, is the headland that overlooks the Minas Channel. It is known as *Cape Split.* This is the legendary home of the great Mi'Kmaq god, Glooscap.

To get into the rugged-nature spirit of things, the vigorous among you may want to make the trek to the end of Cape Split. This is the must-do trek for Nova Scotia's committed hikers, since the spectacular panorama offered by the end of this excursion is unmatched anywhere else in the province. Count on a day's recovery from this trek, so plan to stay either at Blomidon Park, where you can camp, or at a nearby bed-and-breakfast. To get to Cape Split, stay on Highway 101 until you reach exit 11 just outside Wolfville. Turn onto Route 358 and drive north in the direction of Scots Bay and Cape Blomidon.

Just past Port Williams on Route 358, you'll come to Starrs Point and the historic *Prescott House,* which was built from 1814 to 1816 by Charles Prescott. He was a successful merchant who served as a member of the legislature for Cornwallis Township in the early 1800s. His true claim to fame, however, is apples.

Prescott was the man who introduced the Gravenstein apple and other superior apple varieties to Nova Scotia, forever changing the landscape of the Annapolis Valley. In his day all ornamentals, fruits, and vegetable and fodder crops came from European stock or were adapted to the eastern United States. Because of the harsh winters and proximity to the ocean, some did not succeed here until Prescott established strains that thrived in the Nova Scotian climate.

The honorary member of the horticultural societies of New York, Boston, and London offered grafting stock in the way of " . . . scions and buds of any kind to every person who may apply in the proper season . . . ," according to a notice posted by Prescott himself.

The impressive Georgian architecture of Prescott House is complemented by the period furnishings that Prescott's great-granddaughter collected when she restored the house in the 1930s. Surrounding the house are beautiful trees, gardens, and lawns. The vista includes the diked lands of the Cornwallis River. For more information, call (902) 542–3984.

Prescott House is open from the beginning of June to mid-October, Monday to Saturday from 9:30 A.M. to 5:30 P.M., Sunday from 1:00 to 5:30 P.M.

The Prescott House also has a fascinating collection of old Prescott family photos. At various times of the year there are presentations on the family history and the role the Prescotts played in medicine and in World War I. A small admission is charged.

One fine spring day I took a notion to roam out into one of the local apple orchards in full bloom, looking for something gorgeous to paint. The experience was something out of television's *X-Files:* From the road you just can't imagine the terror caused by the ceaseless humming of billions of honeybees. My advice: Go the third week of May, take lots of film, but use a camera with a zoom lens.

Summer comes earlier in this part of the province, and there are many cozy places to stay where you can enjoy the great outdoors early in the season. One nice place is the **Farmhouse Inn** in nearby Canning. The bed-and-breakfast offers standard rates and can arrange packages for its guests. This inn is right on Canning's Main Street. Call (800) 928–4346 or (902) 582–7900, or visit www.farmhouseinn.ns.ca.

Pause at a point on Route 358 called **The Lookoff,** high on North Mountain, for a spectacular view of **Minas Basin,** site of the highest of the Bay of Fundy's record-breaking tides. There is adequate space here for parking, as well as washrooms and picnic tables, so you can take in the scenery while you munch. Sprawling below like a scattered bouquet you can see apple orchards, woods, lazy cows drifting through fields of clover, old farmhouses, and, farther back, spread out like a brown carpet, the muddy waters of the basin.

From this point continue a little past **Scots Bay,** where a walk of slightly more than 5 miles (8 km) begins. In June the red trillium blooms along this path. Far below you can watch eagles and hawks soar above the sea.

There is another hike in this area, slightly more than 10 miles (16 km) long. This hike starts at the campground at **Cape Blomidon,** atop the eroding sandstone cliffs, and then backtracks in a loop through woodlands.

Like the Cape Split hike, this trail demands extreme caution, as erosion is slowly claiming the cliffs. The edge of the headland is dangerous; no barriers are there to protect people from falling to the beach 330 feet (100 m) or so below the footpath. Several times along this path the trail diverges to the edge, so the incautious could plunge to their doom.

Whatever you do, don't whiz past this area after your Cape Split excursion or a visit to Blomidon. Since it is set deep in the heart of a rich agricultural area, with trendy cuisine inspired by the population drawn to the local university, the stretch of road from Kentville to Wolfville has much to offer the gourmet. Try **Paddy's Pub & Brewery,** 42 Aberdeen Street in Kentville, with a great relaxed pub atmosphere. In Wolfville, seek out **Tattingstone Inn,** 434 Main Street, (902)

542–7696, a posh, elegant restaurant attached to an intimate couples-oriented Victorian inn. They're known for their rack of lamb and chicken served with pear and ginger sauce, using pears grown on the property. Also in Wolfville, *Acton's Grill & Cafe,* 402 Main Street, (902) 542–7525, is a local favorite with wonderful chowder, monkfish, and rack of lamb, and great service.

The three communities of Kentville, New Minas, and Wolfville (home to Acadia University) seem to have blended into one another as the population has grown. You must leave the main highway if you wish to drive through some of these charming communities. Take exit 11, drive downhill a short way, and then turn right onto Route 1 and continue on your way through Wolfville. It has a cozy college-town feel, with the university name really tied into the province's most infamous historical event: the expulsion of the Acadians. The proclamation declaring that the Acadians were to leave the now-British territory came in 1755, and was made in nearby *Grand-Pré,* on the shores of Minas Basin; a sign will direct you to turn right about a half mile (1 km) after the exit 10 marker on Route 1. You will then be directed by a road sign to drive just over another half mile before getting to the *Grand-Pré National Historic Site.* The interpretive center will be to your left, just before the railroad tracks. A small church and national monument mark the spot where the expulsion, which continued until 1762, was set in motion.

Here you will see a statue depicting the fictional Acadian heroine Evangeline, immortalized in a poem by Longfellow about a young Acadian girl separated from her fiancé and expelled down south. The center is open from mid-May until mid-October, daily from 9:00 A.M. until 6:00 P.M. A small admission is charged.

If you are there at the right time of year—that is, the third weekend in May—you must take in the Annapolis Valley's *Apple Blossom Festival.* Even if you hardly take in any of the festival events, the scenery here at the end of May is breathtaking. There will be mile after mile of orchards in full bloom and beautiful spring weather. You can also enjoy an assortment of stately old homes for bed-and-breakfasting in the college town of Wolfville.

Nova Scotia's early settlers came from the Atlantic coast of France, which as we all know is a great place to grow wine grapes. When they arrived here they found many similar growing conditions, and, as can be seen in the area of Annapolis Royal, used the same kind of dike building and lowland agriculture as they had employed back in France. So it should come as no surprise that vintners have put down roots here. The province is now home to more than a half dozen successful wineries, making it a valid wine tour destination.

One of the best ways to spend an afternoon in this part of the province is visiting one of the vineyards, *Domaine de Grand-Pré,* which has attached to it the province's only Swiss restaurant, **Le Caveau.** This establishment features exquisite Swiss food served along with their own wines, and has a wonderful vine-covered, pergola-shaded patio for summer dining for up to eighty people. To get there after visiting the national historic site at Grand-Pré, retrace your steps 0.6 of a mile (1 km) back to Route 1, turn right, and drive a half mile back towards Wolfville. Domaine de Grand-Pré is clearly marked on the road. If you decide to visit the winery first, it is only two minutes by car before the historic site, on the same side of the road as you come from Wolfville.

Visiting this setting in mid-August, you will find the grapes starting to ripen and change color, and the outdoor patio is a wonderful way to enjoy a meal in the beautiful setting. The net result of all this is that it has become increasingly popular as a setting for weddings. Often, the bride and groom stay next door at the **Old Lantern Inn and Vineyard,** and, illuminated by a series of lanterns, they walk through the vineyards at sunset to the wedding ceremony at Le Caveau. All the details of a wedding, right down to making the cake, can be handled by Le Caveau.

Domaine de Grand-Pré has joined the econo-museum network, meaning they now have interactive and instructional components to their wine tours, along with an opportunity to sample many of their wines. In the downstairs of their reception center, you will see their huge vats of maturing wine. Upstairs, you'll have a chance to sample many varieties. All Domaine de Grand-Pré wines are made from Nova Scotia–grown grapes. Don't pass up the chance to try their unique ice wine, several varieties of which have won medals in international wine competitions.

Because it is a small vineyard, they do not intend to export their wines, but they do supply wine to many of the province's fine dining establishments, particularly those participating in the Taste of Nova Scotia program. Grapes have been carefully selected to thrive in Nova Scotia's shorter growing season and most of the wines are named for the grape varietals. One exclusive wine they produce, L'Acadie Blanc, recalls the early inhabitants and first grape growers in the region. Their New York Muscat (named for the grape) is a crisp white and my personal favorite.

Wine-making is apparently complicated stuff, requiring many years of study, from the agriculture of the grapes to the complex chemistry of making sure the optimum quality is derived from the wine-making process, and even the pairing of flavors of different grapes. This is a family-run business, with patriarch Hanspeter Stutz taking care of marketing while his son (a graduate vintner) handles the scientific aspect. The daughter and daughter-in-law, Beatrice Jurt and Caecila Stutz, handle the wine tours and organizing weddings, and son-in-law and Swiss-trained chef Alex Jurt is in charge of the restaurant.

The food here is sublime, meaning the Swiss quiche has perfect pastry, the unsurpassed schnitzel is tender and moist, and the desserts (featuring decadent things like three varieties of the finest Swiss chocolate) are out of this world. Enjoyed on the beautiful flagstone patio, the whole experience will leave you wanting to buy a few bottles to take home. Since the vineyard is in the midst of the apple-growing region, they have also produced their own hard apple cider, Stutz Cider.

Tour groups often come through in minibuses. On the day we visited, two bachelorette-party wine tours were just finishing up amid general hilarity. Tours are at 11:00 A.M., 3:00 P.M., and 5:00 P.M. during the summer. Even in other months, the activity continues, with the harvesting of grapes and their cultivation. (Optimum harvesting of the grapes for their gold medal–winning ice wine, for example, takes place in mid-winter, under cover of darkness. Nets are put out to keep the ripe, frozen grapes from falling to the ground.) To make reservations for the restaurant, or to check details of their wine tours, you can call (902) 542–1753, or visit their Web site at www.grandprewines.com. Domaine de Grand-Pré has another vineyard in Canning.

The Glooscap Trail

From this point in the valley, you can easily drive back to Halifax via **Windsor,** home of nineteenth-century novelist and Windsor native Judge Thomas Haliburton—the Mark Twain of Canada. His creation, Sam Slick, the Yankee clock peddler, was an unparalleled smooth talker, whose colorful aphorisms live on to this day. Among Haliburton's pithy clichés are: "Facts are stranger than fiction," "raining cats and dogs," "quick as a wink," "barking up the wrong tree," and "circumstances alter cases."

You can visit this famous wit's Windsor home, **Haliburton House,** since it has been a branch of the Nova Scotia Museum for many years. The house and its lovely grounds can be found just off Route 101 and are clearly marked from the road. The house contains a number of items of local historical interest and effects related to the life of the town's famous author. If you are interested in reading more, get a copy of *The Clockmaker.*

If you have already visited Halifax and are heading out of the province, you may want to try following a route referred to as the **Glooscap Trail.** This nears the shores of Minas Basin, the inner arm of the Bay of Fundy. It is a pretty, unspoiled area, accessed by leaving Highway 101 at exit 5 in Windsor and driving along Trunk Highway 215.

It is with this routing that I will take you out of the province. (If you drive back to Halifax, you can always rejoin the Glooscap Trail in Truro, 60 miles/100

trivia

The originator of the expression "A nod is as good as a wink to a blind horse" was Thomas Haliburton, creator of the literary character Sam Slick.

km past Halifax toward New Brunswick.) To do this take exit 14A or 15 off Provincial Highway 102 outside Truro, to Route 2.

If you travel the considerably less-traveled Route 215, you will be edging the area of the world's highest tides, which reach their peak of 53 feet (16 m) at Burntcoat Head near Noel. Just a few minutes' drive farther down the road, and you will reach **Maitland,** the entry spot for **rafting on the tidal wave.** This wave is otherwise known as a tidal bore, a scientific term for a wall of water created when a large volume of water from the oncoming tide is forced into a much smaller channel. The resulting tidal bore will push passengers up the Shubenacadie River for 18 miles (29 km) aboard Zodiacs— big inflated dinghy-type boats. The entire trip takes half a day, during which time you are pushed by "roller-coaster" rapids of 3 to 10 feet (1 to 3 m). Lunch is included.

Several outfits take rafters on this trip. I'll name the top three here, followed by their phone numbers and Web sites. They are all reliable, experienced, and similarly priced at around $40 per person. Remember that departure times vary depending on the day's tides, which are given on the Web sites. The rafting companies are Shubenacadie River Runners Ltd. (800–856–5061 or 902–261–2770, www.tidalborerafting.com); Shubenacadie River Adventure Tours (888–878–8687 or 902–261–2222, www.shubie.com); and the Shubenacadie Tidal Bore Rafting Park (800–565–RAFT or 902–758–4032, www.tidalborerafting park.com). Tours with this last group end with a barbecue.

If you haven't arrived at the right time for the day's tides, or if you expect you'll be too wet and tired to leave afterward, you can find reasonably priced accommodations at the renovated home of a former sea captain. **The Captain Douglas House Inn and Restaurant** is right on Highway 215. The municipal Heritage property dates back to 1860 and has a country restaurant on-site. For reservations, call (902) 261–2289. Rates are standard to moderate.

The **Shubenacadie Tidal Bore Rafting Park,** mentioned above, is a short distance from the intersection of Route 215 and Highway 102 (marked on the map at exit 10). It features fully equipped housekeeping cottages right on the Shubenacadie River, as well as rafting packages. Call (800) 565–7238 or (902) 758–4032.

The first highlight of the road after Truro is in **Portapique,** where you can pay a visit to the studio and gallery of noted artist Joy Laking. You may have seen some of her prints in other areas of the province. Laking's work is

Giant Pumpkins and Their Seeds

Peter Peter Pumpkin Eater must have lived in **Windsor** once. Howard Dill, a resident of Windsor, is internationally famous for breeding the world's biggest pumpkins year after year, earning Windsor the name of "Pumpkin Capital of the World." The genetics hobbyist took many years to come up with his own patented strain of giant pumpkin seeds, and even when his own pumpkin doesn't win the Giant Pumpkin weigh-ins, you can bet that it was a Howard Dill seed that gave the champion life. Mr. Dill explained his practical method of selective breeding to my son, comparing it with growing good kids. "You start with healthy parents, and go from there."

You can drop in at **Howard Dill's Farm and Visitor Centre,** and buy yourself a packet or two of giant-pumpkin seeds, while you are in Windsor. My favorite time of year to come is in early fall, when the pumpkin patch is overrun by excited children who climb the mountainous fruit (yes, pumpkins are fruit!) to get their pictures taken. Dill's best pumpkins can still make a preteen look like a dwarf. Needless to say, I had to buy a much humbler specimen to fit into my trunk.

You can visit this shrine to the Giant Pumpkin at 400 College Road. The field is overlooked by King's Edgehill School, a private school for which the town is well known. To get there take a left at exit 5 off Highway 101, drive 2.5 miles (4 km), and then turn left onto College Road. You can also call the farm at (902) 798–2728.

There are destinations off the beaten path, and then there are destinations that are offbeat. This next event, the **Pumpkin Regatta,** falls into this category. Held in Windsor's Lake Pizaquid, it generally takes place the second Sunday in October. It's one of the wackiest events in the Maritimes and a big hit with the kids. It starts with a parade of suitably equipped pumpkins, which have been hollowed out in preparation for the race. Accompanying them on their floats are the paddling crews in equally laughable costumes.

The race then gets under way, with a number of heats run throughout the afternoon. Amazingly, quite a few of the giant pumpkins do manage to reach the finish line before sinking. Needless to say, a carnival atmosphere reigns. For details, call (902) 798–2728.

composed of watercolors and serigraphs of a decidedly nostalgic nature—sunny front porches on hazy summer afternoons, lady's slippers and trilliums, and kitchen curtains blowing softly in a summer breeze—all painted with delicacy and liveliness. The *Joy Laking Gallery* is indicated by several signs along Highway 2. You will not see the gallery itself from the road. A driveway leads to a home and the studio, in a separate whimsically decorated outbuilding. The gallery is open year-round. June to August it is open Monday to Saturday from 9:00 A.M. to 5:00 P.M., Sunday from 1:00 to 5:00 P.M. At other times, you can arrange an appointment to visit by calling ahead at (902)

647–2816. The artist also produces serigraphs of her charming works, which may better suit a souvenir hunter's budget than an original watercolor. In Portapique you will also find the remains of an Acadian dike, along the salt marsh that edges the shore.

Apart from its obvious appeal to beachcombers, the rugged Fundy shore of Nova Scotia has much to offer would-be geologists and other rock hounds. The areas of coastline that front the Bay of Fundy contain a wealth of prehistoric fossils just waiting to be gathered like so many wild berries.

If you take a close look at your official "Scenic Travelways" map (available at any tourism information booth), you will note the fossil icons that dot the shores of the Bay of Fundy. They indicate the richest areas for fossil exploration.

Roughly 350 million years ago, long before dinosaurs began decorating kids' pajamas, this area was teeming with life. Lying near the equator, it was wedged between North America and Africa, in the middle of the supercontinent called Pangaea. As the continents started drifting apart, huge rift valleys formed, of which the Bay of Fundy is one. As the tides coursed through this cleft in the continents, water eroded a huge cross section, revealing a window into the world of 200 million years ago and beyond.

The area of the Bay of Fundy is noted as the world's best site of continuously exposed Late Carboniferous Age rocks. Along these same shores are exposed sea cliffs that reveal ancient treasures from the Triassic and Jurassic geological periods. And you would never think of Nova Scotia as a place full of volcanoes, but along these shores you will quite unexpectedly come across rock formations created by ancient lava flows.

The fossilized legacy of some of the world's oldest terrestrial reptiles and the oldest land-dwelling snails have been found along here. Two hundred million years ago, some of the planet's first dinosaurs roamed the desert that was Nova Scotia. And 70,000 years ago mastodons were here. Bones of two mastodons, including a baby, were recently found in a gypsum pit near Halifax.

Apart from rugged basalt cliffs and fossils, the area has other geological delights, noted and treasured for centuries by the native peoples. Mi'Kmaq legend has it that the mighty Glooscap lived across the narrow neck of the Minas Basin, in the area of Blomidon and Cape Split, the breathtaking promontory that overlooks the spot where tides reach 50 feet (16 m) and more. From there the great god of the Mi'Kmaq looked over his children.

Once he was mocked by an animal spirit named Beaver, and his anger caused him to scoop up land from the gorges and fling the clods of earth at the mocking spirit, creating islands that now comprise *Five Islands Provincial Park* (near Economy) and scattering the jewels known today as jasper, agate, onyx, and amethyst. To this day the legendary gifts of Glooscap draw rock hounds from around the world to the shores of the Bay of Fundy. The park is open from mid-May to September.

At Five Islands Provincial Park, on Route 2, you will find camping, a beach, and, of course, five islands: Moose, Diamond, Long, Egg, and Pinnacle.

The picnic areas and the **Estuary Nature Trail** in this park are marked with interpretive displays explaining the geology of the site.

In the **Parrsboro** area you'll run into a lot of geology buffs and rock hounds. The pleasant little town of some 1,600 persons is actually the biggest community along this route, so this is the place to stock up on film or food before exploring the area's coastline. The rock hounds you will meet will be looking for zeolites—semiprecious stones such as amethyst and agate.

From the **Fundy Geological Museum,** on Two Island Road in Parrsboro, paleontologists lead daily tours to the site of the biggest fossil find in North America. A reasonable fee is charged for these tours. Every tide brings more erosion, exposing two different prehistoric periods, the Jurassic and Triassic, 200 million and 350 million years ago, respectively.

There are two types of guided collecting tours: One explores mineral sites; the other, fossil sites. You can generally count on one of these tours occuring daily, but not both. If you have a particular interest or preference, call (902) 254–3814 to confirm the tour's planned itinerary. Tour departure times are dictated by the tides, which can reach as high as 44 feet (14 meters). Less-mobile or rainy-day visitors can opt to cut and polish semiprecious stones at a lapidary workshop at the museum.

If you do go on a tour, be sure to wear a hat and effective sunscreen. The constant breezes can fool visitors into thinking that the sun is not very strong here, but the reflection off the basalt rock can cause a brutal sunburn.

Visitors are prohibited from removing any fossils from the rock face, and no one is allowed to use hammers on the outcrops. There are many loose fossils to be found, however. Every fossil is carefully examined by the tour leader, whose expertise is really needed for identification of each specimen. If you are touring the beach areas, pack a sweater, because when the fog rolls in the temperature can drop quite suddenly.

The museum has a 10-foot-long, 200-million-year-old prosauropod dinosaur in its collection. This herbivore was discovered encased in sandstone, gradually unearthed, and assembled at the museum over the course of several years. The museum also features some interesting workshops during the summer and an elderhostel geological safari in early October. If you want to plan ahead to join one of its programs, visit http://museum.gov.ns.ca/fgm/ for information.

A Visit to Wasson Bluff

On a tour led by Ken Adams, a curator of the Fundy Geological Museum, I visited the site known as **Wasson Bluff,** a pebbly beach at the foot of an eroding cliff. The mouth of the brook that cuts through the bluff is made of reddish-brown 300-million-year-old sandstone and shale beds, where visitors regularly find footprints of ancient amphibians, ancestors of the dinosaurs.

Turning west across a fault line—a fracture in the earth's crust—the rock suddenly changed to a deep greenish-gray basalt and purple sandstone. The basalt is volcanic rock that in places looks like it was squeezed out of a toothpaste tube. Roughly 200 million years old, it was part of a massive lava flow that reached as far south as Boston and created both Brier Island and Grand Manan Island farther out in the Bay of Fundy.

One layer under this lava flow marks the period when almost half the earth's prehistoric animals were suddenly rendered extinct. As the lava cooled, little bubbles formed, and in these bubbles, minerals known as zeolites were formed. Fragments of these zeolites were scattered along the beach. Beyond this point, the fault line forked. The fossils unearthed here come from the Jurassic period and include tiny dinosaur footprints, as well as dinosaur bone fragments.

These volcanic cliffs look much as they did in the age of dinosaurs. The remains of the animals that made these cliffs their homes are found in the red-and-orange sandstone, now packed into cracks left by the volcanic rock. Because the faults move slightly over time, these fossils are often crushed into fragments, which visitors find scattered in the sandstone like chocolate bits in scoops of Rocky Road ice cream.

The museum is open year-round. June 1 to mid-October daily from 9:30 A.M. to 5:30 P.M. Winter hours are Tuesday to Saturday 9:00 A.M. to 5:00 P.M. and Sunday afternoon from 1:00 to 5:00 P.M.

The other highlight along this coast is *Joggins,* reached via two routes after Parrsboro. Route 2 turns inland, leaving you with the choice of taking a small highway (209), which skirts the remainder of the Fundy Coast, or traveling inland along Route 2 and either skipping Joggins altogether or backtracking to Joggins via exit 4, some 13 miles (20 km) from Amherst, and then driving to Joggins on Highway 242. Along this road you can take a break to stretch your legs at *Cape Chignecto,* a wilderness area that includes a number of nature trails. Admission is $3.00. The park is open from mid-May to mid-October.

Joggins is a must if you want to get to the bottom of fossils' mysterious appeal. When you reach the village, turn onto Main Street in beautiful downtown Joggins (population 491), where you will find the *Joggins Fossil Centre.* Guides here will take the time to explain the origins of the area's many 350-million-year-old fossilized trees, ferns, insects, amphibians, and animal tracks. The center is open from June 1 to the end of September and has an extensive collection of fossils on site. For more information, write to the Joggins Fossil Centre, Main Street, Joggins, NS B0L 1A0; or call (902) 251–2727 in season or (902) 251–2618 off-season. Admission is charged.

After Joggins you have merely a 12-mile (20-km) drive to the New Brunswick border, where your travels through mainland Nova Scotia will be complete.

Places to Stay in Western Nova Scotia

ANNAPOLIS ROYAL

King George Inn
548 Upper Saint George
(902) 532–5286
This is one of those massive homes previously owned by a sea captain. Dating back to Confederation, this antiques-filled inn is close to all the town's best sights. Standard.

BEAR RIVER

By the Brook/
The Carriage House
1894 Clementsvale Road
(902) 467–3612
Quaint community set deep in a river valley near the Bay of Fundy.
Standard.

Queen Anne Inn
494 Upper Saint George
Street
(877) 536–0403
(902) 532–7850
Soaking in romance and history. Honeymoon worthy Heritage building close to historic gardens.
Standard to deluxe.

BRIER ISLAND

Brier Island Lodge and
Restaurant
(800) 662–8355
(902) 839–2300
You'll love this place as much for its location as its ambience. Good seafood.
Standard to moderate.

CALEDONIA

Whitman Inn
Route 8
(2.5 miles/4 km south of Kejimkujik National Park)
(800) 690–INNS
(902) 682–2226
A good place to stay if you don't want to leave civilization behind but still want to enjoy the national park. Breakfast for guests.
Standard.

CANNING

The Farmhouse Inn
9757 Main Street
(902) 582–7900
Charming country setting amid miles of apple orchards. Four-star bed-and-breakfast with assorted packages.
Standard.

DIGBY

The Pines Resort Hotel
The Shore Road
Digby County
(877) 375–6343
(902) 245–2511
Luxurious Norman-style château resort overlooking the water. Tennis, golf, and other amenities available. One of the province's poshest places.
Deluxe.

MAITLAND

Captain Douglas House Inn
and Restaurant
8842 Highway 215
(902) 261–2289
Former sea captain's home, now a Heritage property, featuring in-house restaurant.
Standard to moderate.

MAITLAND BRIDGE

Mersey River Chalets
Route 8
(902) 682–2443
Year-round rustic cottages overlooking Mersey River, offering abundant outdoor activities and proximity to national park.
Moderate to deluxe.

MAVILETTE BEACH

Cape View Motel and Cottages
near Salmon River,
off Route 1
Yarmouth County
(902) 645–2258
Best location near spectacular beach.
Also has a diner.
Standard.

PARRSBORO

Parrsboro Mansion
15 Eastern Avenue
(902) 254–2585
An Italian-style mansion on park grounds.
Central location.
Standard.

PORT WILLIAMS

Planter's Historic Inn
Highway 101, exit 11,
then Route 358
(902) 542–7879
The oldest building in Nova Scotia, this English manor–style house seems straight out of *Pride and Prejudice*.
Standard to moderate.

SANDFORD

Churchill Mansion
Route 1
Yarmouth County
(888) 453–5565
(902) 649–2818
You'll find quirky charm in this "haunted" Heritage property. An excellent value.
Standard to moderate.

SANDY COVE, DIGBY NECK

Olde Village Inn
Route 217
(800) 834–2206
Housed in a nineteenth-century building, this antiques-filled inn is tucked away in Digby Neck.
Moderate.

SMITHS COVE

Mountain Gap Resort
off Highway 101,
exit 24 or 25
Digby County
(800) 565–5020
Great setting.
Moderate.

WOLFVILLE AREA

The Blomidon Inn
127 Main Street
(800) 565–2291
Victorian-era inn in former sea captain's mansion.
Moderate to deluxe.

Old Lantern Inn & Vineyard
Highway 1, Grand-Pré
(877) 965–3845
(902) 542–1389
Surrounded by lush vineyards, this inn features modern conveniences in a romantic traditionally styled building.
Moderate to deluxe.

Places to Eat in Western Nova Scotia

ANNAPOLIS ROYAL

Garrison House Inn
350 Saint George Street
(902) 532–5750
Screened-in verandah, Old World atmosphere.

Leo's
222 Lower Saint George Street
(902) 532–7424
Lunch and early-afternoon service only.

DIGBY

The Pines Resort
Shore Road
(902) 245–2511
Posh former Canadian Pacific hotel in the old style; try their scallops.

WOLFVILLE AREA

The Blomidon Inn
127 Main Street
(800) 565–2291
(902) 542–2291
Extensive seafood selection, deluxe pricing.

Le Caveau
at Domaine de Grand-Pré,
Grand-Pré, Highway 1
(902) 542–7177
Gorgeous vineyard setting, Swiss food.

Tattingstone Inn
434 Main Street
(902) 542–7696
Elegant dining in Italianate Georgian mansion.

Cape Breton

Linked to the mainland of Nova Scotia by the world's deepest causeway since 1955, Cape Breton remains very much an island, in every sense of the word.

Here "bilingual" could just as easily mean Gaelic and English as French and English, although all these cultures plus Mi'Kmaq are strongly evident on Cape Breton Island. The Mi'Kmaq, of course, have been here for more than ten thousand years.

Scots came in two basic waves of immigration. After the failed rebellion of 1745, many Highlanders chose Cape Breton as their exile and refuge. Then, in the 1820s, many landlords drove the Scottish tenants off their land and took it over as sheep pasture. The landless Scots left for Cape Breton and points beyond in search of a place where they could continue to live as their ancestors had.

The French actually settled Cape Breton before the Scots but were exiled after the fall of Louisbourg, their stronghold. Many of them returned to France but came back to Cape Breton a few years later and settled in communities only a few miles from the Scots.

At every rest stop on Cape Breton you will see locally produced books, stories of the first Scottish settlers or the French.

CAPE BRETON

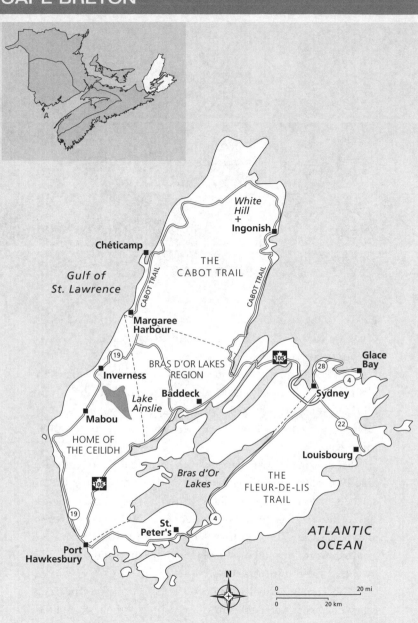

White Hill +
Ingonish

Chéticamp

THE CABOT TRAIL

Gulf of St. Lawrence

CABOT TRAIL

CABOT TRAIL

Margaree Harbour

Glace Bay

105

28

BRAS D'OR LAKES REGION

19

Inverness

4

Baddeck

Sydney

Lake Ainslie

Mabou

22

HOME OF THE CEILIDH

Louisbourg

105

Bras d'Or Lakes

THE FLEUR-DE-LIS TRAIL

19

St. Peter's

4

ATLANTIC OCEAN

Port Hawkesbury

N

0   20 mi

0   20 km

Among the stacks of videotapes, heavily in demand by visitors awed by the island's spectacular scenery, will be those that focus on Cape Breton's native sons and daughters who have managed to carve out their own niche in the music industry with a blend of Celtic traditional and modern rock ballads.

You will be shortchanging yourself if you do not take the time to enjoy firsthand the music and arts that have kept a love of Cape Breton culture foremost even in the hearts of the island's economic exiles who have drifted off in search of opportunity.

Home of the Ceilidh

There is a local festival somewhere on the island at least once a week all summer long. Along the boardwalk that skirts the waterfront of Chéticamp, near the start of the Cabot Trail, one has a chance of catching live performances three times a week. If you happen to spend any length of time in one place you may also be lucky enough to get invited to a traditional Gaelic party, or *ceilidh* (pronounced *kay loo*), at someone's home. If this happens, you're in for a treat, a holdover from the descendants of the hardy group of pioneers who left the difficult times of Scotland to establish a New Scotland for themselves on Cape Breton Island.

With that in mind, the very first thing to do once you cross the causeway is buy a copy of the local paper, the *Cape Breton Post,* turn to the entertainment section, scan the listings, and plan your itinerary accordingly. Then fill up your tank before leaving Port Hastings and turn left onto Route 19 to head north along the scenic western coast.

TRUDY'S FAVORITES

Scarecrow Village,
Cap Le Moine/Monk's Hat

Sunset Art Gallery,
Chéticamp

Cape Breton Highlands National Park,
from Chéticamp to Ingonish

Keltic Lodge,
Middle Head

Amoeba Sailing Tours,
Baddeck

Alexander Graham Bell Museum,
Baddeck

Fortress Louisbourg,
Louisbourg

Wallace MacAskill Museum,
St. Peter's

LeNoir Forge Museum,
Isle Madame

In short order you will come to *Judique.* Along the shore road in this area you will find a number of wharves where you can purchase lobsters straight from the boats.

If you continue on Route 19, you will soon come to *Mabou,* home of the Rankins, who achieved international recognition for their singing, songwriting, and animated performances. Several of them have gone on to successful solo careers. They still retain strong links to the area.

trivia

North America's first coal-miner choir, The Men of the Deeps, was formed in 1966 in Glace Bay, Cape Breton, to prepare for the nation's centennial celebration the next year. They are all miners or retired miners and have now performed worldwide and recorded successful albums.

The pride that Mabou's inhabitants feel in the singers' success is at least partially due to their skill in taking Gaelic singing to the masses, once again putting the spotlight on Mabou as a center of Gaelic language and traditional culture.

In a small part-time museum called *The Bridge,* or, in Gaelic, An Drochaid, eager youngsters line up for fiddle lessons. Located near the bridge on the only piece of highway in the village, the museum also offers day-camp courses in Gaelic, with children from far afield taking the opportunity to learn the ancient language. Formerly a general store, An Drochaid also houses the *Mabou Gaelic and Historical Society Museum,* with artifacts, genealogical and historical records, research, and local music. Admission is free. The little museum is open year-round (upon request). If you don't find it open, you can call locally at (902) 945–2311 or (902) 945–2790.

For a village this size, one can find a remarkable chowder, along with other typical Maritime delicacies, at *The Mull,* situated on the main road. The settlers of this area came from the Isle of Mull in Scotland, and near here you will find the Mull River. The restaurant also sells big rings of Mabou cheese and other local products.

The Mull was started by innkeepers Eleanor and Charles Mullendor several years before they opened the *Duncreigan Inn.* The inn is a modern building, with all the newest comforts, although it was designed to incorporate features of the original farmhouse. At one time it was a charming old home, say the innkeepers, but it had reached the point where, as the locals put it, the building was "after falling down."

At one point the Mullendors headed the local arts council for the Inverness area. They have developed considerable contacts with area artists. In every room in the inn, you will find old-time Chéticamp hooked rugs colored with organic dyes in the traditional manner. They also prepare special meals for their guests, including local Mabou cheeses and *maraq,* also known as "poor man's haggis," a combination of suet, onions, and oatmeal done up like sausage meat in a cow's intestine. Reportedly, it's not a process for the unambitious cooks among us. For reservations call (902) 945–2244 or write to Box 59, Mabou, NS B0E 2T0. Rates are moderate.

Take a look at Mabou from the front deck of the Duncreigan Inn (located just south of the village proper and across the bridge from the community) for a view of the tiny village church, reflected perfectly in the still water. It is easy to imagine a life where time stands still, even though the village has international recording stars living next to the bald eagles and the moose.

Mabou pioneers were determined not to yield to persecution in their homelands. The Scottish settlers who came to this end of Cape Breton and succeeded in making a life of it were of the most hardy stock. Think of it as pioneers' Darwinism: Those who did not succeed moved on. At one point 800 of the Scottish pioneers left Cape Breton en masse for New Zealand. Those who remained and thrived were the toughest of the lot.

Their memory is preserved in the ***Our Lady of Seven Sorrows Pioneers Shrine,*** which looks for all the world like a simple country church from the patio of the Duncreigan Inn. It's a surprising optical trick. From the outside it seems almost too small to accommodate the congregation. But inside, the Douglas fir timbers used to make columns and the skillfully constructed archways make it look like a tiny cathedral.

There are several interesting walks in the area. If you turn toward the sea just before crossing the bridge to exit the village, you can follow the Harbour Road to ***Mabou Harbour Mouth.*** At the tip of land you will find the tiny, pretty lighthouse at ***Mabou Mines.***

bonappétit!

Many visitors get a little queasy when it comes to eating haggis, the ultimate Scottish food. The problem is knowledge out of context.

Haggis is made from the heart, lungs, and liver of a sheep or calf. The organs are mixed with suet, chopped onions, and oatmeal, boiled in a sheep's stomach, and, voilà! Haggis. Sounds terrible, doesn't it? Actually, it's not much different from sausage, which is traditionally made from spiced (and sometimes smoked) organ meats that are dried or cooked and then inserted in animal intestines. The methods used for making both haggis and sausage were developed to preserve meat in the days when the only things refrigerated were your toes on a cold winter night.

Now that you realize that you've been eating similar stuff all along, next time a Cape Bretoner offers you a plate of the dreaded haggis, dig in!

TOP ANNUAL EVENTS

Big Pond Summer Festival,
Big Pond (mid-July to month's end);
no phone

Highland Village Day Concert,
Iona (first Saturday in August);
(902) 725–2272

Cape Breton Fiddlers' Festival,
St. Anns (second to last
weekend in August);
no phone

Fête de St. Louis,
Louisbourg (late August);
(902) 733–2630

From here, provided it hasn't been too rainy, you can walk along the shore for a good distance north. Once thriving, Mabou's mines eventually had to be abandoned when the ore that could be reached safely was depleted and digging under the water became impossible. For the vigorous among you, the walk is 7 to 8 miles (11 to 13 km) and will take you to Sight Point, where you can rejoin a road that leads north to Inverness.

Visit the **Mabou Pioneers Cemetery** at the West Mabou Road. Just after the West Mabou Sports Club and Hall, turn right toward **Indian Point,** which overlooks the harbor. Here you will find the old graveyard of the village's pioneers, punctuated by a cairn (a traditional stone marker) and neat rows of headstones of the area's founders, who came here in the early 1800s. The church in the village originally stood here; it was moved to its current location in 1967.

When it's time to leave Mabou, return to Route 19, head north, and follow the signs for **Inverness.** Ever want to explore the mysteries of Scotch whisky, or perhaps just want an excuse to taste-test quite a lot of it? En route from Mabou to Inverness you will come to the **Glenora Inn and Distillery,** which offers you a unique opportunity. This is the only single-malt whisky distillery in North America and is strikingly similar to distilleries in the old country. The whisky is produced in the traditional copper-pot stills, but cannot be called Scotch unless it is produced in Scotland. Glenora's brew, named Glen Breton Rare Canadian Single Malt Whisky, is available in provincial liquor stores, as well as places as far away as Bermuda, Mexico, Switzerland, Ireland, France, and the United States. The brew is also aged at least eight to ten years. Every day the distillery offers tours from 9:00 A.M. to 5:00 P.M. A whisky museum is part of the distillery tour. The 600-acre property is also home to an inn and Celtic pub, so you could just decide to explore Scottish culture in more depth. The Scottish-style Glenora Pub showcases musicians several times daily. The dining-room specialty is salmon smoked in a whisky barrel. For information, call (800) 839–0491 or (902) 258–2662, or visit www.glenoradistillery.com. Rates are moderate. Just outside of town you will see a sign indicating a provincial picnic park. Just after this the road passes over two rivers. The second of these is fed by *Glenora Falls,* a walk of 0.2 mile (0.4 km) in from the road.

After a brief drive you will come to Inverness. You will notice that after several miles of driving in the interior, you are now along the coast again, and even though you have stayed on the same stretch of highway, you will have made a right turn just as you entered the village.

To your left is a pristine but exposed beach overlooking the Gulf of St. Lawrence, reached by a small boardwalk. On the other side of the street are a number of craft shops, featuring items from as far away as Chéticamp and Judique; they range from tartans to hooked rugs.

Backtrack about a block from the intersection that brought you into town and then drive down toward the government wharf. You will notice a small old-style railway station that has been converted into the *Inverness Miners' Museum.* Outside you will see a cairn, upon which are noted the names of men who died in various local mine disasters before mining was completely abandoned in the 1940s. It is open mid-June through September Monday through Friday 9:00 A.M. to 5:00 P.M. and weekends from noon to 5:00 P.M. A small admission is charged.

If you happen to be in Inverness on a Thursday in July or August, take a room in any of the establishments that line the road on the beach side of town and attend the ceilidh at the fire hall, which starts at 8:00 P.M. The last week in July, there is always the Inverness Gathering, where the ceilidh spirit will prevail.

After years of active involvement in the community arts scene, the *Inverness County Centre for the Arts,* a wonderful arts center, was opened in Inverness in 2003. Along Route 19 in the north end of Inverness, it's on the opposite side of the highway from the Inverness Beach Village. Open from June 1 to the middle of September, the center's hours are Monday through Friday 10:00 A.M. to 5:00 P.M., open two hours later on Thursday, and open after 1:00 P.M. on the weekends. The center houses the work of local and international artists, as well as special events, workshops, and performances. Details of their schedule can be found on their Web site at www.invernessarts.ca, or you could call (902) 258–2533.

Leaving Inverness, continue for a short way along the coast on Route 19. You'll come to a fork in the road at Dunvegan. From here you have the option of continuing along the scenic coastline on a secondary highway, Route 219, or traveling the more modern stretch of highway that leads to *Southwest Margaree.* There are a number of Margarees in this area of beautiful rolling hills and meadows, and the scenery is just as lovely as it is along the coastline.

Of note is the ***Margaree River,*** which in 1991 was designated as a Canadian Heritage River. It is excellent for salmon fishing. You'll see many anglers as you drift along its banks, should you decide to hike in this area. If you want to make an entire vacation of fishing, the Margaree would fit the bill very well.

Continue inland from Margaree Forks into Northeast Margaree. There you can explore the collection of angling and salmon paraphernalia at the ***Margaree Salmon Museum,*** to find out just how special the river is for fishing. For information call (902) 248–2848. The museum is just 0.2 mile (0.3 km) off the Cabot Trail.

Something happens on this stretch of highway. Within a few miles the family names change from MacDonald and MacMaster to Doucet and LeBlanc. Gaelic heritage starts to give way to French Acadian and, just at the Margarees, the transition seems to be at its high point.

It's surprising when you think of it: Two generations ago, just south of Margaree, people lived and worked in Gaelic. To this day their children learn the traditional songs and attend Gaelic classes. And then, just a short stretch of road away, the language changes to French.

The Cabot Trail

Continue along Route 19 north after Margaree Forks until you rejoin the Cabot Trail at ***Margaree Harbour.*** (If you took the coastal route, you're already there.) On both sides of this harbor are pleasant, uncrowded beaches. Beyond the harbor is a small bridge that promptly brings you to ***Belle Côte.*** From here on you will encounter a string of thriving Acadian communities.

Just after the road passes a piece of coast that appears to jut out into the gulf, look to your right. A weathered old barn, which appears to be propped up on one side by poles, has an unusual group of individuals standing around not doing anything in particular. These are the scarecrows of ***Cap Le Moine*** (on some maps this appears as its English translation: "Monk's Hat").

There are more than one hundred scarecrows in all, including a golfer. The proprietor of this ***Scarecrow Village*** has capitalized on these cool lawn ornaments to draw business for a take-out and gift shop that he runs on the same site.

A short drive from here is ***Chéticamp,*** the largest Acadian community in the area and the location of the hospital and other essential services such as a pharmacy. Because of this, it seems much more of a town than a village. During the summer months large numbers of French-speaking visitors come here from the rest of the Maritimes. Roughly 20 percent come from Quebec.

In summer this influx of French-speaking visitors gives Chéticamp the atmosphere of a surprisingly cosmopolitan village.

The origins of Chéticamp are not entirely straightforward. Although the village is unmistakably French in character, its earliest settlers were actually from the French-speaking Channel Islands, under the British Crown. Following the Treaty of Paris in 1763, the French lost fishing rights in the Gulf of St. Lawrence.

Quickly filling the vacuum was Charles Robin, a French Huguenot from the Isle of Jersey. And at about that time, exiled Acadians were starting to come back to these shores. The exiles had been packed off to St. Malo in France, a port just south of Jersey. Robin offered them work, and soon a thriving community of returned Acadians sprang up. For many years afterward the people of Chéticamp were tied to the fortunes of the Robin family. (They weren't the only Acadians to have dealings with the Jersey "French": On the southeastern coast of Cape Breton, you will find other relics of the Jersey connection in St. Peter's and Arichat.)

You might want to visit a replica of the Robin Company Store, re-created to evoke the year 1896, a time when the economic well-being of the village's fishermen depended on the whim of this solitary family-run company. The replica is located in a complex completed in mid-2002 called **Musée La Pirogue** (Pirogue Museum), at 15359 Cabot Trail Road. The museum is a reproduction of an old Acadian homestead and features demonstrations on the making of lobster traps, and the characteristic Chéticamp rag rugs. Admission is charged.

Just before reaching Chéticamp proper, you'll see a sign indicating **L'Auberge Doucet,** or Doucet Inn, which is set far back off the road at the end of a massive sloping lawn that would make a good bunny slope at a ski school. Just behind the inn is an unspoiled view of the Cape Breton Highlands. From the patio that separates the two parts of the inn, you can see a small inlet, and, off in the distance, Chéticamp Island. For information call (800) 646–8668 or (902) 224–3438. Rates are standard to moderate.

The **Coopérative Artisanale de Chéticamp Ltée** is the first eating establishment that you will encounter as you enter Chéticamp. Here you can eat a traditional Acadian meal and then check out the craft co-op in the other wing of the same building. On display are excellent examples of Chéticamp hooked rugs. These are so intricately executed that they look more like needlepoint than the usual hooked rug one finds in hobby shops.

The rug-hooking technique developed in Chéticamp as a way of covering the cold wooden floors of the simple Acadian homesteads. As sometimes happens when necessity and isolation conspire, an original art form developed from the use of objects at hand. At first women used burlap potato sacks, stretched out on a frame and pulled tight. Starting with rags and then moving

trivia

Caid Mile Failté is Gaelic for "100,000 welcomes."

Fishermen call an undersized lobster a tinker.

on to wool yarn, the women drew the fabric through the holes in the burlap, forming a loop. When the intricate pattern had been filled in, the stretcher was loosened and the burlap relaxed. This caused the wool loops to be tightly enclosed by the burlap, and a beautifully patterned rug would result.

One of the early developers of the technique was a woman who was quite noted for the designs she stamped on the burlap backing. As a young girl she had made her materials from rags that she cut from family clothing. Eventually, the industry became lucrative and her entire family became involved in it, sons as well as daughters. But as the matriarch who started the rug business aged, she became more and more determined to produce the rag carpets, so much so that the family had to hide all scissors and fabric from her. She passed away at age eighty-nine, still eager to cut rags at every opportunity.

The home she spent her life in is a Heritage property, out of which a craft shop called **Le Motif** operates. It is painted a deep blue and is located at the northern end of town. The specialty here, not surprisingly, is rag rugs.

Several restaurants operate down along the boardwalk that follows the waterfront from the government wharf to the end of the village's main drag. You can sit in the **Harbour Restaurant** and watch the lobster boats drift off to cast their traps.

Just past Le Motif you will notice that the village is thinning out as you head north. At this point, on your left, you will see a large brightly painted sign for the **Sunset Art Gallery** and an arrow indicating a small wooden building across the street. This is the studio of Bill Roach, one of the province's most noted folk artists. You can't miss his calling: He has a fence made out of people who resemble giant clothes pegs.

Roach's works have been displayed at the Nova Scotia Art Gallery; sent to the Canadian Embassy in Washington, D.C.; and as far away as Aus-

Folk Art at Sunset Art Gallery

tralia. To get an advance peek at Roach's amusing handiwork, you can visit his Web site at www.sunsetartgallery.ca.

You might also want to visit *Chéticamp Island.* For many years this island was in the hands of the Robin family (known locally as "the Jerseys"), until in 1893 a priest and activist, Father Pierre Fiset, arranged the purchase of the island.

From the road that runs along the harbor side of Chéticamp Island, you can get a charming view of the village, punctuated by the large church of St. Pierre, all set against the backdrop of the highlands. The view of the village and the church (built under the direction of Père Fiset) is well worth the trip to the island, where you can also hike and view eagles, cormorants, cliffs, moorlands, a lighthouse, and beaches.

Apart from checking out the village's thriving crafts and arts community, a warm summer day in Chéticamp is best spent strolling along the boardwalk, where there are free concerts three times a week in summer. Once you've fulfilled your need for human company, follow the road leading out of the village at its northern end, toward *Cape Breton Highlands National Park.* Be sure to bring something along to munch and drink, because eating establishments are few and far between along the route you will follow; you may find yourself getting hungry several hours before you reach the next restaurant, unless you curtail all stops. The park is located along the *Cabot Trail,* named for explorer John Cabot, who sailed into Aspy Bay, near Dingwall, in 1497, only five years after Christopher Columbus visited the Caribbean. Soon after Cabot's discovery, European fishermen and fur traders began visiting these shores, eager to make their fortunes from the natural bounty of the area.

The main interpretive center is at the park entrance. In the same building is a bookstore. Apart from the maps and information for sale or offered there, you'll have a chance to explore what has to be the most extensive collection of naturalist books you may ever see.

The park is full of natural wonders—from huge 300-year-old sugar maples, yellow birch, and beech trees, to waterfalls rushing down rugged mountain-sides, to eagles soaring gracefully in their wilderness refuge, to the black bear, which will tolerate no insult from human intruders who roam the park's interior. Take heed and use a telephoto lens to photograph any bears that you may happen to spot. You may also see a moose along the road in the park, so drive cautiously.

The park has been carefully mapped out with twenty-eight suggested trails—some challenging overnight ones, and some just twenty minutes long and on level ground. There are also plenty of places to stop and park so you can get a panoramic view of the ocean or river rapids far below the road, which winds its way around the highlands. Pick up a detailed map at the park entrance, as well as the booklet entitled *Walking in the Highlands,* which outlines the many hikes and has them conveniently arranged with numbers corresponding to indicators on the map.

Soon after you've entered the parkland itself, you will come to an area inhabited at one time by French Acadians. Several trails along the Chéticamp River are reminders of this area's first European settlers. If the long hike to **Pleasant Bay** is not your style, you can still get excellent views of the coastline from several lookout points along this part of the route.

On a very clear day it is worthwhile to make a stop at the **Fishing Cove Lookoff.** Cast your gaze northwest into the St. Lawrence. The islands you will see are 50 miles (80 km) away: Quebec's Magdalene Islands.

From the park entrance to Pleasant Bay takes about an hour by car if you stop only a few times to look around. This little village is just outside the national park, because the highway meanders outside park boundaries temporarily. During the summer months you may be able to dine at one of the few restaurants that operate as part of the motels.

Just north of Pleasant Bay, in the direction of Red River, a **Buddhist monastery** was established after its founder, a Tibetan lama, decided the environment was suitable for contemplation. Once you've roamed around the Cape Breton Highlands for a while, you'll understand why.

When you exit Pleasant Bay along the Cabot Trail you will return to official national park territory within a few minutes. You will then steadily climb uphill while making a number of turns. Be on the lookout for a sign that indicates **Lone Shieling** and parking. If you don't grab a chance to park at this spot, it will be too late to look at Lone Shieling, a replica of a Scottish crofter's hut, except for a perfunctory glance as you whiz past in your automobile.

Lone Shieling on the Cabot Trail

Once you do park, you have before you one of the most pleasant and interesting short walks that the park has to offer. The loop takes about a quarter hour, if you don't count the time you spend at the site. The building was erected at the request of a man named Donald MacIntosh, a native of Pleasant Bay and a professor of geology at Dalhousie University. He donated one hundred acres (forty hectares) in the area of Pleasant Bay, including some virgin forest, to the government in 1934. (The park has 80 percent of the province's remaining virgin forest.) After the land was absorbed into the budding national park, the government built this replica of the Lone Shieling, a crofter's hut like those on the Isle of Skye, the home of this man's ancestors. It's a cleverly constructed little shelter; one can well imagine a shepherd huddled in here with his sheep when storms made the out-of-doors unpleasant.

After viewing the hut, descend a small set of steps and walk along a woodland path in an area of tall, ancient yellow birch and 350-year-old sugar maples. The trail ends with another set of stone steps leading up to the parking area.

Another few minutes' driving time from here will take you high up into the mountains, to a point where scenic views are around every corner. The best panoramic shots are cleverly designated by small lookout symbols and a widening of the road that permits parking. From one of these lookouts, you can see in the distance **Beulach Ban Falls,** which can be reached by a trail at the base of the mountain.

To get to the falls, follow the directions to the Aspy Trail; the entrance is at a turnoff just after the warden station. Take note that while the first part of the trail is accessible by vehicle, the road requires a high wheelbase and good suspension in the spring.

After the trail to the falls, the road once again exits official park territory and leads through a stretch of rural Cape Breton where you won't have an opportunity to eat for miles and miles, until at long last you come to **Cape North** and **Dingwall.** Here, finally, the hungry traveler can find several promising spots at which to eat.

At Cape North the road forks, with the left turn leading to the pretty coastal communities of Bay St. Lawrence, Capstick, and Meat Cove. Then the road stops. If you want to see more of the rugged coast, you can take a whale-watching cruise aboard a Cape Islander boat owned by Captain Dennis Cox in **Capstick.** For information call (888) 346–5556 or (902) 383–2981. In addition to the frequent sightings of whales on this cruise, you'll stand a good chance of seeing eagles, cormorants, lots of puffins, moose, bear, waterfalls, and sea caves.

After Capstick turn your car south and backtrack to the fork in the road at Cape North. (Take note that on a really foggy day, you may as well pass up this detour altogether, because you'll hardly be able to see anything.) If you take the right instead of the left road, and then drive for a moment, you will come to the turnoff for Dingwall, 2 miles (3 km) after Cape North.

This road will take you to *The Markland Coastal Resort* in Dingwall. The Markland features rustic Scandinavian-style pine chalets spread out over seventy acres (twenty-eight hectares) overlooking the ocean. A long, secluded, sandy beach here is complemented by a stretch of inland waterway suitable for water sports. For details call (800) 872–6084 or (902) 383–2246. Rates are moderate to deluxe.

During the summer months the Markland also operates a gourmet restaurant; this is virtually the last place to eat until you get to Ingonish. The restaurant is open only from mid-June to mid-October.

There are two options for heading southeast out of Cape North: You can drive through official park territory, or take the scenic route along a coastal road from Effies Brook to New Haven. Although the scenic route takes a bit longer, it's well worth it. There is a potential picture postcard around every bend.

This loop ends at the tiny community of *Neils Harbour,* which has a lighthouse and a picnic area where you can stretch your legs and roam around amid fishing shacks and lobster traps. Then it's back into the park for another stretch of hilly driving until you reach Ingonish and then *Middle Head,* which is lumped in with Ingonish whenever anyone talks about it as a destination.

Middle Head is the site of *Keltic Lodge,* not Ingonish, as you might hear. Keltic is the granddaddy of all Cape Breton resorts, perched majestically on a

Celtic Colors

Fall foliage season is glorious on Cape Breton. A visit at this time will yield lots of choices for pleasant outdoor recreation, stunning scenery, and the *Celtic Colours International Festival.* This great event brings together entertainers from Scotland and Ireland as well as other parts of Canada and the United States. Celtic Colours has grown in popularity every year. In a typical year the festival entertains thousands, at more than three dozen concerts held in more than twenty-six communities all over Cape Breton. Needless to say, if you don't book well in advance, you'll have to scramble to get tickets. While you're booking your show tickets, be sure to reserve a hotel room, since accommodations, too, will be in short supply. The festival is striving to maintain its rural emphasis, so many performances are held in cozy communities featured elsewhere in this book, with lots of other things to see and do while you are there. The festival kicks off on the Canadian Thanksgiving weekend, which for Americans is Columbus Day weekend. For details of the upcoming festival, call (902) 562–6700 or visit www.celtic-colours.com.

high promontory overlooking Ingonish Beach. It is a lovely setting, and a fabulous picture. The restaurant at Keltic, the posh *Atlantic Restaurant,* is probably the only one on the island that requires male patrons to wear a jacket to dinner. Keltic is adjacent to an eighteen-hole golf course. To one side of Ingonish Beach is a freshwater lake with supervised swimming. For information call (800) 565–0444. Rates are deluxe.

Continuing along the Cabot Trail in the *Ingonish* area, you will soon see a sign on the right for *Lynn Gorey's Craft Shop and Art Gallery.* This is a must-see. Lynn is the wife of widely acclaimed artist Christopher Gorey, whose work is displayed in this shop (as well as at the Art Gallery of Nova Scotia in Halifax).

Along with wonderful full-size original watercolors, Gorey has limited-edition reproductions in sizes that pack easily, unframed. Gorey, whose studio is located in the back of the art gallery, depicts life on this coast with a special sensitivity for his medium. The shop is open mid-May to mid-October. For details call the gallery at (902) 285–2845.

From Ingonish you'll return briefly to the national park to climb one last mountain along a winding road. This is where the advice to travel the trail clockwise from Chéticamp to Ingonish comes in handy: If you went in the other direction, you would be "cliffside" on the road.

Die-hard cyclists love to "do" the Cabot Trail; often you will see one pedaling away in his or her lowest gear up *Cape Smokey.* If this is the case, exercise extreme caution, because cyclists often need considerable leeway on the road and cannot stop quickly.

A pleasant stretch of coastal road awaits you after leaving the national park for good. This area is sometimes referred to as *St. Ann's Loop.* Here there is an eclectic mix of artists and craftspeople who have been drawn to the area by its bucolic charm.

In *Indian Brook* you'll notice a rustic wooden home and shop called *Leather Works* on the right-hand side of the road. Operated by John Roberts, the store features historic reproductions of traditional leather goods, including leather buckets, which modern-day owners use to chill

trivia

When it was founded in 1939, St. Ann's became the first Gaelic college in North America.

champagne or as elegant flower pots. Leather buckets are lighter than wooden ones, so back in the days when brigades of men passed water buckets hand over hand to fight fires, these were the type used. Pitch was used to make them watertight.

Roberts specializes in leather reproductions for national parks and museums across the country. For example, when you visit the Fortress Louisbourg, farther

along in Cape Breton, take note of the fire brigade's leather buckets. These reproductions were made by Roberts.

Along with the buckets and belts, purses, and shoes at Leather Works, you
will find tavern-style aprons in supple leather that are *très chic*.

A few moments' drive after Indian Brook will bring you to a tiny ferry
crossing at Jersey Cove. Here you have the option of driving to South Gut St.
Anns at the head of St. Anns Harbour, or taking a car ferry across the narrow
harbor. Cars and passengers cross for a small fee.

Bras d'Or Lakes Region

On the other side of the harbor is **Englishtown,** which has the distinction of
being the childhood home and final resting place of a famous Cape Breton
giant and one-time P. T. Barnum circus performer **Angus MacAskill.** Just a
minute after you drive off the boat, you will spot a small graveyard where the
7-foot-9-inch (2.4-m), 425-pound (193-kg) giant is buried. Not surprisingly,
his is the biggest headstone.

Five minutes' drive farther down Route 312 will bring you to the **Giant
MacAskill Museum,** which contains all sorts of memorabilia. A sign on Route
312 indicates the museum.

Open from mid-June to mid-September, the house contains artifacts—big
ones, like massive boots and the giant's chair. These items from MacAskill's life
and times provide a fascinating picture of one of the most unusual people of
his day. A full-scale model of the giant (at one time displayed at the Halifax
Citadel) gives you a good idea of the commanding presence of the man. For
information, call (902) 929–2925. There is a small admission charge.

From here the drive to **South Gut St. Anns** is quite straightforward. Route
312 ends momentarily at junction 12, where you will join TCH Highway 105,
headed south. Follow this route for 3.5 miles (5 km) until you reach exit 11. If
you take this exit, you will find yourself in front of the **Lobster Galley at Harbour House.** Complete with its own lobster pound at the inner limit of St.
Anns Harbour, you can guess what the specialty is at the restaurant. While the
seafood at this place is a calorific delight fit to make you swoon, the galley's
view is equally out of this world, overlooking a dramatic piece of the North
Atlantic. (Particularly rave-worthy are the seafood Alfredo, the maple-infused
salmon, chowder, and seafood-stuffed mushrooms.) The Harbour House also
has a gift shop.

Right next door is the **Gaelic College of Celtic Arts and Crafts.** Locally
known as St. Ann's Gaelic College, it is a place where visitors can explore the
legacy of Scottish settlers to North America at the "Great Hall of the Clans."

A Gaelic Language Primer

(Adapted from the Harbour House menu)

A nice touch on the Harbour House's menu is the "Gaelic Language Primer," complete with pronunciations. The English translations alone sound typical of Gaelic speakers, since they use colloquialisms and a sentence structure not wholly English.

Gaelic has only eighteen letters in its alphabet, but it has sounds unheard of in English due to the unusual combination of letters. Here are a few essentials:

Ciamar a tha thu-fhein, pronounced "Kimmer uh ha oo haen?" meaning, "How's yourself?" (It's their translation, not mine.)

De do naigheachd, pronounced "Jae daw neh ochk?" meaning, "What's new?"

Se biadh math a bha sin, pronounced "Sheh bee ugh ma uh va shin," meaning, "That was a lovely meal."

Am feum mi na soithichean a nighe? pronounced "Um faem nuh seh eechyun uh nee uh?" meaning, "Must I wash the dishes?"

There is also a museum and craft shop. For information, call (902) 295–3411. Reach the craft shop at (902) 295–3441.

Now the center of Gaelic education on the island, St. Ann's has an interesting story attached to it. In the last century a group of 800 Scottish settlers decided that life in Cape Breton was just too hard, the soil too unyielding, the winters too long. Led by a Presbyterian minister, they pulled up stakes and moved to New Zealand. Today thousands of New Zealanders can trace their roots to one-time Scottish settlers in this area of Nova Scotia.

Who could have predicted that a century after the Scottish settlers had abandoned their homes in St. Anns, the village would be the center of Scottish revivalism?

The first Scottish attempt at settling Cape Breton was in 1629, when a baronet named Lord Ochiltree promoted Cape Breton and its qualities. The king had established an order of baronets five years earlier, who were to promote and oversee the settlement of 3-by-6-mile (5-by-10-km) tracts of land along the coast. The rough equivalent of modern-day real estate developers, these baronets were gambling not just their personal fortunes, but also their lives.

Soon after Lord Ochiltree landed at Baliene, on the island's east coast, he discovered French fishing vessels in what were supposed to be British waters. The baronet sent a ship to tell them they could stay to fish and trade with the

trivia

The world's tallest true giant (that is, not due to pathological causes) was Angus MacAskill, who at 7 foot 9 inches, or 236 cm, put the tiny village of St. Anns, Cape Breton, on the map.

Mi'Kmaq if they paid him 10 percent of their earnings. Ochiltree and his soldiers then took the first mate hostage and kept three cannons as collateral until the French captain was able to pay.

At about this time yet another declaration of peace was being signed between France and England. Meanwhile, another sea captain named Daniels arrived from France, landing at St. Anns, where some French settlers told him about the Scottish pioneers at Baliene. Peace declarations aside, Captain Daniels determined to teach Ochiltree a lesson, gathered together his hardiest men, had scaling ladders constructed, and went to make a neighborly call on Ochiltree. Once inside Scottish walls, Daniels captured Ochiltree. His men subdued the baronet's armor-clad soldiers. Once again a French flag flew over the island. Baronet Ochiltree was taken prisoner along with all his men and brought to St. Anns, where the most able Scotsmen among them were set to work building the French a fort, chapel, and magazine. By November 1629, Captain Daniels sailed for France with his captives, a number of whom died en route and were thrown overboard. Our hapless land speculator ended up in France, where he made unheeded appeals to the Court of Admiralty in Dieppe. Finally, Captain Daniels sailed off on another adventure, and Nova Scotia's unfortunate baronet was released. The entire misadventure had cost him £50,000 and thirteen men.

From St. Anns drive south back along the same stretch of highway and you will again reach exit 11, which brings you to the TCH. Follow it south until exit 10, which is the junction leading to *Baddeck,* your next destination, and the perfect spot for exploring the beauty of the *Bras d'Or Lakes.*

Nova Scotia is home to one of the highest concentrations of *bald eagles* in North America. There are an estimated 250 nesting pairs of eagles, found for the most part along the shores of the Bras d'Or Lakes. Incidentally, this isn't really a lake at all, but an inland sea with mildly salty water; its 5 percent salt content is sufficient to keep a lobster fishery going. Its total area is 450 square miles (1,165 sq. km).

Because it has virtually no tide, the saltwater arm of the sea freezes solid in winter. During July and August you'll have ample opportunity to see the eagles in their native environment. The birds are sufficiently plentiful and healthy that some newborn eagles are being exported to the United States

Reproduction problems were experienced by many birds in the 1960s, due to DDT and other chemical insecticides in the food chain. In the isolation of the Nova Scotia coastline, these problems did not arise, leaving the province with healthy communities of raptors, including ospreys, hawks, and owls.

Several sailing tours are available in the area, as the lake is a haven for sailors. (Boats can get in from the northern inlet that you recently crossed by ferry or through St. Peters Canal. **Amoeba Sailing Tours** are aboard a 67-foot (20-m) five-sail schooner. Visitors can sail to the Baddeck Light House and Kidston Island, which has a lovely beach; Spectacle Island Bird Sanctuary; and the shoreline of Alexander Graham Bell's mansion. During many tours, visitors will spot bald eagles, since there are many nesting pairs in the vicinity; they can often be seen diving for fish and then returning to their nests to feed their young. Reach Captain John Bryson at (902) 295–7780 or (902) 295–2481.

Helen Sievers, co-owner of **Auberge Gisele's Inn** in Baddeck, capitalizes on the beautiful natural setting of the village by referring guests to a local naturalist who leads them out on wild mushroom hunts. Chanterelles are one find that the inn's chefs freeze and use in their scrumptious meals. In fall, they even find delicious boletes, which are also used in the inn's cuisine, along with fiddleheads, when in season.

Gisele's has a long sweeping lawn built up a hill, giving such a picturesque view of Baddeck that painters sometimes set up their easels there. For reservations, call (800) 3040–INN or (902) 295–2849; fax (902) 295–2033. Rates are moderate to deluxe.

Also in the Baddeck area you can visit the **Alexander Graham Bell Museum and National Historic Site.** Bell spent summers here for many years and quite a bit of time in the winter as well. Displays on his many inventions tell his life story.

Bell was initially involved in speech therapy, as were his father and grandfather. His mother was partially deaf, and Bell eventually married one of his deaf students. His work on the telephone came as a result of his intense interest in communications technology. Along with inventing the phone at age twenty-nine, he worked on airplane development, building the Silver Dart, which was flown over Bras d'Or Lakes. (He used the frozen lake as his tarmac for takeoff and landing.) He also built a hydrofoil, the original HD–40 version of which is on display at the museum. It is open year-round with some reduced services and early closing in the off-season. It's open daily in June from 9:00 A.M. to 6:00 P.M. and in July and August from 8:30 A.M. to 7:30 P.M. Admission is charged.

Baddeck is an anomaly: This tiny village with a population of slightly more than a thousand souls swells to several times this number in the summer without being frazzled. The result is a collection of good eateries along the waterfront and a number of interesting things to do. The community even has a ferry

ia

Cape Breton Island comprises one-third of the entire area of Nova Scotia.

that takes people over to the beach on nearby **Kidston Island** for free.

The **Bell Buoy** provides scrumptuous desserts, delicious seafood, and a great view of the lake, including the little lighthouse on Kidston Island, which is just facing the restaurant. You'll also see a lot of yachts. Since it's a charming little community with a good marina, it has become a haunt of yachters who love the Bras d'Or for its excellent sailing.

Bell's stately summer home overlooks the inlet where the village is nestled, just across from a small island and lighthouse. The home's setting couldn't be prettier.

Another cozy restaurant operates out of the **Telegraph House,** which has been an inn for more than a century. In the late 1880s it was the home away from home of Alexander Graham Bell before his mansion was built on the stretch of headland overlooking the lake. The building also housed the telegraph office at one time. Room number one, Bell's room, has been left in very much the same state as when he used it. For information, call (902) 295–1100. Rates are standard.

Moving from the Baddeck area into the forest hinterland, you can take the time for one of the most scenic walks in this end of the country, culminating at **Uisage Ban Falls,** Gaelic for "white water." To get there you will have to backtrack about 1 mile (1.6 km) to the Cabot Trail (which terminates at Baddeck) on Route 105, just after the TCH junction leading to Baddeck.

A sign indicating a left turnoff will direct you to the falls. Follow the signs to a parking lot, where you can leave your vehicle and proceed on foot up a moderately steep incline for about 1 mile (1.6 km), past a stream that runs through a thick stand of birch and evergreens. At the end your reward will be the sort of astoundingly beautiful ice-cold waterfall that could have appeared in a Robin Hood movie.

Once you're on the road again and have left Baddeck behind, turn south on Route 105 in the direction of Little Narrows. From here you can take another little ferry across a narrow arm of the lake onto a small patch of land, the **Washabuck Peninsula,** which is practically an island itself.

You will have a choice of two directions as soon as you get off the ferry. Choose the road to your right, the southern end of Route 223. This road will take you through rolling hills that yield a beautiful view of the lake, an area that seems completely untouched by the modern world. It is a likely setting for the **Highland Village,** in **Iona,** just before the recently built bridge that spans the Barra Strait.

Just before you approach the bridge, turn right and follow the shore road a short way. High on a hilltop overlooking the Bras d'Or, you will find a replica of an old Scottish pioneer village. There are homes from 1830, 1865, and 1900, as well as a thatch-roof Hebridean Black house, of the type used by the earliest settlers, and a log house. There are also a school, forge, carding mill, and barn. Costumed guides will show you around. On the first Saturday in August each year they hold Highland Village Day, with traditional Scottish music. Admission is $7.00 for adults, $2.00 for children ages five to eighteen, families $14.00, seniors $6.00. For information call (902) 725–2272.

Iona is also one of the venues for the ***Celtic Colours International Festival,*** held the second week in October. Over the years the little village's Legion Hall has been the stage for performers from Scotland and Ireland, as well as local entertainers. Ticket information for this particular concert is available by calling the number for the Highland Village listed above. For other Celtic Colours Festival tickets, call (800) 565–9464 or (902) 564–6668. Tickets go on sale in mid-August, and I would strongly advise you to book well in advance.

From Iona drive across the bridge to ***Grand Narrows.*** This is a wonderful, unspoiled spot worth your time. There is good swimming with warm water at ***Pipers Cove,*** just after Grand Narrows.

You can take either Route 223, along St. Andrews Channel on the northern end of this peninsula, or the southern route past Eskasoni, a large Mi'Kmaq community. Regardless of which end of highway you choose, head to Sydney so that you do not find yourself trying to get to Louisbourg on secondary roads with rough patches.

Sydney is a good spot for a rest stop. There are a number of interesting things to see here. You will enter the city on Route 4, which quickly becomes King's Road, until you reach the city center. This is a city built by the coal and steel industries of the past century. These days there is a small university here, and the city serves as a service hub for the island.

Sydney was first settled by United Empire Loyalists fleeing the revolution, and has several interesting houses that date back to its founding. One block away from the Esplanade, you will find two of the oldest still-standing buildings in this part of the island. ***Cossit House,*** at 75 Charlotte, was built between 1785 and 1787 and is the oldest. The slightly younger ***Jost House,*** built in 1787, is across the street and a few houses up, at 54 Charlotte Street.

trivia

To put it delicately, Alexander G. Bell liked to relax *in puris naturalibus,* meaning he was a nudist.

During the Second World War, a passenger ferry on the Sydney–Port aux Basques route was sunk.

Bran Bonnach

You may be wondering what kind of food the early settlers ate. Here is a recipe for bran bonnach (pronounced *ban-auch,* with a hearty gutteral ending), as made by the highland Scots. Similar to biscotti, a bonnach is a flat homemade oatcake sometimes cooked on a griddle. The recipe is courtesy of the Highland Village in Iona.

1 egg

1 cup bran (softened in warm water and drained)

⅓ cup brown sugar (optional)

¾ cup rolled oats

1 cup buttermilk

½ cup melted bacon fat or lard

2½ cups flour

3 teaspoons baking powder

1 teaspoon baking soda

1 teaspoon salt

Preheat oven to 400°F (182°C). In a large bowl, lightly beat the egg and add bran. Add brown sugar (if desired), rolled oats, buttermilk, and melted bacon fat. In another bowl, mix together flour, baking powder, baking soda, and salt and add to mixture. The dough should have the texture of lumpy biscuit dough. Roll out on a floured board. Take care when rolling: The rolled dough should be the thickness of scone or biscuit dough. If rolled out too flat, the oatcakes will be hard and dry. Mark with a fork, and place on a nonstick baking sheet (or brush the pan with butter). Bake for 40 minutes.

Cossit House was built to house the British Garrison's first Anglican chaplain for Sydney. Tours of the home include handwork demonstrations by costumed guides, who demonstrate the many skills practiced by women of that era. The building is authentic in every detail, and was refurnished according to an inventory taken of Reverend Cossit's possessions at the time of his death in 1815. Of particular interest is the kitchen, with its huge hearth. Cossit House is open from June through mid-October, Monday through Saturday 9:30 A.M. until 5:30 P.M., and Sunday from 1:00 to 5:30 P.M. A small admission is charged.

Across the street and three houses down, at Jost House, you will find a home built under orders of Governor DeBarres in 1787 as a repayment of a debt he owed to a merchant and shipowner named Samuel Sparrow. Sparrow took possession of the house, but decided that the harsh winters of Cape Breton were not for him, and he quickly moved south. By 1836, the house was purchased by Thomas Jost, whose family retained possession of the home until 1971. Artifacts and construction in this house span three eras. In the oldest part of the house, in the eighteenth-century kitchen, you will find a cooking fireplace and a separate beehive-shaped oven for baking. A closet with exposed lathes built adjacent to the hearth served as a "drying room" for the family's laundry during inclement weather. The house has an impressive collection of Victorian-era artifacts. Upstairs a marine display recounts the city's marine history, along with the 1942 sinking of the Newfoundland ferry, the *Caribou,* which cost 136 lives. Ship models, including one of the *Caribou,* underscore the city's marine heritage. In another room you will find a display of apothecary items and the tools used by pharmacists to extract medicinal compounds in the early twentieth century. Jost House opens from June 1 to October 30. During summer months, it is open from Monday to Saturday from 9:00 A.M. to 5:00 P.M. In September and October, the hours shorten to 10:00 A.M. to 4:00 P.M.

Another interesting historic home has been made into a charming country inn. ***Gowrie House*** is located in Sydney Mines, at 840 Shore Road. This is not adequately marked on maps or road signs, but is just to the north of the Newfoundland ferry terminal, which straddles the communities of North Sydney and Sydney Mines, along the Shore Road. Gowrie House dates back to 1832, and was the home for many years of the Archibalds, a wealthy shipping and shipbuilding family. Thomas Dickson Archibald served in the provincial government, and became a senator in the federal government at the time of Confederation. The home remained in the family for a century and a half, until it was converted into an inn. Gowrie House has been tastefully decorated with an eclectic mix of modern, abstract, and representational paintings; sumptuous wall coverings; and tasteful antiques, making it worthy of a story in a home decor magazine. In fact, its dining room was once used as the setting for a Rita MacNeil Christmas Special. Innkeeper Ken Tutty is a great source of information about the art scene in the area. The inn has many nice touches, like a great selection of "vacation" reading material and an inviting garden. They have a much-sought-after dinner sitting at 7:30 P.M., so you need to reserve early. They are not licensed to sell liquor, but inn guests receive a complimentary half liter of wine at dinner. Diners not staying at the inn are permitted to bring their own wine. They are closed during the winter months, except during the Christmas season. To reserve ahead for dinner, or to book a room, call (800) 372–1115 or (902) 544–1050. Room and dining rates for this four-and-a-half star establishment are deluxe.

The Fleur-de-Lis Trail

Once you've seen enough of Sydney, take Highway 22, which runs straight off George Street downtown. Highway 22 is the most direct route to take to see Fortress Louisbourg, North America's largest and most authentic historical restoration, but there are many other routes.

Highway 22 takes you across the **Mira River,** which has been immortalized by one of Cape Breton's most popular ballads. (If you're in the Maritimes for any length of time, you're bound to hear "Song for the Mira.")

Just 2 miles (3 km) east off Route 22 at exit 17 in **Albert Bridge,** you will find **Mira River Provincial Park,** where there are facilities for swimming and picnicking. Because the land at this part of the river forms a peninsula, there are several little coves and secluded swimming areas as well as launch sites for canoes. Many locals have summer cottages along this river and in Catalone, just 2 miles (3 km) farther along Route 22.

There are two routes to take from Louisbourg to Sydney, or vice versa. The direct route is a modern, direct, and reliable highway. The other route is much more fun. On a sunny day with a full tank of gas, driving the coastal road from Louisbourg through Main à Dieu will make you feel as if you are inside a video game, complete with winding roads that snake through gorgeous scenery with quaint coves and secluded shoreline. Give yourself plenty of time if you decide to take this route. In Main à Dieu you will find a series of boardwalks that edge the grassy dunes, and the Coastal Discovery Centre, one of the lone pit stops along this route.

Between Main à Dieu and Sydney is the community of Glace Bay, which seems to blend right into Sydney. The must-see attraction here is the **Cape Breton Miners' Museum** complex. Follow the blue museum markers until you come to a large museum complex along Glace Bay's shoreline, marked by a giant black iron wheel. This was used at one time to haul the huge worker-filled steel cages up to the surface from deep in the mine shaft. The museum offers audiovisual presentations on the history of mining in this end of the province, along with displays of everything from early stretchers designed to transport injured miners along the rails underground, to mining helmets and documentation about the work of Draegermen, whose job it was to rescue miners (or retrieve bodies) after a cave-in. If you are feeling adventurous, take an underground tour into a mine shaft. Plan ahead and wear well-treaded footwear and a sweater, because underground the temperature hovers about 53°F (12°C) and it's damp and a bit slippery. Your guide will direct you to suit up and the tour down below will take more than an hour, so don't go on an empty stomach. (There is a small restaurant on-site.)

Mining has a 250-year history in Cape Breton, and much of it involved a very hard life for miners and their families. Part of the museum involves a series of buildings depicting the mining community in days past. Although the outside of these buildings is in a modern state, the interiors are authentic in every detail. One of these is the company store, complete with the accounting methods used in olden times to track the forever-mounting debts of the miners, who were paid in credit at the company store rather than in hard currency. Debts of dead miners were inherited by their families, and a miner's pay never met all the bills. All of this contributed to the hardscrabble existence of the miners, whose entire lives were essentially spent in indentured servitude. In the 1800s, boys would have been put to work in the mines at eight years of age. Right away they had to purchase their gear from the company store and the cycle of insurmountable debt would begin. Miners' wives would have been able to make a small supplement to the family coffers by putting up single miners in a room at the back of their house, which would have been shared by two mining families. Families averaged ten to fourteen children, who would sleep in a boys' bedroom and a girls' bedroom upstairs, often averaging seven to a bed made of a sack of straw suspended over a frame laced with rope. The miner's house is divided down the middle, depicting two eras: one side the mid-1800s, the other more modern.

Admission is charged. Summer hours are daily 10:00 A.M. to 6:00 P.M. (Tuesday until 7:00 P.M.); winter hours (September to June) are Monday through Friday 9:00 A.M. to 4:00 P.M. For more information, call (902) 849–4522 or visit www.minersmuseum.com.

On Route 22, just before you reach Louisbourg, you will come to the old *Sydney and Louisbourg Railway Museum.* It features two wonderful full-size turn-of-the-twentieth-century railway coach cars in mint condition, a caboose, an oil car, and a freight car—sufficient paraphernalia to satisfy any railway buff. The museum also chronicles the salad days of Louisbourg, when shipping, mining, and the railway made this excellent harbor a thriving community. The building that houses what is left of the railway is the station, which, along with the freight shed, was constructed in 1895, an era when this little stretch of rail had more than four million tons of coal a year hauled across its ribbon of steel.

Sadly, the original roundhouse is gone. But an exact replica has been constructed and is used to house the rolling stock during the winter. For more details on the local area, visit the railway museum information center.

Along with railway memorabilia, the museum has many photographs chronicling the three transatlantic Marconi wireless stations established by Italian inventor Guglielmo Marconi. At the turn of the twentieth century, Marconi spent several years near Glace Bay setting up his wireless stations.

Upstairs in the museum is a display on various shipwrecks, including the *Titanic* and the passenger ferry the *Caribou,* which was sunk by a German U-boat off the coast of Newfoundland in 1942. Until the railway was shut down, the Newfoundland ferry would occasionally dock in Louisbourg harbor when ice blocked Sydney harbor. Passengers were then shuttled to Sydney via this small line, which apparently kept casual hours and random stops.

There is one other little museum in the town. The **_Louisbourg Marine Museum_** on Main Street has a real treasure trove of material related to sunken ships in the area, and the divers who search for their contents. Most significantly, the museum chronicles the wreck of the French ship *Le Chameau,* which held the payroll of the French soldiers at Fortress Louisbourg. Open from mid-June until the end of September from 10:00 A.M. to 8:00 P.M.; donations are welcome.

The biggest draw in **_Louisbourg_** will forever be **_Fortress Louisbourg,_** at the far end of the community along the coastal road. Louisbourg was a fishing village for many years, with the fortress little more than heaps of rubble left behind when the British blew it to tiny bits back in the mid-1700s. Then in the early 1960s the federal government slowly began reassembling the fortress. Now that the local fishing industry has experienced a seemingly irrevocable downturn, the former pile of rubble has been the town's lifeblood, bringing in much-needed tourists during the summer months. The fortress was located here because of the magnificent harbor discovered by the Europeans in 1713, which led to the founding of the town. Unfortunately, its exposed location made farming difficult, and the fortress an easy target. Nevertheless, at its peak, Louisbourg was the third-busiest seaport on the east coast of North America. Since its location was far closer to France than the scattered settlements along the St. Lawrence River, no price seemed too high to pay in the defense of the "Gibraltar of the North."

The restoration has been arranged to re-create life in the town during a summer's day in 1744, the peak of French power in the New World. Along with a garrison of 600 soldiers was a permanent population of approximately 2,000 administrators, clerks, innkeepers, cooks, artisans, and fishermen. The restored fortress includes fifty buildings (one-quarter of the original town). Local residents, many descended from the original French settlers, portray the residents of the French garrison town.

When you arrive at the fortress gate, you are immediately accosted by a French "soldier," who demands to know your business there. One hundred interpreters in full costume explain intricate details of life at Louisbourg in 1744.

If you time your visit right (just after noon), you will likely see the daily "punishment" being meted out by soldiers who march the day's designated miscreant down the Rue Toulouse, then up to the pier, where his or her list of offenses is read out and then the criminal is briefly subjected to public restraint. This is short lived, and the honor is conferred on a rotating basis. (A conversation overheard amongst the costumed staff: "Are you getting punished today?" "No. That was three days ago. I think it's Megan's turn." "What was she supposed to have done?" "Stole a chicken, maybe?")

Elsewhere in the fortress, you will notice entrances festooned with spruce bows. These were used to designate the inns that were permitted to sell liquor. At the fortress's zenith there were twenty-five inns and taverns, not counting the illegal ones. In 1744, the military comprised only one-third of the total inhabitants of old Louisbourg. Another third included tradesmen, and the last third were the middle and upper classes, including officers and their wives and children. Roughly one thousand fishermen and their families lived in about one hundred homes that stretched from outside the fortress walls to the location of the modern town. Land inside the fortress had been designated for a church for the common people, but when it became apparent that they would have to pay for it themselves, it was never built. Instead, everyone went to the impressive fortress chapel.

In the chapel, which is part of the fortifications, tiny model ships hang in the window. These traditionally were built by fishermen as a way of expressing their gratitude to God for a good catch. Only the elite sat in the church; all others stood, so it held hundreds at a single mass.

The governor's wheelchair in his chambers dates from that era. His room is adorned with carefully reproduced portraits and period furniture.

Take note of the open fireplaces, where meat was roasted on spits. Cooks would turn a mechanical device that would evenly rotate the spit, untended, for a half hour or so before the cook had to attend to the basting.

Ultimately, the location that made winters severe and cultivation difficult also led to the downfall of the fortress. In 1745, one year after the summer's day you see reenacted, an expedition of New England volunteers laid siege to Louisbourg's barely complete defenses. The fortress garrison held out for several weeks.

During the following winter, 900 of the victorious New Englanders died of cold and starvation. The dead had to be buried under floorboards until the spring thaw.

Finally, the New England soldiers mutinied and drowned their sorrows in drink. When reinforcements arrived, the new British governor ordered their rum confiscated. A total of 64,000 gallons was seized.

Three years later, Louisbourg was briefly returned to the French. In 1758, a year before the fall of Quebec, a force of 15,000 British soldiers and more than 150 ships attacked, blowing the fortress to smithereens.

For years afterward Louisbourg was nothing more than a source of cut stone and hardware for buildings as far away as the newly founded Halifax. Eventually, because the fortress did not have a modern city constructed over it, the ruins allowed for an amazingly authentic restoration.

This is a National Historic Site, covered by the same admission structure as other national parks. Louisbourg's fortress is open from May through October, but access during May and October is by guided tour only, arranged for groups through the visitor center. During the summer months, hours are daily from 9:30 A.M. until 5:00 P.M., opening a half hour earlier in July and August. Parking is at the reception center. You will then be bused to the fortress.

There are several pleasant places to stay in Louisbourg. The **Point of View Suites** are at one end of town, literally the last stop on the way to the fortress, which you can see clearly from the front of the building. These suites offer kitchenette facilities and the comforts of a home away from home, and have an on-site laundromat, as well as hook-ups for visiting RVs. Their dining room serves breakfast and dinner, if you are not inclined to cook. For information call (888) 374–8439.

At the other end of the same road, shortly after you enter the town, about two minutes' walk from the Louisbourg Playhouse, you will find a pair of refurbished historic homes that have been converted into bed-and-breakfast establishments. The **Louisbourg Harbour Inn** and the **Heritage House Bed and Breakfast** are both owned by Parker and Suzanne Bagnell and offer scrumptious breakfasts. The Heritage House was originally the rectory of the church next door. Built in 1886, it features Victorian rooms, some with balconies overlooking the harbor and fortress. The top-floor room encompasses the entire story and features all the special touches worthy of its four-and-a-half star rating. Rates are moderate to deluxe. Call (888) 888–8466 or (902) 733–3222 to make reservations at either inn.

While in the area, be sure to take in a summertime show at the **Louisbourg Playhouse,** one block downhill from Main Street, overlooking the harbor. This is a large wooden octagon-shaped building modeled on Shakespeare's Globe Theatre. The playbill varies a bit during the summer months, but generally you can count on excellent performances from some of the island's most talented performers. The evening I attended, the *Lyrics and Laughter* show included excellent performances from an East Coast Music Award nominee and his cohorts, who sang, step-danced, and traded off musical instruments constantly in an authentic demonstration of virtuosity. Prices are modest, and during intermission guests are invited upstairs to the balcony level to enjoy tea and oatcakes from a local bakery. It's good to arrange tickets through your hotel-keeper, since people come from all over this end of Cape Breton for the ceilidh. For information, call (902) 733–2280.

After Louisbourg you have no option but to return almost to Sydney on Highway 22, then exit to Highway 4 southbound, just outside the city. From here you will skirt the southern end of the Bras d'Or Lakes until you reach **St. Peter's.**

The reward of this slight backtracking to Highway 4 will be self-evident: The road passes through breathtaking scenery, particularly late in the day as the sun sets over the lake.

Rita's Tearoom in Big Pond is actually a large modern building over-looking the Bras d'Or Lakes. It houses a pleasant restaurant featuring enough parking for busloads. The complex has pretty decor, decent food, and a room full of music-industry memorabilia chronicling the rise of Rita MacNeil's successful international music career. Roughly 35,000 people per year visit the tearoom, and browse in its excellent souvenir shop. Open July 1 to October 15, daily 10:00 A.M. to 6:00 P.M.

In St. Peter's the land narrows so much that, for want of a few inches of water, Cape Breton would consist of two major islands instead of one. One hundred and forty years ago, the opportunities presented by this geographic fact led to the building of the ***St. Peters Canal.*** Before that time, the area was the haunt of French fur trader and adventurer Nicolas Denys, who eventually became the governor of New France in the late 1600s.

Everything there is to see in St. Peter's is within walking distance of the rustic log structure of the charming ***Bras d'Or Lakes Inn,*** which fronts the lake. If you stay at the inn, take note of the log-construction hardwood chairs and furnishings. These were made by a local furniture artisan.

It is open year-round. Rates are moderate. For reservations call (800) 818–5885 or (902) 535–2200.

A short walk from the inn will take you to the canal, along which you can walk for a considerable distance. On the north side you will find ***Battery Park,*** a pleasant place where you can stroll around the point of land or turn southward and cross the canal along walkways that form the tops of the locks.

Lobster Boat in St. Peters Canal

Between the lake and the ocean there is a differential of 8 inches (20 cm) of water between high and low tides. Because of the calm seas, it is a haven for pleasure boaters, many of whom use the canal to enter the Bras d'Or.

On a hill overlooking the south side of the canal is the **Nicolas Denys Museum.** This is a reconstruction of the famed French explorer's fur-trading post, circa 1650. This was just one post run by Nicolas Denys, who also traded in the Gulf of St. Lawrence and had a post on Miscou Island before he decamped to Bathurst. Denys used oxen to haul ships across the narrow strip of land that separated the Atlantic Ocean from the Bras d'Or Lakes. This track eventually became the canal. The museum has artifacts from the pre-British occupation of the area, right up until modern times. Among the collection of local memorabilia is a rattan wheelchair of the type used in the early 1900s. The museum is open from the beginning of June until the end of September. A very small admission is charged. Hours are June 1 through September 30 daily from 9:00 A.M. to 5:00 P.M. For more information, call (902) 535–2379.

Another worthwhile stop in St. Peter's is a short walk from the canal. Situated on Main Street (Highway 4) is a small, unassuming 120-year-old house, the birthplace of one of the country's most famous photographers. The **Wallace MacAskill Museum** contains well over one hundred photographs, many of them hand-tinted, as well as biographical material of the famous marine photographer.

MacAskill literally made Peggys Cove into the tourist icon it has become. His photographs from the 1930s, when it was depicted as the ultimate sleepy little fishing village, set the stage for the growth of the tourist industry in this province. His most famous photograph is accessible to millions: Just reach into your pocket and pull out a Canadian dime. That's a MacAskill of the original *Bluenose*. The museum guide will point out that the dime is a mirror image of a 1937 photograph that hangs just to the left of the front door. The museum is open daily in July and August and on September weekends from 9:30 A.M. to 5:30 P.M. Admission is free; donations are welcome.

Right next door to the MacAskill museum, at 4 MacAskill Drive, is the ultimate shopping stop for those with a fetish for all things Celtic. **MacIsaac Kiltmakers and Celtic Giftshop** has a fantastic selection of pewter ornaments, jewelry, and (my favorite) assorted pewter whisky flasks with a Celtic emblem in their center that pops out and serves as a glass for having a *"wee dram."* They have every item of Highland wear that your Celtic heart desires, and make kilts to order that can be sent worldwide. These represent a considerable investment, and the staff point out that the material comes in two different weights, with prices ranging from six hundred to roughly a thousand dollars for a full outfit. For those considering a return to their Scottish roots for a formal occasion, they rent kilts and formal jackets for the groom and make custom-designed Celtic wedding dresses. They also feature less serious items, including the Cape Breton passport, which appears to be a serious document until it undergoes more careful scrutiny. If you left town without buying that item you now regret not getting, you can recover from "non-buyer's remorse" by visiting their Web site at www.mackilts.com.

With St. Peter's your tour of Cape Breton is almost complete, except for a stop at the *LeNoir Forge Museum* on *Isle Madame.* Leaving St. Peter's, you can continue along Highway 4 or take Highway 104. Either way, to visit Isle Madame you will have to turn off at exit 46, near Louisdale, and drive to *Arichat*. Here again you will find an Acadian community, many of whose residents are descendants of exiled Acadians who returned to these shores. Added to this mix is the trail of Jersey Island money and investors in the fishing industry who moved into the area as soon as the land was ceded to England.

Isle Madame is now a sleepy, pretty seaside place with scenic vistas and the North Atlantic at its doorstep. But a century or more ago, the seven-by-ten-mile island was one of the most important seaports in the province. Soon after 1492, French, Basque, and English fishermen started using it as a temporary seaport. By 1718, fishermen settled in the northern part of the island at D'Escousse. After the fall of Louisbourg in 1758, more Acadians arrived on Isle Madame, retreating from the disaster of the obliterated fort. After the English takeover of Nova Scotia, until 1784, there were many restrictions of the region's French Catholics. As a result, an opportunity arose for French-speaking Protestants from the British Channel Islands to establish themselves as businessmen associated with shipbuilding and trading fish. Eventually they settled in Arichat, the largest community on Isle Madame. By 1811, the island's population was 1,200, 90 percent of whom were Acadian. Soon after, the island experienced an influx of Irish, Scottish, and English immigrants. In the 1800s, Arichat was a hugely successful seaport, with five shipbuilding enterprises and factories lining its waterfront.

The island thrived during the golden age of sailing ships. At its peak, from 1821 until 1867, Arichat was the fourth-largest port in Nova Scotia, behind Halifax, Yarmouth, and Pictou.

In 1811, two brothers from France, Thomas and Simon LeNoir, set up a blacksmith and locksmith shop along the shore, using a ship's chandlery that was established in 1793. It had a deep-water wharf and slip, adding to the ship chandler business (which supplied all kinds of hardware such as chains and anchors for fishing ships). It underwent many incarnations, from a ship's chandlery and forge, to a trade school, to a coal shed and warehouse, to an ice house. Eventually the family business closed down around 1902, when the shipbuilding business went into decline in this area, following the opening of the St. Peters Canal and the growth of industry in the Sydney area. The forge fell into severe disrepair, until the local historical society decided to restore the building and catalog all the forge's tools that played a part in Arichat's shipbuilding heyday. In the summer students from local universities act as tour guides. The forgery has been expanded to now include a small gift center that also carries a few books on the area, and another building with artifacts not directly related to work at the LeNoir Forge. As well, a small outdoor stage is in the middle of the complex, so that local concerts can be held from time to time.

Two roads run in parallel through Arichat. The low road skirts the coast and gives a whiff of salty air and seaweed, along with great scenery. You will find the LeNoir Forge at the far eastern end of town. The high road is a two-lane highway where you will find most businesses.

Although many of the region's young people have left, the community is now also home to a collection of telecommuting creative types, artists, and people who have returned to the home of their ancestors. One example is a couple from the United States, Peggy and Charles Bosdet, who have established the largest candy store east of Montreal at *The Candy Shop,* downstairs and to the side of Dooley's Pharmacy on Arichat's main road. Charles Bosdet, who was born in Winnipeg but moved to Chicago in his youth, is a descendant of an original inhabitant who came to Isle Madame from Jersey in 1842. The shop's signature treats come from its own chocolate manufacture on-site. Their on-staff *chocolatier,* who hails from Austria, makes unbelievably delicate chocolates, some of them insanely complicated (like the tiny ones complete with a tiny musical score on the top). They make delicious fudges in a variety of mixtures. They've even made one surprisingly tangy and inviting fudge called the Cape Bretoner, which involves layers of milk chocolate, lemon cream, and infused tea. One unusual product is popcorn coated in white chocolate and sprinkled with bits of toffee. This is far more delicious and less kooky than it sounds. The shop also features the unique Wolf Bait, a confection of white chocolate, dried cranberries, and cashews. The Candy Shop's owners' next venture, underway at press time, was the establishment of a factory so that these delicacies will be available to people who don't manage to get to Arichat. If you do visit, however, plan to spend a bit of time sampling the treats.

The Candy Shop is directly across the street from *L'Auberge Acadienne,* or the Acadian Inn. This is a cozy inn on a sufficient elevation where you get a good view of the coastline. The inn's pretty dining room has traditional decor and heightens your experience of the area by playing music by Cape Breton performers, some of them from the region of Isle Madame. (Selections seem to run the gamut from Gaelic to French to English.) They have a delicious, reasonably priced menu and wine list. You can have a set three-course menu, or choose from their bar selections. Both are excellent value.

Check out the bar even if you eat in the dining room. The walls feature vibrant paintings of Louisbourg's costumed interpreters reenacting life in the ill-fated fortress. Innkeeper Pauline Bona is another returned descendant of Isle Madame who is eager to impart information on things to do in the local area. There is a small reading room and some gift items in a room adjoining the inn's reception area. The inn also carries a selection of local maps and other information. Bona says people often use the inn as a staging ground for exploring the whole Acadian shore.

If you have visited Isle Madame, you will need to return to exit 46 via either Highway 206 or 320. From exit 46 southbound you can take either Highway 104 or the slightly more scenic Highway 4 to Port Hastings, the Canso Causeway, and beyond, bringing to a close your tour of Cape Breton.

Places to Stay in Cape Breton

ARICHAT, ISLE MADAME
L'Auberge Acadienne
2375 High Road
(902) 226–2200
Good choice on this coast in terms of cleanliness, convenience, and location.
Moderate.

BADDECK
Auberge Gisele's Inn
Shore Road
(800) 304–0466
(902) 295–2849
Nice rooms and excellent restaurant.
Moderate to deluxe.

CHÉTICAMP
L'Auberge Doucet Inn
Cabot Trail
(800) 646–8668 or
(902) 224–3438
View of Chéticamp Island on one side and Cape Breton Highlands on the other. Nice rooms.
Standard.

DINGWALL
The Markland Coastal Resort
3 miles/5 km off the Cabot Trail
(800) 872–6084
(902) 383–2246
Excellent outdoor setting. Rustic Scandinavian-style cabins set amid beaches, mountains, and dunes.
Moderate to deluxe.

GLENVILLE
(midway between Inverness and Mabou)

Duncrelgan Country Inn
Route 19
(902) 945–2244
Intimate setting overlooking picturesque Mabou Harbour. Open year-round.
Moderate.

LOUISBOURG
Louisbourg Heritage House B&B and **Louisbourg Harbour Inn**
(888) 888–8466
(902) 733–3222
Renovated Victorian-era homes, four and a half stars.
Moderate to deluxe.

Point of View Suites
15 Commercial Street Extension
(888) 374–8439
(902) 733–2080
Great view of fortress; modern suites include kitchenette.
Moderate to deluxe.

MABOU

Glenora Inn and Distillery
Route 19
(6 miles/9 km north
of Mabou)
(800) 839–0491
(902) 468–6516
Occasional free ceilidh, some
rustic cabins available on this
lovely, tranquil property.
Moderate to deluxe.

ST. PETER'S

Bras d'Or Lakes Inn
Route 4
(800) 818–5885
Pleasant inn with log
cabin–style dining room.
Adjacent to St. Peters Canal.
Within easy walking distance
to park and nature trails.
Standard.

SYDNEY MINES

Gowrie House
840 Shore Road
(902) 544–1050
Eclectic decor mixing elegant
Victorian and modernist elements with particular flair.
Moderate to deluxe.

Places to Eat in Cape Breton

ARICHAT, ISLE MADAME

L'Auberge Acadienne
2375 High Road
(902) 226–2200
Standard, reliable fare.

BADDECK

Telegraph House
Chebucto Street
(902) 295–1100
Charm dating back to
Alexander Graham Bell.

BIG POND

Rita's Tearoom
on Route 4 (25 miles/40 km
west of Sydney)
(902) 828–2667
Friendly staff, pleasant food
and decor.

CAPE NORTH

**Morrison's Pioneer
Restaurant**
The Cabot Trail
(902) 383–2051
Quaint artifacts and seriously
decent food at good prices;
one of the only places to eat
in this area.

INGONISH BEACH

The Keltic Lodge
Cabot Trail
Middle Head Peninsula
(800) 565–0444
Most formal dining on the
island; top-notch prix fixe
dinner menu included in
room rate.

LOUISBOURG

Cranberry Cove Inn
12 Wolfe Street
(902) 733–2171
Cozy dining room in Victorian
property; excellent food
including homemade biscuits
and molasses.

MABOU

The Mull
Route 19
(902) 945–2244
Great salads. One of western
Cape Breton's hot spots.

MARGAREE VALLEY

The Normaway Inn
Egypt Road
(exit 7 off Highway 105)
(800) 565–9463
Good food in secluded valley.
Local singers and dancers
make frequent appearances.

ST. ANNS HARBOUR AT SOUTH HAVEN

The Lobster Galley
(exit 11 off TCH 105,
12 miles/19 km north of
Baddeck)
(902) 295–3100
Excellent menu choices,
very good seafood.

SYDNEY MINES

Gowrie House
840 Shore Road
(902) 544–1050
Historic setting.

Index

About the Author

Trudy Fong has worked as a journalist in Canada and in Southeast Asia. For a time she was a reporter for the *Hongkong Standard,* and then she turned to magazine writing. Before she settled into a steady job, she traveled around the world for three years with her husband, Greg, during which time she visited and wrote about more than twenty-five countries. Trudy speaks several languages, including French, which was especially useful while researching this book. She lives in Nova Scotia with her three sons and her husband, who owns the Garden View Restaurant (famous for its all-meat egg rolls) on Main Street in Dartmouth. If you happen to find her there, be sure to ask her to autograph your book for you, and give her an update on your own travels to these shores.